PORTRAITS *of* EXCELLENCE

A HERITAGE OF ATHLETIC ACHIEVEMENT AT THE UNIVERSITY OF KANSAS

KU

Quality Sports Publications

For information write:

Quality Sports Publications
#24 Buysse Drive
Coal Valley, IL 61240
(800) 464-1116
(309) 234-5016
(309) 234-5019 FAX
www.qualitysportsbooks.com

Duane Brown, Project Director
Melinda Brown, Designer
Susan Smith, Editor

Printed in the U.S.A. by
Walsworth Publishing Co.
Marceline, MO

Publisher's Cataloging-in-Publication
(Provided by Quality Books, Inc.)

Niedens, Lyle.
        Portraits of excellence : a heritage of athletic
achievement at the University of Kansas / by Lyle Niedens and
Steve Buckner ; portraits by Ted Watts. -- 1st ed.
        p. cm.
        Includes index.
        ISBN: 1-885758-14-6

        1. University of Kansas--Sports--History.   I. Buckner,
Steve. II. Watts, Ted, 1942- III. Title.

GV691.U542N54 1998   796'.07'1178165
                                QBI98-1386

To Mom and Dad,
for the sacrifices you made
and the lessons you taught.

Lyle Niedens

To my wife, Tammy,
who supports and believes;
To our children, Brenna and Gannon,
who inspire; and
To my late parents, Art and Ruth,
who taught with love.

Steve Buckner

The campus of the University of Kansas.

Table of Contents

Jayhawk Boulevard cuts through the heart of the KU campus. The Chi Omega fountain (lower center) marks the west end of the boulevard.

Acknowledgments

Producing this book involved more than just our effort. We would like to thank the dozens of people who helped make this project a reality.

We especially thank our publishers, Duane and Melinda Brown of Quality Sports Publications, for their encouragement and guidance – and for taking a chance on two first-time authors.

We also thank Ted Watts, the talented artist who painted the portraits featured in this book, for sharing our enthusiasm about this project. Even as we conducted hours of research, Ted painted portraits of new University of Kansas Athletics Hall of Fame inductees. He proved he's as much of a sports fan as he is an artist, even providing reference materials about the KU subjects he's painted during the past 20 years.

In addition, we thank those who guided us through researching volumes of historical material. Steve Jansen, director of the Watkins Community Museum of History in Lawrence, allowed us to sift through reams of the museum's files and even conducted additional research about Kansas sports during the early 20th century. His influence gave us another historical perspective from which to write.

Ned Kehde and Barry Bunch with the University Archives in the Spencer Research Museum provided indispensable facts, files and photographs. They truly do an excellent job recording historical events at KU.

Within KU's athletics department, Doug Vance, Associate Athletics Director Media Relations; Dean Buchan, Sports Information Director and the Kansas Sports Information staff allowed us to view their files and photographs upon numerous requests.

Without the help of Becca Green, formerly with the KU Williams Fund office, and Kathie Whalen with the KU Alumni Association, we would not have been able to contact so many former KU sports personalities. We sincerely appreciate their help.

Also, reporter John Unrein contributed to our effort in various ways, from conducting last-minute research to serving as a courier across northeast Kansas. We're grateful for all his help.

A number of other people assisted us in one way or another from the moment we hatched this idea. They include: Sam Colville, Tom Eblen, Mac Engel, Mike Fisher, Bob Frederick, Heidi Hammrick, Glenn Kappelman, Richard Konzem, Jeannette Kratz, Jason Lamb, Mandy Leibold, John Milburn, Judy Morris, Audrey Novotny, Alisa C. Salmons, Jean Thoma, Bob Timmons, Bill Wachter and Phil Wilke.

Finally, we can't forget those who took the time to talk with us about KU's Hall of Famers, including many of the inductees themselves. Those who were particularly helpful include Bill Alley, Ernie Barrett, Bob Billings, Dave Bingham, David Blutcher, B.H. Born, Lynn Bott, Larry Brown, Hal Cleavinger, Joe DeMarco, Tamecka Dixon, Howard Engleman, Ray Evans, Max Falkenstien, Don Fambrough, Bob Frederick, Tim Friess, Gordon Gray, Kalum Haack, Herald Hadley, Theo Hamilton, Dick Harp, Charlie Hoag, Scott Huffman, David Jaynes, Rebecca Jensen, Monte Johnson, Bruce Kallmeyer, John Keller, Gary Kempf, Kristi Kloster, Nora Koves, Raef LaFrentz, Jill Larson, Clyde Lovellette, Janet Manfred, Bob Marcum, Glen Mason, Chuck Merzbacher, Billy Mills, Jack Mitchell, Bud Moore, George Mrkonic, Jim Neihouse, Bill Nieder, Ted O'Leary, Ted Owens, Fred Pralle, Gil Reich, Dave Robisch, Pepper Rodgers, Michelle Rojohn, Jim Ryun, Wes Santee, Otto Schnellbacher, Gary Schwartz, Herb Semper, Dean Smith, Camille Spitaleri, Bud Stallworth, Wade Stinson, Eddie Sutton, Floyd Temple, Bob Timmons, Billy Tubbs, Mark Turgeon, Marian Washington and John Zook.

The Authors

I also would like to thank my colleagues in the Kansas City and Chicago bureaus of Bridge News Service. I always will appreciate accommodations they made while I juggled financial news reporting and writing a book.

But above all, I would like to express special thanks to my wife, Caryl: I'll never forget your support and understanding while I tackled this challenge. You've always wondered what possible good could ever come from the "useless" sports trivia that rattles around in my head.

Here is my answer.

Lyle Niedens

As with Lyle, I would like to thank my co-workers in the Lenexa, Kan. and Tampa, Fla., offices of Vance Publishing Corp. I appreciate their enthusiasm and encouragement for this project – it has been a big help.

I also would like to say a heartfelt "thank you" to my family, especially to Tammy, my wife. Her love and support have been a constant throughout our marriage and this book. From researching some people of whom she had never heard, to taking our children to the pool so I could have some quiet time to write, she has thoughtfully supported me every step of the way. Her efforts played an enormous role in the completion of his book.

Steve Buckner

Two hallmarks of the KU campus: The Campanile (left) and Fraser Hall.

Billy Mills celebrates his amazing victory in the 10,000 meter run at the 1964 Summer Olympics in Tokyo. Mills is the only U.S. runner to win this event at the Olympics.

Foreword

Although the central topic in Lyle Niedens' and Steve Buckner's *Portraits of Excellence* is a collection of insightful stories about members of the University of Kansas Athletics Hall of Fame, this book also is a reflection of the commitment to excellence by the University as illustrated through its former and current sports personalities.

From my opportunity to associate with a group of student-athletes at the University of Kansas and learn from the coaching staff, I was witnessing and participating in the preparation of individuals to gain prominence in their chosen fields of endeavor – far beyond sports.

When I won a gold medal in the 1964 Olympic Games in perhaps the greatest upset in Olympic history, it was apparent that the University and its athletics programs had played a significant role in helping prepare me for the ultimate challenge of my sports career.

This book speaks for the greatest contribution I believe athletics can offer humanity: the achievement of unity by understanding the beauty and dignity of diversity. These athletes all came from diverse backgrounds to become our heroes and later our mentors. In many cases, merely ordinary men and women aspired to achieve extraordinary things.

In an exciting and easy-to-read manner, *Portraits of Excellence* will inspire and motivate you long after you turn the final page. This is must reading for any sports enthusiast and those willing to challenge the depths of their abilities and perform to the highest of their potential.

Billy Mills
Olympic Gold Medalist
National Spokesperson, Running Strong for American
      Indian Youth
B.S. in Education, University of Kansas, Class of 1962

Dyche Hall at sunrise.

Preface

Thousands of University of Kansas sports fans have viewed them. In fact, if you attend a KU basketball game at Allen Field House, you can't miss them. They adorn the east lobby and hallways of that venerable structure, ensuring all who enter see and hopefully appreciate the history and tradition they represent.

But who are they, these dozens of men and women immortalized by paintbrush on canvas within a wooden frame? And what makes their place among thousands of former and current KU sports personalities so special as to deserve a portrait that freezes their achievements in time?

If nothing else, we hope this book answers those core questions. In fact, writing *Portraits of Excellence* served as a way to answer them for ourselves.

Regardless if you're a fan of the Jayhawks, it's hard to overlook the undeniable tradition and historical significance that emanate from the home of Kansas basketball. Portraits that identify members of the KU Athletics Hall of Fame are a part of that atmosphere.

When you're in the building, perhaps it's easy to forget that KU's athletics tradition is not limited to basketball.

But the Kansas tradition, one of the most unique in college athletics, encompasses much more. It extends beyond the Lawrence campus, or even the playing fields and indoor courts of the school's opponents. In some ways, it transcends the games from which it is derived, as well as the enthusiasm – and controversy – those games often create.

Kansas athletes have won Olympic gold medals. Kansas coaches have revolutionized their sports. Kansas athletics directors have helped define and redefine the purpose of college athletics. In one way or another, they all have helped shape the world of sports, and in some cases, society as a whole.

This book profiles the most prominent among those individuals: the struggles they faced, the obstacles they overcame, the accomplishments they achieved ... the lives they lived.

Separately, each portrait has a story to tell. Pieced together, they depict the history of Kansas athletics.

We hope you enjoy reliving that history.

Lyle Niedens
Steve Buckner

**Right and below:
Allen Field House,
home of KU
basketball since
1955.**

The University of Kansas Athletics Hall Of Fame

In October 1976, led by athletics director Clyde Walker, the University of Kansas began preparations for a Hall of Fame that would honor the most outstanding individual athletes and teams in the history of KU sports.

By April 1977, with the aid of gifts from that year's senior class and associates of the late Skipper Williams, who helped created KU's athletics scholarship program, the Hall of Fame became a reality.

In less than two years, dozens of portraits honoring individual members of the Hall of Fame appeared in the east hallways and lobby of Allen Field House, where they still hang today.

***

The KU Athletics Hall of Fame honors individual athletes who:

- won an Olympic medal;
- set a world record recognized by the particular sport's national governing body;
- set a U.S. record recognized by the particular sport's national governing body;
- earned first-team All-America status in football, basketball, baseball, volleyball, soccer or softball; or
- won NCAA championships in individual sports, including cross country, indoor track and field, outdoor track and field, golf, swimming and diving, tennis or rowing.

The Hall of Fame honors coaches of:

- an NCAA championship team;
- an NCAA basketball Final Four team;
- a football team that appeared in a bowl game; or
- a team that finished in the top eight of NCAA championship competition.

The Hall of Fame also honors KU athletics directors who served at least two years or served while a KU team qualified for the Hall of Fame.

In addition, the Hall of Fame honors individuals whom its executive officer (the KU athletics director) deems worthy of entrance because they contributed to and/or accomplished feats in a particular sport at such a high stature that they brought KU considerable national distinction and honor.

Each individual member of the Hall of Fame is honored with a 16-inch by 20-inch portrait that hangs in Allen Field House's east hallways or lobby.

This book focuses on the 147 individual members of the Hall of Fame (as of summer 1998). They are honored by a total of 134 portraits. Seven portraits contain more than one individual, and four individuals – Forrest C. "Phog" Allen, Arthur C. "Dutch" Lonborg, Karl Salb and Wes Santee – are honored in two portraits apiece (Allen is honored as a coach and athletics director, Lonborg is honored as a basketball All-American and athletics director, Salb is honored by himself as an NCAA champion and also appears and with fellow shot putters Steve Wilhelm and Doug Knop, and Santee is honored by himself as an NCAA champion and also appears with fellow members of a 1954 world-record sprint medley relay team).

Teams inducted into the KU Hall of Fame are honored with photographs that hang in Allen Field House and/or other memorabilia in the main lobby.

KU teams qualify for induction into the Hall of Fame when they:

- appear in a football bowl game and final national rankings
- appear in an NCAA basketball Final Four
- appear in the College World Series in baseball or softball
- finish among the top four in NCAA championship competition in cross country, outdoor track and field, indoor track and field, golf, swimming and diving, tennis, volleyball, rowing and soccer. After 1996, teams that finish in the top eight of NCAA competition may be considered for induction, as may teams whose accomplishments during a particular season warrant consideration.

The following teams have been inducted in the Hall of Fame:

Baseball
- 1993 College World Series

Men's Basketball
- 1922 Helms national champion
- 1923 Helms national champion
- 1940 NCAA Tournament runner-up
- 1952 NCAA Tournament champion
- 1953 NCAA Tournament runner-up
- 1957 NCAA Tournament runner-up
- 1966 NCAA Regional Finals
- 1971 NCAA Tournament Final Four
- 1974 NCAA Tournament Final Four
- 1986 NCAA Tournament Final Four
- 1988 NCAA Tournament champion
- 1991 NCAA Tournament runner-up
- 1993 NCAA Tournament Final Four
- 1996 NCAA Regional Finals

Men's Cross Country
- 1950 NCAA fourth-place finish

The Campanile stands guard over Memorial Stadium, providing one of the most picturesque settings in college football.

- 1951 NCAA second
- 1953 NCAA champion
- 1954 NCAA fourth
- 1955 NCAA second
- 1956 NCAA second
- 1961 NCAA fourth
- 1963 NCAA fourth
- 1966 NCAA champion
- 1989 NCAA sixth

Football
- 1948 Orange Bowl
- 1961 Bluebonnet Bowl
- 1969 Orange Bowl
- 1973 Liberty Bowl
- 1975 Sun Bowl
- 1981 Hall of Fame Bowl
- 1992 Aloha Bowl
- 1995 Aloha Bowl

Softball
- 1972 Association of Intercollegiate Athletics for Women World Series
- 1973 AIAW World Series
- 1974 AIAW World Series
- 1975 AIAW World Series
- 1976 AIAW World Series
- 1977 AIAW World Series
- 1979 AIAW World Series
- 1992 College World Series

Men's Indoor Track and Field
- 1965 NCAA tenth
- 1966 NCAA champion
- 1967 NCAA third

- 1968 NCAA fourth
- 1969 NCAA champion
- 1970 NCAA champion
- 1971 NCAA fourth (tie)
- 1973 NCAA second (tie)
- 1975 NCAA second
- 1978 NCAA fourth
- 1979 NCAA fourth
- 1980 NCAA fourth (tie)
- 1989 NCAA fourth (tie)

Women's Indoor Track and Field
- 1979 AIAW third place

Men's Outdoor Track and Field
- 1932 NCAA tenth
- 1933 NCAA sixth
- 1952 NCAA ninth
- 1953 NCAA sixth
- 1955 NCAA fourth
- 1956 NCAA second
- 1957 NCAA fourth
- 1958 NCAA second
- 1959 NCAA champion
- 1960 NCAA champion
- 1968 NCAA sixth
- 1969 NCAA second
- 1970 NCAA co-champion
- 1971 NCAA fifth
- 1972 NCAA fifth
- 1974 NCAA seventh
- 1975 NCAA fifth
- 1976 NCAA ninth

KU's Memorial Stadium opened in 1921 with a capacity of 22,000. It seated 50,250 when a significant renovation began in late 1997.

Forging Tradition

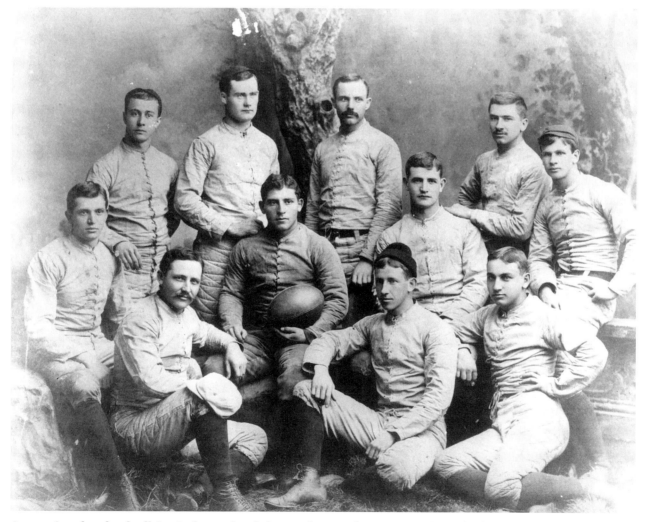

Inventing basketball isn't the only claim to fame of James Naismith (back row, standing second from left). As a college rugby player, he also created the first football helmet. He later coached the first basketball team at the University of Kansas.

THE ORIGINAL KU LEGEND

First All-American gained hero status

A 6-foot x 4-foot portrait honored him in old Robinson Gymnasium. Flags flew half-staff to honor him at the 1935 football homecoming game. And in voting for the 1932 *Jayhawker* Yearbook, which glorified him as "the man who gave his life for Kansas," Kansas coaches unanimously selected him as the school's all-time greatest football player.

If ever an athlete reached mythical proportions at the University of Kansas, Tommy Johnson did.

Reasons vary when rationalizing why the status of certain prominent individuals surpasses sheer popularity, approaching passionate homage instead. Like ancient Greek gods, their legend often arises from a potent mix of precise circumstances and tragic conclusions.

In the least, that's perhaps the most conceivable way of explaining the adoration Johnson inspired.

He grew up in a time of dime-store novels, which, if not inventing the ideals of American heroism and self-sufficiency, undoubtedly championed them as never before.

Johnson's life practically served as a Horatio Alger tale. During his youth, he suffered a kidney condition that may have been related to tuberculosis (historical accounts are vague regarding the exact ailment). It hindered him considerably and left him frail.

By the time Johnson entered Kansas in the fall of 1905, though, few could match his athletic ability. He and a fellow first-year student, Forrest C. "Phog" Allen, led KU to a 12-7 record in the 1905-06 basketball season, only the second winning season since the Jayhawks began playing basketball eight years earlier.

Inexplicably, Johnson left school after his freshman year. In a day that didn't feature stringent amateur eligibility rules, he returned to Kansas for the 1907-08 basketball season. With Allen as coach, the Jayhawks claimed by far their best record to that point in the program's history, 18-6.

The next fall, Johnson immediately stepped in as KU's football quarterback, leading the Jayhawks to an undefeated 9-0 season. KU played its first six games at home that year and concluded the season by defeating Missouri 10-4 in Kansas City, Mo.

By then, Johnson had established himself as the most well-known athlete in KU's brief history but had not yet fully constructed the foundation of his legend.

He cemented it, though, in a game against Nebraska in 1909. Kansas fans of the day hated the Cornhuskers and Missouri with equal vigor, and the Jayhawks entered the game with a 16-game winning streak dating to 1907.

The only score in the game came on a 70-yard touchdown punt return by Johnson, and KU won for the second straight year in Lincoln 6-0.

"The playing of (Verne) Long and Johnson at forward was characteristic of the work of the whole team. Their clever dodging and throwing of the most difficult goals early, won for them a place in the hearts of the basket ball fans."

– *Jayhawker* Yearbook comments on Johnson leading the way.

Twenty days later, Missouri knocked Johnson dizzy in the season finale, and the Tigers ended KU's 18-game winning streak 12-6. It was the first Missouri victory in the series in eight years. The *Kansas City Times* described a "wobbly" Johnson after he was struck on the back of the head returning a punt in the first half. Playing with what probably was a concussion, Johnson fumbled several times at the end of the half and "failed to produce any of the startling runs which have set the Kansas rooters wild so many times."

Partially because of Johnson's injury, KU's Regents, led by famous newspaper editor William Allen White, for whom the Kansas journalism school is named, voted to prohibit football in early 1910 until rule changes made the game safer. To the dismay of many, the school encouraged rugby in football's place. University elections that spring centered on the debate. One newspaper advertisement bellowed:

> ### Vote for Prof. H. A. Rice and the FOOTBALL Ticket
> --------------------
> ### DOWN WITH ENGLISH RUGBY

Meanwhile, Johnson shook off the football injury in time for the 1909-10 basketball season. In coach W.O. Hamilton's first season after Allen entered osteopathy school in Kansas City, KU won its third straight conference title.

Johnson "threw" 58 field goals during the season and led the Jayhawks in scoring with 9.9 points per game. His performance made him KU's first All-American in any sport. KU finished 18-1, its only loss a 16-15 defeat by Washington University of St. Louis.

TOMMY JOHNSON
Basketball, football and
track and field,
1905-06, 1907-10

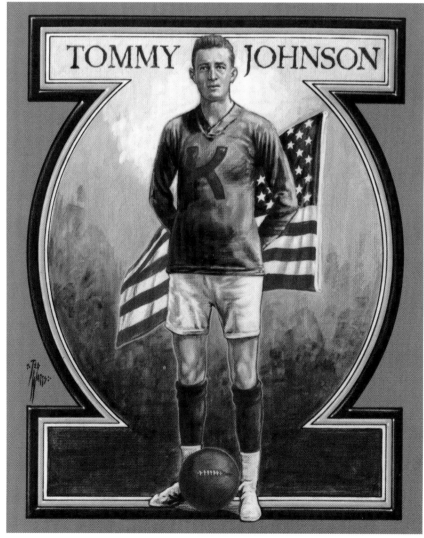

After already earning nine varsity letters in three sports (he also was a standout for KU's track and field squad), Johnson, along with American football, returned for his final year of KU athletics in 1910. He led the Jayhawks to a 6-1-1 record, including a 5-5 tie with Missouri that partially avenged the previous season's defeat.

However, he again suffered an injury against the Tigers. At one point during the game, two Missouri defenders sandwiched him, aggravating his kidney ailment from years earlier.

This time, Johnson did not recover. The former football and basketball captain didn't play basketball that winter as his condition worsened. On Nov. 24, 1911, exactly a year after he played his last college football game, Johnson died at Bell Memorial Hospital in Kansas City, site of what is now KU's Medical School.

In his 1947 book, *Phog Allen's Sports Stories for You and Youth,* Allen wrote that a teammate of Johnson's visited him in the hospital months before he died.

Allen wrote that the teammate said, "It's a darn tough break, Tommy," to which Johnson replied, "Don't feel sorry for me, pal. I've had a swell time. I've lived more in my twenty-two years that a lot of guys do in seventy."

Allen then wrote about his dear friend: "Tommy Johnson was Kansas' greatest all-around athlete. He took advantage of all the time he had. Achievements, not years, must be Time's answer to people seeking reasons why."

It's no wonder Allen, who was instrumental in bringing Memorial Stadium to the northern edge of Mount Oread, later said he would have pushed to name the stadium "Tommy Johnson Memorial Stadium" had Kansas students not died in World War I. The stadium instead is dedicated to those students.

Nevertheless, Kansans remembered Johnson. A 1935 KU homecoming tribute honored him as the school's greatest athlete; the *Lawrence Journal-World* named him as such.

As for that homecoming game, just as they had in Johnson's last game in any uniform, Kansas and Missouri tied.

"Tommy Johnson, the greatest athlete ever to wear the colors of Kansas University..."

– Lawrence Journal-World
Nov. 29, 1935

FOOTBALL FEVER

With good reason, Kansas has earned its reputation as a traditional college basketball power. But that budding tradition took a backseat to football during Tommy Johnson's days at KU, even though his All-America status stemmed from his basketball exploits.

Football was by far the dominant college sport in the late 1890s and early 1900s, especially at state-supported schools such as Kansas. Consider these newspaper accounts during Johnson's days as a KU quarterback:

"Everything in Lawrence is suspended to-night in celebration of the victory of the Jayhawker football team in Lincoln this afternoon. Hundreds of students are parading the streets shouting and singing, and the whole town is overjoyed at the news. The crowds began to collect directly after dark, and a parade was formed at the park on South Massachusetts street, and after marching all over town, the search began for material for a mammoth bonfire ..."

– Nov. 14, 1908, edition of the *Kansas City Star*, reporting how KU's 20-5 victory earlier that day at Nebraska affected Lawrence.

"This is turkey day, chrysanthemum day, football day and the old town will be in the possession of the rah-rah students from the Universities of Kansas and Missouri until late in the night and into wee hours of the morning ... The students from Lawrence, Ks., and Columbia, Mo., began to arrive yesterday morning and every train from the university towns brought its quota of rooters. A special train from Columbia arrived here about 6 o'clock last night bringing 500 students. The team arrived at 10 o'clock and was accompanied by 300 students. Two specials will bring 500 rooters from Topeka and 1,000 from Lawrence this morning. The Kansas team will arrive at 10 o'clock and by that hour the city will be in the hands of the football throng ..."

— Nov. 25, 1909, issue of the *Kansas City Times*, setting the stage for the annual Thanksgiving Day matchup in Kansas City between Kansas and Missouri.

Finally, in the "some things never change" category:

"... After the game the Missouri crowd broke through the wires and swarmed over the gridiron. Never had the Association Park, the staid old home of the second division ball clubs, been the scene of a wilder, more hilarious demonstration. One of the goal posts was pulled up and at the top was crucified a black hen, the nearest thing to a Jayhawk the frantic Missourians could find. Lifting this Jayhawk effigy aloft, the Tiger rooters fell in behind the Missouri band and paraded around the gridiron. The Missouri student rooters, a thousand strong, cheered until their throats were dry and their lips were parched ... Missouri followers from everywhere throughout the state, Missourians who never before had seen a Tiger team beat Kansas, fell in with the gay paraders ..."

— Nov. 26, 1909, edition of the *Times*, describing Missouri's 12-6 victory, its first against KU in eight years, at old Association Park in Kansas City, Mo. The park, featuring grandstands that could seat 11,300, was located at 19th and Olive streets, east of what is now the Crossroads district.

PREACHING ATHLETICS

Inventor of basketball concentrated more on helping others

We all know how James Naismith invented the popular sport of ... vrille?

"Vrille, a game originated by Dr. James R. Naismith, professor in physical education, is arousing interest in the University at the present," read the lead to a story in the Feb. 15, 1924, edition of the *University Daily Kansan*.

The story explained how Naismith invented the game while serving with the YMCA as a chaplain for U.S. soldiers in France during World War I.

The indoor court game pitted two teams against one another. Points accrued in a similar manner to tennis. The object of the game consisted of serving and returning a small rubber ball, using only one bounce, off a 4-foot-by-8-foot target in the middle of the court. Failing to do so resulted in points for the opposition.

Not exactly a sport that conjures images of cheerleaders and championship trophies. Hylo, a cross between English rugby and soccer that Naismith created during the early 1920s, also didn't fuel the competitive fire of aspiring athletes or raucous fans – if it ever had any.

Then again, loud bands weren't playing the cold December day in 1891 when Naismith, a 30-year-old instructor, posted the original 13 rules of basketball on bulletin board outside the gymnasium at Springfield (Mass.) YMCA College. Yet that simple act represents the birth of the most famous sport to trace its origins to U.S. soil.

Born in Canada of Scottish descent, Naismith never sought worldwide acclaim. At the time, inventing basketball merely fulfilled an order from his boss, Dr. Luther Gulick, to develop an indoor sport that would interest bored students suffering from cabin fever during the long New England winter.

But in a larger sense, Naismith invented basketball for the same reason he conceived vrille and hylo.

"I had prepared for the ministry at McGill University (located in Montreal, Canada) and had turned to the YMCA only because I thought the opportunities for helping young men lay more through exercise than through preaching," Naismith wrote in an article for *The Rotarian* several months before he died Nov. 28, 1939.

In 1932, he explained to the KU News Bureau how he arrived at that conclusion. It happened at McGill, after he heard a string of profanity roll from the lips of a football teammate.

"I had never said anything to him about profanity, nor even winced when he used that kind of language, for I had been all my life in the lumber camps of Canada," Naismith said. "I began to wonder what it was that led men to do this...

"When I was in college, athletics and gymnastics were considered inventions of the devil, intended to lead young men astray. Somehow, I couldn't help feeling that if athletics had a power to attract young men, that power should be used to attract them to better ways of living, for I had found a great satisfaction in the feeling of physical well-being that regular exercise gave me.

"Although I was graduated from a theological seminary, I felt there was a new field in which good could come for mankind, as well as in preaching."

So Naismith never practiced as a full-time Presbyterian minister, although he often conducted Sunday church services in various towns surrounding Lawrence. Otherwise, he limited his preaching to members of the First Kansas Infantry guarding the U.S.-Mexican border during Pancho Villa's insurrection in 1916 and to U.S. troops in World War I. During his early years at KU, he also served as chapel director, which basically consisted of leading students in a morning devotion and leading the football team in pregame prayers.

Naismith also never worked as a physician, even though he received a medical degree in 1898 from Gross Medical College in Denver.

Shortly after that, he accepted a position as director of physical education at Kansas. Amos Alonzo Stagg, famous college football coach and a friend of Naismith's at Springfield, recommended him for the job.

For the next 41 years, Naismith's life centered on physical education, his family and the city of Lawrence. He directed physical education at KU until 1924. After that, he continued teaching courses such as anatomy, kinesiology and "freshman hygiene," a sex education course, until he was 75.

At KU, Naismith developed a fascination for the human physique. He tracked physical measurements of incoming freshman as they progressed through college and compared the data of different years.

Paul Endacott, a KU basketball All-American in the early 1920s, wrote that Naismith's 20 physical measurements of incoming freshman ranged from height and weight to wrist circumference. In addition, Naismith liked people to know he worked hard to stay physically fit. One summer, he worked on a highway construction crew to prove he maintained abundant physical energy.

Endacott's account sheds light on another peculiarity regarding Naismith. He developed a great deal of pride about inventing basketball. But outside of serving on rules committees, he somewhat kept a distance from the game, generally guiding students to other activities.

"All he was basically interested in was fencing and wrestling," says Ted O'Leary, a KU basketball All-American in the 1930s who also knew Naismith while growing up in Lawrence. "He came to all the games, and he watched attentively, but I wouldn't say he was a fan. We never thought to ourselves, 'We're playing in front of the guy who invented the game! This is something special.'

"While we were practicing every day just a floor above him (in Robinson Gymnasium), I don't remember him ever coming up just to watch practice. Offhand, you'd think he'd be kind of interested, occasionally at least, to see what was going on up there, to see what Doc (F.C. "Phog" Allen) is telling them about the game. But he never came up."

Perhaps that's because he and Allen had a professional but not extremely friendly relationship, says O'Leary, who thinks Allen considered Naismith as sort of a rival.

"But Naismith never thought of Allen that way," he says. "He was not a flamboyant character in any way. He didn't think of himself as a famous man. He never gave any indication of vanity."

Although he later stayed out of Kansas basketball affairs, Naismith started KU's program in 1898-99 and guided it through its early years. Most remember him as the only Kansas coach with an all-time losing record (55-60).

But when reviewing his coaching record from 1898-1907, one should consider Naismith usually did not travel to road games, which accounted for most KU games before the first Robinson Gymnasium opened. Naismith's demands for a home court led to Robinson's construction, which finished a season after he quit coaching.

Physical education always captured his utmost interest, though. Despite his reserved nature, Naismith liked to tell a good story, said Gordon Gray, a basketball player who studied physical education in the mid-1930s.

"I think one of the things I enjoyed most were the stories he told in and out of

Naismith's trademark mustache still was jet black when he served in World War I as a chaplain.

"He regarded basketball pretty much as just another game that was played in gymnasiums in conjunction with physical exercises and gymnastics. However, he held such an intense interest in researching and recording the physical measurements of individuals that this was looked upon as being virtually an obsession."

– Paul Endacott described Naismith's devotion to physical measurements

JAMES NAISMITH
Head basketball coach, 1898-1907 • Head track and field coach, 1901-06
Physical education director and instructor, 1898-1937

class," said Gray, who died in December 1997. "He'd tell us stories about Alonzo Stagg and his life's story, so to speak. We just relished it."

Those stories could have included how Naismith invented the first football helmet by splitting a football in half and using it to cover his ears. Maybe they divulged how basketball passes were the impetus for another change in football: the legalization of the forward pass.

Possibly, Naismith told how both of his parents died when he was a child, or how he eventually dropped out of high school and spent nearly five years drinking, swearing and cavorting as a lumberjack during the early 1870s.

He returned to high school after an old family friend spotted him in a saloon one day and gave him a sobering reminder.

"Your mother would turn over in her grave to see you now," the friend said.

Four decades later, in 1918, Naismith wrote *The Basis of Clean Living*. By that time, he had been married to his wife, Maude, for 26 years. They had three daughters and two sons.

Life wasn't always easy for Naismith, especially once the Depression started. Never having financially capitalized on basketball, he lost his house in a 1934 mortgage foreclosure, and Maude died in 1937. Two years later, only months before he died, Naismith married Florence Mae Kincaid.

Through it all, he maintained dignity and sense of honor.

Perhaps Robert Ellsworth, a Kansas congressman and son of long-time KU Alumni director Fred Ellsworth, said it best in a 1961 speech to Congress. Ellsworth was proposing a stamp to celebrate the 100th anniversary of Naismith's birth:

"… His every concern was to urge physical habits upon young Americans that would develop strong bodies and minds. He has left a great imprint on all sport-minded Americans and certainly a very strong influence on the University of Kansas."

"He deplored any form of discrimination, segregation or prejudice, and helped me to surmount glaring institutional discriminatory practices during my junior and senior years … There's no question that my life would not have been anywhere near what it has become if I had not had Dr. Naismith as my adviser."

– John McLendon,
Hall of Fame
basketball coach
New York Times, 1996

PENNIES FROM HEAVEN

James Naismith never profited from his greatest invention. Yet he traveled to the 1936 Olympic Games in Berlin after high schools across the nation collected pennies from basketball fans during the 1935-36 season. The donations created a fund Naismith used to pay his trip expenses to see the first Olympic basketball competition.

In Berlin, Naismith watched the game he invented played on an outdoor court, and he posed for photographs with each of the 21 countries that fielded basketball teams.

He also attended swimming events with Adolf Hitler. The *University Daily Kansan* reported that when Naismith returned to the United States, he told friends and students how much German unification and nationalism impressed him.

During the games, Naismith had access to almost every area of Berlin's Olympic venue, called the "Reichfield." The lone exception: Hitler's private suite.

SHAKY START

The man who invented basketball was Kansas' coach AND the referee in the school's first hoops game Feb. 3, 1899.

Despite James Naismith's presence, the Jayhawks still lost. In fact, as far as deficits go in those low-scoring days, Kansas got crushed 16-5 by a more-experienced Kansas City, Mo., YMCA squad.

KU was lucky to have scored that many points. *The Lawrence Daily Journal* described how Kansas captain Will Sutton scored one of the team's two field goals:

"Sutton made one of the most sensational plays of the game. The ball was thrown to him and he rolled it for three yards. He was viciously beset by two YMCA men, and bending backward, he threw the ball fully 12 yards and got a goal."

Twelve yards translates into a 36-foot shot — a tremendous heave, especially backward.

The game also featured a prominent name on Kansas City's squad.

"Jesse James, the young man who has lately come into prominence by his alleged connection with the recent train robberies in Missouri, played a rough, and at times, a very ungentlemanly game. He was cautioned and punished by the referee several times during the game," the *Kansas University Weekly* wrote.

Actually, the player probably was the son of the well-known train robber. The elder James — who at age 15 joined William Quantrill's gang — died of a gunshot wound in 1882. Quantrill, of course, was the infamous Confederate guerrilla leader. In 1863, he and his raiders ransacked Lawrence, burning the town and killing about 150 men and boys.

STANDARD OF PERFECTION

"Lefty" exemplified ideal physical traits of a pre-World War I athlete

Height: 6 feet 2 inches. Weight: 175 pounds.

Nearing the new millennium, unless you're a lightning-quick ballhandler à la Jacque Vaughn or a Rex Walters-style three-point threat, those physical specifications won't get you any closer to the Kansas men's basketball team than a courtside seat.

Before World War I, Kansas forward Ralph Sproull parlayed those exact measurements into All-America status and a declaration by basketball's inventor, Dr. James Naismith, as the standard of perfection by which other KU athletes should be judged.

Times certainly do change.

Naismith based a large part of his continuing study as a physical education instructor on that basic fact of life. He required detailed physical assessments of every man who entered the University, including such arcane measurements as arm length and sizes of various muscles. As the years passed, he used the information to compare differences between incoming classes.

In Sproull, Naismith found the physical model after which he thought other athletes should fashion themselves. With all Sproull accomplished at Kansas, it's hard to argue with Naismith's appraisal.

"Lefty" was the best player among a slew of former Lawrence high school stars, including Ray "Stuffy" Dunmire and Art Weaver, who formed the heart of Kansas teams between 1910-15. Lawrence had won the Kansas high school championship in 1910-11, Sproull's senior year.

At Kansas, Sproull racked up scoring records other KU players didn't touch until after World War II. He led the Missouri Valley Conference in scoring each season he played, peaking with 17.8 points per game during his senior season of 1914-15. No Missouri Valley, Big Six or Big Seven conference player averaged more in league contests until KU's Clyde Lovellette poured in 23 points per game in 1949-50.

In 1913, Sproull set a school record with 40 points as the Jayhawks blitzed conference foe Washington University of St. Louis 68-8. The scoring barrage broke the previous mark of 26 points set by F.C. "Phog" Allen in the only year he played for Kansas, 1905-06. No one exceeded it until Lovellette scored 42 against Southern Methodist 39 years later.

Kansas won two conference championships during Sproull's career, running away with the title his junior and senior years. The Jayhawks lost one game apiece in each of those seasons, both to the Kansas State Aggies by a combined seven points.

Despite his strong physical traits, Sproull was not immune to afflictions that bothered other players of the era. Illness was a bigger fear than injury. Childhood vaccinations taken for granted today were almost unheard of then, and antibiotics were limited.

Sproull suffered bouts with the mumps, tonsillitis and once, blood poisoning in his leg. All hindered his play at various times. But they didn't prevent him from becoming the greatest scorer fans at KU's Robinson Gymnasium ever witnessed.

Admittedly, his scoring records benefited from the pre-1924 rule that allowed one player to shoot all of his team's free throws. Charity shots often were rewarded for numerous violations by opposing teams, not just fouls. In addition, players during Sproull's era could not return to the game after they were replaced. Consequently, he played every minute of every game in 1913-14.

Sproull, who died in 1981 at age 87, also played baseball and competed in track and field at Kansas. In fact, he twice ran in final sprint trials for the Olympics. But above all, he cherished his basketball memories, often corresponding about Kansas hoops with former KU sports information director Jay Simon in the late 1960s and early 1970s.

"I know I was lucky to be playing all three years with Art Weaver and Stuffy Dunmire," he wrote once from his California home. "Anyone should score with those guys to help."

But Naismith and the record books agreed – Sproull wasn't just anyone.

RALPH SPROULL

RALPH "LEFTY" SPROULL
Basketball, baseball and track and field,
1912-15

Basketball's primitive nature in the early 20th century is illustrated by a story Ralph "Lefty" Sproull related to the *Lawrence Journal-World* during a visit to his hometown in the late 1960s.

Sproull recounted a game during his sophomore year of 1912-13 against Washington University of St. Louis. Three weeks before the game, Sproull had set KU's one-game scoring record of 40 points versus Washington in a 68-8 KU victory in Lawrence.

But in this contest on Washington's home court, the score was close with time running out. However, Sproull didn't know the exact score or how much time remained because Washington's gymnasium contained no game clock or scoreboard.

"I was dribbling down the floor when the coach (W.O. Hamilton) yelled at me and said the score was 29-28," Sproull said. "I knew the game was about over and I thought he meant we were behind. I hurried down the floor and fired up a left-handed shot from the corner. It bounced off the rim and didn't go in just as the final buzzer sounded.

"I was walking dejectedly off the court when the official came out and announced the final score: 'Kansas 29, Washington University 28.' "

Of course, Sproull's dejection quickly turned to elation. Maybe clocks and scoreboards were too much to ask for at the time. After all, only six seasons earlier, KU's home games were played in the basement of Old Snow Hall. Not only was the Snow Hall court smaller than a regulation-size floor, but players had to dodge a support beam in the middle of the court.

Home games moved to the new $100,000 Robinson Gymnasium, which sat on the site now occupied by Wescoe Hall, for the 1907-08 season.

CARL RICE / TOM POOR

LEAPING INTO THE SPOTLIGHT

High jumpers commanded early attention for KU's track squad

Long before Bill Easton, Al Oerter, Jim Ryun and others took the University of Kansas track and field program to a higher level and produced one of the most respected reputations in amateur athletics, KU athletes were distinguishing themselves in both intercollegiate and international track competition.

Only three years after James Naismith started the Kansas track team, KU's Ray Moulton competed in the 1904 Olympic Games in St. Louis, winning a bronze medal in the 100-yard dash and placing fourth in the 200-yard dash. Later, KU's Everett Bradley won a silver medal in the pentathlon at the 1920 Olympics in Antwerp, Belgium.

But two high jumpers probably did more to lay the foundation for KU's track tradition than any other athletes during an era marked by the first World War, Prohibition, flappers and women's suffrage. It also was a period in which track and field shared a spotlight in the American sports scene with major league baseball, college football, horse racing and boxing.

The two, Carl V. Rice and Tom Poor, dominated U.S. high jumping as the

Troubled Teens melted into the Roaring Twenties. Along with Tom Scofield in the late 1940s, Randy Smith and Barry Schur in the early to mid-1970s and Nick Johannsen in the mid-1990s, they remain two of the most prominent men's high jumpers in Kansas history.

Rice was the first. A 16-year-old from Coffeyville, he entered the University in September 1914 resembling a thoroughbred jockey more than a high jumper. At the time, he stood just 5 feet 8 inches and weighed only 128 pounds. His athletics experience was limited to unorganized town-team baseball and basketball games.

Rice didn't consider college athletics until his sophomore year, when a friend urged him to begin distance running. Once, while "fooling around," as Rice put it in a 1975 account of his time at KU, he discovered he could jump almost as high as KU's No. 2 high jumper. He then worked out on his own until he caught the eye of track and field coach W.O. Hamilton.

He eventually joined the squad and won one dual meet in 1916, enough to earn a varsity letter. An athletics scholarship, which in those days translated into working four hours a day for 25 cents an hour, followed. But Rice's best was yet to come.

For five straight years, 1917-21, Rice won the high jump at a prestigious national meet sponsored by the Kansas City Athletic Club. He won the

TOM POOR
Track and field,
1923-25

CARL RICE
Track and field,
1916-18

1918 Penn Relays, becoming the first KU athlete to win an event in that meet, and also placed third in the javelin, the only time he ever competed in that event.

In addition, Rice won Missouri Valley Conference championships, tied for a national championship in the 1917 Indoor Intercollegiate gathering and placed second in the 1917 Outdoor Intercollegiate, both of which were precursors to the annual NCAA meet.

But Rice didn't routinely clear 6 feet until after he graduated from KU with a law degree in 1918. Later that year, he won the national meet sponsored by the Amateur Athletic Union, earning a spot on Spalding's All-America team.

After a brief stint in the service, Rice went to Parsons to practice law. In May 1919, KU track coach Karl Schlademan asked him to demonstrate proper high-jump techniques. While doing so, Rice cleared a personal-best 6-5 3/8, which prompted the Army to ask him to rejoin and represent the United States in the Inter-Allied Games in Paris. He placed second, becoming the first KU athlete or alumnus to win a medal on foreign soil.

But the Paris trip would veer Rice from athletics to politics. There he met President Woodrow Wilson, who was attending the Paris Peace Conference promoting his League of Nations, the forerunner of the United Nations. Years later, Rice was a delegate to the 1932 Democratic National Convention in Chicago. After Franklin D. Roosevelt won the presidency, he appointed Rice as counsel for the Reconstruction Finance Corp., a Depression-era program in Kansas City, Mo.

By the time he retired in the 1960s, Rice had made a fortune in manufacturing, invented a mechanism for coin-controlled vending machines and had frequented the White House on several occasions. He regularly visited his Kansas City law office well into his 80s. He told the Kansas City Business Journal in a 1983 interview his secret for a long life: "Live an interesting life. Drink good whiskey. Vote Democratic."

As Rice's high jump career was ending, Poor's was beginning. He arrived on campus in the fall of 1921 and broke the school record not long thereafter.

By the time he left KU in 1925, "The Kansas Grasshopper" had placed fourth in the 1924 Olympic Games in Paris, jumped as high as 6-5 1/2 (KU's school record now is 7-4 1/2, set by Tyke Peacock in 1982), garnered KU's first individual NCAA track championship in 1923 and broken meet records 10 different times.

Poor also won the conference meet three consecutive years and established the league's all-time mark of 6-3 1/8.

Perhaps Poor's finest hour, though, came in 1925. In a four-week period, he won the Texas, Kansas and Penn Relays, accomplishing a rare college high-jump triple crown. He won the the first three Kansas Relays, which began in 1923, and also won the Drake Relays twice.

It's difficult to understate Poor's impact on high jumping. Decades before the Fosbury Flop revolutionized the event, his rise coincided with the the addition of the Kansas and Texas Relays to the spring outdoor circuit, which increased track's popularity during what many still refer to as the Golden Age of American sports.

The 1925 Jayhawker Yearbook adequately assessed Poor's career heading into his final college campaign: "Tom Poor is perhaps the most consistent winner in his event that the Valley has ever seen ... Poor has gained world-wide fame for his ability as a high jumper."

World-wide fame indeed. Though their records were eclipsed, Rice and Poor nursed KU's budding track and field tradition, helping jump-start decades of success.

ATHLETICS TO AUTOS

First Kansas athletics director gave it up for new business

Critics often equate unscrupulous college basketball coaches to sleazy used car sales representatives. In 1919, a University of Kansas athletics director and basketball coach gave up a 23-year career in coaching and sports administration to ... open a car dealership.

But William Oliver Hamilton, whose reputation squeaked cleaner than a freshly waxed floor, proved honesty and integrity can be hallmarks of both professions.

In 10 seasons as KU's basketball coach from 1909-10 to 1918-19, Hamilton's teams won or shared five Missouri Valley Conference championships. He won 125 games and lost 59, a .679 winning percentage that places him behind Roy Williams, Larry Brown and Forrest C. "Phog" Allen among the seven head coaches in Kansas men's basketball history.

Not bad, considering he served as KU's track and field coach and athletics director at the same time. Hamilton's background, though, had prepared him for various tasks in athletics.

He grew up in Liberty, Mo., where his family moved in 1879 when Hamilton was just 3. He attended college at Liberty's William Jewell College, where as an undergraduate, he formed the Midwest's first basketball team only a couple years after James Naismith invented the game.

William Jewell also gave Hamilton his first job. From 1896 to 1902, he directed the school's physical training department.

In 1902, Hamilton and his new bride, Annie, moved to Kansas City, Mo. For the next seven years, he was in charge of the physical education department at Kansas City's old Central High School.

He arrived at KU in 1909, where he took over as basketball and track coach. Allen was basketball coach the previous two seasons before leaving to attend osteopath school in Kansas City after the 1908-09 season.

Hamilton had an auspicious beginning at Kansas. Led by All-American Tommy Johnson, the basketball team finished 18-1 and won the conference title. The track team also won the conference meet, the only time it accomplished the feat in his tenure as coach. During that same year, he assumed the role as KU's first athletics director.

His association with Kansas athletics didn't end at work. During his years at KU, several Kansas athletes lived in Hamilton's large house on Mississippi Street in Lawrence.

By the end of the 1914-15 basketball season, Hamilton's teams had won 90 games and lost 22. But his last four seasons weren't as successful. The Jayhawks suffered losing records twice and didn't finish higher than third in the conference, which contained six teams when Hamilton started at KU. The conference expanded to seven when Kansas State joined in 1913 and to eight when Grinnell (Iowa) joined in 1918.

W.O. HAMILTON
Head track and field coach,
1910-18
Athletics director and head basketball coach,
1909-19

Hamilton quit as track coach after the 1918 season, and after the 1918-19 school year, he resigned from Kansas altogether. Ironically, the man he replaced as basketball coach – Allen – replaced him as athletics director.

Hamilton then opened a Chevrolet dealership in Lawrence and operated it for 12 years. He ran a Ford dealership for several years after that. During World War II, he worked in vehicle maintenance at the large Sunflower Ordnance Works in DeSoto, about 15 miles east of Lawrence. The Sunflower plant manufactured munitions for the U.S. war effort.

Hamilton never retired. He stayed in the automobile business until he died Dec. 30, 1951, at age 75. His pallbearers included Kansas athletics director A.C. "Dutch" Lonborg, former KU football coach Adrian "Ad" Lindsey, Loren "Red" Brown and Frank Mandeville. All four played basketball for him at Kansas.

Basketball Takes Center Stage

Paul Endacott	34	Albert Peterson	43
Charles T. Black	38	Gale Gordon	43
Tusten Ackerman	41		

The 1922-23 Kansas basketball squad did not lose a game in the Missouri Valley Conference and was named the National Champion by the Helms Foundation. Coach F.C. "Phog" Allen (far left) led the Jayhawks to a 17-1 record. The team included three players later named to the KU Athletics Hall of Fame: Paul Endacott (second from left), Charles T. Black (third from left) and Tusten Ackerman (third from right).

FINE PLAYER, FINER MAN

Longtime KU benefactor succeeded in many ways

The University of Kansas basketball team milled about a Sedalia, Mo., hotel, waiting for the east-bound train to Columbia. The Jayhawks were tired, having returned to Lawrence just two days earlier after a grueling trip across Iowa. On this particular Tuesday morning in mid-January 1923, the season was only 13 days old, yet KU already had played six games.

The Jayhawks had won every one, including three in three days against Iowa State, Grinnell and Drake during the recently completed Iowa tour. But as newspaper reports the day before indicated, each of KU's five starters were suffering various injuries as they prepared to face their biggest test of the season: Missouri.

Kansas' captain and starting guard, Paul Endacott, felt his badly sprained wrists throb periodically that morning. While waiting for the 6 a.m. train, he possibly contemplated that night's game against the powerful Tigers. The season before, Missouri had tied KU for the Missouri Valley Conference championship.

Or maybe he simply listened to his growling stomach. Because of a mixup at its stop the night before in Pleasant Hill, Mo., the team's only meal since leaving Lawrence had consisted of a few sandwiches.

In any case, as the team waited, a strange man suddenly appeared at Endacott's side. He quickly shoved a note into the balding player's hands and darted outside the hotel.

Confused, Endacott opened the crumpled piece of paper and read four scribbled words: *"To Hell with Kansas."*

A lifetime resident of Lawrence to that point, Endacott knew his ancestors had settled in northeast Kansas shortly before Congress approved the Kansas-Nebraska Act of 1854. Born in 1902, he had heard the stories of "Bleeding Kansas," the violent Civil War period when pro-Union forces from Kansas clashed with Confederate sympathizers from Missouri.

No one knows whether the note spurred Endacott's performance against the Tigers that night. But he played the key role in KU's 21-19 victory.

Unfortunately, as the years passed, Kansas coach F.C. "Phog" Allen embellished Endacott's heroics – so much so that an embarrassed Endacott wrote a letter in his personal basketball archives to set the record straight. It detailed how he had not controlled 16 straight jump balls in the last two minutes of the game and virtually collapsed afterward, as Allen always suggested:

> *"It is certain that he greatly exaggerated that incident, and I respectfully told him so. Unfortunately, he insisted that this was not the case and that he had a record to prove it, although he never showed it to me."*

Maybe Allen recalled it that way because he had considered quitting as coach if KU didn't beat Missouri twice and win the conference in 1922-23. But Endacott, who countered his 5-foot-10-inch frame with great leaping ability, remembered controlling only three or four straight jump balls (players in that day could tip a jump ball directly to themselves).

Tusten Ackerman, a sophomore who led KU in scoring that night with 11 points, also remembered Endacott only forcing three or four jump balls, which allowed time to run out. But during an interview shortly before he died in May 1997, Ackerman also recalled that his teammate's tenacity saved the game.

"He was a fine man, a fine player," Ackerman said. "He NEVER gave up."

Growing up in Lawrence, where James Naismith taught his Sunday school, Endacott never had much to give up. At 9 years old, he worked part-time in a factory and on a farm to provide extra money for his family. His parents never owned an automobile or even a horse. His home had no electricity or running water.

But by the time he was 8, less than two decades after Naismith invented the

PAUL ENDACOTT
Basketball,
1920-23

game, Endacott was playing church-league basketball, scoring 44 points in one game.

He graduated from Lawrence High School in 1919, the same year Allen returned to Kansas as athletics director.

Originally a walk-on, Endacott later made first-team all-conference twice and All-America twice. He scored only 50 points during the 1922-23 season, when KU went 17-1 while winning the conference title outright for the first time since 1914-15.

Nonetheless, the Helms Foundation retroactively named Endacott as the national player of the year for that season. The Jayhawks outscored their opponents by an average of 31.5 to 16.6, and no team scored more than 27 points against Kansas all year.

Paul Endacott went from working in a factory at age 9 to one of KU's most generous financial contributors.

Endacott and KU's other starting guard, Charlie T. Black, led the Jayhawks' stingy defense.

"Endacott and Black at guard positions broke up counter attacks and wrested the ball from the hands of rival forwards with ease time after time during the majority of games," the 1923 *Jayhawker* Yearbook wrote. "In Endacott, Kansas had the best defensive player in the entire conference."

A Missouri correspondent to the *University Daily Kansan*, covering the KU-Missouri game that Allen later embellished, described how Endacott's defense could change the flow of a game: "Time after time he broke up the short-pass floor work of the locals and generalled his team so well that the Tigers were forced to shoot from the center of the court."

Although he hardly scored, few players of his era surpassed Endacott's other abilities. In 1943, the Associated Press asked several college coaches to name all-time All-America teams. Endacott, the only former KU player selected, made the second team. (Legendary UCLA coach John Wooden, who played at Purdue in the early 1930s, made the first team along with the man who popularized the jump shot, Hank Luisetti of Stanford.)

Endacott continued making various all-time teams until his induction into the Basketball Hall of Fame in 1972.

His basketball achievements withstood time, but Endacott's success during an illustrious career with Phillips Petroleum Company had greater lasting impact on American life.

Unlike many former college basketball players who joined Phillips merely to play for its famous amateur team, Endacott had studied engineering at Kansas and seriously desired a position with a growing oil and gas company. Instead of playing more basketball, Endacott wanted a career that could provide money for his parents.

During the summer of 1921, Endacott used his background as an engineering student while helping build KU's Memorial Stadium. KU appointed one of his professors, J.O. Jones, as the surveying engineer for the stadium's construction, and he hired Endacott to assist.

Later at Phillips, Endacott contributed considerably to the company's growth. He developed its employee relations department and also received about 20 patents for innovations that changed the oil and natural gas industries.

His most famous invention occurred when he was only 25 years old. As a plant manager, he developed a system that allowed homeowners outside main natural gas lines to use propane as a substitute. In the process, Endacott virtually started the liquid petroleum gas industry.

His 44-year career with Phillips ended when he retired as vice chairman of the board in 1967. At that point, he started paying more attention to basketball again.

Before, Endacott and his wife, Lucille, had organized reunions for the 1923 team. He also underwrote a gift of about $1,000 that paid for an oil painting of Allen that now hangs in the east foyer of Allen Field House. But he rarely attended KU games and only played briefly for the Phillips squad after leaving Kansas.

Once he retired, though, Endacott grew concerned about how increasingly tall players dominated basketball. In 1968, he wrote a lengthy letter promoting a three-point shot to Press Maravich, head coach at Louisiana State and head of the National Association of Basketball Coaches' rules committee. He also contacted Ed Steitz, who led the NCAA men's basketball rules committee.

His persistence, along with that of countless others, paid off years later. Steitz, the primary force behind the introduction of a shot clock and the reinstatement of the dunk, led the introduction of the first three-point shot for all college games. The rule began in 1986-87.

Although somewhat reluctant to constantly talk basketball, Endacott always supported Kansas. A lifetime trustee of the KU Endowment Association, he also served stints as a director and president of the KU Alumni Association. In 1977, he received the Fred Ellsworth Medallion, one of the University's highest honors, for outstanding lifetime service to the school.

Endacott also contributed money to form the KU Retirees' Club. His architectural sketch for a retirees' center eventually became a blueprint for the first floor of the Adams Alumni Center. The center is named after K.S. "Boots" Adams, a former president of Phillips to whom Endacott served as an assistant in the late 1930s and early 1940s.

Kansas has retired Endacott's basketball jersey, and he donated his personal basketball archives to the KU Sports Information Department a few years before he died in January 1997 in Bartlesville, Okla. Those archives, which provided some historical material for this book, contain mountains of information regarding his playing days. They also include background on the careers of Allen, Naismith and famous Kentucky coach Adolph Rupp – Endacott's backup guard at KU.

Allen may have stretched the truth regarding Endacott's exploits at Missouri in 1923. But his assessment in 1972, when Endacott received membership to the Hall of Fame, hit the mark:

> "In this case they have picked a bona fide all-time, All-American, not only in basketball but in life. He was a Lawrence boy who worked his way through school, made All-America in college and was an all-time player.
> "There just isn't a finer man to be found. I'm proud to have had the chance to coach Paul."

HARD WORK, OUTSTANDING PLAY

Combination proved fruitful for "Kansas' greatest living athlete"

Huey Black preached hard work. In a bygone time when many thought high school was a luxury and only the rich considered going onto college, Black thought any son of his should be earning his keep by age 16, if not earlier.

Charles Terence Black, by all accounts a modest teenager, appeased his father. After classes and sports practices in Alton, Ill., ended for the day, young Charlie worked at a munitions factory that cranked out materiel for the U.S. effort in World War I.

Through the night, he alternated an hour's work with an hour's sleep in a setting less than conducive for a good night's rest, especially for a high school student-athlete who occasionally suffered from severe headaches. Shortly after dawn, he returned to school, and the routine started again.

His arduous life might have continued into adulthood. Fortunately, for Black and the University of Kansas, fate stepped in and changed the future of both for the better.

In this case, fate's name was Walter Wood, a former quarterback for the Kansas football team and athletics director at Alton High School. Knowing Black's desire to attend college, Wood told him about Lawrence.

Go there, Wood said, and knock on the door of the Sigma Alpha Epsilon fraternity.

And that's how a runaway F.C. "Phog" Allen later described as "Kansas' greatest living athlete" arrived at KU.

The fraternity supplied Black with meals and living quarters. A "scholarship," consisting of a job as a janitor in Robinson Gymnasium, supplied Black with needed spending money.

Black, in return, gave Kansas perhaps its most versatile athlete ever – and convinced his father to pay college expenses for his younger siblings.

In football, Black was a quarterback and left end who still holds the Kansas record for points scored in a game (29). Black set that record and the KU record for touchdowns in one game (four) in an 83-0 victory against Washington (Mo.) University in 1923. Only June Henley, against Texas Christian in 1996; Tony Sands, against Missouri in 1991; and Quintin Smith, against Louisville in 1989, have matched the latter mark.

In baseball, Black helped lead Kansas to a Missouri Valley Conference championship in 1923. And in basketball, he was a two-time All-American who piloted KU's second undefeated conference season and two Helms Foundation National Championship squads.

During his senior season of 1923-24, Black served as captain for all three teams. Although the baseball team struggled with a 5-9 record, he led the football team to a share of its first conference championship since 1908, the second year of the Valley's existence. As for the basketball team, it won its third consecutive conference title.

Yet if Black was proud, no one knew it.

"Charlie is a natural athlete," KU football coach George "Potsy" Clark told the *Jayhawker* Yearbook in 1923, "with a modest personality."

It's a typical description of Black, whose humble 5-foot-9-inch, 160-pound stature belied his abilities. But humble is how others viewed him.

"I never knew he was a great athlete until I was a teenager," says Janet Manfred, Black's oldest daughter. "My father was a very modest man."

Since then, Manfred has learned that were he so inclined, her father could have justifiably boasted about his playing days at Kansas. His retired basketball jersey hangs in Allen Field House, honoring his accomplishments in the sport that gained him the most fame.

Black was the best ballhandler Kansas fans had ever seen. A newspaper account of KU's 23-20 victory against Missouri in the final game of the 1922-23 season, a game that clinched the first undefeated season for any Missouri Valley team, called Black a "whirlwind on dribbling down the court."

KU's *Graduate Magazine* said, "Black's play is marked by his brilliant dribbling, his coolness and his fine handling of the ball."

Black's primary position – Allen called them "quarterbacks" – was akin to the modern-day point guard. He and All-America Paul Endacott formed the back-court that Helms later called the national champions in 1921-22 and 1922-23, but Black also played forward during parts of 1922-23. The next year, Black was the national college player of the year, another honor later bestowed by Helms.

Shortly before his death, Tusten Ackerman, a starting forward from 1922-23 through 1924-25, said Black's dribbling and passing skills overshadowed his ability to score.

"He was a great player, an all-around athlete," Ackerman said. "He was a good shooter, but guards didn't do much shooting in those days. Forwards did most of the shooting."

Besides dribbling and passing skills, Black earned the reputation as a clever player, as the "coolness" remark by the *Graduate Magazine* attested. A highly dramatic account by Allen in his 1947 book, *Phog Allen's Sports Stories for You and Youth*, exemplifies Black's savvy.

The incident occurred during the final two minutes of KU's last game of 1922-23 at home against Missouri. The Jayhawks were undefeated in the conference; Missouri's only loss had come to KU earlier in the season.

With the Jayhawks leading by two points, Black had the ball in KU's half of the court. In those days, however, no 10-second rule for getting the ball across midcourt existed. The Tigers guarded Kansas closely, so closely that Black was unable to free himself or find an open teammate. A turnover seemed imminent.

What happened next, according to Allen, must have been a spectacle:

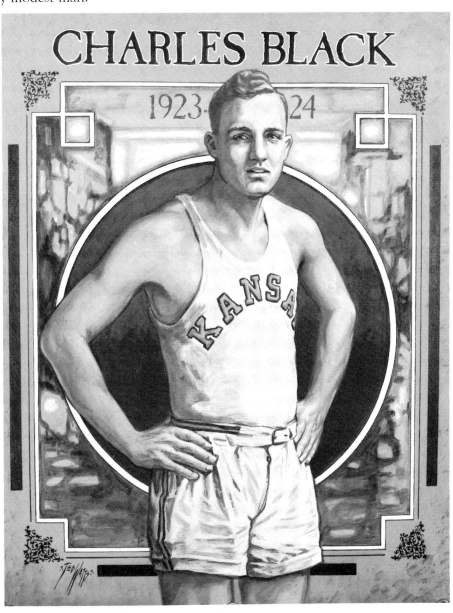

CHARLES T. BLACK
Basketball, football
and baseball,
1921-24

"… in this awful moment, Charley (sic) Black of 1923, apparently disregarding his crouching Tiger opponent, stopped and with complete nonchalance, placed the ball on his hips, as if time had been called out, and turning toward his teammate, Waldo Bowman, he motioned for him, saying,

"'Hey, Bowman, come over here.'

"His opponent stood mute and looked at him while his teammate, Bowman, walked ten or more feet to his comrade.

"This coup d'etat had caught the Missourian off-guard and, apparently thinking that Black had called time out, had relaxed his guarding vigilance.

"Black whispered a word of caution in Bowman's ear, and the two flashed down the floor into open territory, amid the frenzy of an overwrought partisan throng. Black had seized his opportunity and with a smashing dribble drove into safe territory. Figuratively the roof blew off. Black had saved the game by his daring coolness under fire."

Black's achievements are all the more impressive considering he suffered from cluster headaches throughout his life. He risked passing out if he didn't lie down within 30 minutes of their throbbing onset.

The headaches lasted late into Black's life, when he finally discovered they were caused by a strong allergic reaction to milk, Manfred says.

Black overcame them, though, during a productive post-KU life that began in coaching. He was head coach for two years at Grinnell College in Iowa, which was a conference foe of Kansas before the Jayhawks joined the Big Six Conference in 1928.

After that, he was Nebraska's head coach for six seasons, from 1926-27 to 1931-32. His 51-57 record with the Cornhuskers included a 5-7 record against his mentor, Allen. In his first year with Nebraska, the Cornhuskers gave KU, the Missouri Valley champ, one of its two losses.

Black's coaching career ended with a 3-17 season in 1931-32. He then went to work with the Owens-Illinois Glass Co. in Toledo, Ohio. He remained with the company in various capacities, including personnel manager, until he retired. Outside of work, he often officiated sporting events as a hobby, Manfred says.

A golf lover, Black remained physically active until his death at age 86 in 1988, the same year he shot his last hole-in-one.

From a munitions plant in 1918 to a golf course 70 years later, it seemed Black never stopped working or playing.

SOMEBODY PLEASE SCORE

Charlie Black's basketball career at Kansas overshadows his other athletic accomplishments. But as captain of the KU football team in 1923, he led a squad that didn't give up a touchdown and only surrendered two field goals in eight games.

Despite a 5-0-3 record, KU finished tied for first in the conference with Nebraska because the Jayhawks and the Cornhuskers played a scoreless tie on Oct. 20 in the first game played in Nebraska's Memorial Stadium. Proving that offense was a precious commodity in early 1920s college football, KU and Kansas State played a scoreless tie the next week in Lawrence.

That season, KU established a school record by scoring 83 points in a game against Washington University of St. Louis (the 1947 team broke the mark with 86 against South Dakota State). The Jayhawks averaged only six points in their other seven games, yet still finished the season without a loss.

HARVEST CREWS & BASKETBALL SHOES

Scoring leader's summer approach unheard of today

Today, high school players who qualify as potential college All-Americans spend summers honing their skills against the best high school players in the nation. They attend basketball camps sponsored by large shoe companies, where dozens of college coaches watch, salivating at the thought of attracting them to their school.

It's safe to say not one college coach traveled to western Kansas in the summers between 1918 and 1921 to watch Tus Ackerman harvest wheat – despite his stellar performances for Lawrence High School's basketball team.

But Nike and Converse were decades away from controlling summer basketball camps, and Kansas farms needed bodies after World War I service decimated summer harvest crews. So Ackerman joined hoards of young men riding westbound freight trains to help cut wheat.

He eventually made All-America twice in college, anyway, and saved $300 from his harvest experiences. (Back then, high school players who qualified as potential college All-Americans didn't receive full scholarships that paid for books, tuition and meals, either.)

By the time Ackerman entered the University of Kansas in 1921, his harvesting days were over. Focused on books and basketball, he provided scoring punch at forward and center that helped KU win 50 games and lose only five while winning the Missouri Valley Conference each year during his three varsity seasons from 1922-23 to 1924-25.

The son of a former professional baseball pitcher and the first grandson of one of the founders of Russell, Kan. (the renowned hometown of another prominent Kansas alumnus, Bob Dole), Arthur Tusten Ackerman was born Oct. 7, 1901, in Elk City, Okla. He moved often as a child, actually living in Columbia, Mo., during grade school.

"I didn't care for Columbia," Ackerman said a month before he died in May 1997.

It's a good thing, then, that his family eventually settled in Lawrence, or he might have played basketball at the university he wound up loathing.

At Lawrence High, he played for a program

TUSTEN ACKERMAN
Basketball,
1922-25

that had developed a pipeline to KU beginning in about 1910. In fact, Lawrence claimed six of the 11 players on KU's 1922-23 Helms National Championship team.

In a 1965 letter to Kansas coach Ted Owens, Ackerman called his coach at Lawrence High, Julius Uhrlaub, "one of the finest basketball technicians I played for" – high praise considering he also played for F.C. "Phog" Allen. Uhrlaub had twin sons, Ernst and Rudolf, who played at Kansas shortly before and after World War I for Coach W.O. Hamilton, Ackerman's future father-in-law.

Ackerman's first varsity game at KU foreshadowed the dominance he and his teammates enjoyed during the next three seasons. The Jayhawks pounded Creighton in Omaha, Neb., 29-7, allowing the Bluejays just one field goal.

During that season, Kansas held its opponents under 20 points 12 times while compiling a 17-1 record. KU's only loss was a 27-23 defeat against the Blue Diamonds of the Kansas City Athletic Club, the U.S. amateur champions. Ackerman and fellow engineering student Waldo Bowman were KU's starting forwards throughout the season.

Ackerman made All-America the next two seasons, alternating time between foward and center. As KU's captain in 1924-25, he led the conference in scoring, averaging 10.3 points per game.

In the 1965 letter, Ackerman told Owens he didn't think the records of Kansas teams in the early 1920s could be duplicated in the so-called modern era:

> "You, of course, know that the game in the '20s was very different from the game today. There was a center jump, which slowed the game. It was harder to score because possession of the ball was all important and fewer shots were taken. Closer guarding was allowed; in other words there was more contact. In addition, the basketball was not a perfect sphere and I am sure the present day ballplayer's technique has improved."

In the same letter, which summarized his activities at KU, Ackerman wrote that he was honored when James Naismith included him as a forward on KU's all-time team. But what Ackerman cherished most was never losing to Missouri.

In 1922-23, the Jayhawks defeated Missouri twice by a combined five points. In the first of those two encounters, Ackerman scored 11 of KU's points in a 21-19 Kansas victory in Columbia.

Allen often credited Ackerman's performance in that game to a pre-game speech. Allen had urged Ackerman to imitate one of his boyhood heroes, Tommy Johnson, KU's first All-American. Tragically, Johnson had died in his early 20s when Ackerman was only 10 years old, and Allen suggested Ackerman play in honor of Johnson's memory.

After more than 70 years, Ackerman couldn't recall the details of that speech, but he remembered how much he enjoyed beating the Tigers.

"We played seven times, and I never lost to Missouri," he said proudly. "We had a couple of squeakers, though."

Three years after graduating from Kansas, Ackerman married Mary Hamilton. Their daughter, Ann, married Claude Houchin, captain of the 1949-50 Kansas basketball team.

After KU, Ackerman spent most of his career with Equitable Life Assurance Society, retiring in the 1960s as a vice president of the group insurance giant. During his career, he assisted more than 100 companies in developing and maintaining employee retirement programs.

"I enjoyed life," Ackerman said shortly before he died. "I was pretty good. I made All-America two years. But it (basketball) didn't pay any bills."

That's another thing that has changed – or eventually changes – for most of today's All-Americans.

KANSAS CITY COOKING

Sometimes-forgotten duo carried Kansas hoops in mid-1920s

Somewhat unheralded among the pantheon of great Kansas basketball teams are the squads that succeeded the undefeated Missouri Valley Conference champions of 1922-23 and preceded the powerful collections that dominated the Big Six Conference in the 1930s.

But two players from Kansas City certified the Jayhawks would barely skip a beat in the mid-1920s.

Albert Peterson and Gale Gordon likely never were mistaken for brothers. With thick legs, broad shoulders and wavy hair, Peterson commanded campus attention the same way Douglas Fairbanks and Rudolf Valentino did in the era's popular silent pictures.

Gordon's lack of movie-star features rendered him less recognizable among KU's approximately 5,000 students. Instead, a receding hairline and gangly build ensured a certain degree of anonymity.

On the other hand, KU basketball players were the toast of campus, maybe even more so than today because of its cozy size. And feats on the court definitely distinguished Gordon and Peterson as KU's stars.

Both were two-time All-Americans, but oddly, neither enjoyed that honor their senior year of 1926-27. Peterson, who split time between forward and center, made all-conference three times. But Gordon, a guard who later switched to forward, made all-conference only once, and that occurred in 1925-26, his poorest individual year of three varsity seasons.

Whatever vagaries accounted for their postseason honors, Gordon and Peterson kept KU consistent on the court. In their three years together, Kansas won 48 and lost just five, capturing three more conference championships that extended its streak to six.

Peterson led the conference in scoring during his junior and senior seasons, averaging 9.0 points and 10.3 points per game, respectively. As with all centers before rulesmakers eliminated the center jump after each basket in the mid-1930s, his ability to control jump balls largely determined his success.

He mastered that skill as no other KU center before him, yet he was a versatile player, often shooting from long range. In late 1941, F.C. "Phog" Allen, naming a team of KU all-stars covering the

ALBERT PETERSON
Basketball,
1924-27

first 25 years he coached the Jayhawks, named Tusten Ackerman and Peterson as the centers.

"Peterson was the most coordinated man I ever coached," Allen told the *Kansas City Star* at the time.

Years earlier, in 1935, Allen told *The Daily Oklahoman* that Peterson was one of the best ballhandlers, "long shots," rebounders and jumpers he ever coached. Of centers he saw play in the Missouri Valley and Big Six, Allen said Peterson was the "finest all-around player of the lot."

Gordon, with a scoring average of 8.3 points, combined with Peterson to score more than half of KU's points in 1925-26. Versatility was Gordon's forte, the 1926 *Jayhawker* Yearbook said.

However, Gordon struggled that season compared with his sophomore year, says Ted O'Leary. As a high school player in Lawrence, O'Leary watched Gordon play at old Robinson Gymnasium on Jayhawk Boulevard.

"I remember Gordon had a great sophomore year," says O'Leary, who made All-America at KU in 1931-32. "Then he had a poor junior year.

GALE GORDON
Basketball,
1924-27

"Allen discovered he had practiced during the summer before his junior year, and Allen said, 'I know what's the matter with him. I don't want my basketball players to go near a basketball court during the summer.' So Gordon didn't work out the next summer, and came back his senior year and played quite well."

O'Leary says Allen occasionally gave him the same advice, fearing he would go "stale" if he played too much. "That was an old phrase that was very common in those days," O'Leary says.

Apparently, Gordon and the rest of the Jayhawks stayed fresh in 1926-27. The Jayhawks held their opponents to an average of 22.2 points per game while scoring 30.5 points per contest on the way to a 15-2 record.

The following year brought change to Kansas basketball. The Jayhawks played their final game in Robinson Gymnasium before moving home games to newly built Hoch Auditorium.

Meanwhile, without Gordon and Peterson, KU didn't win the conference for the first time since 1920-21, finishing fourth with a 9-9 record. Records show that in the season's home games, Kansas had only a .265 team field goal percentage. That figure actually resembled shooting by most teams of the era, compared with the usual 40-50 percent team shooting in the 1990s.

The season also was the last of the old Missouri Valley. Kansas, Missouri, Oklahoma, Iowa State, Nebraska and Kansas State formed the Big Six in 1928.

The other Valley schools – Drake, Washington University of St. Louis, Grinnell (Iowa) and Oklahoma A&M – went their separate ways. Oklahoma A&M eventually changed its name to Oklahoma State when it rejoined its former conference mates 30 years later. At that point, the Big Seven, having previously added Colorado, became the Big Eight.

Olympic Ambitions

Gwinn Henry (center) succeeded F.C. "Phog" Allen as Kansas' athletics director in 1937 and was named head football coach two years later.

QUICK TURNAROUND

Fiery guard led Jayhawks out of despair

> *"He was strong as an ox. He could bring the ball down well, and he was a good shot, a good long shot. We all shot set shots. Nobody ever shot one hand, except when we drove to the basket. I think Frosty was the best player I ever played with."*
>
> – Ted O'Leary

Unmitigated disaster.

That's about the only way to describe the 1928-29 basketball season at the University of Kansas, which had won six straight Missouri Valley Conference championships between 1921-22 and 1926-27. But only two seasons after its last title, the Jayhawks won just three games during the 1928-29 campaign.

Three.

Only once in its already proud history had KU won so few games in a season. That came in the second year of the program's existence, 1899-1900, when the team only played seven games.

Maybe the Jayhawks should have stopped after seven in 1928-29. They won their first game of the year in the seventh contest, a 24-23 victory against California, before finishing the season 3-15, including 2-8 in the new Big Six Conference.

Kansas fans should have seen it coming. After all, the captain of the squad, Forrest "Frosty" Cox, was a sophomore playing his first year of varsity competition.

Cox was a point guard, or "quarterback" as they were called, from Newton. He was one of the best high school athletes Kansas ever produced. The fact he served as captain his sophomore year probably was as much a testament to leadership skills he later used as a successful college coach as it was to KU's lack of talent.

"He was fiery," says Ted O'Leary, who received many of Cox's passes. "Frosty would just chew your butt out if you weren't playing your best. You admired and liked that in him, you wanted to be driven like that. When you would see him come down the court, the look on his face was one of absolute determination."

With additional talent in 1929-30, including the arrival of O'Leary, a future All-American, the Jayhawks won their first 13 games on the way to a 14-4 record. Cox gained All-America status that year, then led KU to a 15-3 record and a conference championship during his senior season of 1930-31.

"He was strong as an ox," O'Leary says. "He could bring the ball down well, and he was a good shot, a good long shot. We all shot set shots. Nobody ever shot one hand, except when we drove to the basket. I think Frosty was the best player I ever played with."

The 1931 *Jayhawker* Yearbook also praised Cox: "The secret of the Jayhawkers' success ... lay largely in an airtight defense, built around 'Frosty' Cox and Lee Page, who combined exceptional guarding ability with the ability to hit the basket at crucial moments."

Cox didn't limit his strength and desire to the basketball court. He also played halfback for the KU football team, forming a powerful backfield with Jim Bausch when the Jayhawks won the conference in 1930. Cox received all-conference honors that season.

When his KU career concluded in 1931, Cox received the Big Six honor medal, which each conference school awarded to an athlete who excelled both in sports and academics.

Cox came a long way from a poor background, said Gordon Gray, who played guard at KU from 1932-35. Gray knew Cox while the two were growing up in Newton.

"He never had a lot to start with," Gray said months before he died in December 1997. "His athletic ability is what really got him a scholarship.

"Frosty talked me into coming to KU. He was the freshman coach up here at the time and the assistant varsity coach. He had more to do with (the varsity) than you can imagine. He was the detail man. He actually did more coaching of the varsity than 'Phog' (Allen) himself, and it got so Phog resented his input with the varsity squad, and they had some bad blood."

Unfortunately, the bitterness escalated, Gray said, when Cox accepted the head coaching position at Colorado without telling Allen he had interviewed for the job.

Cox then decided not to play a team Allen coached unless necessary. The two avoided one another until 1942, when Colorado and Kansas met in the first round of the eight-team NCAA Tournament, which Allen had helped create four seasons earlier.

FORREST "FROSTY" COX
**Basketball and football,
1928-31**

With four starters who had played high school basketball in Kansas, Cox and the Golden Buffaloes defeated KU 46-44, giving Colorado's program its first of two Final Four trips.

Cox stayed at Colorado through the 1949-50 season. By that time, the Golden Buffaloes had joined the Big Seven Conference. In eight more Cox-versus-Allen matchups, Colorado won five.

After a five-year layoff, Cox returned to coaching with Montana in 1955-56. Five seasons later, he left coaching for good after a dispute with Montana's administration. His record in 18 seasons as a head coach was 203-151.

Cox died May 22, 1962, in Missoula, Mont., at age 54, two days after suffering a heart attack.

JARRING JIM

Olympic champion earned title of 'world's best athlete'

Piecing together the Jim Bausch Story proves difficult, if only because of the knack he showed for arriving somewhere, making his mark, then moving on.

Calling Bausch, the 1932 Olympic decathlon champion, one of the world's greatest American athletes of the first half of the 20th century is anything but difficult – or inappropriate. But he also was one of the most controversial athletes of the early 1930s.

His tale makes for a compelling yet complex chronicle. Maybe that's why lasting fame escaped a man once officially recognized as the nation's best amateur athlete.

To tell it, let's start where James Aloysius Bausch started. He was born March 28, 1906, in Marion, S.D., to parents whose recent ancestry traced to Germany. His younger brother, Frank, played football with Jim years later at the University of Kansas.

By the early 1920s, Bausch's family had settled in the Wichita area, and he enrolled in Augusta Junior High School in the fall of 1923.

Immediately, he gained attention as an outstanding football player, and high schools throughout south-central Kansas desired his talents. Bausch eventually decided to attend high school in Garden Plain, 17 miles west of Wichita.

There, he dominated small-town opponents for two seasons, which isn't surprising considering he was 18 years old as a high school sophomore.

But his time at Garden Plain also coincided with his introduction to track and field, the sport that would later lead him to an Olympic gold medal. A Nov. 2, 1930, story by *Wichita Beacon* sports editor Jack Copeland stated, "He could have run for mayor of the little city and been elected. But Bausch wanted new worlds to conquer."

So he transferred to Wichita East High School. Several months later, he transferred to Wichita Cathedral High School.

By then, Bausch regularly attended college track meets across the state, watching shot put competitions. Once they ended, he would stroll to the throwing pit to ask which competitor threw the farthest. Invariably, he would take the shot and pitch it comfortably farther than the winning distance.

That coolness and confidence preceded him when he entered Wichita University. But again he left after one year, this time for KU.

Football, track, basketball – you name it, Bausch played it at Kansas. In 1929, he was an all-Big Six Conference selection at fullback. The next year, "Jarring Jim" – the nickname his fierce play elicited – earned the same distinction at halfback when the Jayhawks won the conference championship.

In basketball, Bausch, a bruising 6-foot-2-inch, 200-pound center, helped the 1929-30 KU edition finish second in the conference. And in track, he won the 1930 conference indoor shot put title and won the shot put, discus and pole vault at the conference outdoor meet the same year. He also enjoyed first-place finishes in various events at the Kansas, Drake and Texas Relays.

Football episodes against Kansas State exemplify Bausch's disdain for any result other than victory. In 1929, early in a 6-0 loss to the Aggies in Lawrence, Bausch left the game, "probably from an accidental low blow," a 1977 article in *Kanhistique* magazine said. He returned in the fourth quarter but not in time to lead a comeback.

Reviewing the game, Manhattan sportswriters called Bausch an "all-star yellow-belly." He didn't forget.

In 1930, Bausch returned the intrastate contest's opening kickoff in Manhattan 98 yards for a touchdown. He kicked the extra point, giving KU a 7-0 lead. In the second half, he intercepted a K-State pass and returned it 68 yards for a touchdown. Again, he kicked the extra point. Final: KU 14, K-State 0.

"You just marveled at what he did," says Ted O'Leary, a KU basketball teammate of Bausch and later a correspondent for *Sports Illustrated*. "There was nothing he couldn't do. He was the greatest athlete I've ever known."

O'Leary and Gordon Gray, another of Bausch's basketball contemporaries at KU, agreed his size belied his speed. And O'Leary adds that almost always, Bausch channeled his quick temper to improve rather than detract from his athletic ability.

In retrospect, dominating the 1930 Kansas State game probably shortened Bausch's college career. Shortly after that, Missouri and other conference schools began questioning his job representing an insurance agent in Topeka. The University refused to declare Bausch and several other KU football players ineligible because of alleged recruiting and job improprieties, and he led Kansas to the conference title, capped by a 32-0 demolition of the Tigers.

But the push from conference foes to oust Bausch proved too strong as 1930 neared an end. After failing a couple of fall classes, Bausch declared he would be KU's first representative in the East-West Shrine game, thereby relinquishing his final year-and-a-half of eligibility.

Although conference schools had refused to schedule 1931 football games against Kansas if Bausch played, he retained his standing in the Amateur Athletic Union – even though the AAU's rules often were more stringent than most college conferences in an era when the NCAA had yet to take center stage as a rules enforcer. He trained with KU track and field coach Brutus Hamilton throughout 1931, even though he didn't compete with the Jayhawks.

The training led to his greatest accomplishment. Competing for the Kansas City Athletic Club at the 1932 Olympic Games in Los Angeles, he shattered the official world record in the decathlon. After sitting in fifth place heading into the last day of events, Bausch placed first in the discus and javelin and tied for first in the pole vault, raising his final point total to 8,462.

Northeast Kansas residents eagerly awaited news of Bausch's Olympic progress. The *Lawrence Journal-World* reported the day after his victory that "hundreds of telephone calls were received Saturday night at the *Journal-World* office for the final returns of the Olympic decathlon... and a crowd of about 25 persons waited in the office most of the evening for scores."

Bausch's total exceeded Jim Thorpe's unofficial point total of 8,413 in the 1912 Olympics. Ironically, track and field officials later disregarded Thorpe's total when he encountered the same "professionalism" charges that Bausch suffered at Kansas. The official world record at the time Bausch broke it was 8,255 by Finland's Akilles Jarvinen, who won the silver medal behind him in Los Angeles.

Interestingly, two other Lawrence athletes competed in the 1932 Olympic decathlon, Clyde Coffman of KU and Wilson "Buster" Charles of Haskell Institute. Charles finished fourth.

"He is the only one who could really come close to (Bausch) as an all-around athlete," Gray said of Charles.

Bausch received the 1932 Sullivan Award, honoring the nation's top amateur athlete. But by the mid-1930s, he had retired from sports altogether after playing three seasons with the Chicago Cardinals in the NFL. He also played professional baseball briefly in Washington, D.C.

It appears Bausch, who was offered movie scripts after receiving his Olympic gold medal, somewhat struggled to find a niche once his athletic endeavors ended. An accomplished singer, he tried a nightclub singing career without much success. He also worked for the Bureau of Internal Revenue as a traveling auditor, sold insurance in Tulsa, Okla., and worked for the U.S. Department of Agriculture in Hot Springs, Ark., before retiring in the early 1960s.

He faced other battles outside of his career. According to the *Kanhistique* article, Bausch contracted osteomyelitis, an inflammatory bone disease, while serving with the Navy in the South Pacific during World War II. It afflicted him the rest of his life. He also battled but eventually overcame alcoholism shortly before dying July 9, 1974, at age 68.

Discuss the top U.S. decathletes of all time, and most people mention Dan O'Brien, Dave Johnson, Bruce Jenner, Rafer Johnson and Bob Mathias. Rarely do they recall Bausch. But adjusted for scoring changes since 1932, Bausch's Olympic and world record point total would rise to 8,896. That's five points higher than O'Brien's world record set in 1992.

Adjusted for changes in scoring methods, Jim Bausch's 1932 Olympic decathlon point total would be a world record today – more than 65 years after he set it.

However, Bausch is a charter member of the College Football Hall of Fame and is a member of the National Track and Field Hall of Fame. When the *University Daily Kansan* conducted voting to name the best athlete in KU history for the school's 75th anniversary in 1939, Bausch secured the most votes.

Some people remembered him after all.

BIG SIX UPROAR

As the popularity and business aspects of college athletics have grown side-by-side, especially during the era of sports television, pundits critical of what they perceive as an overemphasis on college sports cry for the days of pure, wholesome intercollegiate competition.

Problem is, those days never existed, at least not to the degree many idealists think. If nothing else, Jim Bausch's 1930 case proves that.

As Kansas marched to its first Big Six Conference football title that season, questions about Bausch's work for a Topeka insurance agent increased. College athletes of the day were allowed to have jobs, so long as they actually performed the work for which they were paid.

However, conference rules at the time prohibited coaches or sports administrators from contacting high school students about their college plans. In other words, recruiting was illegal.

As accusations regarding Bausch gained momentum, conference schools widened their allegations against KU, charging illegal recruiting and other severe violations. Kansas chancellor E. H. Lindley and athletics director F.C. "Phog" Allen vehemently denied the accusations.

Specifically relating to Bausch, conference foes led by Missouri and Oklahoma coach Adrian "Ad" Lindsey (a former KU football player) suggested the lofty sum of $75 per month he reportedly received as an insurance company representative was improper, even though jobs were considered acceptable as part of athletic scholarships. Questions about whether Bausch actually sold insurance also arose.

Newspaper accounts gave varying views on the fight between KU and its conference foes. Some also questioned the role of college athletics in society. Westbrook Pegler, a famous sportswriter, wrote in a column that appeared in the *Kansas City Times*:

"...*Now it is legal and ethical for a man to hold a job or to play football but there is something in the chemistry of American sport which causes poisonous vapors to arise and fume up the atmosphere when a man does both.*"

Generally, Kansas newspapers defended Bausch and KU, citing envy about the Jayhawks' successful football season as a basis for the allegations. Most thought opposing conference schools merely wanted to get rid of Bausch:

"*No single collegiate athlete has ever caused such a wave of public sentiment and today Kansas University stands virtually ostracised from the Big Six – all because Bausch was destined to become one of America's foremost football players and is being paid wages by a man who has no connections to KU whatsoever.*"
– Jack Copeland, sports editor, in the Nov. 2, 1930, edition of the *Wichita Beacon.*

When KU refused to declare Bausch ineligible for the remainder of the 1930 season, opposing conference schools met secretly and decided they would refuse to schedule games against Kansas for the 1931 season, effectively forcing KU out of the conference. Eventually, every conference school but Kansas State, which abstained, voted to throw Kansas out of the conference if it didn't declare Bausch ineligible.

The controversy, which by that time had gained nationwide attention, culminated in early December 1930. With little choice, Kansas prepared to declare Bausch ineligible for the upcoming basketball season and his entire senior year of 1931-32. But Bausch saved KU the trouble by declaring he would play in the East-West Shrine all-star football game. Doing so forfeited his remaining college eligibility.

So who was right? Did the rest of the conference unfairly railroad Kansas, or did KU knowingly break conference rules? Usually, such issues aren't entirely clear-cut,

and this case is no different.

Bausch had left Wichita University (now Wichita State) after one year when the Topeka agent offered him a job. It appears the offer at least partly was an enticement to get Bausch to transfer to KU. Moreover, the money Bausch received far exceeded wages most KU athletes received for jobs waiting tables at fraternity houses or punching cash registers at clothing stores.

However, once they knew Bausch would no longer play at KU, opposing conference schools didn't pursue their other allegations – charges never fully explained – against Kansas.

If KU broke rules against recruiting and illegal payments, it was no different from most other conference schools at the time. In the Dec. 22, 1932, issue of the *Olathe Mirror*, the newspaper reported "Missouri was paying dearly" for athletes and entertaining senior high school stars from Kansas City at the time the school led the fight against Bausch. The newspaper also said Nebraska was housing 40 freshman football players in apartments above a store in Lincoln, another violation of conference rules.

In addition, when the allegations against him first surfaced, Bausch issued a public letter. In it, he said the Missouri athletics department had approached him with a financial offer to transfer to Columbia after he had enrolled at KU. An investigation by the *University Daily Kansan* later uncovered other cases in which Missouri tried to entice KU athletes to transfer.

Finally, the *Kansan* found a Missouri athletics department representative who admitted its entire protest was aimed at getting rid of Bausch.

Time heals all wounds, though, and they apparently healed quickly for Kansas. Less than two years after the front-page headline in the Dec. 6, 1930, edition of the *Kansan* blared "*KU STAYS IN THE BIG SIX CONFERENCE,*" the University hired Lindsey, who had helped instigate the Bausch ordeal, as its football coach.

SELF-MADE CHAMPION
Olympic wrestling champion learned sport through correspondence

Pete Mehringer never succeeded in athletics without a struggle, but the greater his struggles, the greater his successes.

The challenges Mehringer faced started long before he attended the University of Kansas, where he earned Big Six Conference honors as a football tackle and excelled on the wrestling team.

Mehringer grew up on a homestead farm outside of Kinsley, the 10th – and last – child of German immigrants. He became interested in wrestling in his early teens and learned about the sport through a correspondence course he picked up from a subscription to "Frank Gotch and Farmer Burns School of Wrestling and Physical Culture."

By high school, Mehringer showed how well he had learned his lessons. As a sophomore, he coached the Kinsley High School wrestling team (the school's football coach wanted nothing to do with wrestling) to a fourth-place finish in the state. Mehringer won his first Kansas state championship at the same tournament.

The Kinsley team couldn't afford to return to the tournament the next two years because of the Great Depression. But Mehringer found his way to the state tournament his senior year by hitchhiking across the state. He made the most of his trip and won his second state title.

As a 214-pound tackle on the Jayhawks' football team, Mehringer was named all-conference in 1932 and 1933. In a 1932 loss to Notre Dame in Lawrence, Mehringer's nose was broken and both eyes were blackened. Notre Dame named him to its all-opponent team that year.

The next year, Kansas traveled to South Bend, Ind., for a rematch with the Fighting Irish. Mehringer again played superbly, garnering more than half of the Jayhawks' tackles and blocking two punts. The game ended in a scoreless tie.

Mehringer played in the first College All-Star football game in 1934. He later played nine seasons of professional football.

But Mehringer made a name for himself in wrestling at Kansas. In 1932, he won the conference and Missouri Valley Amateur Athletic Union heavyweight championships without losing a single fall. At the National Intercollegiate Meet, he lost the college heavyweight title to Jack Riley of Northwestern.

A few weeks later, Mehringer and Riley squared off again to determine who would represent the United States as its heavyweight wrestler in the 1932 Olympic Games in Los Angeles. Mehringer pinned Riley twice in six minutes. Despite the victory, the U.S. coach wanted Riley as the team's heavyweight and asked Mehringer to wrestle at the 191-pound level.

This request meant Mehringer had to lose 17 pounds in 12 days before the Olympic competition. He did, barely, as a concoction of citrate-of-magnesia and a last-minute session in a steam box reduced his weight to the required limit just before the final weigh-in.

Strengthened rather than weakened by the ordeal, Mehringer pinned the defending gold medalist in the first-round match and then earned a decision against a passive

Canadian grappler. He won the gold medal against an Australian opponent, who blackened one of Mehringer's eyes.

Mehringer returned to Lawrence for his final two years of collegiate competition as an Olympic champion – and as the Jayhawks' coach. Leon Bauman, who helped groom Mehringer into a champion, quit as coach to enter medical school. Mehringer then inherited his second coaching job, which paid nothing.

Money, or the lack of it, plagued Mehringer in college. He waited on tables at his fraternity house for a small stipend. According to *Westways* magazine, he did not graduate on time with his class of 1934 because F.C. "Phog" Allen, then KU's athletics director, took his campus job away, forcing him to work elsewhere.

The magazine also reported that Allen would not send Mehringer to the college wrestling championships during his junior and senior years. These times, Mehringer couldn't hitchhike his way to a title, so he never got a second chance at a college championship.

Despite these events, the 1934 *Jayhawker* Yearbook hailed "The Kansas Whirlwind" as follows:

"All Mount Oread now joins in praise of Pete Mehringer's years of meritorious service as he leaves Kansas University competition. Pete's versatility in athletics made him valuable in more than one sport, and his sportsmanship and sense of fair play have brought athletic prestige and secured universal commendation from opponents and officials alike."

While in Los Angeles during the professional football off-season, Mehringer worked as a movie extra in "Knute Rockne, All-American," with Ronald Reagan, as a stunt man in a Tarzan movie and in Bob Hope's "Road to Zanzibar."

Mehringer's work in the Los Angeles Department of Public Works far outlasted his movie career. He became an expert in erosion control and special excavation, and his career highlight was the completion of the Sepulveda Boulevard tunnel under the Los Angeles International Airport's runways.

Mehringer, honored as a distinguished member of the National Wrestling Hall of Fame in Stillwater, Okla., died Aug. 27, 1987, at age 77.

PETE MEHRINGER
Wrestling and football,
1931-34

ELKHART EXPRESS
"Iron Horse of Kansas" was nation's greatest miler in the 1930s

"As long as you believe you can do things, they're not impossible."

– Glenn Cunningham

He simply didn't see the hole.

The date was June 17, 1934, and Glenn Cunningham – winner of the 1933 Sullivan Award as the top amateur athlete in the United States, Big Six Conference and NCAA champion and pride of the University of Kansas (indeed, the entire state of Kansas) – prepared to compete in one of the biggest U.S. track and field events of the outdoor amateur season.

The 40,000 spectators who jammed a New Jersey track stadium for the Princeton Invitational considered the mile run as the day's main feature, and Cunningham played the leading role. But because of the hole, Kansas track coach Bill Hargiss almost summoned an understudy.

Almost.

Cunningham, after completing a warm-up jog, went down in a sideways, twisting heap of pain and agony as his foot hit a divot in the track. But minutes later, with a generous supply of athletic tape choking a newly sprained ankle, he lined up to start the race.

He never believed much in pacing himself. That day, Glenn Cunningham ran the fastest third lap of the four-lap mile to that point in U.S. track history. That day, Glenn Cunningham, known for his fast down-the-stretch "kicks," ran the last quarter mile in 59.1 seconds.

That day, Glenn Cunningham, with an ankle that swelled so much the tape holding it tightly at the beginning of the race exploded off his leg during the middle of it, ran the fastest time over the course of one mile that any human ever had. For the next three years, he kept the world record of 4 minutes, 6.7 seconds, adding it to his world records in the indoor mile and 1,500 meters.

"As long as you believe you can do things, they're not impossible," Cunningham said in a newspaper interview 44 years later as he lived virtually destitute after years running homes for troubled children. "You place limits on yourself mentally, not physically. People say something's never been done, so it can't be done. But that's not so. It's never been done because no one has set about the task of doing it."

When he was 8, Cunningham's primary task was learning how to walk again.

The story of how he survived a fire that permanently scarred his legs is the most popular example of Cunningham's mettle. But it bears repeating, for it shaped the rest of his life.

The winter of 1917-18 remained grim throughout. The United States had entered World War I, the nation's first armed conflict since the Spanish-American War 20 years earlier. But a world war was a world away in extreme southwest Kansas, where Floyd Cunningham and his younger brother Glenn attended classes in a one-room schoolhouse.

Winters are harsh on the prairie, and one of Floyd's jobs upon arriving at school every morning included starting a fire in a kerosene stove.

Before one particular morning, though, a delivery service inadvertently left gasoline instead of kerosene at the school. Unaware, Floyd put the gasoline in the stove.

The stove exploded immediately. The resulting fire killed Floyd and left Glenn in critical condition for six weeks. Even after doctors determined he would live, they told him he would never walk again on his severely burned legs, which they had considered amputating.

He was walking in six months.

He jogged a few months later.

By the time he was 12, he won his first school race.

Cunningham often credited his strong will for helping him defy doctors' predictions. But he also credited his mother, who massaged his legs four hours a day "until her hands and arms were numb."

As if he needed a reminder, grotesque scars never let Cunningham forget the cold winter morning when his brother died – or the months of painful recovery that followed, when his legs remained wrapped virtually 24 hours a day.

But Cunningham never really tried to forget. Instead, he used the experience as a motivating tool, both for himself and others.

"I was miserable at the thought of being an invalid all my life," he wrote in a piece for *Guideposts* magazine in 1968. "And I might have been, had I not had a mother who was filled with such great hope and faith that she wouldn't let me give up.

"...Maybe it was this early handicap that made it so much fun to run. I ran in some big races – including the Olympics – but no race was more important than that race I ran at (age) 12."

***

Elkhart straddles the Kansas-Oklahoma border in the far reaches of southwest Kansas. It's where Cunningham went to high school, and its where he developed into a national high school star.

In 1929-30, a senior at age 20, Cunningham played fullback for Elkhart High's football team, center for the basketball team and set a U.S. record in the mile run at the National Interscholastic Meet in Chicago. He bought a new pair of shoes for that race and completed it in 4:24.7.

In the fall of 1930, he entered KU. In the fall of 1931, the conference named him its outstanding cross country runner. The next spring, he began a routine he would repeat until he graduated in 1934: running the half-mile (880 yards), mile and two-mile runs in the same track meet. He won every race he ran in the conference in 1932, and won the mile at the NCAA Track and Field Championships.

That summer, while Kansan Jim Bausch won the decathlon at the Olympic Games in Los Angeles, Cunningham placed fourth in the 1,500.

GLENN CUNNINGHAM

GLENN CUNNINGHAM
Cross country and
track and field,
1931-34

In 1933, Glenn Cunningham was the second athlete in a row with KU ties to win the prestigious Sullivan Award as the top U.S. amateur athlete. Jim Bausch won the award in 1932.

He won the mile at the NCAA meet again in 1933, when he also set a record in the 880 at the conference meet with a time of 1:52.2. He won every amateur race he entered in the winter of 1932-33.

By the time he graduated, Cunningham had won the mile run in the conference indoor and outdoor championship meets for three straight years. In 1933 and 1934, he won the conference outdoor titles in the 880 and the mile on the same day, an unprecedented feat.

In 1936, he again ran in the Olympics, this time in Berlin. After a poor indoor season, he had a fine outdoor season heading into the 1,500 meters on Adolf Hitler's home turf. Cunningham ran that race faster than any previous runner. But New Zealand's Jack Lovelock ran it one second faster, setting a new world record. Cunningham settled for the silver medal.

By 1938, Cunningham had run the mile in an amateur race (not including high school) 60 times. He had won 50. That year, he ran his fastest time in the event, 4:04.4, but track officials did not recognize it as an official record because a runner set the pace for Cunningham.

Nevertheless, the time only enhanced the reputation of the man who symbolized U.S. track and field throughout the 1930s.

Cunningham also symbolized clean living. By the time he entered college, he possessed amazing stamina in his upper body. He astounded fellow KU athletes with his ability to walk on his hands for up to 30 minutes at a time. Even more impressive, he could scale the steps of Memorial Stadium walking on his hands.

He thought that sort of extraordinary athleticism stemmed partly from his vehement refusal to drink or smoke. In fact, when he ran his fastest mile at Dartmouth University's indoor track in 1938, not a soul lit a cigarette during an era when indoor arenas often resembled dimly lit nightclubs.

After he retired from competition in 1940, Cunningham often spoke against the evils of smoking and drinking, even leading a 1948 "Temperance Tornado" campaign that opposed the repeal of prohibition in Kansas.

In 1940, Cunningham took a job as director of student health and hygiene at Cornell University. But after he returned from serving in the Navy during World War II, he moved back to Kansas, where he grew crops and raised cattle on a ranch southwest of Emporia.

Eventually, the ranch turned into a home for wayward youth and wards of the state. From the 1950s until about 1970, at the ranch near Emporia and at a smaller ranch east of Wichita, Glenn and his wife, Ruth, raised their 12 children and provided a home for a total of 8,300 others at one time or another. Grocery bills often ran $130 per day, but the Cunninghams thought they were serving a societal purpose by offering guidance for troubled children.

Judges and Kansas welfare officers sent the Cunninghams children by the dozens but offered little financial backing. Running the homes turned the Cunninghams from a financially prosperous farm family shortly after World War II to one that nearly was broke by 1968.

That's the year the Kansas Health Department determined the Cunningham ranch did not meet necessary environmental and sanitary standards to obtain a state license. In January 1969, Glenn and Ruth were accused of illegally boarding two 16-year-old boys without a state license. They eventually were fined $100 but were declared legal guardians of the boys.

However, the experience caused the Cunninghams to leave the state.

"Our only interest is trying to help some of these kids through a difficult period in their life, and I think we have helped some," Glenn Cunningham told the *Wichita Beacon* at the time.

He and Ruth moved to Arkansas, where they continued housing troubled youth. After he quit competing, Cunningham rarely followed track, save for the progress of KU sensation Jim Ryun. But his state high school mile record stood for 18 years, his conference mile record stood for 20 years and his Kansas Relays time of 3:53.3 in the 1,500 remained a record for more than 20 years.

In 1974, Cunningham, a man the media often called "the Iron Horse of Kansas" was inducted into the National Track and Field Hall of Fame. And in 1978, he received his biggest honor when he was selected the most outstanding track performer in the 100-year history of New York City's Madison Square Garden.

But the man whom track fans worldwide identified with Kansas remained in Arkansas. In March 1988, while feeding animals from his pickup truck on his farm near Menefee, Ark., Cunningham died of a heart attack. He was 78.

A CHARMED LIFE

Basketball player, journalist loved growing up in Lawrence

Imagine yourself as an All-American basketball player at the University of Kansas. You're king of the hill, right? Most popular person on campus?

Well, Ted O'Leary was an All-American forward in 1931-32, but he arguably wasn't even the most popular "O'Leary" on campus.

That distinction went to his father, who taught English at the University from 1895 until his death in 1936. Professor R.D. O'Leary was the first editor of the *Graduate Magazine*, the forerunner of today's *Kansas Alumni* magazine, and one-time president of KU's Phi Beta Kappa chapter. Thousands of KU students walking to class have passed the building that bears his name on the northwest edge of campus, Carruth-O'Leary Hall.

Theodore Morgan O'Leary was born in England during the one-year sabbatical his father spent studying at Oxford University. But he grew up in Lawrence.

Although his father showed little interest in athletics, young Theodore idolized KU basketball players in the late 1910s and 1920s. It's little wonder: he and KU basketball coach F.C. "Phog" Allen's son, Forrest Jr., were close friends who lived in the same Louisiana Street neighborhood.

O'Leary links one of his first painful memories with Forrest Jr., who died of typhoid fever when the two were in junior high.

"It was my first experience with death," he says. "It was quite a terrible experience

TED O'LEARY
Basketball and tennis,
1929-32

for a kid."

But mostly, O'Leary lived a charmed, Norman Rockwell childhood.

"I think I shot more baskets at Robinson Gym than anybody in history," he says. "I think I started sneaking in through the south door when I was 7 years old.

"As kids, we'd have hoops out in our yards. They were very primitive; we'd have maybe an oil drum hoop or something and throw a tennis ball through that. I remember all the kids imitated our favorite players. I just worshiped them all."

When O'Leary accepted his KU Hall-of-Fame portrait decades later, he recalled Tusten Ackerman, a two-time KU All-American in the mid-1920s, as his favorite.

"Ackerman was there, and I said, 'I just never dreamed when I was a little kid learning to imitate how Ackerman played, that I would ever follow in his footsteps and play on a KU basketball team,'" he says. "But I had him down cold, I just knew exactly how he shot everything."

O'Leary continued imitating Ackerman as a high-scoring forward for the Jayhawks in the early 1930s. During his senior season in 1931-32, he led the Big Six Conference with 11 points per game in league contests, averaging about one-third of KU's points.

Kansas won two conference titles during O'Leary's three years on the varsity, and his teammates included three other KU Hall-of-Fame athletes: Jim Bausch, Frosty Cox and William Johnson.

O'Leary also dominated as a tennis player, controlling the No. 1 spot on KU's team. Later, he earned a No. 3 national ranking in handball.

Despite his father's disinterest, athleticism ran in O'Leary's family. His two older brothers, Dorman and Paul, both set school sprint records as KU track and field athletes during and shortly after World War I.

But basketball always commanded center stage with Ted, although he acknowledges the game in those days sometimes hinged on boredom.

"We didn't have the 10-second rule," he says. "We had a Missouri and Kansas game in Columbia where Allen told us not to go out after their guys if they stalled. It was a frequent thing then – you'd stall in your own half of the court. You didn't have to cross the center line.

"Anyway, they took the ball back in their half of the court. Four guys sat down on their team and one guy stood up and held the ball. And four sat down on our end of the court and one guy stood up in case they should make a dart for the basket.

"That went on for over 15 minutes, and the clock just ran. I think the score at half was 4-2 or something like that. So it made for a pretty dull game. That Missouri game was a stupid game."

O'Leary also played in the days when officials brought the ball back to the center circle for a jump after each basket. Getting rid of that rule before the 1937-38 season benefited the game, he says.

"Putting the 10-second rule in and eliminating the center jump (after every basket) really revolutionized the game," says O'Leary, who worked 25 years as a correspondent for *Sports Illustrated*.

Although he loved playing basketball, O'Leary professes to a few distractions during his days as a student-athlete – a time he referred to as the "happiest period thus far in my life" in a 1942 letter to Allen on his 25th anniversary as a coach.

"I remember one day before our last game (in 1932) against Oklahoma," he says. "It was the time of year when it starts getting warm outside, and you're in the gym and you look out, and the girls are in their summer outfits, the sun's out and the campus is pretty. Basketball just suddenly ceases to be fun.

"I said, 'Doc (Allen), in practice I can't hit a damn thing,' and he said, 'You're stale. Just don't practice for two days, just stay away from the place.' Imagine Roy Williams doing that?"

O'Leary took the advice. Days later, he scored 14 points in a 33-29 victory against the Sooners, leading KU to its second straight conference title.

Like his father, O'Leary graduated Phi Beta Kappa with a degree in English. But finding a job during the Depression proved difficult until C.E. McBride, sports editor of the *Kansas City Star*, arranged for O'Leary to meet an old friend at George Washington University in Washington, D.C. There, O'Leary was head coach for two seasons, winning 26 games and losing nine.

But O'Leary never desired coaching as a profession. Instead, he returned to Kansas City and worked as a reporter on the city desk of the *Star* during one of the city's most colorful and corrupt eras – the reign of mayor and political boss Tom Pendergast.

"I was fortunate to cover city news all the time," he says. "Covering city news in the Pendergast era was just the greatest experience in the world."

O'Leary, who has lived in his suburban Kansas City home in Fairway, Kan., since 1940, also reviewed books for the *Star*. Even today, thousands of books, stacked to the ceiling in some places, fill his home.

His father would be proud. But what O'Leary wrote Allen in 1942 still holds true, despite his vast experiences as a journalist.

"I enjoyed going to school," he says. "It was fun. I just couldn't have been happier there in Lawrence. I remember that I never stepped on the court for a practice or a game without a feeling of exhilaration.

"It never got old."

WILLIAM JOHNSON

OKIE CITY'S SKINNY
Lanky player flourished in days of center jump

A 6-foot-4-inch center from Oklahoma City helped lead the University of Kansas basketball team to three straight Big Six Conference titles in the early 1930s. He made All-America in 1932-33. He had an outstanding amateur basketball career after leaving KU. He was enshrined in the Basketball Hall of Fame in 1976.

But William Johnson, who spurned his home state in favor of Kansas, provided the subject for one of F.C. "Phog" Allen's favorite stories. That story and Johnson's legacy will forever intertwine.

Time and again, Allen described how "Skinny" Johnson returned home for his father's funeral in late February 1932, just days before KU's final game of the year against Oklahoma in Lawrence. As the game neared, almost everyone thought Johnson would miss it.

To win the conference title, Kansas needed a victory and a Missouri loss against Kansas State that same Saturday night. Otherwise, the Sooners or Tigers would

BILL JOHNSON

WILLIAM JOHNSON
Basketball,
1930-33

capture the championship. Without Johnson, many feared the Jayhawks had little chance.

In subsequent books and magazine articles, Allen relived how Johnson appeared just before tip-off, lifting the spirits of his teammates and dashing Oklahoma's hopes. Of course, the story wouldn't carry the same appeal had KU not won 33-29 while Missouri lost. Johnson's miraculous return had saved the day – or so Allen said.

"That has been completely distorted in many ways," says Ted O'Leary, an All-American in 1931-32 and KU's leading scorer that season. "His father died on Wednesday, so we knew that chances were pretty good he wouldn't show up for the game. Allen was pretty gloomy about it."

But the day before the game, Allen arranged to fly Johnson back to northeast Kansas in time to play. Only he told no one except O'Leary, a team co-captain.

In the meantime, Allen moved the starting time for the game back 30 minutes. That gave Johnson more time to return but also meant the Missouri game likely would end before KU's contest concluded.

After KU players finished dressing for the game that night, O'Leary says Allen divulged to the team that Johnson indeed would return and play. But he ensured Johnson didn't enter Hoch Auditorium, KU's home court, until just before the game started.

"He said, 'I'm going to send him upstairs (at Robinson Gymnasium) and have him warm up there because I don't want Oklahoma to know he's coming,' " O'Leary says. "None of us saw him before we left the gym for Hoch.

"So about five minutes before the game was ready to start, who should walk down the aisle of Hoch but Bill Johnson. I looked over at the Oklahoma players, and their faces just completely collapsed because they had been so happy they weren't going to have to play Bill."

Despite the theatrics, Johnson was ineffective. Instead, O'Leary played the key role for the Jayhawks, scoring 14 points in his final game.

But O'Leary never will forget how Allen orchestrated the Johnson airplane episode, which actually may have shocked the Sooners enough to account for the final four-point margin.

"Doc wanted to wring every ounce of drama out of it he could," he says. "It was a helluva game."

It's one of the few games Johnson failed to dominate. In the days when the center jump still occurred after every basket, many thought no college center jumped better.

"I really was considered tall in those days," Johnson said shortly before his Hall of Fame ceremony in 1977. "Naturally, if you could control the center jump, you could pretty well control the game. That is what I was able to do pretty consistently."

Johnson battled foul trouble most of his career, when four fouls, not five, rendered disqualification. Nonetheless, he was so good, rumors flew that Kansas wanted to cancel the Oklahoma game Allen memorialized.

"He was very graceful," O'Leary says. "He didn't weigh much more than 160 pounds. But he could jump, and he was good at following in shots and tipping them in. He got a lot of shots from under the basket."

Johnson may have gained more fame, though, during an extended career playing for amateur teams. Shortly after he received All-America honors in 1932-33, he decided to join a Kansas City team in time for the national Amateur Athletic Union tournament, which began only days after KU's season ended.

Apparently, Johnson toyed with not playing that soon after the season. So when he announced he would play, a *Kansas City Times* article flashed the news, much like today's go-professional-or-stay decisions by undergraduate college players. The headlines read:

K.U. STAR TO TEAM HERE
STAGE LINERS GET BILL JOHNSON FOR NATIONAL TOURNAMENT

The Tall Jayhawk Center, Outstanding in Big Six for 3 Years,
Enhances Bus Club's Chances to Win Basket Ball Classic

A steady scorer who averaged 8.4 points per game in college, Johnson joined a select few who received All-America recognition in high school, college and AAU basketball. The youngest of six brothers, his talents were well known in an era when conference schools could not actively recruit athletes.

Before he played a varsity game at Kansas, Johnson had his eligibility questioned. It occurred in December 1930, just weeks after KU's Jim Bausch, a football and track and field star, gave up his remaining eligibility. Bausch did so in the midst of a fight between Kansas and other conference schools regarding his job as an insurance representative.

Oklahoma coach Hugh McDermott made the allegation against Johnson, charging that he violated a league rule by playing a non-scholastic game about a year earlier in Oklahoma City. But his accusations quickly faded after Johnson publicly stated that McDermott approached him three times in high school, also an infraction of league rules.

After silencing McDermott, Johnson played college and amateur basketball through World War II. In addition, he embarked on a diverse career after leaving KU.

First he was a passenger agent for Southern Kansas Stage Lines, then moved to a job as an assistant merchandise manager with the Jones Store in Kansas City, Mo. In 1937, he joined Artophone Corp. in St. Louis, which distributed Philco radio equipment. He rose to vice president of sales before opening his own Philco distributorship in 1951 in Wichita. But in 1960, he switched gears and began working as an investment broker.

Likable and easy-going, Johnson savored his basketball experiences until his death in 1980. However, he also thought they carried a higher purpose. As captain of the 1932-33 KU squad, he wrote a piece reflecting on his days at Kansas for that year's *Jayhawker* Yearbook.

Bill Johnson used his height and tremendous wingspan to help KU dominate Big Six Conference basketball in the early 1930s.

"My experiences with the coaching staff have convinced me that their primary interest is not in victories at any cost, but rather the development of character, and the preparation of the athlete, under their guidance, for the problems of later life.

"My contacts with the men participating in basketball have indicated to me that they are the highest type of student found upon the campus. In my estimation, it is the combination of these things that has made it possible for the University of Kansas to achieve the position it now enjoys, in the the realm of sports."

– William C. Johnson, Honorary Captain

SWEET LORRAINE
High school legend gave KU its first NCAA shot put title

Like many other tiny central Kansas towns, Lorraine lost its high school years ago. The consolidated district of Quivira Heights meshes the town's students with those from other area hamlets, and the kids of Lorraine now take a southern Ellsworth County road south to K-4, take a right and drive a couple miles to attend high school in Bushton.

Many of those teenagers probably don't realize that only months after Wall Street's Black Tuesday signaled an end to 1920s prosperity and foreshadowed 1930s despair, a short, husky farm boy from Lorraine High School set a U.S. scholastic track and field record that would span the Great Depression and almost all of World War II.

Five years later, the boy, Elwyn Dees, capped his track and field career by winning the first NCAA field event championship by a University of Kansas athlete.

Dees threw the shot put, and he threw it as no other athlete from the Great Plains had before. From Lorraine to Lawrence to Los Angeles, site of his 1935 NCAA title, the iron ball took a rural boy to the city lights, and along the way, Dees rarely lost.

In fact, in the Big Six Conference, he *never* lost. He won every dual meet against a conference foe, and he never lost a conference championship meet, winning three straight league indoor and three straight league outdoor titles from 1933 to 1935.

Dees' high school record throw of 58 feet, 10 inches stood until Tex Coulter, later a star football lineman at Army, broke it in 1945. His KU record of 51-7 stood for 19 years. (High school athletes compete with a 12-pound shot, college athletes throw a 16-pound version.)

He twice broke the conference outdoor record, setting the mark at 50-1 3/4 in 1934 then eclipsing it the next year with a throw of 51-3 3/4. Twice, he finished second at the Kansas Relays before winning in 1935, and he won the Drake Relays in 1933 and 1935.

Despite his success, Dees' personal nature never wandered from his central Kansas upbringing, said Gordon Gray, a teammate, fellow physical education major and college roommate of Dees.

"He was just a good, old hard-working farm boy," said Gray, a two-time conference champion in the pole vault who died in December 1997. "He was very simple. He was a nice guy."

Gray also said Dees was a good student, which helped propel him to a job as KU's athletics trainer shortly after he graduated. He didn't stay at Kansas long, though, before taking a job as head trainer at Oklahoma A&M in the summer of 1937. He later accepted a similar position at Nebraska.

Dees died Aug. 16, 1995, 60 years after he won the NCAA title with a heave of 51-1 1/8. Shot putters today must throw six to twelve feet farther just to qualify for the NCAA meet. But those who do rarely dominate their college conferences as Dees did the Big Six in the early 1930s, and even fewer grow up in the Lorraines of the world.

ELWYN DEES
Track and field and football,
1932-35

ELWYN DEES

Elwyn Dees didn't limit his athletics competition at Kansas to the shot put. Although he never played football in high school, the 210-pound thrower helped anchor the KU offensive and defensive lines with Pete Mehringer, Dick Sklar, Dean Nesmith and Milo Clawson during 1932-34. In those years, the Jayhawks finished second once and fourth twice in the Big Six Conference but outscored Missouri in three games by a combined 54-0.

Dees also played in one of the biggest Kansas football games of the 1930s. With a 2-0 record, the 1933 Jayhawks traveled to South Bend, Ind., to play Notre Dame. KU partially avenged a 24-6 loss to the Fighting Irish in Lawrence the previous season by tying the home favorite 0-0.

Undefeated after three games, Kansas appeared on the way to a memorable season. Forgettable is how it turned out.

The Notre Dame tie started a streak of five straight games in which KU failed to score a point. In the process, the Jayhawks lost to Tulsa, Kansas State, Oklahoma and Nebraska. They won their final three games, ending the season with a 5-4-1 record, but left Kansas faithful muttering about what might have been.

GWINN HENRY

FROM ANATHEMA TO ALLY

Former rival coach took reins of Kansas athletics

Imagine Dan Devine as athletics director of the University of Kansas.

No, it probably wouldn't happen in a million years. But once upon a time, another former successful Missouri football coach DID replace a popular Kansas athletics director.

Of course, the former coach, Gwinn Henry, probably couldn't fully appreciate the scope of replacing F.C. "Phog" Allen when he accepted the job April 7, 1937. Allen had returned to KU 18 years earlier, not as basketball coach but as athletics director. He loved the job, and he hated giving it up.

But the fate of Kansas football during Allen's tenure as athletics director worked against him. Before 1920, Kansas had built a strong football tradition, winning 166 games, losing 66 and tying 17. The Jayhawks' combined record versus Missouri, Kansas State, Oklahoma and Nebraska during that period was 49-32-7.

From 1920 to 1936, though – including Allen's one year as head coach in 1920 – KU football teams went 61-65-16. Meanwhile, Allen feuded with several football coaches.

"Allen was accused almost always of deliberately hurting football so it wouldn't be successful," says Ted O'Leary, KU's All-American basketball star of the early 1930s who also worked on the *Jayhawker* Yearbook staff and later wrote a biographical piece on Allen for the *Kansas City Star*. "The charge was he wanted basketball to be the successful sport at Kansas. All the football coaches who came there and failed, nine times out of ten they'd blame their failure on Allen for failing to back them up."

GWINN HENRY
Athletics director,
1937-43
Head football coach,
1939-42

Some KU students and alumni accepted that theory. In the mid-1930s, pro-Allen and anti-Allen camps formed concerning his position as athletics director. Finally, Allen retained his position as head basketball coach but, under pressure from the school and the Kansas Board of Regents, relinquished his position as athletics director in favor of heading KU's newly created undergraduate physical education department.

Enter Henry. He came to KU after three years as head football coach at New Mexico. Before that, he was the head coach at Missouri from 1923 to 1931, winning 49 and losing 26 while beating powerhouse Nebraska three years in a row. Before he arrived at Missouri, the Tigers had managed to score against the Cornhuskers just once in 26 years.

Henry was familiar with the Sunflower State. He had served five years as head coach at Emporia Teachers College (now Emporia State), where his teams went 37-3 before he departed for Missouri.

Still, alumni and newspaper writers were surprised not so much that KU selected Henry, but that he took the job.

"Kansas will ask Henry to live a year with an athletic widow and her family – with no assurance he won't be booted if everyone isn't happy," wrote the *Lawrence Journal-World*, referring to the one-year contracts common for athletics directors at that time. "Will Gwinn Henry want any part of that? (We) doubt it."

But Henry, a former world-class sprinter who missed the 1912 Olympics because of illness, accepted the challenge. One year later, he found himself coaching football again after structuring a five-year contract with the KU Physical Education Corp., a predecessor of the current KU Athletics Corp., instead of the state of Kansas. Doing so sidestepped a new regents rule that prevented athletics directors from coaching. The *Journal-World's* Earl Potter called the contract "revolutionary in KU athletic history."

But Henry only served four years as head coach, forging a forgettable 9-27 record from 1939 to 1942. He left KU and athletics for good in 1943, entering the real estate business in Albuquerque, N.M. He died in 1955.

Henry's stint as athletics director preceded a more successful era under famous umpire and referee E.C. Quigley. But his quiet, stern yet unpretentious nature proved a needed salve for an athletics department wounded from controversy.

SCORING KINGS
1930s pair provided
abundant offense

It's a good thing Ferdinand "Fred" Pralle never aspired to a landscaping career.

A boisterous German kid from St. Louis, Pralle earned a basketball scholarship to the University of Kansas in the mid-1930s. Most scholarships then included a mandatory job that paid about 35 cents an hour.

Pralle, though, didn't have a scholarship athlete's most enviable job. He mowed lawns.

Not just any lawns, mind you, but those of two prominent Lawrence residents: his head coach, F.C. "Phog" Allen, and the inventor of basketball, James Naismith.

Pralle (pronounced Praylee) chuckles as he recalls doing yardwork 60 years ago.

"Naismith always said I could shoot baskets better than I could edge his lawn," he says.

Yard-care shortcomings aside, Pralle developed into one of the best basketball players in Kansas history.

"He was a one-man team, really," says Clint Kanaga, a sports editor for the *University Daily Kansan* in the late 1930s, referring to Pralle's senior season of 1937-38. "He could shoot a high-arching shot from almost near the center of the court, and if they came out to guard him, he would go around them."

Pralle was two years younger than a silky smooth scorer named Ray Ebling. As a senior in 1935-36, the third consecutive season he led the league in scoring, Ebling tied a Big Six Conference record for points scored in one season. He also led the Jayhawks to the conference's first undefeated season.

"When he (Ebling) was out on the court, he always looked like a gazelle as he slid across the floor." said Gordon Gray, a KU guard in 1932-35. "He could move."

Pralle, an in-your-face guard, and Ebling, a finesse-oriented forward, played together just one season. But that season, 1935-36, remained in the hearts of Kansas basketball fans for years.

With Ebling, who averaged 12.2 points per game, and Pralle providing nearly half the Jayhawks' scoring, Kansas reeled off 21 straight victories to start the season. No KU team matched that feat until the 1996-97 Jayhawks opened with 22 victories.

Unfortunately for Allen, the Jayhawks finished 21-2. Kansas lost two straight games to Utah State in a three-game playoff to determine the U.S. representative in the first Olympic basketball competition.

Allen had played a key role in making basketball an Olympic sport, and he wanted the Jayhawks to

FRED PRALLE
Basketball,
1935-38

FRED PRALLE

RAY EBLING
Basketball,
1933-36

"What Notre Dame was to football, KU was to basketball."

– Fred Pralle

win the gold medal at the 1936 Games in Berlin.

"Phog was very disappointed," Pralle says, surmising the pressure of an undefeated record may have hurt the team.

Allen instead settled for KU's fifth conference championship in six years. For the second straight year, Ebling, a dentist's son from Lindsborg, Kan., made at least one All-America team.

"He was a great offensive player," Pralle says, calling Ebling the best KU player with whom he played. "He would take a long step toward the basket, fake a shot, then go underhand. They counted on us to score."

Ebling, whose younger brother Don played with Pralle in 1937-38, continued playing amateur basketball after college while working with Phillips Petroleum Company in Kansas City, Mo.

Pralle joined him after completing his KU career. During his three seasons, the Jayhawks won conference titles each year while he made All-America twice. As a senior, during the first season without a center jump after each basket, he led the conference with 12.1 points per game in league contests.

Pralle needed 22 points during the final game of his career at home against Missouri to win the conference scoring championship. Late in the second half, with a 56-36 KU victory imminent, he started shooting.

"Within a few points of his goal, teammates began feeding Fred as the crowd called for him to shoot," the spring edition of the 1938 *Jayhawker* Yearbook said. "When his twenty-second point swished the netting, Fred Pralle was through for Kansas. Three thousand, five hundred fans arose to cheer the player to whom was due, more than any other, Kansas' thirteenth championship."

Shortly after the season ended, he received most valuable player honors while leading Kansas City's Healy Motors to the Amateur Athletic Union championship in Denver.

"He could shoot the ball from thirty to thirty-five feet if he wanted to," says Dick Harp, a sophomore guard during Pralle's senior year. "He could go to the basket. He had exceptional quickness. He was 6-(foot)-3, just an unusually capable basketball player for that time. I always remember Fred."

Harp and other former teammates have hinted Pralle's talents would have thrived in today's up-tempo game. Pralle dismisses that notion but says, "I would have liked the three-point shot, and I could dunk a little bit."

Pralle and his family moved in 1953 to Gainesville, Fla., and he's lived there since. But he returned to Lawrence with scores of other former KU players in February 1998 to celebrate the school's 100th year of basketball.

"KU was the greatest thing," he says. "Even today, people say, 'You played at Kansas?' Kansas basketball just sticks out, even down here."

He also recalls how the nation perceived Kansas basketball when he and Ebling, who died in 1983, were scoring kings.

"What Notre Dame was to football," Pralle says, "KU was to basketball."

In that sense, not much has changed since he cut Naismith's grass.

Fred Pralle died November 6, 1998 in Gainesville, Fla.

SOMETHING TO TALK ABOUT

Professor enlivened games, enhanced student life

Sometimes that detached voice you hear over the public address system at sporting events is more attached to the action than you might think.

Take Edwin R. Elbel, for example. Known as "the voice" that handled the P.A. chores at the University of Kansas' football and basketball games from the early 1930s through 1966, Elbel was known for his one-liners about the games and other extra-curricular activities. Here is a sampling of Elbel's observations from his perch in the organ loft above the right side of the stage at Hoch Auditorium, where KU played basketball from 1927 to 1955:

- During a relatively silent moment in a basketball game, he often commented, "Quiet isn't it?" or "Somebody say something."
- In waning moments of games, he often said, "Immediately following the game, we will have one of those very unofficial summaries."
- Once he reminded students during a game that final exams were to begin the next day. Later that season during a halftime bull-whip demonstration, he noted that with finals over, perhaps there were some students who would enjoy seeing certain professors on the receiving end of the whips.

But "Doc" Elbel's accomplishments far exceeded quips about whips. He was born Nov. 24, 1895, in South Bend, Ind. He earned a bachelor's degree in 1920 from Springfield (Mass.) College and then became director of physical education at Ottawa University for five years. He returned to Springfield for a master's degree in 1925, then took an associate professor position at KU in 1928. He earned a doctorate degree in 1938 at the University of Iowa.

He directed KU's intramurals, considered one of the leading programs of its kind, from 1928 to 1942. In the

EDWIN R. "DOC" ELBEL
Intramurals director, 1928-42,
Physical education instructor and Kansas relays manager, 1928-66

EDWIN R. "DOC" ELBEL
Kansas Relays

Nov. 25, 1941, edition of the *University Daily Kansan*, sports columnist Clint Kanaga recognized the associate professor for his dedication:

"One of the best-liked men on the University of Kansas campus is Dr. E.R. Elbel. In directing the men's intramural program for 14 years, Elbel has had a man-sized job. Included in his actual instrumental routine is listening to endless complaints, drawing up brackets and tournaments for individual and team play, arranging numerous postponements, disciplining guilty athletes, securing competent officials and handling an intramural board of ten students who aid in the running of the program."

"One of the best-liked men on the University of Kansas campus is Dr. E.R. Elbel."

– University Daily Kansan

Besides intramurals and announcing, Elbel also taught physical education and was clerk of the course for the Kansas Relays. Elbel excelled at organizing the Relays and made the events run with military-like precision.

"He kept everybody in line and was always calling the heats and arranging everybody at the starting blocks," says longtime Jayhawks' broadcaster Max Falkenstien. "Without Ed Elbel, I don't know where the Kansas Relays would have been. He was the glue that held the Relays together for decades."

In 1942, at age 46, Elbel left the University to serve in the technical training command of the U.S. Army Air Corps, which meant he trained men who were non-fliers.

"I certainly am going to miss my contacts here," said the World War I veteran of KU.

At the time, Elbel assured his colleagues and students that he did not relish the idea of leaving, but thought he should do it given the circumstances. As the *Kansan* reported March 13, 1942, "To Dr. Elbel the emergency in the United States is very real and it is his impression that any small contribution that a person can make is a step toward victory."

When Elbel reported for duty, it was said it would take three men to replace him as manager of the Relays. In 1997, the Kansas Relays used nine people as clerks of the course.

After the war, Elbel returned to the University, resumed his former duties and directed the University's Veterans Services bureau. Elbel also was nationally known for his research in physical education, specifically exercise physiology. In 1948, the American Academy of Physical Education conferred its national research citation to him.

Despite his association with swift, powerful and graceful athletes, Elbel, who died in 1983, kept a watchful eye for students with limited athletic ability. He urged the physical education faculty in 1961, to "Do something for the boy or girl, man or woman without obvious athletic talent. Your job is to teach, not eliminate. Your greatest thrill may come when some unpromising lad bursts with pride at reaching a goal that was difficult for him."

Hoop Heroes, Gridiron Glory – and World War

Head Coach George Sauer (leaning on football) led Kansas to Big Six Conference Championships in 1946-47. His staff included longtime trainer Dean Nesmith (far left) and Don Pierce (second from left), KU's first sports information director.

START OF A SCORING PARADE

A hot-shooting forward played integral part in 1940 NCAA run

"Howard was an alert player on the floor. He had touch around the basket. He was always thinking what the next play would be. He was just an outstanding guy."

– Dick Harp

When University of Kansas basketball fans discuss the most prolific scorers in school history, rarely do they mention a skinny forward with blond curls who answered when teammates hollered "Rope."

But five decades before Raef LaFrentz, four decades before Danny Manning, 16 years before Wilt Chamberlain and nine years before Clyde Lovellette suited up for the men's varsity, Howard "Rope" Engleman redefined scoring prowess at Kansas and earned All-America honors in the process.

In his senior season of 1940-41, Engleman scored 16.1 points per game, an almost unheard of average in those days. Since 1923-24, when college basketball's hierarchy rescinded the rule allowing one player to shoot all of his team's free throws, no KU player had averaged more than 12.2 points per game for an entire season.

Engleman accounted for 39.5 percent of KU's points in 1940-41, and his 16.5 average in Big Six Conference games set a league record. By comparison, Manning accounted for 32.9 percent of the team's points while averaging 24.8 per game and garnering nearly every national player-of-the-year award during KU's 1988 NCAA championship season.

It's almost as if Rope, who never saw a college basketball game before playing in one, opened the floodgates for dominant scorers at KU. Two years later, future football All-American Otto Schnellbacher, only a sophomore, led the Jayhawks with 16.3 points per game. A steady stream of scorers followed – Charlie B. Black, Lovellette, B.H. Born, Chamberlain, Wayne Hightower, right up to LaFrentz.

KU had outstanding offensive stars before Engleman. But Rope, who surmises his nickname must have arisen from the light-colored locks that have since faded to silver, may have been the first KU star whose name was synonymous with scoring.

"Howard was an alert player on the floor," says Dick Harp, a senior guard in 1939-40, the year Engleman hit a shot with 15 seconds left in the NCAA Western Region final, lifting KU past Southern California 43-42. "He had touch around the basket. He was always thinking what the next play would be. He was just an outstanding guy."

Not unusually, Engleman sat on the bench for a significant portion of that USC game – bad news in an era when players could only re-enter a game twice. But defense always came first with head coach F.C. "Phog" Allen, and Rope's defensive inadequacies were almost as well known as his stellar offensive skills.

"Yeah, I wasn't too good on defense," Engleman says. "Sometimes I'd find myself on the bench. I probably didn't work on it as hard as I should have."

But with Harp, Phog's son Bob, Johnny Kline and Don Ebling providing more than enough defense, the 1939-40 squad needed scoring punch. Future Hall-of-Fame coach Ralph Miller provided some, but reflecting on the season, the March-April 1940 issue of the KU *Graduate Magazine* declared:

"It was undoubtedly the rise of Howard Engleman, brilliant scoring ace in the latter part of the season, that gave them the necessary power at the last. He was crippled and in bad form earlier."

Engleman's "crippling" injury was a mysterious knee ailment that caused him to miss seven games. He still blames the concrete directly beneath KU's former home floor at Hoch Auditorium, which supplied abundant shin splints.

Once he returned, the Jayhawks surged. But after the USC game, Kansas lost to Branch McCracken's "Hurryin' Hoosiers" from Indiana 60-42 in the final game of the fledgling NCAA Tournament.

"Of course, we didn't have television, we didn't know what Indiana had," Engleman says. "A KU alum living in Bloomington (Ind.) sent a 12-page handwritten report to Phog about Indiana's personnel. That and newspapers were all we had. We had no idea they were capable of scoring 60 points. I know they fast-breaked and threw long passes that we had just not seen before."

Harp says, "That was a really bad one to take. In retrospect, had we played as well as we should have, we might have had a chance to win. But Indiana had basketball players running out of their ears in those days. They began running with the ball, and we got a little lazy."

It was the only NCAA Tournament in which Engleman played, even though the Jayhawks tied for the conference championship during his senior year. During his sophomore year of 1938-39, the tourney's first year, the Jayhawks saw their berth disappear by losing to Missouri at Columbia in the conference finale for both teams.

"I was too young to be disappointed," Engleman says of that loss to the Tigers. "But I remember we played in old Brewer Field House, and there were pigeons all over the damn roof inside. That place – they just had a wooden floor at one end with bleachers.

"Missouri and Oklahoma tied for the title. Missouri didn't know there was such a thing as a tournament, and (Coach) Bruce Drake at Oklahoma was knowledgeable. So Oklahoma went."

Engleman recollects another odd moment in Columbia. This one occurred in 1947, when he had moved from freshman to varsity coach in the middle of the season as a substitute for Allen, whom doctors ordered to rest after he suffered a head injury during a collision with a player in practice.

"We played Missouri the second to the last game of the year over there, and they had a flu epidemic," he says, "so the chancellor wouldn't let anyone go to the game. So we just played in that empty barn, and we beat Missouri without any crowd, which we probably wouldn't have with a crowd."

It's a wonder Engleman found time to coach anyone in the 1946-47 school year. But the $300 per month he earned coaching the freshman team helped pay for taking 15 semester hours in law school. He also played for the M & O Smokies, a local amateur team. Then suddenly, in early January, Engleman found himself coaching the varsity.

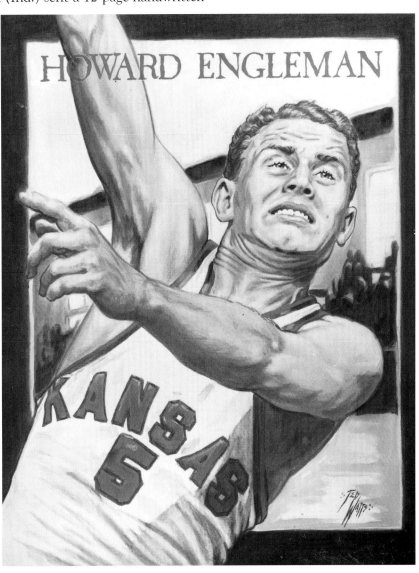

HOWARD ENGLEMAN
Basketball,
1938-41

"I had no plans to ever go into coaching," he says. "It was a tough situation. We had guys coming back from the war and young guys coming up."

Engleman won eight and lost six as a head coach, but under his direction, the Jayhawks won eight of their last 11 after losing their first three by a combined 10 points. Later, another loss came to Kansas State in Manhattan, breaking KU's 22-game winning streak against its cross-state rival. It was only the fifth win for K-State in the series since 1930.

After the season, Engleman left coaching for good. The Arkansas City native has practiced law and golf with the same zeal in Salina since leaving KU with a law degree. But he still keeps close tabs on college basketball, and memories of his scoring heyday occasionally surface.

"When the middle was open, that's where I got most of my shots," he says, crediting Bob Allen for often setting him up with wonderful "feeds."

"I'd cut across the lane and fake and shoot with either hand, or fake and go around my man," Engleman says.

You can bet, too, Rope never has forgotten the desired end result: the sight of a leather ball gently falling through a hoop.

TWO SEASONS OF GLORY

Football coach swept in, out of Kansas, leaving Big Six titles behind

Otto Schnellbacher, moments after catching the winning touchdown pass in the first road victory by a Kansas football team against Nebraska since George Sauer was 5 years old, sauntered up to Sauer, KU's head coach. The two discussed the 13-7 victory as they walked off Memorial Stadium's field that Saturday in November 1947.

"Coach, we stuck it to 'em today," Schnellbacher said.

A smiling, seething Sauer replied, "You're damned right we did."

Sauer had every reason to love the Cornhuskers. He was born in southwest Nebraska, raised in Lincoln and played football for the Cornhuskers. His coach was Dana X. Bible, one of the top college football coaches in the first half of the 20th century.

Sauer was a three-time All-Big Six Conference fullback and an All-American in 1933. When he played, Nebraska never lost a conference game. He and his wife, Lillian, named their first-born child after Sauer's coach and idol. They called her Dana.

But in early 1946, Sauer also was a runner-up for the Nebraska coaching job. Bernie Masterson, who played with Sauer at both Lincoln Central High School and Nebraska, got the job instead.

So Sauer took the job at Kansas, and during his two years as coach no one despised the Cornhuskers more than he did. It filtered down to his players, and the animosity grew after the Jayhawks lost a 16-14 heartbreaker to the Cornhuskers at home during Sauer's first year, 1946.

Nonetheless, KU shared the conference title with Oklahoma that season. Those two teams shared the title again in 1947. As it turned out, Sauer's desire to beat Nebraska mirrored his overall competitive fire, a fire he stoked in the Jayhawks.

"George, we loved him," says Ray Evans, a key component of KU's success during Sauer's brief tenure. "We played like hell for him, just fought like hell. We were lucky in those years because we didn't have a lot of injuries. We didn't have a lot of depth. We might have been outmanned or outsized, but boy I'll tell you, we were fightin' sons a bitches."

Don Fambrough, an all-conference guard and middle linebacker on Sauer's teams, remembers Sauer leading more by example than with fiery platitudes.

"He really wasn't the gung-ho type," Fambrough says. "George was tough, he worked his players hard. The players liked Sauer; they didn't get too close to him. But that was the way coaches were in those days, they kind of kept their distance from players."

Sauer's first season also was the first year most schools were at full strength after World War II. At Kansas, longtime physical education instructor Henry Shenk had coached the Jayhawks from 1943 to 1945. Considering the limited talent available during the war, he compiled a respectable 11-16-3 mark.

But after the war, KU athletics director E.C. Quigley looked elsewhere and found Sauer, who had played briefly with the Green Bay Packers in the mid-1930s before coaching New Hampshire from 1937 to 1942. There, his teams won two Yankee Conference championships before he served as a Lt. Commander aboard the Navy vessel *Enterprise* during the war.

Sauer's immediate task at KU was to meld older war-time veterans, including Schnellbacher, Evans, Fambrough, Hugh Johnson and Red Hogan, with younger players fresh from high school. Despite his inclination to keep players at a distance, he often sought advice from older players who had played service football. He also changed KU's offense from the dying single-wing set to the trendy split-T formation.

The results speak for themselves. Before Sauer, the Jayhawks hadn't claimed a conference title since 1930 and have captured only one since he left. Of KU's 34 coaches, Sauer's .786 winning percentage remains the fifth-highest, and the highest since A.R. "Bert" Kennedy went 53-9-4 in 1904-1910.

Despite beating Nebraska once, Oklahoma once and Missouri twice, Sauer's biggest accomplishment was taking the 1947 Jayhawks to their first bowl game. Throngs of Kansans followed the Jayhawks to the Orange Bowl in Miami, and despite losing to Georgia Tech 20-14, Sauer's popularity threatened to make KU football the state's annual top sporting attraction, even ahead of F.C. "Phog" Allen's basketball squads.

"He could have been governor of the state of Kansas," Evans says. "They gave him a new car, and he drove off in it and went to Navy."

GEORGE SAUER

**GEORGE SAUER
Head football coach,
1946-47**

With that, Sauer was gone, shortly after he signed a four-year contract extension at $10,000 per year. Only a month after KU's first bowl game, he accepted the same position at the U.S. Naval Academy.

"I regret very much leaving Kansas," he told the *Kansas City Star*. "But I just feel that the opportunity to take over as head coach at Navy is one that I can't pass up."

Sauer and Quigley rarely saw eye-to-eye regarding financial support of the football program, but Chancellor Deane Malott and Quigley thought they had met Sauer's requests with the contract extension.

"They had their disagreements, no doubt about it," Evans says of Sauer and Quigley. "He used to run a tight ship, Quigley did. Of course, every coach wants to spend money to do this and that, to upgrade their program. We were in an old, dilapidated stadium in those days.

"People were bitter. They never forgot. I know he would have liked to come back to KU to be athletics director when he was down at Waco, Texas."

Sauer had an ignominious two-year stint at Navy, where his teams went 3-13-2. He became the head coach at Baylor in Waco in 1950. His 1951 Baylor team again played Georgia Tech in the Orange Bowl, and again Sauer's team lost 17-14.

Later, he became general manager of the New York Titans in the American Football League and served as director of player personnel after the Titans became the Jets. He was instrumental in acquiring the talent – including his son, George Jr. – that shocked the Baltimore Colts in Super Bowl III. He then served as general manager of the New England Patriots from 1969 to 1971.

Sauer, who is enshrined in the College Football Hall of Fame as a player, died in 1994 in Waco at age 83. His death brought mere four-paragraph mentions in the *Star* and the *Lawrence Journal-World*. One wonders how extensive those obituaries may have been, and how the legacy of KU football might have developed, had he and Quigley worked out their differences 46 years earlier.

OTTO SCHNELLBACHER

'SNELLY'

Two-sport star traded
Dust Bowl for Orange Bowl

Nothing discredits the notion that Kansas – all 81,823 square miles of it – is an endlessly flat, windswept domain more than Mount Oread, upon which the University of Kansas sprung to life in September 1866.

Nothing epitomizes the same notion more than Sublette.

A diminutive southwest Kansas town, Sublette only briefly interrupts a tediously uniform landscape that rises imperceptibly, invading Colorado before finally succumbing to the powerful Rocky Mountains. Whereas the KU campus and Lawrence caress the scenery surrounding them, Sublette and other High Plains communities forlornly impede the natural horizon.

But while Otto Schnellbacher grew up in Sublette, the horizon sometimes altogether vanished as thick, black clouds of dust literally choked the town, not to mention the hopes of its residents.

As if the Depression wasn't difficult enough, southwest Kansas, which still depends heavily on its annual wheat crop, suffered through continuous drought that annihilated fields and spawned monumental dust storms, the type current conservation practices have all but rendered extinct.

Schnellbacher's youth, then, was not unlike the life his neighbors endured.

"We were a poor family," he says. "We all worked to eat. I had a job where I got to play sports and work second, and I could pick my own hours to work. Also, the man I worked for fed me. That made it nice."

Somehow, between attending school and working at a service station, Schnellbacher found the time to play sports, and he played them well. He even led Sublette to a state championship in basketball.

By then, it was the early 1940s. The "Dirty Thirties" were over, and Schnellbacher's own skies were clearing, as well.

Word had spread to F.C. "Phog" Allen's ears in Lawrence of a fine high school basketball player living 350 miles away. Jack Gardner also heard at Kansas State. Former KU All-America Frosty Cox heard at Colorado. And legendary Henry Iba heard at Oklahoma A&M.

Each of those coaches wanted a kid later dubbed the "Double Threat from Sublette." Schnellbacher had older brothers who played for Washburn University and Emporia State, so he briefly considered smaller schools in eastern Kansas. But his siblings convinced Otto his talent suited a Big Six Conference school.

He felt pressure from the K-State majority throughout southwest Kansas, and he "loved" Iba. But he decided to follow in the footsteps of Ed Hall, another Sublette native who played basketball and football for the Jayhawks in the late 1930s and early '40s.

"You had tryouts everywhere you went in those days," Schnellbacher says. "When I first got to KU (for a tryout), as far as I was concerned, it was love at first sight."

Even after he arrived for his freshman year, though, the limited budget to which Schnellbacher was accustomed continued. He didn't have a full business suit during an era when get-togethers were consider-ably more formal than today's college scene.

"I had a coat that fit, and (fellow basketball player) Armand Dixon had a pair of pants that matched," he says, recalling how the two shared. "But both of us couldn't go to the same affair dressed up. That's how we got through our freshman year."

Schnellbacher worked various jobs during home football games at Memorial Stadium to supplement his income waiting tables at a fraternity. But once the foot-ball coaching staff found out he was working Saturday home games – jobs usually reserved for freshman football players – they threatened to have him removed from the payroll. So he asked Allen what he should do.

"Go out for football," Allen replied.

OTTO SCHNELLBACHER
Football,
1942, 1946-47
Basketball,
1942-43, 1945-48

Thus began one of the most celebrated two-sport careers in KU athletics history.

Schnellbacher eventually became one of only three KU athletes to serve as captains of both the basketball and football teams. (Tommy Johnson in 1909-10 and Charlie T. Black in 1923-24 were the others.)

He benefited from an NCAA rule that gave some athletes who served in World War II an extra year of eligibility. As with other freshman of the era, he was ineligible for varsity athletics but wound up playing four years of varsity basketball anyway. He received all-conference honors each season.

"He was a horse on the boards," says former KU All-American forward Howard Engleman, who was Schnellbacher's coach briefly in 1947. "He'd kill Oklahoma State every time we played. Iba told him after his last game, 'I'm glad you're graduating.'"

Schnellbacher made all-conference twice in football, and he remains one of the best ends in KU history. In all three years he played varsity, he led the Jayhawks in pass receiving, finishing his career with a total of 58 catches for 1,069 yards. Those figures stood as school records for 22 years.

Against Nebraska in 1947, Schnellbacher caught two touchdown passes, including the winning grab with 42 seconds left. KU's victory was its first in Lincoln in 31 years. The 1948 *Jayhawker* yearbook called it the most crucial play during Kansas' march toward its first bowl game.

"We only threw four to five times a game," Schnellbacher says, "and I'd catch half of them."

But "Snelly," as his teammates called him, will be remembered more for one catch than any other. It wasn't a reception, really, more of a toss from star halfback Ray Evans in the 1948 Orange Bowl against Georgia Tech.

Late in the fourth quarter as Kansas, trailing 20-14, neared the Yellow Jackets' goal line, Evans ran three yards before pitching to his fellow All-American at end. Schnellbacher straddled the sideline into the end zone for what appeared to be the tying touch-

Football coach George Sauer presented Big Six Conference title rings to Ray Evans (far right) and Otto Schnellbacher (second from right) at a 1947 Kansas basketball game.

down.

"Some said he was in, some said he wasn't," Evans says. "By that time of the game, there were a lot of people down there, near the out-of-bounds line. Of course, from our point of view, he wasn't out."

But in the official's view, he stepped out of bounds at the 10-yard line. Schnellbacher still doesn't know whether the call was correct.

"The only thing I know is I used an official who was in the way as I was trying to score," he says, smiling wryly. "He's the one who called me out of bounds, and I do know I shoved him into a player. So he had to be close, and I don't think it matters now."

Later, KU quarterback Lynne McNutt fumbled as he tried to sneak in the end zone from the 1. After officials finally unraveled the ensuing pileup, Georgia Tech had the ball and the victory.

The game ended Schnellbacher's college football career, and his college basketball days ended months later. He briefly continued his two-sport ways at the professional level, playing a season with Providence and St. Louis in the Basketball Association of America, a forerunner of the NBA.

But as in college, he gained more notoriety in professional football. In the four years he played with the New York Yankees of the old All-America Football Conference and the New York Giants in the NFL, he intercepted 34 passes and was named All-Pro defensive back three times. However, he retired before the 1952 season and entered the insurance business.

"I had been selling insurance part time," he says. "I was making more money selling insurance than I was playing football."

Since then, the pay scale for an All-Pro certainly has soared farther than that for an insurance salesman, even successful ones like Schnellbacher. But he's not complaining as he eases back in his chair in his west Topeka home, reflecting on his insurance career and why he chose to live in northeast Kansas.

"It's a feeling you get about KU," he says. "I didn't want to get too far. I thought Lawrence was too small, Kansas City was too big, so that's why I chose Topeka. And I'm very happy I did."

TIME OUT FOR WAR

Early in his career, Kansas fans associated Otto Schnellbacher's name more with basketball than football. As a sophomore in 1942-43, he was an integral part of KU's 22-6 squad that raced through the Big Six undefeated.

As World War II intensified, that season bided time for most team members who already had volunteered for military duty. Had they not volunteered, they likely would have been drafted and missed the entire year.

As it was, Armand Dixon and All-American Charlie B. Black left for the service before the season ended. Seven more, including Schnellbacher and Ray Evans, left for Fort Leavenworth to begin their tours of duty hours after beating K-State 47-30 and claiming the conference title March 6, 1943.

The circumstances caused Coach F.C. "Phog" Allen to withdraw KU from NCAA Tournament consideration. More KU play-

ers, including a sophomore backup and future politician named Bob Dole, entered the service later that spring and summer.

College athletics wouldn't be the same for the next two years. Schools struggled to fill rosters while most prime athletes served their country. Meanwhile, Schnellbacher says winning the conference title but not having a chance to play in the NCAA Tournament is somewhat bittersweet.

"The 1942-43 team was the best ballclub I played on at KU," he says. "We would have won the NCAA if we could have gone."

Indeed, the Jayhawks' victory total was the second-most in school history at that time. Other than losing twice to Missouri Valley Conference champion Creighton, including a March 4 game that Evans, Schnellbacher and Hoyt Baker missed while they were visiting their families one last time before going to Fort Leavenworth, the only teams that beat Kansas were service

teams featuring a mixture of several college and even a few professional athletes.

Schnellbacher and Black, KU's two main scoring threats, were named all-conference along with Evans and John Buescher. The Jayhawks defeated their conference opponents by an average score of 48-32.

Schnellbacher, Evans and Black returned in the winter of 1945-46, leading the Jayhawks to a 19-2 record and another undefeated conference title. As in 1942-43, one school defeated KU twice. Eventual NCAA champion Oklahoma A&M (now Oklahoma State) and 7-foot, three-time All-American center Bob Kurland dropped Kansas by 18 points in late December and by nine points in a first-round NCAA Tournament matchup.

"We couldn't beat Bob Kurland," Schnellbacher says. "Of course, in those days you could goaltend. He just went back and knocked everything out. Every shot, he just had his hand over the rim."

CAMPUS CELEBRITY

Two-sport star gained unparalleled popularity

Great athletes at the University of Kansas, it seems, always perform well against Missouri. Or maybe it's a chicken/egg, what-comes-first scenario: performing well against their arch-rival is what qualifies Kansas athletes for greatness.

Either way, no KU athlete ever personified success against the Tigers more than Raymond Richard Evans.

Take the 1947 football game. Missouri, arriving with a 6-3 overall record, 3-1 in the Big Six Conference, came to Lawrence looking for a share of the conference title.

Undefeated Kansas, meanwhile, sought its first bowl invitation after sharing the conference championship the previous season.

Otto Schnellbacher, an All-American end for KU that season, remembers how Evans, playing defensive back, saved the game for the Jayhawks late in the fourth quarter.

"A Missouri back went up the line and cut to the left," Schnellbacher says. "When I turned around, I thought he was gone.

"Ray came across the field and nailed him at the 10-yard line. I didn't think there was a chance anybody could get him."

Once Evans did, he unleashed a hit that marked his love for defense.

"I don't know whether you understand the feeling – to hit somebody and knock them on their ass was a great feeling," says Evans, who also ran, threw and caught for 194 yards in the game, representing half of KU's total offense. "You'd rather do that than get hit yourself."

After the tackle, KU's defense held its ground and blocked a field goal. The Kansas offense then marched down the field, running back Forrest Griffith scored a touchdown with about 45 seconds left, and the Jayhawks escaped with a 20-14 victory.

Escape is what Evans did during one memorable play the previous year in Columbia. On the last play of the first half, with Kansas trailing the Tigers 12-7...

"... Ray dropped back to throw the football," says Don Fambrough, a guard who provided blocks that often sprung Evans for long runs, "and ended up running 50-some yards for a touchdown."

Fifty-four yards, to be exact. That day, Evans scored one more touchdown and passed for yet another in a 20-19 Kansas victory, its first at Missouri since 1934. The *Kansas City Star*'s sports editor, C.E. McBride, waxed eloquent about Evans' performance:

"The victory, which you might refer to as Ray Evans 20, Missouri 19, gives Kansas a tie with Oklahoma for the Big Six championship ... Evans really was the difference between the two teams, and by long odds the best football player on the field. Not only was he a sensational unit in the Kansas offense, but he played with a savage ferocity on the defense."

McBride especially liked the touchdown run at the halftime gun:

"... Evans fell back to throw a pass. Then came one of the all-time dazzlers of play

between Missouri and Kansas. Evans found no receiver open, so he started to run toward his own right side, completely hemmed by Tigers racing in a group. Quickly Evans cut, shifted the ball from one hip to the other and almost before the crowd realized what was under way, the fleet and elusive Kansan was on his way toward the opposite sideline, moving swiftly, leaving the astonished Tigers to the far siding, picking up a pair of blockers and racing all the way to the Tiger goal line. It was a 54-yard sprint, a great back in his fanciest rehearsal."

Evans remembers the run this way: "It was supposed to be a pass. I was lucky to get down to the other end. When you're scared, you run like hell."

***

Ray Evans' list of athletic achievements are almost too numerous to mention. Among them: he's the only KU player named first-team All-America in both football and basketball, the only KU athlete to have his jersey retired in two sports, a member of the College Football and Helms Foundation College Basketball Halls of Fame and a five-time all-conference selection. He was the national leader in pass completions with 101 in 1942, a one-time college record-holder for most passes thrown without an interception (60) and a member of five KU sports squads that won conference championships.

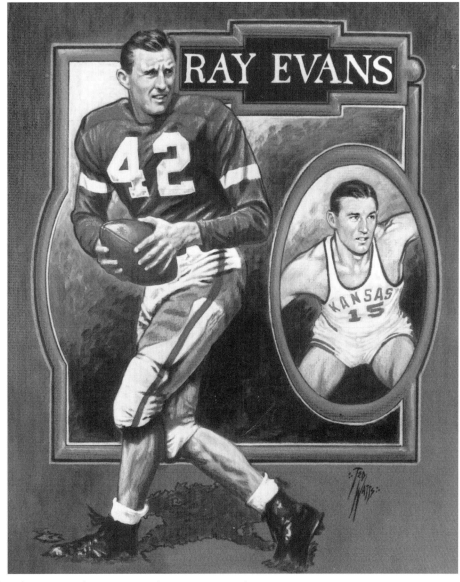

But statistics and honors, including having KU's indoor football practice field in Anschutz Sports Pavilion named after him, merely serve as a barometer of Evans' sheer athletic skill and leadership. For instance, more from his era remember the interception he made in front of his own goal line against Oklahoma in 1947, preserving a 13-13 tie, than the fact he still holds the KU record for most career interceptions with 17.

"Ray had the ability to make the great play at the crucial time in the game," Schnellbacher says.

And, as he did against Missouri, he had the ability to dominate games. Two games before his memorable 1946 performance against Missouri, he had a hand in a double-lateral for KU's first touchdown against Oklahoma.

Then, on a 41-yard field goal attempt with only 1:20 left and the game tied, he received the center snap and held the ball with *two* hands, one on top and one on bottom, to lift it slightly above a muddy field. The adjustment worked as kicker Paul Turner booted the ball through the uprights, securing a 16-13 victory against the Sooners. The next week, Evans scored three touchdowns in a 34-0 pasting of Kansas State.

Even in KU's 20-14 loss against Georgia Tech in the 1948 Orange Bowl, Evans scored both KU touchdowns, ran for 31 yards, passed for 61 yards and caught a pass for 12 yards. For the game, KU only totaled 235 total yards, and Evans accounted for almost half of them.

"We just loved to get out there and play," Evans says. "When we played, we didn't

RAY EVANS
Football,
1941-42, 1946-47
Basketball,
1941-43, 1945-47

> *"Any time you stepped in the huddle and called a play, and it involved Evans, you just did something a little extra, because of the type of person he was."*
>
> – Don Fambrough

keep statistics like they do now. They're so sophisticated; we didn't worry about any of that stuff.

"The Orange Bowl ... that was a big thrill to see. We had never been to a bowl. Students got these big trailers that had big signs, 'Orange Bowl or bust.' That was the only time we ever flew to a game."

The son of Czechoslovakian immigrants living in the Strawberry Hill section of Kansas City, Kan., Evans loved to play any sport, seemingly from the time he was born Sept. 8, 1922. His father, Joseph, who had changed the family's surname to Evans from Ivanco, died when Ray was young. But his mother and five older sisters and brothers looked after Ray, the self-professed "baby of the family."

Even before arriving at KU in fall 1940, Evans had earned the reputation as one of the state's best athletes at Kansas City's Wyandotte High School.

"Now, kids have TV and all sorts of things to watch," he says. "We didn't have that in our day. We just went to the school lot across the street. All the neighborhood kids would meet, and that's all we did was play whatever was in season – basketball, football or baseball. And that carried over into high school."

(By the way, in case anyone wonders about Evans' baseball ability, the New York Yankees once offered to pay for his college tuition if he played for one of their minor league teams on the West Coast.)

Ray Evans eludes a tackler, a common sight during KU's 1947 Orange Bowl season.

At Kansas, Evans gained more national fame in basketball than football before leaving for World War II. As a guard, he was an All-America selection on KU's conference championship teams of 1941-42 and '42-43.

KU's football fortunes, dismal during Evans' pre-war stint, soared when he returned after the war. He also convinced several teammates, including Fambrough, from the Second Air Force team on which he played to follow him back to Kansas.

Evans' campus celebrity extended outside of football.

"He brought more to KU than just athletics," says Bruce Hoad, a mid-1940s KU student – one who distinctly remembers the muddy Oklahoma victory.

A solid student in the KU business school, Evans served as president of the his senior class. His All-America season in 1947 occurred after he chose to return to Kansas for a final year of football rather than turn professional. He received a business degree in February 1948.

Evans played just one season, 1948, in the NFL. While at KU, he often said professional football didn't appeal to him much, and it certainly didn't after the battering he took playing about 55 minutes a game on offense and defense for the lowly Pittsburgh Steelers.

"I'd be so sore on Mondays, I couldn't even go downtown to get my paycheck," he says of his autumn in Pittsburgh.

What's more, Evans still was enduring flat feet that gave him painful bunions throughout his athletics career. He regularly wore arch supports during games.

So he came back to the place he always wanted to live, the Kansas City area. He began a career in banking, eventually rising to president of Traders National Bank. He enhanced his celebrity status by helping bring a professional football team to Kansas City; he later served as president of the Chiefs Club.

Evans also was chairman of the board of the Kings, the city's one-time franchise in the NBA, and served as president of the Kansas Board of Regents, which oversees the state's public colleges and universities. In 1963, he received the Man of the Year award at Kansas City's All-Sports awards dinner.

But Evans, whose father and three older brothers died of heart disease, retired in 1975 after two open-heart surgeries. He resigned from Traders shortly before he and three other prominent Kansas City businessmen were indicted by a federal grand jury for conspiring to misapply bank funds for use as political contributions. Evans pled guilty to that charge and an additional charge of preparing a fraudulent tax return. He was fined $15,000.

Since then, he's watched a son, Ray D. Evans, play defensive back at Kansas and otherwise observed KU athletics. But mostly, he's battled a weak heart.

"I've had several angiograms, angioplasties, bypasses, whatever," he says. "I'm just lucky to be here today."

Fambrough says anyone who had the chance to play with Evans or merely watch him dash across Memorial Stadium's field, his red jersey and silver trousers blurring in a rusty hue, also is fortunate.

"Any time you stepped in the huddle and called a play, and it involved Evans, you just did something a little extra, because of the type of person he was," Fambrough says. "He wouldn't say five words during a football game, but you've heard the old saying 'he led by his actions' – well, he invented that term, in my opinion."

CHARLIE B. BLACK

A NEW ATHLETICISM

Many considered KU's first 1,000-point scorer ahead of his time

Newspapers across the United States hailed Charlie Black as one of college basketball's biggest stars of the 1940s.

Name any 1940s Kansas contemporary of Charlie Black's, and they have a favorite story that recounts his sheer athletic ability.

How about you, Otto Schnellbacher?

"They had tryouts in those days, and I came up to KU for a tryout," Schnellbacher says, referring to a scrimmage with KU players at the end of his senior year in high school. "I almost went back home after I saw Charlie.

"He went up and caught the ball off the backboard with one hand and brought it back down. Of course, Phog chewed him out right in front of everybody: 'Get two hands up there, Charlie!' But I was thinking, 'My goodness!' "

Okay, your turn, Howard Engleman.

"In those days, they would have jump balls, and they would take it to the free throw line to jump," says Engleman, who had replaced an ailing F.C. "Phog" Allen as the Jayhawks' coach during the last half of 1946-47, Black's final season at KU. "(As the jumper) Charlie would jump and just tip it in the basket off a jump ball, and I had NEVER seen that done in a jump ball situation."

Are you finished, Howard?

CHARLIE B. BLACK
Basketball and
track and field,
1941-43, 1945-47

"Every time I was around him, I was just always amazed at his physical ability to do things they do now."

– Otto Schnellbacher

"When we would go on trips, at the hotel, most of the restrooms, you had to put a dime in to get into the stall," he says. "Charlie could reach clear over the top of the stall and knock the thing open without putting a dime in it. He'd do that all the time. He had tremendously long arms."

Yeah, the arms. That's what Ray Evans remembers.

"He had those long arms that damned near drug the floor," Evans says. "And he was big – 6-feet-4, that was big for those days – but Charlie could move, he could run, he could lead a fast break, he could rebound, and being as agile as he was, he got his share of points."

That he did. Black, benefiting from the NCAA ruling that gave some World War II veterans – such as he, Evans and Schnellbacher – an extra year of eligibility, was the first Kansas player to score 1,000 points. Every year he played, he made at least one All-America team, the only KU men's basketball player ever to accomplish that four times. And the players with whom he played are positive he's one of the few stars of the 1940s who could have played today.

"He would have been ideal dunking a basketball," Schnellbacher says.

Dunking was forbidden in Allen's practices. But Schnellbacher admits now, "We would try it on our own when he wasn't around."

Evans isn't sure Black could shoot as well as most 6-foot-4-inch players do today. But he is sure Black would have found a niche, especially because he played defense so well.

Black prided himself on defense. His nickname, "Hawk," derived from his expertise at stealing the basketball. He often guarded the opposing team's post position from his "post guard," or forward, spot.

"Charlie was one of the best athletes I've ever seen. Period," Evans says.

Given that Black also competed in the decathlon for the Kansas track team, it's hard to argue with Evans. As with his KU namesake 20 years before (the two were not related), Black laid claim as one of the most versatile athletes in KU history.

Charles B. Black took a circuitous route to Kansas. Born in Arco, Idaho, he lived in Hutchinson, Wichita and Topeka before attending Southwest High School in Kansas City, Mo.

He then spent his freshman year in college at the University of Wisconsin, where he planned to study horticulture. But Black transferred to Kansas for the 1941-42 season.

He was an immediate success, teaming with future college coach Ralph Miller to provide the bulk of KU's scoring as the Jayhawks won 17 and lost five while sharing the Big Six Conference title with Oklahoma.

The Jayhawks lost a first-round NCAA Tournament game 46-44 against Colorado, whose coach, Frosty Cox, was an All-American guard 12 years earlier at KU. Proving what a hotbed Kansas was for high school basketball players, four of Colorado's starters grew up in the Sunflower State.

The next year, Black was a part of Allen's "Iron Five," consisting also of Schnellbacher, Evans, John Buescher and Armand Dixon. KU went 22-6, but Black played only 18 games, leaving toward the end of the season to join the Army Air Corps as the brooding skies of World War II beckoned.

During the next two years, he flew 51 missions as a reconnaissance pilot in Europe and attained the rank of captain. He returned to Kansas for the 1945-46 season, probably the best of his four years at Kansas.

Buoyed also by the return of Schnellbacher and Evans, KU went 19-2, winning the conference with a 10-0 mark. But as they did earlier in the season, the Jayhawks lost to Oklahoma A&M in their opening NCAA Tournament game.

Oklahoma A&M coach Henry Iba called Black the best post guard in the nation. But even Black couldn't stop Bob Kurland, Iba's 7-foot center who dominated Kansas in the two games in 1945-46. (Oklahoma A&M won back-to-back NCAA titles in 1944-45 and 1945-46.)

Still, Black led the conference in scoring, averaging 17.3 points per game in conference contests. For the season, he scored 326 points, the second-most in KU history at the time, and averaged 16.3 points.

Black's final year coincided with Allen's absence during the last half of the season because of a head injury. By KU standards, the Jayhawks struggled, losing five straight at one point and finishing 16-11. Black's scoring average fell to 11.3 points per game, yet he still received first-team all-conference honors for the fourth time, the first player to accomplish that feat, and made some All-America teams.

An article before Black's final game at KU in the March 14, 1947, edition of the *University Daily Kansan* indicated the depth of his celebrity at Kansas and throughout college basketball:

"For the majority of Midwest coaches, the exit of the 'Hawk' will be cheering news, and if Black's big shoes are never filled again, that will be soon enough. Some of the Big Six cage fans rate the angular 6 foot, 4 1/2 inch two-time (consensus) All-American as the greatest player who ever came off Phog Allen's endless assembly line."

Black played five years of professional basketball in the National Basketball League and the NBA. Oddly, he returned to Lawrence only twice after leaving KU, once for the dedication of Allen Field House in March 1955 and once when KU dedicated the men's basketball locker room in his honor. His retired jersey hangs in the field house.

Black was a successful farmer and managed a welding supply company before retiring in 1984, whereupon he took life easy just outside of Rogers, Ark. He died there in December 1992 at age 71.

Although he's gone, memories of Black's abilities still linger, especially with his former teammates.

"There wasn't anything he couldn't do naturally," Schnellbacher says. "Every time I was around him, I was just always amazed at his physical ability to do things they do now."

Black's long arms and extraordinary leaping ability gave him an advantage over most opponents.

"YOU CAN'T DO THAT," BUT HE SURE COULD

Success distinguished colorful official and athletics director

In August 1945, an envelope from Europe, listing no address, arrived at the University of Kansas via U.S. mail.

It simply bore the inscription, "You Can't Do That, U.S.A."

Nonetheless, anyone associated with KU at the time, or even a lukewarm sports fan, would have had no problem identifying the letter's intended recipient.

It belonged in the mailbox of E.C. Quigley, director of athletics.

A man no one could intimidate in an administrative office or on the field, Quigley popularized his signature admonishment "Y-o-o-o-u-u-u CAN'T do that," during years of work as a major-league baseball umpire, college football referee and college basketball official. But at Kansas, "can't" rarely entered Quigley's vocabulary – unless the request involved what he considered lavish spending.

Colorful and convincing, yet cautious and conservative, Ernest "Ernie" Cosmas Quigley guided the reformation of Kansas athletics and paved the way for KU's post-World War II success.

With the exception of F.C. "Phog" Allen's basketball squads, the war and a turbulent period within the athletics department in the late 1930s and early 1940s stripped the luster off most KU programs. The department languished in debt when Quigley took over Aug. 1, 1944.

He hadn't served as an athletics director in 30 years, and at 63 was only two years short of the state's mandatory retirement age of 65. But few questioned Chancellor Deane Malott's hiring of Quigley, whose stern reputation combined vanity and honesty. The interesting mix proved a superb tonic for what ailed KU athletics.

Born in New Brunswick, Canada, and raised in Concordia, Kan., Quigley's entire adult life revolved around sports. He entered KU in 1900 and promptly made a name for himself as a football halfback. Against Missouri, Quigley returned a second-half punt 65 yards for a touchdown, saving Kansas from defeat in a 6-6 tie.

Missouri fans never forgot, especially several years later when Quigley, in his more famous role as a basketball referee, assessed 17 consecutive technical fouls against a rowdy Missouri crowd in Columbia.

Quigley never graduated from college. While playing at Kansas in 1901, he took a job as football coach of Warrensburg (Mo.) Normal College (later Central Missouri State University). He then accepted a position in 1902 as athletics director at St. Mary's (Kan.) College for $50 per month.

Quigley also coached baseball, football, basketball and track and field at St. Mary's. During summers, he played minor league baseball in the Wisconsin-Illinois League until breaking his right hand in 1910.

The fracture led to a break of another kind. He previously had worked as an umpire in the Kansas State Professional League, but as he prepared to return to Kansas after his injury, an umpire asked Quigley to replace him so he could return home and tend to business. Quigley accepted, and he made extra money as a minor league umpire during the next four summers.

In 1913, he got a chance at major league baseball. He left St. Mary's a year later. By the time he ended his career as a National League umpire at the end of 1936 to take over as the league's public relations director and supervisor of umpires, Quigley estimated he called 5,400 games (likely an inflated figure, considering teams played 154 games each season.)

During that time, he was an umpire in six World Series, including the infamous 1919 Series that inspired the best-selling book and movie "Eight Men Out," which detailed how the Chicago White Sox schemed with gamblers to intentionally lose the series.

Quigley also traveled overseas to call games in the Japanese World Series, where he called 13 balks in the first inning of a 1927 series game.

"It's a wonder Pearl Harbor didn't come years earlier," columnist Maury White wrote while referring to the incident in the Feb. 10, 1975, edition of the *Des Moines* (Iowa) *Register*.

Quigley's officiating wasn't limited to baseball, though. For 40 years, until 1943, he was a college football official in about 400 games. He worked three Rose Bowl games, one Cotton Bowl and five Yale-Harvard games, the nation's top rivalry in the early 20th century. In the early 1930s, demand for his services was so great that Yale and Harvard officials paid him $500 per game plus expenses when other college officials routinely earned $50 per game.

Quigley also officiated about 1,500 college basketball games, mostly in the Midwest, in 37 seasons before bowing out of that sport in 1942. He officiated 19 straight national Amateur Athletic Union championship tournaments, one NCAA Tournament and the U.S. Olympic playoff tournament in 1936.

Kansas fans, players and basketball coach F.C. "Phog" Allen knew him well; he officiated many of the Jayhawks' games from about 1915 to 1940. In fact, many remember Quigley as a part of KU lore more for his officiating antics than his term as athletics director. But there's no doubt which had more impact on KU.

When he took the job as athletics director, Quigley made retiring the $113,000 debt on Memorial Stadium, which had been built two decades earlier, his No. 1 goal. Not far behind was cutting other expenses.

A noted penny-pincher, colleagues often found him in his office wearing overalls

E.C. QUIGLEY
Football,
1900-01
Athletics director,
1944-50

and chewing on his beloved pipe after touching up paint at the stadium. Before leaving for his home on Stratford Road or his pig farm just northwest of Lawrence, Quigley often stopped by the stadium to ensure locker room light bulbs weren't burning and other light switches in the structure's bowels were switched off after late afternoon football practice.

"I don't see why everyone associated with the department shouldn't have an idea of thrift," Quigley told the *Kansas City Star* in 1950, shortly after announcing his retirement.

His thriftiness irked George Sauer, the coach who led KU to two straight Big Six Conference football championships in 1946-47. Sauer wanted more money for himself and his assistants, and even after signing a contract extension, he left for the U.S. Naval Academy in January 1948 after guiding the Jayhawks to the Orange Bowl.

But by the time Quigley left, KU had paid off the stadium debt through bonds and direct donations. Eliminating it allowed Quigley to lobby the Kansas Legislature for money to build a new basketball arena. The legislature's $750,000 appropriation in 1949 began the drive to build Allen Field House.

He also supervised the beginning of KU's first athletics scholarship fund, started by Dick, Skipper and Odd Williams. Founded in 1949, the Outland Club was named for John Outland, the famous football mind who was Quigley's coach in 1901 at KU. Today, it's known as the Williams Educational Fund and is the primary scholarship provider to all Kansas athletes.

Quigley, elected to the Basketball Hall of Fame in 1961, also had an eye for hiring coaches. Besides Sauer, he hired J.V. Sikes, one of KU's most successful football coaches. He also hired Bill Easton, who led the KU track

As a major league baseball umpire and college football and basketball referee, E.C. Quigley wore many hats before returning to Kansas as athletics director. He earned additional fame as a motivational speaker and radio talk-show host.

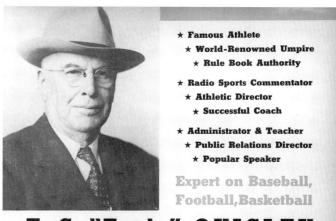

and field program to 12 outdoor conference championships, 11 conference indoor championships and back-to-back NCAA championships in his 18 years as head coach.

The Kansas Board of Regents allowed Quigley to skip the mandatory retirement age of 65 so he could realize his debt-cutting visions. But he was forced to retire at age 70, and Quigley left months before that.

From then until two years before his death at age 79 in December 1960, he toured the Midwest, urging thousands of high school students to attend college. A precursor to today's popular sports talk-show hosts, Quigley also continued conducting a radio show three times a week on Topeka station WIBW.

"It is with a pronounced degree of regret that the final whistle has blown to end a delightful, interesting, and I hope, successful tenure as director of athletics at the University of Kansas," Quigley said when he announced his retirement in January 1950.

If success can be determined by the lasting impression Quigley left on KU, then his hope indeed has been realized.

SLAP-HAPPY ERNIE

Nowadays, sports fans generally desire game officials with an inconspicuous presence. But boisterous Ernie Quigley, an antonym for anonymity, often attracted more attention than the teams he officiated.

Basketball fans repeated his famous "Y-o-o-o-u-u-u CAN'T do that" phrase when calling a foul. But most players hated his slap on their back and his index finger in their face more than the phrase.

"Quigley liked to leave five fingerprints on your back when he called a foul on you," Ernst "Dutch" Urhlaub, a KU basketball player in the late 1910s, told the *Topeka Journal* in 1967 while describing an incident between Quigley and another KU player, Howard "Scrubby" Laslett. "Scrubby didn't like to have Quig slap him. One time Scrubby ran all the way out the door to get away from Quigley, but Quig chased him all the way."

The victim of the foul often fared no better. Instead of simply handing the ball to a free-throw shooter, Quigley usually slammed it into the shooter's gut.

Quigley left little doubt he, not the coaches or players, controlled the game.

"You get back to the bench," he once told a coach at a game in St. Louis. "And

I'm going to give them (the opposition) a free throw for every step it takes."

Early in his career, he often officiated basketball alone. Later, he and one other official usually patrolled the action.

"If the ball went out off two guys' hands out of bounds, he'd ask who touched it last," says Howard Engleman, KU's All-American forward in the early 1940s and later a freshman coach during Quigley's tenure as athletics director. "And by God, if you lied to him, you were in trouble. He'd just test you that way."

Fred Pralle, KU's All-American of the late 1930s who notoriously broke the seemingly bygone rule that prohibits palming the ball while dribbling, remembers how he once spouted off at Quigley.

"What kept us from being better offensive players – we had to dribble the ball with our hands on top of it, and they were strict about it," Pralle said, referring to a time Quigley called him for palming. "Quigley said, 'You can't do that,' and I said, 'You can't do what, goddammit?'

"He threw me out of the game."

Ted O'Leary, the great Kansas guard of the early 1930s, recalls how Quigley could catch a player doing something against the rules, then file it away for future reference.

"Bill (Johnson, the All-American KU center in the early 1930s) had a terrible habit of fouling," O'Leary says of Johnson's first year of 1930-31. "E.C. Quigley reffed Johnson's first game, and if he ever caught a player in his first two or three games doing something frequently, he'd never forget it and he would watch him like a hawk.

"Bill had a habit, while everybody else was looking up at the basket, of pushing the other guy down low in the back (to gain position). Quigley caught him doing that the first time, and I think he fouled Bill Johnson out 12 times that first year."

O'Leary says Quigley definitely knew he was a fine official. However, he liked to be reassured. After his last game as a senior, O'Leary recalls telling Quigley how he admired him.

"He said, 'Young man, will you write me a letter to that effect?'" O'Leary says. "He was a very vain man, but a man you could absolutely rely on to give you an honest call."

Scaling Championship Heights

Oklahoma A&M's legendary coach, Henry Iba (left), congratulates F.C. "Phog" Allen after Kansas defeated Iba's Aggies in February 1952. At the time, records showed the victory as the 700th in Allen's half-century coaching career.

DREAM DENIED, DREAMS FULFILLED

Lawrence via West Point proves right path for versatile athlete

It could have been the opening chapter of a great American tragedy:

Pennsylvania high school hero attends U.S. Military Academy. Stands by his convictions yet gets booted from West Point amid a highly publicized scandal.

As the story unfolds, the hero's dreams vanish, replaced by a meager, meaningless existence.

Gil Reich knows Chapter One. He lived it.

But for Reich, a riches-to-rags saga never materialized. Ironically, he thinks his only real tragedy would have been not leaving West Point.

And in the almost 50 years since, his life's record is anything but meaningless.

"The best thing that ever happened to me was going to KU," Reich says. "At the time, I couldn't have said that. But it was a very refreshing place. It was a second home. I wish I would have gone (there) directly from high school."

No regrets?

"I was devastated when I had to leave (West Point) under the circumstances," says Reich, who had idolized Army's Mr. Inside and Mr. Outside, Heisman Trophy winners Doc Blanchard and Glenn Davis, while growing up in central Pennsylvania in the mid-1940s.

But he also realizes what might have happened had he finished school at West Point, graduating with a commission as second lieutenant.

"I'd be a white cross at West Point cemetery from Vietnam," he says, his voice trailing off in a faint tone of relief. "Not that I wouldn't have done my patriotic duty, but it turned out just fine."

Here's Reich's story: An all-state football and basketball player, he arrived at the academy in the fall of 1949, fulfilling his boyhood dream.

Quickly rising to the top three in a class of 800, he thrived at West Point until 1951. That's when the academy's administration discovered several cadets, including some members of the football team, had received advanced information regarding a test.

The academy's honor code demands cadets reveal any knowledge of cheating. But Reich and his teammates refused to disclose who among them had cheated. Had they done so, the violators would have faced possible expulsion.

**GIL REICH
Football and basketball,
1952-53**

"We weren't willing to 'squeal' on our teammates," Reich says, adding that's not how his parents raised him and his two younger brothers. "My dad would have been awfully tough if he would have found us squealing on each other."

Because no one came forth, the academy instead decided several sophomores and juniors on the football team should leave for not honoring the academy's code. Actually, most players, including Reich, resigned rather than faced what they deemed unfair disciplinary measures.

Schools and athletic conferences across the country had made it clear they would not allow West Point transfers to compete in varsity sports because of the scandal. Nevertheless, Reich transferred to Kansas, enrolling in fall 1951.

A month after classes started, Reich declined another appointment to West Point. The Big Seven Conference, spurred by KU Chancellor Franklin Murphy and columns by Bill Mayer, a sports writer with the *Lawrence Journal-World*, then changed its stance regarding transfers from Army. But Reich only gained one year of varsity eligibility and had to sit out 1951-52.

When fall 1952 arrived, Reich was more than ready to compete again, and he made the most of his opportunity. In the first nationally televised game in college football history, he threw two touchdown passes as the Jayhawks defeated Texas Christian 13-0 in their season opener.

Throughout the year, Reich split time with Jerry Robertson as KU's quarterback, helping lead the Jayhawks to a 7-3 record.

"Why Gil wasn't our quarterback all the time, I never really understood," says Hal Cleavinger, a teammate of Reich's on the 1952 squad. "When he would come into a game, it was instant leadership. He was just a person who commanded respect."

Maybe head coach J.V. Sikes saved Reich for defense, where he teamed with Cleavinger and John Konek in a 6-2-3 alignment, forming one of KU's best defensive backfields ever.

"Gil was outstanding in run support," Cleavinger says. "He would recognize immediately that it was a run, and in those days, the thing you had to worry about was the halfback pass."

Reich saved the Jayhawks' 21-12 victory against Colorado with two goal-line tackles of star fullback Carroll Hardy. He also returned punts for touchdowns against both Santa Clara and Iowa State on his way to All-America recognition as a cornerback.

But Reich, who also led the team in punting, didn't stop with football, despite breaking a finger in a season-ending 20-19 loss at Missouri. He took his quickness to the basketball floor. After the finger healed, he played an integral part in KU's drive to repeat as NCAA champions in 1952-53.

KU fell short by one game, losing by a point to Indiana in the NCAA final. But Dick Harp claims the Jayhawks wouldn't have come that close without Reich.

"If we hadn't had him, we probably wouldn't have gone to the championship game," says Harp, Phog Allen's assistant coach in the early 1950s. "He was as determined a player as you'll ever see. He never accepted defeat. Never."

Despite the loss, Reich says the 1953 national championship game is the "highlight of my athletic career," even more than playing in the 1950 Army-Navy football game, perhaps the marquee college football game at that time.

He graduated with a civil engineering degree in 1954, served two years in the Air Force, then spent his entire professional career with Equitable Life Assurance Society, an insurance company from which he retired as a senior vice president.

Reich now lives in Savannah, Ga., where he is an admitted golf addict. But he also found time to serve as the national chairman of KU's Alumni Association during 1996-97 and remains active in the organization.

A meager existence? Hardly. So much for the great American tragedy.

"Gil," says B.H. Born, Reich's former teammate and most valuable player of the 1953 Final Four, "is one of the top people I have ever known."

OF STEEL MILLS AND WHEAT FARMERS

Two hard-nosed All-Americans anchored KU's line in early 1950s

George Mrkonic's colossal hands tell a story. If any doubt exists that he's a former football lineman who learned the game amid the steel mills of western Pennsylvania, his giant fingers and mighty handshake immediately erase it.

Young men in western Pennsylvania, especially in the 1940s, "cut their teeth on football," as Mrkonic puts it. The region remains one of the sport's most fertile grounds for high school football prospects.

Mrkonic was one of those prospects. But like other high school stars he knew as a standout in McKeesport, Pa., southeast of Pittsburgh, he planned on not straying too far to play college football. In the days before letters-of-intent bound high school players to the college of their choice, he turned down Penn State, Ohio State, Michigan, Pittsburgh and Kentucky, enrolling instead in the summer of 1949 at Purdue University.

That was before Kansas assistant coach Pop Werner talked to an old friend – Mrkonic's high school coach. Werner then spoke with Mrkonic.

"Pop said, 'You ought to come out here to Kansas and take a look around,' " Mrkonic says.

He gave Werner a typical Eastern response.

"I said, 'Kansas? What's out there, a bunch of wheat farmers? Indians? I don't know.' I had never been out of Pennsylvania," Mrkonic says.

But he visited and ultimately chose Kansas over Purdue.

"I tell you, it was the finest choice I ever made," Mrkonic says almost 50 years later. "All the alumni were so dedicated. You felt as if you were really wanted."

As for wheat farmers, Mrkonic soon met one in Oliver Spencer, a sharecropper's son from Ulysses, located in Kansas' southwest corner. Together, they would anchor one of the best offensive lines in KU history.

"They were excellent blockers," says Charlie Hoag, the former Kansas halfback who ran behind both during the early 1950s. "They were big, but both could run well and were fierce competitors. Ollie, in particular, was awfully quick getting out of his stance. He sort of picked that up from Mike McCormack."

McCormack was the all-Big Seven Conference right tackle whom Spencer replaced in the 1951 season, after McCormack – a future All-Pro with the Cleveland Browns who was named to the Pro Football Hall of Fame in 1984 – graduated. It was quite a task for Spencer, a former high school fullback.

"J.V. Sikes (KU's head coach from 1948-53) used to recruit a lot of fullbacks from around the state and convert them into linebackers and lineman," Hoag says. "It seemed to work."

During that era, though, high school fullbacks often were their team's best players, so Sikes knew he was recruiting good athletes. Even while Spencer waited for McCormack's eligibility to expire, he showed promise playing defensive tackle in practice.

> *"I said, 'Kansas? What's out there, a bunch of wheat farmers? Indians? I don't know.' I had never been out of Pennsylvania … I tell you, it was the finest choice I ever made. All the alumni were so dedicated. You felt as if you were really wanted."*
>
> – George Mrkonic

GEORGE MRKONIC
Football,
1950-52

OLIVER SPENCER
Football,
1950-52

"That Spencer is half what's wrong with our centers," Sikes said after a spring scrimmage in 1950. "He's giving them so much hell they can't snap the ball, let alone block him."

Mrkonic recalls how Spencer, who was 6 feet 3 inches tall and weighed about 230 pounds, dominated opposing lineman.

"He just had great fundamentals," he says. "He looked kind of awkward, but I tell you, he was able to make those blocks. Ollie was unassuming, but he couldn't stand to lose. You wouldn't think, looking at Ollie, that he was that dedicated, but what a tremendous athlete. He and McCormack were cut out of the same cloth, I thought."

Once Spencer played regularly, he stuck primarily to right offensive tackle. But Mrkonic, who weighed about 10 pounds less, played left offensive guard, defensive tackle and even punted.

One of Mrkonic's finest games highlighted his versatility. In a 27-7 victory at Nebraska on a blustery day in 1951, he punted six times in a 35-mile-per-hour wind for a 32-yard average; none were returned. The Associated Press also named him its "Lineman of the Week" for his performance on defense.

The fall 1950 edition of the *Jayhawker* Yearbook had alerted readers to Mrkonic, telling them to "look for him in two years on the All-America selections." Actually, he made it only a year later, in 1951. Spencer was a second-team All-American that season and a first-team pick in 1952.

During their three seasons together, the pair played on KU teams that won 21 and lost just nine. Despite coming close, they never could beat an Oklahoma team in the midst of winning 12 straight conference championships. That shortcoming still irritates Mrkonic.

"In 1950, we had them 13-0," he says. "Then they beat us 33-13; we just fell apart. And in 1951, we should have beaten them down there. We had them in the first half, then we started throwing the ball in the second half when we should have kept running ... Oh, that was a big disappointment. Losing to Oklahoma three years in a row was the biggest disappointment ever."

But Mrkonic and Spencer enjoyed success against Jim Weatherall, Oklahoma's outstanding two-time All-American lineman who won the Outland Trophy in 1951. Mrkonic holds his unanimous selection to the Sooners' "all-opponent" team three straight years in higher esteem than any of his other honors.

"The all-star games, they don't mean much: it's your team-mates, your peers, the teams that you play against," says Mrkonic, who spent 14 years with the marketing department of Phillips Petroleum after a brief stint in the NFL with the Philadelphia Eagles and a year in the Canadian Football League. He also served in the Air Force Reserves, officiated high school and small college football games and coached youth football.

A smile spreads across his face as he hearkens back to other stories, such as the time KU traveled to Missouri during 50-degree weather in 1950, then played the Tigers in brutally cold temperatures the next day after seven inches of snow had fallen.

Mother Nature's surprise might not have mattered had KU's equipment staff been prepared. But the Jayhawks played that late November game with the same gear as they would have worn in an a September contest.

"What a day," Mrkonic says of a game the Jayhawks lost 20-6. "We had no long johns, no gloves ... it was the coldest day I ever played."

But fonder memories include his former teammates, players such as Hoag, Gil Reich, Galen Fiss and others.

And, of course, he'll never forget Spencer, who played nine seasons in the NFL and the American Football League with Green Bay, Detroit and the Oakland Raiders. He was the Raiders offensive line coach in 1962-1979. After that, he ran an insurance agency in Danville, Calif., until dying abruptly of a heart attack in 1991 at age 60.

"Ollie was like a brother. He was a good coach, a good friend," Mrkonic says. "They were all outstanding individuals. What a super bunch of guys, great citizens, now and back then. It was great to be associated with them."

JUST SHY
Record-breaking hurdler barely missed 1952 Olympics

BOB DeEVINNEY
Track and field,
1950-52

Heartbreak is hitting the last hurdle and losing the U.S. Olympic Trials in a photo finish.

Bob DeVinney knew heartbreak.

The former University of Kansas track star was among the favorites to compete for a gold medal in the 400-meter hurdles at the 1952 Olympic Games in Helsinki, Finland. But at the qualifying race, he saw his Olympic dream fade away when he struck the final hurdle, fell to the track and barely lost third place at the tape. He stayed home instead.

Charles Moore of Cornell, the lone U.S. qualifier in the 400 hurdles, captured the gold in the Olympics, winning the event in 50.8 seconds. The previous year, Moore and DeVinney had gone head-to-head in the National Amateur Athletic Union Senior championships, where Moore had won.

Leading up to the Olympic Trials, 1952 was DeVinney's year. The KU star, who was the Jayhawks' captain that year, won the 400 hurdles at the 1952 NCAA Outdoor Championships in 51.7 seconds, an NCAA record. He won his only Big Seven Conference title earlier that year in the 220-yard low hurdles, and he set a national record in the 440-yard hurdles with a time of 52.4 seconds at the Drake Relays.

Teammates remember him as an intensely competitive sprinter who had just one gear: full-speed ahead.

"Bob was another guy who was hard-nosed," says Herb

BOB DeVINNEY

Semper, a former KU track star and 1952 teammate of DeVinney's. "He worked at it. All of (coach Bill Easton's) boys worked at it, and we believed in ourselves."

DeVinney, recruited heavily by Easton, was an all-state hurdler in Anderson, Ind. DeVinney came to KU in 1948 and quickly established himself as one of the Big Seven Conference's top sprinters and hurdlers. In dual meets, the team often called on him to fill slots wherever the Jayhawks needed points. During his career he ran all distances from 60 yards to the half-mile, including the 440 relays, and performed long and high jumps.

In 1950, he ran the anchor leg of KU's mile-relay team that upset Oklahoma in the conference outdoor championships. His split time was 48.2, a world-class effort in his day. He improved that time to 47.1 seconds at the 1952 Drake Relays as the Jayhawks again won the mile relay.

DeVinney won the National Junior AAU championships in the 400 hurdles in 1950 and placed second in the 1951 Senior AAU meet, where he set a new school record of 51.3 seconds.

In the 1952 conference indoor championships, DeVinney dashed to a second-place finish in the low hurdles and third place in the high hurdles. He also placed in both events as a sophomore.

After college, DeVinney worked in the insurance business in Dallas.

HERB SEMPER

FOR DAD AND TEAM

Cross country star shared his greatest accomplishments

"If there was a guy who ran two or three miles at night, I'd run four or five miles. I did more exercises. I devoted myself to the task at hand. You've got to. If you're going to excel in life, you've got to work at it, that's all there is to it."

— Herb Semper

As the first member of his family to go to college, Herb Semper never forgot where he came from and what a privilege it was to attend the University of Kansas.

When he left Forest Park, Ill., for Lawrence, Semper gladly acknowledged he would share any of his track and field accomplishments with his father. That's because Helmuth Semper had quit high school after his junior year to support his family. In time, the elder Semper became a successful, self-made man. By studying on the job, taking night courses and passing a state exam, he advanced from clerk at a drug store to become a registered pharmacist.

Still, leaving school early had left a void in Helmuth Semper's life. As with his son, he had run track in high school and had enjoyed it. So when Herb departed for Kansas, Helmuth Semper supported him every step of the way.

"Dad kind of relived his fondest wishes and desires in what I accomplished," Herb Semper says. "That's what gave me the greatest satisfaction in competing. Whatever I accomplished, Dad shared it with me. It made it doubly nice.

"There's a lot of self-esteem and self-reward and stuff like that, but to share it with others, especially that close, that's what made it all worthwhile."

Herb Semper shared a bounty of achievements with his father. He won the

NCAA cross country championship in 1950 and 1951. He finished third in the two-mile run in the NCAA Outdoor Track and Field Championships those same years. He also prevailed three straight years in the Big Seven Conference's indoor two-mile competition. As the 1952 *Jayhawker* Yearbook noted:

"It would take nearly every superlative in the book to do justice to Herb Semper. The red-headed Phi Gam senior … has wiped every two-mile record in the Big Seven Conference off the boards in his three-year career on the cinders. He holds the outdoor loop standard for his specialty at 9:21, the fall two-mile record at 9:14.9, and he erased his own indoor meet mark this spring when he negotiated the Municipal Auditorium boards in Kansas City at a blazing 9:07 clip. This last performance was the fastest two-mile ever run indoors by a Big Seven athlete."

While he drew his inspiration from his father, Semper credits his success to former KU track and field coach Bill Easton. But opportunity precedes success, and Semper is thankful that Easton gave him the chance to be a Jayhawk.

"He sought me out. Nobody else did," Semper says. "I did well in high school, but I wasn't top dog or anything like that. Bill was the type of guy that would see something good in somebody and he would develop it from there. He was a tremendous, tremendous coach."

For Semper, developing into a champion meant going the extra mile(s).

"If there was a guy who ran two or three miles at night, I'd run four or five miles," he says. "I did more exercises. I devoted myself to the task at hand. You've got to. If you're going to excel in life, you've got to work at it, that's all there is to it."

After he graduated, Semper worked in sales, touting everything from building materials to office supplies. Currently, he works as a technician assisting pharmacists with Walgreens in Omaha, Neb. As he reflects on his achievements at KU, Semper says running for the Jayhawks taught him the value of teamwork and self-reliance.

"What I think the career did for me, as well as my teammates, it made men out of us," he says. "Although we competed individually in our events, you put them together and as a team, we were just unbelievable in what we accomplished. We had a camaraderie like I've never seen in my entire life.

"But I think what it taught me personally, is that you've got to count on yourself. Unlike other sports, there are no timeouts, no substitutions, no rest periods; when the gun went off, the only thing that stopped you was the finish line. If you were ill, you competed. If you were hurt, you competed. No matter what, you overcame because that's what Bill instilled in us."

Not a bad legacy to share with your father. Or a legion of Kansas fans, for that matter.

HERB SEMPER
Cross country and
track and field,
1949-52

SHORT-CIRCUITED
Lifetime ban curtailed promising track career

As one of the best distance runners in the world, Wes Santee never encountered difficulty breaking the tape at the end of a race.

But getting untangled from the red tape of his star-crossed career proved a problem. A big, insurmountable problem.

Santee, the Kansas farm boy whom the media dubbed the "Ashland Antelope," was a star performer for the University of Kansas track and field team in the early 1950s. He set two world records in the indoor mile: 4 minutes, 4.9 seconds in 1954 and 4:03.8 in 1955. He set a world record in the outdoor 1,500 meters, 3:42.8, in 1954 and was a member of the world-record sprint medley relay team that same year.

He won college championships. He captured first in the 5,000 at the 1952 NCAA Outdoor Track and Field Championships and won the mile a year later. In the fall of 1953, he finished first in the NCAA Cross Country Championships, which helped Kansas to its first and only team title in that sport.

Santee's legacy also grew for what he almost did. In 1954, he ran several mile competitions in 4 minutes and a fraction of a second. He seemed poised to become the first runner to conquer the 4-minute mile. But what a big fraction the split second turned out to be: On May 6, 1954, a British medical student named Roger Bannister broke the four-minute barrier with a time of 3:59.4 at Oxford, England.

Finally, though, Santee became embroiled in a series of controversies involving the bureaucratic morass of the U.S. Olympic Committee and the Amateur Athletic Union. In time, the AAU banned him from competition for life, costing him a shot at the 1956 Olympics and other athletic glory.

Despite his problems, the Wes Santee story is a success story. But it might have been even more successful had understanding, compassion and common sense prevailed.

Santee learned hard work growing up on a cattle ranch southwest of Ashland. He often worked six to eight hours on the ranch with his father, sometimes missing high school classes to do so.

The state-champion miler picked Kansas because of coach Bill Easton, whom he eventually adored.

"He was virtually my second father," Santee says. "When I went to KU, I didn't have any money, I didn't have any place to go, so I spent a lot of time at the Easton household."

But work came first for Easton. And the former ranch hand was ready.

"When I got here to Kansas, Easton had researched distance running, and we started doing more (training) than had been done," Santee says. "It was duck soup for me. Workouts were by far tougher than track meets, but due to my manual work background, this was not a very strenuous thing."

Hard work never hurt anybody, the saying goes, and Santee flourished in Easton's program. With four world records, three NCAA championships and a near-miss on the four-minute mile, Santee seemed destined to become one of track's greatest

> *"When I got here to Kansas, (Coach Bill) Easton had researched distance running, and we started doing more (training) than had been done. It was duck soup for me. Workouts were by far tougher than track meets, but due to my manual work background, this was not a very strenuous thing."*
>
> – Wes Santee

stars. But starting with an AAU meet at the end of his freshman year, continuing with a dispute at the U.S. Olympic Trials in 1952 and picking up again with the AAU, petty bureaucracies threw Santee's destiny into a loop.

The first problem occurred the summer after his freshman year. Santee competed in a national AAU meet at both the junior and senior levels. He won the junior 5,000 and took second the next day in the same event at the senior level. His top-six finish in the senior race assured Santee a place on a touring AAU team bound for Japan.

Enter the bureaucracy. The KU track office mailed in the entry form for the Japan trip. Herb Semper, a KU varsity runner, joined Santee on the tour. The entry form read "The KU Track Club" for their affiliation.

The problem: Santee still was considered a freshman, and freshmen were ineligible for varsity competition at that time. So Santee's affiliation should have read, "Unattached." It was a simple, honest mistake.

But not to the AAU.

"Some of the coaches, when they saw this, said 'A-ha! He's ineligible for his senior year,' " Santee says.

A movement to that effect started among coaches. Easton, KU basketball coach F.C. "Phog" Allen and KU athletics director Dutch Lonborg fought that movement for three years, and eventually Santee had to sit out one track meet as punishment for a clerical error.

"How asinine," Santee says. "When the NCAA and AAU have those kinds of idiotic rules, and they still have some of them, I certainly haven't much support for that type of thing."

Santee offers some background information as an explanation behind this ordeal:

"You have to understand that in that time frame, there's several things going on. Number one, Phog Allen was primarily instrumental in getting basketball into the Olympics, but he was not particularly well thought of by the AAU and the Olympic committee. You also have to realize that the same person wore the same hat: the person might be an NCAA official, an AAU official and an Olympic official."

The AAU dominated the track and field scene in those days, he says. And when the AAU picked a team to tour abroad, AAU officials went along.

"Phog Allen had quite a battle with them, and I think one of his most famous quotes was when he called them, 'Trans-Atlantic, oceanic hitchhikers,' " Santee says. "And you have Easton, who was a very no-nonsense guy. They did not like us."

Santee's problems with these organizations worsened. In 1952, he won the NCAA title in the 5,000, which was a qualifying meet for the U.S. Olympic team. He won the 1,500 at the AAU meet, which also qualified him for the Olympic team.

At the trials, Easton told Santee to run the 5,000 on one day and the 1,500 the next. Easton then wanted Santee to go to the Olympics in the event in which he ran best. Santee finished second in the 5,000 and was happy because he made the Olympic team.

The next day, he was standing at the starting line for the 1,500, his stronger event, when an official grabbed his arm and pulled him off the track. Easton ran over and told Santee: "They've decided you're not good enough to run both races, and they won't let you pick and choose, and they're not going to let you run."

The gun sounded for the race while Santee stood off to the side trying to sort out the ruling. He's still bewildered by it.

"Who are they to make that kind of decision?" he asks four decades later. "There's nothing in the rule books that addresses that."

At the Helsinki Games, the 19-year-old Santee was bunched in the 5,000 with a veteran field and did not qualify for the finals. The U.S. entrant in the 1,500 finished second in the race. Santee never lost to that runner, and later defeated the Olympic champion, Joseph Barthel of Luxembourg, when they met in a race.

Still, Santee was young. He'd only be 23 in 1956 and the prime age of 27 in 1960 when the next two Olympics occurred. He had plenty of time to run for a gold medal, right?

Wrong.

By 1954, Santee was in full stride to break the 4-minute mile. Although Bannister broke the barrier first, Santee drew interest from track meet promoters after his collegiate eligibility expired that year.

As a common practice, meet promoters covered expenses for the athletes competing at their meets. For someone with Santee's stature, the expenses were padded. Santee admitted to taking the money, more than $10,000 in 1955. In an article for *Life* magazine, Santee explained he used the money for travel expenses and for training.

"I was not the first to receive padded expense money via the little brown envelope," he wrote. "Nor will I be the last."

The AAU ruled on Santee's status in 1956. At a hearing in Kansas City, Mo., AAU officials voted 21-7 in Santee's favor not to ban him from competition.

"The rule book at that time was $12 a day," he says. "I never argued that I took more than $12 a day. It said train transportation, and I was flying (to meets)."

The rule book also stated that anyone on the committee wanting to appeal the vote had 10 days to do so. The 10 days passed, and Santee dismissed the incident. A couple of months later, one of the dissenters complained to the national AAU office about the verdict.

The national office reviewed Santee's case. He was not allowed to appear on his behalf. The AAU then decided to ban Santee for life.

Santee sued the AAU for the right to compete and won a temporary injunction against it. So the AAU sent officials to warn college track coaches not to let their athletes compete against Santee or they would declare the athletes ineligible.

WES SANTEE
Cross country and track and field,
1951-54

Santee did win in the court of public opinion. He was allowed to run against other military runners (Santee was a lieutenant in the U.S. Marine Corps) in a meet at Madison Square Garden in New York. The crowd cheered wildly throughout the mile race. The next race featured college milers, and the crowd booed them every step of the way.

Former KU teammate and fellow distance runner Al Frame says he's amazed by Santee's problems with the AAU, especially compared with the millions of dollars made by today's top runners.

"There wasn't any doubt about that he was getting paid, but other people were getting paid, too," Frame says of the Santee era. "But what he was getting paid was chicken feed to what they get now strictly above board. So we're just amazed that he was booted out of running for what happened at that time."

Santee takes the lifetime ban in stride.

"If they don't follow the rule book, and I haven't followed the rule book, how do you win?" he says. "Of course, when they wanted me to run in the Masters in 1977, they gave me another ticket."

After he finished his Marine hitch, Santee operated a successful insurance agency from 1957 to 1981 in Lawrence. He retired from that agency and then worked on such local projects as the James Naismith Memorial at Lawrence's Memorial Park Cemetery.

Today, he splits his time between a State Farm insurance agency in Arizona and his lakefront home in Eureka. He considers himself a staunch alumnus and basketball fan. And he pays basketball coaches Roy Williams and Marian Washington the ultimate compliment: "I see in Roy and Marian a lot of the characteristics of Easton and Allen," he says. "It's fun to watch them function."

ALLEN FRAME

STEADY IMPROVEMENT

Scholarly distance runner became a national champion

Some athletes start early in their sport and use the experiences to their advantage. University of Kansas distance runner Al Frame falls into that category.

As a fourth-grader, Frame outran three high school boys in a half-mile race. Granted, the race didn't amount to much. The boys ran over a measured course along the sidewalks of their Seattle neighborhood. But the competition raised a consciousness in track that Frame kept with him.

By high school, Frame's family had moved to Wichita, where his father worked as an efficiency expert for Beech Aircraft. Frame attended East High School and ran cross country and track. As a senior, Frame ran a nondescript 4-minute, 37-second mile for third place in the state meet.

But what caught KU track and field coach Bill Easton's eye was Frame's winning time in the University's annual prep cross country run the year before. He took the two-mile race over rugged terrain in 9:56.7, a mark that topped Wes Santee's time of 10:04.2 two years earlier.

The other thing that Easton liked about Frame were his grades. Easton always sought good students for his teams, and in Frame he found one of the best. Frame earned a Summerfield Scholarship to attend Kansas, one of 10 students in the state to receive the award.

ALLEN FRAME
Cross country and track and field, 1953-56

Frame's running style presented Easton with a challenge. Frame ran with low knee action and a bowed head, which was contrary to Santee's classic form and that of other Kansas greats. Although Easton never cured Frame of his shuffling style, Frame did benefit from his tutelage.

"He made me what I was," Frame says of Easton. "When I got out of high school I was about a 4:35 miler, and he put me through his Easton training program and turned me into what I was."

What Frame developed into was a champion. He won the Big Seven Conference Indoor Track and Field Championship in the two-mile race his sophomore year and narrowly lost the mile race. As a junior in 1954, he won the conference cross country meet in 15:16.7 over three miles.

A week later, he captured the NCAA Cross Country championship at East Lansing, Mich., in 19:54.2 across four miles. Frame's kick in the last half-mile made the difference, as he distanced himself from the pack and won by 35 yards.

"I didn't feel much pressure because we had won it as a team the year before," Frame says. "I just beat the guys I was supposed to beat."

He continued his winning ways in the conference outdoor track championships. Frame took first place in the mile run in 4:16.5. Kansas runners finished in the top four spots of the race.

A month later, Frame placed third in the two-mile run at the NCAA Outdoor Championships with a time of 9:09.1, his best mark. Kansas finished fourth in the competition, its best showing to that time.

His cross country teammates elected Frame as their captain for the second straight year in 1955. He also led the KU senior class of 1956 as its president. In November 1955, Frame finished fourth in the NCAA Cross Country meet.

"I felt the pressure that year," he says.

After graduation, Frame served two years in the U.S. Army before returning to Kansas for a year of post-graduate studies. He later graduated from KU's school of law.

Frame now practices law in Kinsley, Kan. He calls his NCAA championship a source of pride, but he doesn't dwell on the achievement.

"Other things happen," Frame says. "I raised five kids and put them through school, and that to me is as much of an accomplishment as anything else."

SUCCESS IN ALL FIELDS

Relay team made mark on and off the track

After setting a world record in the sprint medley, Ralph Moody spotted cinder-covered University of Kansas teammate Frank Cindrich.

"What in the world happened to you?" Moody asked Cindrich.

"You took off too fast," replied Cindrich, who opened the race with a 440-yard leg before passing the baton to Moody. "I couldn't quite get to you, so I made a final leap at you. Fortunately, we connected."

Thus, a record was established by the skin of their teeth, plus the skin on Cindrich's elbows and knees. The team – with Moody's near-miss 220-yard leg, Dick Blair's 220-yard effort and Wes Santee's 880-yard anchor leg – ran the combined mile distance in 3 minutes, 20.2 seconds on April 2, 1954 at the Texas Relays in Austin.

"It was a great honor (to run with) the three other fellas who were the caliber they were," Moody says.

Blair says coach Bill Easton entered the meet with the record in mind.

"I thought we had a chance," he says. "I was still somewhat surprised. It was a very exciting thing."

For Santee, whose accomplishments are chronicled elsewhere in this book, the world record was one of four that he owned during his collegiate career. For Blair and Moody, the record is one of a string of accomplishments each man has enjoyed in life.

Blair served as captain of the Jayhawks in 1956, his senior year. He finished second in the 220-yard dash at the NCAA Outdoor Championships that year and was an alternate for the U.S. Olympic team in the 200-meter competition. He won seven Big Seven Conference championships for KU: the indoor 60-yard dash in 1955 and 1956; the outdoor 100-yard dash in 1955 and 1956; and the outdoor 220-yard dash in 1954, 1955 and 1956.

In the summer of 1955, Blair traveled to Europe with the Amateur Athletic Union team. He won all of his races except for one competition on a soggy English track. The team was the first of its kind to travel behind the Iron Curtain; Blair called the airplane trip from East Berlin to Prague, Czechoslovakia, "haphazard."

The Osborne native earned a bachelor's degree in history in 1956 and then entered KU's medical school, from which he graduated in 1960. Blair practiced as an internist in Lawrence for 18 years before moving to California. He serves as associate chief of staff at the Palo Alto Veterans Administration Medical Center and is an associate professor of internal medicine at Stanford University's medical school.

Moody, a Minneola native, came to KU on a football scholarship. He gained 637 yards as a halfback during his three-year career and served as co-captain in 1955. He displayed great versatility on the gridiron by performing as a punter, placekicker, defensive back, kickoff returner and punt returner.

Moody calls his education at KU, where he earned a bachelor's degree, "The rock

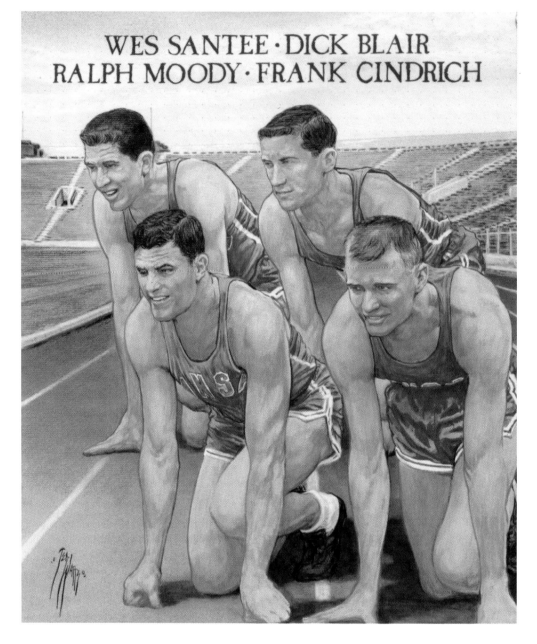

WES SANTEE · DICK BLAIR
RALPH MOODY · FRANK CINDRICH

and base that I continue to move from. An education is a strong background that helps you survive wherever you go."

His education has taken him many places. Moody has taught high school in Kansas, New York and California, where he presently teaches math and science at Washington Unified High School in West Sacramento. He earned a master's degree from Canisius College, Buffalo, N.Y. and a doctorate in education from the University of the Pacific, Stockton, Calif. In between teaching jobs, Moody has worked in administration at Fresno State University, Fresno, Calif., and Napa Valley College, Napa, Calif.

Cindrich, from Wyandotte High School in Kansas City, Kan., also played football at KU. As a halfback, he ran for 380 yards and three touchdowns in slightly more than two seasons. He twisted a knee as a senior in 1953, which limited his playing time.

Moody calls his late teammate one of the most competitive people he knew.

"He was a great guy, always upbeat," Moody says of Cindrich. "He was a very bright competitor. He always seemed to know how to do the right thing."

All three survivors have succeeded in life since that warm spring day in Austin more than 40 years ago. Balance, Blair says, is the key.

"Young athletes should balance their athletic and academic careers," he says. "Successes in each are actually complementary."

TWO GREAT HOOKS

Phog nabbed prep star, whose trademark shots brought NCAA title

In the first half of the 20th century, two states produced a disproportionate number of high-quality college basketball players. College coaches recognized those two states, Indiana and Kansas, as high school basketball hotbeds. If Springfield (Mass.) YMCA College was the birthplace of James Naismith's invention, then the sport's cradles rocked in the Hoosier and Sunflower states.

Hoosier boys always attended the University of Indiana or Purdue, maybe Notre Dame. Likewise, Kansas high school stars played at the University of Kansas. Once in a while they went to Kansas State. Or maybe Colorado, Oklahoma A&M or Oklahoma. But prep stars from either state never roamed too far. That's just the way it was, no questions asked.

Until Clyde Lovellette.

In 1948, Kansas coach F.C. "Phog" Allen faced a crossroads. At 62, his reign as the kingpin of college basketball teetered on the brink of collapse. Just a year earlier, he sat out the second half of the 1946-47 season after suffering a head injury in practice during a collision with a player. Then, his 1947-48 squad went 9-15, KU's first losing mark in 20 seasons. The Jayhawks tied for last in the Big Seven Conference.

Allen, though, regained his coaching focus, recruiting players as never before. He received commitments from three key Kansas high school players: Bob Kenney from Winfield, Bill Lienhard from Newton and Bill Hougland from Beloit.

What he needed, though, was a dominant big man. For that, he looked east to Terre Haute, Ind. That's where he found Lovellette, a 6-foot-9-inch behemoth at Garfield High School.

"All through four years of high school, you're sort of brainwashed with that idea of which way you're going," Lovellette says of his home state's expectations. "So there really wasn't a lot of recruiting by Indiana as far as I was concerned."

CLYDE LOVELLETTE
Basketball,
1949-52

Branch McCracken, Indiana's coach, simply assumed Lovellette would attend college there. He assumed wrongly, even though Lovellette told him he would play for the Hoosiers.

"I never knew who Phog Allen was, but when he recruited me, I enjoyed him," he says. "What Phog said was right off the shoulder, nothing fancy. But on the other hand, being a poor kid, I didn't want to get very far from home."

Allen persisted. Finally, one day in mid-1948 when Allen was scheduled to speak to a group in St. Louis, he asked Lovellette to meet him. But Lovellette asked a brother-in-law to drive to St. Louis to tell Allen he was going to Indiana.

Allen returned to Terre Haute with Lovellette's brother-in-law.

"So he corners me," Lovellette says of the Kansas coach, "and he's told me this before: that he has a group of individuals that by the time they're seniors, they're going to win the national championship, go to the Olympics and win the gold medal. And it's going to be a tremendous year."

Allen convinced Lovellette to return with him to St. Louis. From there, they headed to Lawrence. Allen promised Lovellette he could return to Indiana if he didn't like it.

"You get to some places, people just start patting you on the back and they don't mean it," he says. "Kansas wasn't like that. When I got to Lawrence, the people were just like Indiana folks, I thought, just real great people. I enjoyed the town. It was small; I wasn't a number. At Indiana, you're just a number."

That's how Allen hooked the future two-time All-American. In 1952, he led KU to the land Allen promised four years earlier.

"To my recollection, I didn't enroll (at Indiana), but if you talk to Indiana folks, I did enroll, and I was ready to go to class, and then Phog kidnapped me," says Lovellette, who maintains Allen broke no recruiting rules, despite suggestions otherwise.

Lovellette's presence during his first year at KU, when freshman still weren't eligible to play varsity sports, gave hope to Kansas fans who once again watched the Jayhawks tie for last in the conference.

The next year, 1949-50, Lovellette proved he was worth his press clippings. Still developing a potent arsenal of hook shots, he averaged 21.8 points per game and was the main reason KU shared the conference title with Nebraska and Kansas State.

By then, sportswriters and fans already had cloaked Lovellette with a number of nicknames: the Great White Whale, High Pockets, the Leaning Tower of Lawrence and the Ponderous Pachyderm of the Plains, to name a few.

He may have warranted the last of those monikers. Allen chided Lovellette's weight in an August 1950 letter to KU players:

"A couple of weeks ago, I saw Clyde Lovellette, and he looked as if he had a watermelon stuffed into his abdomen. He weighed exactly 250 pounds, and thirty pounds of that was that watermelon. I am not sure whether Clyde lives to eat or eats to live.

"Now this is enough time devoted to my picking on Clyde's obesity (Clyde, look up the word 'obesity'), but it will serve a purpose. If any of you fellows have any excess poundage, try to get it off before you get up here, because it's going to be a rough fall."

Kansas State, led by All-American guard Ernie Barrett, dominated the conference in 1950-51 while Kansas and Missouri tied for second. But Barrett remembers the difficulty of stopping Lovellette, who averaged 22.8 points and received All-America honors for the first time.

"Clyde was truly an outstanding player," Barrett says. "We had an outstanding ballclub during those years, and we had very good success against Clyde. On occasions, we'd play a 1-3-1 zone and tried to front him and put someone behind him so he couldn't get the ball.

"With that sweeping hook shot, he had just an outstanding touch."

Few defenses stopped Lovellette during his senior season. KU surpassed K-State, won the conference and captured the NCAA title – just as Allen predicted. Seven Jayhawks, including Lovellette, won an Olympic gold medal in the 1952 Games in Helsinki, Finland.

Lovellette, who scored 141 points in four 1952 NCAA Tournament games, made All-America the second straight year. By the end of the year, he had shattered virtually every KU and conference scoring record, and he still is the only player to lead the NCAA in scoring while playing for the national champion.

In Final Four victories against Santa Clara and St. John's, he made a combined 24 field goals and 18 free throws. He finished the year averaging 28.4 points per game, the second-highest one-season mark in college basketball history at the time. He remains third behind Danny Manning and Raef LaFrentz on KU's all-time scoring list with 1,888 points.

But possibly the greatest testament to Lovellette's scoring ability is that during 77 college games, he failed to hit double figures only once. In that game, a loss at Oklahoma during his sophomore year, he scored nine points.

"He just always did a good job, he was very consistent," says John Keller, a junior college transfer who was Lovellette's backup before starting at forward in the second half of 1951-52. "He couldn't run very fast, and he didn't jump at all. But he was so big and strong that he just blocked out his side of the floor wherever he was. Of course, he was a tremendous shooter."

Lovellette compensated for his lack of finesse with toughness.

"When I first went up there, I was playing against Clyde more because I was the substitute center," says Keller, who stands seven inches shorter than Lovellette. "I'd

Despite drawing crowds of defenders, Clyde Lovellette led the Big Seven Conference in scoring during each of his three varsity seasons.

go ahead and scrimmage against him, and if I ever caused him any problems, I'd get an elbow right in the chest."

Lovellette lost control of his intensity in a December 1951 game against Missouri. It occurred during the bygone, preseason conference tournament in Kansas City, Mo. During a rebound battle underneath the basket, Missouri player Winfred Wilfong fell, and Lovellette stepped on his chest. Lovellette immediately was ejected, but if not for Missouri coach Sparky Stalcup soothing pro-Missouri rooters, a riot may have ensued.

Off the court, Lovellette projected a fun-loving, carefree image. He even had a radio show on WREN in Topeka that grew out of a class assignment in a radio speaking class. The Saturday evening show, "Hillbilly Clyde Lovellette," included country music recordings and Lovellette's musings.

"Most people liked Clyde," Keller says. "He was kind of a clown, but most people respected him. He was very outgoing."

Kansas State coach Jack Gardner, though, could never figure out why game officials liked Lovellette so much – or so he thought.

"If the fouls that Lovellette always makes offensively are called Saturday night, we won't have too much to worry about from him," Gardner said before KU's visit to Manhattan in January 1952.

The referees must not have listened: Lovellette scored 31 points and committed just three fouls. But K-State won 81-64, dealing 13-0 Kansas its first loss. KU also lost its next game against Oklahoma A&M, but only lost once after that.

"I don't feel there was ever a moment that if we lost two-three in a row, that we would sit around pointing fingers," Lovellette says. "I never heard that. I think we knew what more kids don't know today: that people have roles to play."

Lovellette's love for playing the game diminished somewhat during a successful 11-year NBA career. He played in three All-Star games and played with NBA championship teams in Minneapolis and Boston. He was inducted into the Basketball Hall of Fame in 1988.

"I think the greatest time I ever had was in high school and college, playing ball for no pay and just the glory of playing for a team," he says. "When I walked away from the pros, I walked away from the pros. I don't watch the pro game anymore, I don't associate with the pros anymore. I don't relish the pros. I relish coming back to Kansas. That's what I cherish the most."

A self-professed "jack of all trades, master of none" after his NBA career ended, Lovellette entered a variety of ventures. Before retiring from full-time work, he even was sheriff of Vigo County, Ind., until finding his niche at White's Institute in Wabash, Ind., a reform school where he still helps as a substitute teacher and basketball coach.

For many years in the late 1960s and 1970s, Lovellette yearned for an assistant coaching position with the Jayhawks. But it never happened.

"I want somebody to tell me why I couldn't have been an assistant coach at Kansas," he says, without the trace of bitterness that once existed. "I played the game, I could recruit, I could speak, I'm presentable. I might not be the prettiest thing, but I'm not the ugliest, either. Why not?"

But Lovellette, who says a turning point in his life came when he embraced Christianity at age 50, refuses to let a perceived slight fade his fond memories of Kansas.

"The tradition is there, and the tradition is that if somebody comes back that played basketball at KU, hey, he is something," Lovellette says. "I feel more at home when I come out here than I do in the town of Terre Haute or even in Wabash. You have to bond with something, and if you don't bond with a town, you're just living in it. I bonded with Terre Haute, but after I came out to Kansas, I never bonded again with Terre Haute.

"But when I come out to Kansas, I bond, even though I've been gone since 1952."

PERSEVERANCE REWARDED

Lanky center took over where Lovellette left off

A beating.

That's what Clyde Lovellette gave his backup, Bertram "B.H." Born, every day in practice for two years.

"Clyde didn't want any competition for his job," says Charlie Hoag, a guard on University of Kansas basketball teams of the early 1950s. "Many times I remember (trainer) Deaner Nesmith going out with the smelling salts and breaking it over B.H.'s nose. He would get up, and that was it for the day.

"He certainly was intimidated by Clyde. During his first two years, I don't think he could even make a layup in practice."

John Keller, also a veteran of Lovellette's vicious elbows, remembers how the All-American targeted Born.

"He beat up on B.H. pretty bad, really he did," Keller says in a sympathetic tone for his one-time road roommate. "That was one thing – I always felt like maybe Phog (Coach F.C. "Phog" Allen) should have said something."

He did. Dick Harp, KU's assistant coach, recalls Allen throwing Lovellette out of practice one day.

"That night, when I got home, Clyde was on my doorstep," Harp says. "He said, 'What am I going to do?' I said, 'You're going to apologize.' I told him no more with B.H. So he did that. But Doc was legitimately mad with how Clyde treated B.H."

But nobody remembers better than Born, then a naive, quiet kid from south-central Kansas.

"He was pretty tough on me," Born says. "He outweighed me by 65-70 pounds."

Lovellette didn't limit his abuse of Born to the court. Putting gum in Born's shoes and dousing his clothes with cold water in the middle of winter were just a few other ways Lovellette let Born know who controlled the center position at Kansas.

"I get along with Clyde fine now," Born says, acknowledging the punishment almost made him transfer to another school. "But he was a real pain."

A sheepish Lovellette pleads guilty to bruising, badgering and bedeviling Born. He recalls yet another time Allen kicked him out of practice. Afterward, Allen told him punishing Born in practice was okay, as long as he didn't do it "maliciously."

B.H. BORN
Basketball,
1951-54

"I said, 'Could you define maliciously?' " Lovellette says. "From that time on, every time I got a chance to hit him, I hit him ... There are a lot of things that probably went on in those practices that I'm not aware that I did. I just knew I was a hard-nosed ballplayer.

"Yes, I punished Born as much as I could punish him. But B.H. wouldn't quit ... B.H. stuck it out and stuck it out, and whether I had a big part of him becoming the ballplayer that he was, I don't know. But I'd like to think that if I could give him that much punishment, and he survived and didn't quit, that that made him a better ballplayer."

An All-American is the "ballplayer" B.H. Born was. The year after Lovellette, a senior, led KU to the NCAA championship in 1952, Born led KU right back to the brink of another national title.

"I'll tell you what ... B.H. surprised me," Hoag says. "He turned into one of the best defensive players in the nation and was a good offensive player, too."

Harp thinks Lovellette's punishment quickened Born's progress.

"B.H. probably learned more that way because he had to defend himself," he says. "B.H. was 195 (pounds), maybe less. But he was much quicker than we realized. He was quick across the lane. He looked awful with the ball, but he got the ball. His early part of the year when he was a junior, he just didn't 'look' like a player. But when you watched him play, he had a good sense of the game."

Good enough by the end of his junior year to break the Big Seven Conference record for points in a league game. In the game against Colorado at Lawrence, Born hit 16 of 26 shots from the floor and scored 44 points, tying Lovellette's school record.

A left-hander, Born broke his right thumb with four minutes left in the game. The injury, he says, caused him more problems after the game when, "about 150-200 people shook my hand."

It's somewhat silly that Lovellette, an All-American, thought Born could move ahead of him as Kansas' starting center. However, Born arrived at Kansas with a salty résumé.

The 6-foot-9-inch recruit from Medicine Lodge probably had received more widespread attention than any prep star in the state's history to that point. He was one of only 20 high school players invited to an all-star game in Murray, Ky., in 1950, and more than 100 colleges contacted him.

Born, whose father died before he was born and who was raised by his mother and various uncles and aunts, got his chance as KU's starting center in 1952-53. He struggled early; Allen told reporters he hoped the player Lovellette harassed for two years could average 12 points a game.

But by the end of the season, Born led KU on both halves of the court. He lacked Lovellette's brute strength but made up for it with quicker moves. He led the conference with 22.5 points per game in league contests and averaged 18.9 points in all games.

Few thought the underdog Jayhawks were poised for another run at an NCAA championship. But Born's unexpected development provided the spark for an otherwise undersized Kansas team.

Other than Born, forward Harold Patterson was the tallest starter at 6-1. But Patterson, guard Gil Reich and the Kelley brothers, Allen and Dean, all averaged between eight and 13 points per game, giving Kansas a balanced attack.

The Jayhawks advanced to the Final Four by defeating Oklahoma City and Oklahoma A&M at the Midwest Regional in Manhattan's Ahearn Field House. Buoyed by an emotional speech by Allen, Kansas then destroyed Washington 79-53. The Jayhawks were a game away from another NCAA title.

But 22-3 Indiana, with center Don Schlundt's 25.4 points per game, stood in the way. Making matters worse, Born had a cold and an inner ear infection that affected his equilibrium.

I would have been a decent ballplayer without playing behind Clyde, but I think he toughened me up."

– B.H. Born

At halftime, the score was tied at 41. When KU went to its locker room, Allen was more concerned with Born's condition than addressing the team.

"We used to have all kinds of people in the locker room at halftime," Born says, recalling KU Chancellor Franklin Murphy's presence at halftime of the 1953 final. Murphy shook his head as Allen spent most of the halftime reviewing proper gargling techniques with Born, hoping that would temporarily alleviate his cold symptoms.

Born wasn't too pleased, but maybe it worked. He scored 26 points before fouling out with 5:36 left. After that, the Jayhawks stayed close, but Schlundt's 30 points allowed Indiana to escape with a 69-68 victory.

Voting for the Most Valuable Player award of the Final Four, however, occurred before Born fouled out. As a result, he was the first player from a losing team named Final Four MVP.

Kansas repeated its 10-2 conference record in 1953-54, Born's senior season, but tied with Colorado for the conference title. In a time when only one team could represent a conference, a tie meant drawing straws for an NCAA tourney berth. The Golden Buffaloes drew the longer of the two, and KU's season ended.

Born averaged 18.9 points per game for the second straight season and finished his career with a 7.1-per-game rebounding average. He didn't repeat as an All-American but made all-conference again. In in his three varsity seasons, Kansas, in the middle of a 33-game home court winning streak, never lost at Hoch Auditorium.

Born and both Kelley brothers joined the Caterpillar Tractor Co. in Peoria, Ill. They played amateur basketball for the Peoria Caterpillars through the 1950s. In 1958, Born played on the first team of any kind to visit the Soviet Union.

He retired as an executive with Caterpillar in April 1997. As Born looks back on his basketball career, one moment stands out more than any other – and it happened long after he quit playing.

"The biggest accomplishments were all the friends I made," he says. "But one of the high-lights was getting my jersey retired, with 17,000 people cheering and me standing out in the middle of the (Allen Field House) floor."

Many of those fans undoubtedly had no idea what Born endured to achieve that honor.

"I would have been a decent ballplayer without playing behind Clyde," he says, "but I think he toughened me up."

B.H. Born was one of the most highly recruited high school basketball players the Sunflower State ever produced, but he barely played his first varsity season at KU.

MORE THAN BASKETBALL

Icon's impact on Kansas, all of athletics, transcends one sport

Forrest Clare Allen's contributions to basketball at the University of Kansas – indeed, to basketball in general – speak for themselves.

They called him "Phog," after the tone of voice, similar to a foghorn, he used while working as a baseball umpire in the early 1900s. But his players and good friends called him "Doc," a label he earned as a doctor of osteopathic medicine.

Some also have called him the father of basketball coaching. Whatever he's called, testaments abound to his impact on the game James Naismith invented in 1891:

- His prodding made basketball an Olympic sport for the first time at the 1936 Games in Berlin. A proud Allen was buried in his U.S.A. sweatsuit.
- He developed and promoted the idea of an NCAA Tournament. The first tournament lost money, but that didn't deter him. Eventually, it turned into one of the nation's biggest sporting events.
- He turned Kansas into one of the nation's elite college basketball programs. Two of his disciples, Adolph Rupp at Kentucky and Dean Smith at North Carolina, turned programs they ran into dynasties, as well.
- In 39 years as KU's coach, in 1907-09 and 1919-56, Allen won 590 games and lost 219, a .729 winning percentage. Combined with seven years as coach of Warrensburg (Mo.) Normal (now called Central Missouri State) and brief stints at Haskell and Baker, Allen won 746 games and lost 264. Through 1997-98, only five coaches in the history of Division I college basketball – Smith, Rupp, Jim Phelan, Henry Iba and Ed Diddle – had won more.
- At KU, Allen's teams won or shared 24 Missouri Valley, Big Six or Big Seven Conference championships and finished second four other times.
- His teams had a 10-4 record in the NCAA Tourney he helped create. He guided the Jayhawks to the NCAA title in 1952, and KU lost in the NCAA final in 1940 and 1953. In addition, the Helms Foundation retroactively named KU's teams of 1921-22 and 1922-23 as national champions.

Of course, KU's Allen Field House bears the name of the man who played just one season of college basketball, 1905-06. But basketball accounts for only part of Allen's overall contributions to the University of Kansas and the sporting world.

When did Allen find time to sleep? He returned to KU from Warrensburg Normal in 1919 not as a coach, but as its athletics director. He relinquished that job in late 1936. But he had taken over as KU's basketball coach shortly after arriving from Warrensburg. He stayed on the bench until state law forced him to retire after the 1955-56 season.

In 1920, Allen was in his only year as KU's football coach when the Jayhawks, down 20-0 at halftime, rallied to tie powerful Nebraska 20-20. The rally served as the impetus Allen needed in his drive to build a football stadium to replace McCook Field. Memorial Stadium, built on the site where McCook previously

DR. F. C. "PHOG" ALLEN
"The Father of Basketball Coaching"

DR. F.C. ALLEN

FORREST C. "PHOG" ALLEN
Basketball and baseball,
1905-06
Head football coach,
1920
Athletics director,
1919-36
Head basketball coach,
1907-09, 1919-56

stood, opened in 1921.

Another Kansas tradition, the Kansas Relays, in large part owes its life to Allen. Unequaled in the Midwest as a promoter of college athletics, Allen insured the first Relays in 1923 with Lloyds of London. If only a tenth of an inch of rain fell during the Saturday morning of the meet, KU would get $5,000. Five years later, the famous insurance company, tired of sending checks to KU each year, refused to insure the event.

Perhaps Allen's greatest Relays stunt, though, occurred when he negotiated to bring five Tarahumara Indians from Mexico's Sierra Madre mountains to the 1927 Relays. Three Tarahumaran men ran 51.2 miles from Kansas City to Memorial Stadium, and two of the tribe's women ran 30.6 miles from Topeka to Memorial Stadium.

Their jogs gained international attention – just what Allen wanted for the young Relays. Two years later, he staged the first Relays parade. In 1930, he promoted a rodeo in Memorial Stadium as a Relays draw. According to the April 1990 edition of *Kansas Alumni*, the rodeo occurred the Friday night before the final day of Relays competition.

Allen proved ahead of his time treating injuries. One of the first to advocate team physicians, he once said, "I won more games on the treating table than I ever won on the athletic field."

He developed a liniment called Salbenthol, later called "Phog's Liniment." The product gained widespread popularity before trainers phased out liniments as injury treatments. His ability to heal muscle aches through lengthy rubdowns attracted several professional athletes to Lawrence, including Hall-of-Fame pitcher Grover Cleveland Alexander.

Born Nov. 18, 1885, in Jamesport, Mo., and raised in Independence, Mo., Allen also wrote off-season newsletters to his players. And during World War II, he corresponded with KU athletes through a newsletter called *Jayhawk Rebounds*.

Allen warned of gambling's potential influence on college athletics years before betting scandals rocked college basketball. But he defended college athletics on nearly every front, despite a running feud with the Amateur Athletics Union. In a series of letters he exchanged with Pulitzer Prize-winning newspaper editor William Allen White of the *Emporia Gazette*, he cordially responded to White's notion that universities placed too much emphasis on athletics:

"...I notice that you have been uneasy and unhappy about the overstressing of athletics in the University. I do not believe that athletics are overstressed at the University of Kansas. In fact, the outcry over the state is more to the effect that we inhibit athletics here more than we should. I assure you that I believe firmly in sane athletics. I love the University of Kansas, I assure you I would not want to cripple its good name in any way.

"... Many academicians feel that we cannot have a school where people can meditate and study, and at the same time have athletics of a competitive and spectacular nature. I believe we can ... I wanted you to feel that we are still trying to play the game squarely here at Kansas. We will not overemphasize athletics to the detriment of academic responsibility."

– Phog Allen, in a letter to William Allen White, Feb. 19, 1927.

REMEMBERING PHOG

Here's how some players, coaches and longtime observers have remembered the most renowned basketball coach of his time:

"...The season was 1913 or '14; KU had played games at Missouri and Washington; on the return trip we stopped for a game at Warrensburg. We had taken only eight players on the trip and Red Brown was declared ineligible (scholastically) while on the trip; Art Weaver had sprained an ankle in St. Louis and could not play in Warrensburg; that left us with six 'for duty.'

"Stuffy Dunmire fouled out with four personals and that brought us down to the five left on the floor. With several minutes left to play, Charles Greenlees got his fourth personal foul and we would have had to go on with only four men – except that Phog Allen stepped in and said, 'No, we're not playing any four-man team; Greenlees stays in the game!' We won the game, but one Phog Allen won the admiration of a lot of people that very evening ...

"Again, I say what a man."

> – Ralph "Lefty" Sproull,
> All-American Kansas forward,
> 1912-15

"He was dramatic. He would get you down on the floor, all holding hands, and get a big cheer going ... I think that was his biggest attribute: psychology.

"I had one memorable night. I think we were playing Nebraska. They clamped down on (All-American forward) Ray Ebling. He could not get a shot off. I was the point guard. I was the playmaker ... I didn't really shoot that much, and without Phog telling me to, I started shooting long.

"The old man always had that quart bottle of water over there. The first long shot I took, I nearly tore the net off the basket. The old man – I can see him yet, picking up that quart bottle of water, shaking his head. So I don't know how close I came to getting my butt sat down on the bench. But he didn't sit me down, and so we come down again, and our guys couldn't seem to jerk loose. You know I hit six straight from way out. After about the third or fourth shot, they started loosening up on Ebling.

"I was a senior. If I'd have been anything else, he'd have put my butt on that bench real quick."

> – Gordon Gray,
> Kansas guard, 1932-35

"... His fundamentals were very good. He prepared us very well. We made almost no mistakes. I don't remember ever being connected with any team or seeing any team that made as few ballhandling errors. And that was a very big factor in his success ... He made you completely believe in yourself. We weren't supposed to lose. That was it. He just drummed that into us. We never even considered that we would lose a game. I think that was probably one of his most important strengths. That, his fundamentals and his ability to teach us not to make mistakes."

"... I started the Kansas State game (in 1930), which was a big game for us, and I had never started a game before ... K-State had a wonderful athlete named Elden Auker, who became a pitcher for the Detroit Tigers. Under the basket at old Hoch (Auditorium), it had pieces of iron that held the goal up. When I took off after a layup, he took after me and hit me and knocked me against this iron thing that held up the goal. This hand – I still have a scar – it popped open like a frankfurter. But I was able to finish the game.

"But the thing got all swollen up, and we had to play Missouri four days later, and Doc was counting on me. He came down to my house after that game at 10 o'clock, heated up a pan of hot water in my kitchen and sat with me from 10 o'clock to one o'clock in the morning bathing this hand. Now imagine Bobby Knight or any of the famous coaches doing that?

"Every night after practice, he would stay there until 7 o'clock, and each one of his five guys (starters) got rubdowns. Not from the trainer. Doc gave us each a rubdown. Now imagine a coach doing that today? It made you feel great, and you were grateful to him. Stuff like that made you love the man, and you would want to win for him. I have nothing but the greatest esteem for him."

> – Ted O'Leary,
> All-American Kansas forward,
> 1929-32

"...The boys who have played under you do not only thank you for coaching them, but for the many lessons of life which they have learned.

"The things that you have done for the University are so many that they need not be mentioned, but they will be remembered long after you have retired from our school..."

> – Ralph Miller,
> Kansas forward, 1938-42 and future
> Hall-of-Fame coach in a 1942 letter celebrating
> Allen's 25th year in coaching

"I consider the value of my association with you at KU in '36, '37 and '38 priceless. University life and even basketball would have definitely lacked something vital without your friendship and more especially, your teaching.

"I have always felt that you have given all your boys much more than prowess in a game. We were taught to fight and win in life."

> – Sylvester C. Schmidt,
> Kansas forward, 1935-38, in a 1942 letter

"He always sought out and got an alumni luncheon for noontime the day of a (road) game. KU people would come to the luncheon, and he would speak. That actually cemented the fact that we were going to play basketball as well as we knew how. But he could motivate emotionally in a lot of ways.

"Doc was a great person to be around. You had a good time anytime (you were) with him."

> – Dick Harp, Kansas forward, 1937-40;
> Kansas basketball coach, 1956-64

"Doc had a routine on game day. You'd always go down to the Eldridge Hotel, take a nap, when you'd wake up, you'd always take a walk around the block. Then we would go to the Hawk (Jayhawk Cafe) and have celery and honey and toast. In those days, you weren't supposed to drink a lot of water, you'd just have this light little protein drink.

"On game days, Phog didn't want you to be on your feet any more than you needed to be. Today, they talk about these shoot-arounds before a game – that would have been unheard of then."

> – Howard Engleman,
> All-American Kansas forward, 1938-41

"He didn't mind it a bit having basketball players play football. Phog had the philosophy that nobody could come down the middle (of the lane) and score. They could come down the middle if they didn't score. But if they scored, you wouldn't play. He had a little bit of (current Missouri coach) Norm Stewart in him. Phog meant for your fouls to be worth time. But if you hurt somebody, he'd run you out of town; you better do it right.

"I met Phog Allen, that was the world. He was a mentor. He backed up his players. Phog was like Roy Williams. He loved his players, he was honest with his players. He taught values. We had a sign up that said, 'What you give you keep, what you don't give you lose forever.'

"... Phog could recruit. He could sell. He would have been great with a bottle of tonic someplace. He would have been a worldbeater with a tonic wagon.

"Phog was a great man. He was an unusual person."

> – Otto Schnellbacher,
> Kansas forward, 1942-43, 1945-48

"Dr. Allen could get the best out of his talent of anybody I've ever seen ... (Allen and George Sauer, Kansas' football coach in 1946-47) both wanted to win in the worst way. And both were great coaches. They were knowledgeable, they knew what they were doing, and both were great influences on the players."

> – Ray Evans,
> All-American Kansas guard,
> 1941-43, 1945-47

"We have been sitting here, on press row, in Kansas University's basketball arena for the past half-hour watching 62-year-old Forrest C. Allen prep his basketball team for its soon-to-start game against the Buffaloes from Colorado University. What a man! First, "Phog" Allen doesn't look 45. Nor does he dress it – an eye-shattering green suit, dotted with red; plaid socks, yellow predominating, and a tie you hear rather than see. And down underneath more pep, more fire, more enthusiasm for the coming hour than will be engineered during the heat of battle by all spectators in the stands.

"Everybody who reads the sports pages knows of "Phog" Allen. It would be impossible to be unaware of him. For it is doubtful if there is a man today in the world of sports who has been so cussed and discussed; who is loved more, hated more; who is damned and who is praised more that this doctor of osteopathy who, over the past 38 years, has made his home a synonym for the game he loves above all – basketball."

> – Jack Carberry, sportswriter,
> The Denver Post, in a 1947 column

"Doc was sort of getting to the end of his coaching career. The game was beginning to pass him by a little bit. But Phog was a great coach. He was a strong man with great beliefs. He stood by his convictions. Phog deserves every accolade he ever got."

> – Charlie Hoag, Kansas guard, 1950-53

"Phog and (Kansas State coach) Jack Gardner were enemies. In my opinion, it's too bad we don't see more of that today. It became very heated from time to time. I just think it made for a good rivalry. They badgered each other an awful lot. They pointed fingers at each other and really got after it.

"I probably was the only K-Stater who attended Phog Allen's funeral. I had a lot of admiration for him. I found him to be a genuine person."

> – Ernie Barrett, All-American guard at
> Kansas State, 1950-51

"Phog was getting older and probably had calmed down a little. Dick (assistant coach Dick Harp) was very intense. Both of them were pretty tuned in to what was going on.

"I always thought it was funny: I was sitting on the bench one time, and Doc turned around and said for somebody to get in the game. It was a name I never recognized. I said, 'Dick, who did he say?' and he said, 'Oh, he graduated about 15 years ago.' I thought, 'How strange,' but then I got into coaching, and I could see how that could happen.

"We won the (1952) Midwest Regional in Kansas City. We heard that Jack Gardner was going to be on the plane flying out to Seattle (site of the Final Four), and everybody thought, 'uh-oh.' They got on the plane, and Doc and Jack sat side-by-side all the way out there.

"...We jumped rope for 15 minutes before practice. We took jump ropes on trips with us. Then we'd run a few setups, run offensive patterns. We worked on fundamentals all season long. Doc was a great believer in fundamentals – pivoting, passing, dribbling, and we worked on defense. Our practices usually would run about three hours, from the time you got on the floor to the time you left the gym ...

"Phog was a great motivator. When I wasn't starting, Phog would always sit the starters on the bench in the locker room before the game and he would talk to them. And I never thought much about it, I thought, 'Well, here's this great coach, and he's not very motivating.' Finally, when I got to start and I sat on that bench, he had some way of getting to you, individually. He would talk not directly to you but had some way to motivate you, you would be ready to go out and fight bears with a switch, so to speak.

"I owe him a lot. He was always fair and straightforward. I think the guys would have fought until the end for him, simply because he was that type of individual. That's probably the one regret, and I'm speaking for most of the guys that played, was the fact that we didn't beat Peoria (in the 1952 playoffs to determine the U.S. Olympic team). That would have made him Olympic coach instead of assistant coach. I think that was the one thing that everyone was very sorrowful about, and we should have been."

– John Keller, Kansas center, 1950-52

"The defense would be the main thing I took from him. The pressure defense. In the middle of the season in 1952, we changed the defense. People taught in those days to stay between your man and the basket. We were the first to go out and get in the passing lanes."

– Dean Smith, Kansas guard, 1950-53 and former North Carolina head coach

"... He is a great individual and did so much for the game of basketball."

– Henry Iba, legendary basketball coach at Oklahoma A&M (later Oklahoma State)

"The hours of practice – it was grueling, just grueling. At 66-67 years old, (Phog) could do push-ups on his fingertips. Seventeen-18-20 years old, we had to do it. A lot of guys couldn't.

"... Phog was a great psychologist. He could get you up for the game when you felt that you couldn't get up for the game ... He didn't particularly care about the Xs and Os, he was more interested in the team concept – that if five guys were playing together, they would win.

"Because of what the man had done prior to us and the success he had, it was like 'Hey, you want me to jump through the hoop? I'll do it. You want me to run through the wall? I'll do it. Whatever you want me to do, Phog.' That was the way I felt. And I'm sure everybody felt that way on that ballclub."

"I've heard many times that (assistant coach) Dick Harp was the brains of that team. But Dick Harp couldn't get me up for a ballgame like Phog could. Dick was a strategist, but it had to come from Phog."

– Clyde Lovellette, All-American, NCAA scoring champion and Kansas center, 1949-52

"Tonight marks several milestones in the life of the University of Kansas ... The name itself is meaningful. It honors a man not so much for his winning record as a basketball coach as for his development of sound men. His many former players here tonight attest how well he has taught, through sports, the good life."

– Chancellor Franklin Murphy, March 1, 1955, marking the first game in Allen Field House

"His activities were so wide-ranging that his file in the Star library fills nine envelopes, the greatest number for any sports figure ... A man as strong-minded and as outspoken as Allen was certain to have enemies. His eastern critics sometimes called him the Big Wind of the West and the Kansas Hayshaker, but in verbal exchanges Doc, as his players called him, gave much more than he got.

"... Allen had an inventive mind, and he was willing to take risks and try new things while men with less vision hung back and carped at him."

– Joe McGuff, sports editor, *Kansas City Star*, Sept. 17, 1974, a day after Allen died at age 88

"He harbored in his heart a burning loyalty to the University of Kansas and Lawrence. He was not ready to quit coaching when the mandatory retirement age of 70 cut him down to what he called 'statutory senility.'

"During his coaching hey-day, many of his countless friends urged him to seek the Kansas governorship. But regardless of his obvious popularity, he declined. He said he was so outspoken he wouldn't last a week ...

"His successes and achievements were many, but among all of them, he probably would be preferred to be remembered as having played a part in the development of hundreds upon hundreds of young men."

– Editorial in *Topeka Daily Capital*
Sept. 19, 1974

"Mere words do not have the capacity to rear a fitting memorial to the life and influence of a person so versatile and exceptional as Dr. Forrest C. Allen. His deeds already have spoken his eulogy...

"Phog Allen is more than just a legend in the world of sports. He dispersed his talents and boundless energy into many different channels. As with a fine diamond of many facets, no aspect of his life could be dull – each had to sparkle."

– Paul Endacott,
  All-American Kansas guard, 1920-23,
  at Allen's funeral

THE JAYHAWKER

DR. FORREST C. (PHOG) ALLEN
Manager of Athletics

Dr. F. C. Allen came to the University of Kansas from Warrensburg, Missouri, where he coached the Normals and made an enviable record as a basket ball strategist. He was appointed athletic manager here to succeed W. O. Hamilton, and has done big things at K. U. this year.

Athletics   *Page 46*

1920

"Keep the rules. Keep faith with your comrades. Keep your temper. Keep yourself fit. Keep a stout heart in defeat. Keep your pride under in victory. Keep a sound soul, a clean mind and a healthy body."

– F.C. "Phog" Allen's,
  "Code of a Sportsman"

The 1920 *Jayhawker* Yearbook shows F.C. "Phog" Allen in his mid-30s, just after he returned to Kansas as athletics director.

NEAR GIVEAWAY

Generosity almost cost javelin champion

Because of a kind deed, Les Bitner almost gave away an NCAA title.

The near-disaster for the University of Kansas javelin competitor happened at the 1955 NCAA Outdoor Track and Field Championships in Los Angeles. Bitner, one of the leading contenders in the event, loaned his spear to Al Cantello of LaSalle. Cantello barely had qualified for the finals with a weak 216-foot throw the day before.

But armed with Bitner's javelin, Cantello unleashed a throw of 245 feet, 3 inches on his first attempt. Bitner saved himself by throwing 246-1 on his first try. That distance withstood the other competitors and Bitner became a NCAA champion. Kansas finished fourth in the meet, its best team finish to that point in the program's history.

Bitner also set a collegiate and NCAA record with his throw. He and Cantello were the first collegians to throw the javelin 240 feet.

Had Bitner been defeated by his own generosity, it would have been a case of "turnabout is fair play." Two months earlier at the Arkansas Relays, Bitner borrowed a new-styled Held model from Dick Ganslen, a former pole vault champion from Columbia University. Ganslen worked in the physiology department at the University of Arkansas and had been researching the Held model.

**LES BITNER
Track and field,
1955-56**

The javelin was named for its inventor, Bud Held, a former Stanford thrower who set the world record at the time with a throw of 263-10. Held's javelin sported a fatter shaft that still met weight and length specifications.

Kansas track and field coach Bill Easton ordered Bitner and two teammates to use their own javelins in the first two rounds of the Arkansas Relays and then try the Held model the rest of the day. Less than thrilled, the Jayhawks followed Easton's command. Bitner, in a full sweatsuit, threw the Held model 215 feet on his first attempt, which convinced the team of the spear's merits.

Bitner was just getting started. He also let fly throws of 223 feet, 230 feet and 236 feet before the meet ended. The 236-foot toss ranked as the best in the nation that season, less than two feet off the college record, which he broke in Los Angeles.

"None of us wanted to use that Held model at first," Bitner said afterward. "It's a psychological matter, I guess. That javelin is bigger, and you wonder about trying to throw it. But you can get a better grip with it, you get no vibration at the release and it seems to take the trajectory better."

Regardless of javelin preference, Bitner was fortunate to compete collegiately. As a senior at Wyandotte High School in Kansas City, Kan., he tried out for the school's track team only after his brother, former KU distance runner Norm Bitner, insisted that he do so. Les

barely could clear five feet as a high jumper, so he turned his attention to the javelin.

The younger Bitner fared little better in the new event. He threw the javelin only 125 feet in his first competition. He improved to 160 feet by the end of the season, but he didn't qualify for the state meet and almost didn't earn a letter in track.

Still, Bitner earned a spot on the Kansas City (Kan.) Junior College track and field team. He improved as a thrower and won the state title with a 180-foot toss. His best throw in junior college measured 189 feet.

But before he enrolled in a four-year school, Bitner served in the U.S. Air Force for three-and-a-half years, including a stint in the Korean War. While in the service, Bitner continued throwing the javelin and won the 1952 Missouri Valley Amateur Athletic Union competition with a 195-foot throw. His distance increased the next year, but a 201-foot mark placed only second in the same competition.

Former Kansas sports information director Don Pierce described the red-headed Bitner as "no giant of obvious power. But he's not slight either. He carries 180 pounds of freckled sinew on a 6-foot frame."

Despite that description, Bitner's teammates respected his abilities.

"He was a great javelin thrower," says distance runner Al Frame. "He produced at the right time. He was a great competitor and always kept in great shape."

Bitner downplayed his Arkansas Relays showing. He said, "I just want to prove to myself that the good throw was no accident."

But Easton knew a potential champion when he saw one.

"He is a keen student of the event," the coach said at the time. "He pays enough attention to detail to continue to get better."

Which Bitner did, of course, even though his thoughtfulness almost cost him a championship.

JOHN TROMBOLD

SURVIVING AND THRIVING
Baseball player overcame disease then fought ones like it

"Memories of college are most enjoyable. I enjoyed baseball at KU so much..."

— John Trombold

The old baseball field at the University of Kansas sat just south and east of Memorial Stadium. With a short right field fence that separated the diamond from Mississippi Street only 290 feet away from home plate, the park was a dream for most good, left-handed hitters.

John Trombold was a good, left-handed hitter, good enough to be KU's first All-American. But Floyd Temple, who began a 28-year career as KU's coach in Trombold's senior season of 1954, says the slick-fielding first baseman never fully took advantage of the park's friendliness toward left-handed pull hitters.

"John Trombold was just a smooth, smooth hitter, a great young man," Temple says. "But he couldn't pull a baseball. His brother Jim came along a year or so later, and he couldn't pull the ball, either. Their power was to left-center, which was toward the tennis courts. He (John) got some home runs, but had he been able to pull the ball, he probably would have hit cars and houses up there on Mississippi Street, because it wasn't very far."

Temple was fortunate Trombold was still around to hit a ball anywhere when he paced the Jayhawks' attack from 1952 to 1954.

Trombold attended Wichita East High School, where he played baseball well enough to earn a tryout with the Brooklyn Dodgers after he graduated in the spring of 1950. In a sort of surrealistic dream, Trombold traveled to St. Louis for the tryout, where famous Dodgers' first baseman Gil Hodges let him take infield practice in his place.

So there was John Trombold, a teenager fresh out of high school, taking grounders alongside legendary Dodger greats Jackie Robinson and Pee Wee Reese. But walking up the steps of the stadium that day, Trombold remembers feeling "funny."

It wasn't a good feeling. But it continued occasionally, worsening after he went to KU in the fall. Finally, doctors found he had a rare blood disease called aplastic anemia.

Trombold almost died that autumn. He endured 28 blood transfusions and an operation to remove his spleen. He still takes cortisone every other day to help cope with the condition. But he says he considers himself "lucky," especially after surviving his freshman ordeal almost 50 years ago.

"I guess I was meant to go on," he says.

Go on he did, turning into one of the best first baseman Kansas has had. Less than two years after the blood disease nearly killed him, the Chicago White Sox drafted Trombold.

He stayed at KU, though, not a surprising decision considering his background. His father, George, played first base and third base at KU in the early 1930s.

"I came from a baseball family," he says. "I never heard about any other school but KU from my dad, that's for sure."

Trombold fondly remembers growing up in a time when "everything was so positive."

"It was a really a big deal to go to Lawrence," he says of boyhood trips to KU's campus. "We were still pretty provincial then. I remember going on the train to Lawrence to watch the Orange Bowl (football) team play in 1947. What a thrill!"

During his senior season, Trombold led the Jayhawks to their best winning percentage, .667, since 1923. But the team only played 15 games, winning 10.

Trombold, who says he can't comprehend how today's college baseball players can play 50-60 games and still go to school, recalls enjoying his glovework around first base as much as spraying balls all over the field as a hitter.

"I always thought of myself as a craftsman at first base," he says. "I always used to challenge people if they got a ball past me, I'd give them five dollars."

After graduating, Trombold played one summer in the minor leagues. But the blood disease spurred him to enter KU's School of Medicine in fall 1954. He now specializes in blood diseases and cancer and is medical director of the Scripps Health cancer center in La Jolla, Calif.

Despite the distance, Trombold maintains close ties to Kansas. He played a key role in turning KU's Quigley Field into Hoglund-Maupin Stadium in the 1980s and has set up an endowment for KU baseball.

In early 1997, Kansas announced it again would renovate Hoglund-Maupin Stadium with a $1 million donation from Forrest Hoglund, Trombold's co-captain in 1954. Trombold and other private donors provided an additional $400,000 for the renovation, which will increase the stadium's capacity from 1,320 to 2,500.

"Memories of college are most enjoyable," Trombold says. "I enjoyed baseball at KU so much that I'm really enthusiastic about giving back to sports at KU, baseball in particular."

JOHN TRUMBOLD
Baseball,
1952-54

SMILIN' DUTCH
Gentle leader fashioned many lasting contributions

Eighty years ago, Arthur C. "Dutch" Lonborg chose the University of Kansas because he wanted to attend the college he regarded as the best in the state of Kansas.

Fortunately for Kansas athletics, the University proved wise enough to return the favor.

For 14 years, from 1950 to 1964, Lonborg presided over KU athletics. During that time, Kansas enjoyed some of its most spectacular sporting achievements: 38 Big Seven or Big Eight Conference championships, four NCAA team championships and three all-sports conference championships.

But Lonborg's success is measured by more than championships. His contributions, which ultimately led to his induction into the Basketball Hall of Fame in 1973, moved both KU athletics and the NCAA Men's Basketball Tournament into the sporting world's modern era.

Quite a résumé for guy who turned down scholarship offers from smaller schools for a chance to walk on KU's football team in 1916.

"...No one ever asked me to come to KU," Lonborg said in a December 1984 interview for KU's Retiree's Club. "I told the coaches in the Kansas Conference that would come to talk to me, 'I want to go to KU, it's the best school in the state of Kansas, and that's where I want to go. No reason asking me to go someplace else.' So I walked on."

He and about 130 other prospective football players tried out that fall. But given the chance, Lonborg, who grew up about 65 miles north of Lawrence in Horton, made his presence known.

By the time he graduated with a law degree in 1921, Lonborg had attained all-Missouri Valley Conference honors three times in football, made all-conference twice in basketball and started for three years at third base for KU's baseball team.

In addition, he earned All-America honors in basketball in 1918-19 (despite KU's 7-9 record that season). Later, in 1921, he was an Amateur Athletic Union All-American while helping the Kansas City Athletic Club win the AAU national tournament, the top U.S. amateur tournament at the time. In 1917, the *Chicago Tribune* selected him as an end on its All-Western football squad, and Walter Camp chose him as a second-team All-American at quarterback in 1920.

Lonborg's accomplishments still would be etched in KU history had he applied his law degree as an attorney, never making sports headlines again.

But he didn't. In fact, he never practiced law. For 29 years after graduating, he practiced coaching instead.

Four years after playing on an AAU national championship team, Lonborg was the coach of the last college team to capture an AAU title. That team, the 1925 Washburn University squad, won the title two years after Lonborg gave up his first coaching job at McPherson (Kan.) College.

Lonborg's four-year record of 68-19 at Washburn propelled him to a job in Evanston, Ill. There, he guided Northwestern University for 23 seasons, compiling a

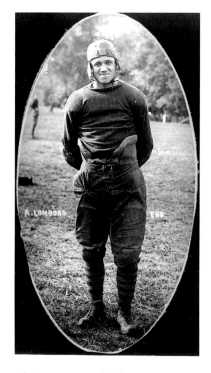

Thirty years before directing Kansas athletics, A.C. "Dutch" Lonborg was a star quarterback for KU's football team.

A.C. LONBORG

237-198 record.

His enthusiasm as a player spilled into his coaching. Once, while sitting on the bench at the end of a close game, Lonborg leaped into the air with his elbows flying after a Northwestern player hit a game-winning shot. In the process, he knocked out two players, one on each side of him. They didn't wake up until most spectators left the gymnasium.

Lonborg also served as an assistant coach for the Wildcats' football team. One of the best players he coached was Otto Graham, an outstanding multisport athlete who led the NFL's Cleveland Browns to six straight league championships as a quarterback from 1950 to 1955.

***

When Lonborg died in 1985 at age 86, KU Chancellor Gene Budig said Lonborg, "never said no to the University of Kansas." That isn't exactly true, however.

Although Lonborg did agree to serve as interim athletics director in 1973 after officially retiring, he initially turned down a chance to return to KU as athletics director in 1937. Instead, the school chose Gwinn Henry.

But 13 years later, Lonborg couldn't refuse KU when the state of Kansas no longer would overlook its mandatory retiring age for E.C. Quigley. On July 1, 1950, Lonborg

A.C. "DUTCH" LONBORG
Football, basketball
and baseball,
1917-20

A.C. "DUTCH" LONBORG

replaced Quigley as KU's fifth full-time athletics director.

By then, Lonborg had been instrumental in developing the NCAA Tournament and had ascended to a position as chairman of the event. He remained chairman until 1960. During that time, the tournament expanded from its original eight teams to 25 teams and overtook the National Invitational Tournament as the most popular college postseason playoff format.

At Kansas, Lonborg quickly gained the admiration of coaches and athletes alike.

"He was a great individual," says Clyde Lovellette, KU's All-American basketball center of the early 1950s. "I enjoyed Dutch Lonborg because he was friendly. Whenever you wanted to see him, his door was always open."

The same went for coaches.

"He was a lovely, lovely man," says Dick Harp, whom Lonborg hired in 1956 to replace the incomparable F.C. "Phog" Allen as basketball coach. "He didn't ever want to hurt anybody. He was just a very nice human being. I'd go in and we'd talk about basketball, and we'd talk about football.

"I guess you could say that if you spent time around Dutch and wanted things done, some of the things you might ask him to do, he might be a little slow on them. But he was good for me. I really liked Dutch. I liked him a lot."

Other than Allen, no KU athletics director served longer than Lonborg (Bob Frederick celebrated his 11th anniversary as athletics director in May 1998). During his term, Lonborg continued a process that Quigley started: moving Kansas into the modern era of college sports.

He supervised the construction of Allen Field House, now one of college basketball's most historic shrines. In addition, he directed the expansion of Memorial Stadium and construction of Quigley Field, forerunner of Hoglund-Maupin Stadium. At the time, Quigley Field was the only completely enclosed baseball diamond in the conference.

Lonborg also directed the construction of the parking lot east of Memorial Stadium, as well as the refurbishing of KU's indoor track in Allen Field House and the outdoor track at Memorial Stadium.

But he made perhaps his most lasting impact by inaugurating scholarship programs for baseball, swimming, tennis and golf. Today, Kansas routinely finishes in the upper half of the Big 12 Conference in a variety of non-revenue producing sports.

Lonborg's accomplishments at Kansas weren't confined to the University. One of his greatest honors occurred in 1960, when he served as manager of the U.S. basketball team at the Olympic Games in Rome.

Kansas law at the time forced Lonborg to retire as athletics director in 1964, but he remained on the Kansas staff as director of events into the 1970s. He was KU's interim athletics director while the school searched for a successor to Wade Stinson in 1973 and served as a consultant to the athletics department into his 80s.

Although his association with Kansas athletics spanned the development of the football facemask, the aluminum baseball bat and varsity eligibility for freshman athletes, one thing never changed about Lonborg's approach to sports, particularly as an administrator at Kansas.

"I tried to stress that we were going to be honest in our program," he said in the 1984 interview. "We were going to try to get the good athletes, and we were going to treat them right. Hopefully, they would come to our school because of our academic situation; because it was a good school.

"This was someplace where a good athlete could get a good education."

Just as Lonborg did.

THE GAME THAT BUILT A STADIUM

He carved his national reputation with numerous contributions to basketball. But one need only glance north from the Campanile towering above the University of Kansas to see another of Dutch Lonborg's legacies.

In 1920, plans already were in motion to replace old McCook Field with a modern football facility. But not until a spirited Kansas effort on a crisp November day did those plans find the spark needed to make them a reality.

With F.C. "Phog" Allen as their coach, the Jayhawks were 5-1 when they faced Nebraska that day. But by halftime, gloomy Kansas fans had watched the Cornhuskers roar to a 20-0 lead.

Lonborg, KU's senior quarterback, then went to work. Early in the third quarter, he hit Frank Mandeville with a 42-yard touchdown pass. KU added the extra point but still trailed by 13 points.

Shortly after the fourth quarter began, Lonborg hooked up with Mandeville again for another touchdown toss. KU added the extra point and trailed by only six.

In a day when quarterbacks called their own plays, Lonborg then stuck to running plays after the Kansas defense stopped the Cornhuskers again. Later, though, John Bunn, another future Basketball Hall of Fame inductee, hit Mandeville with a 10-yard touchdown pass. KU's extra point failed, and the game ended in a 20-20 tie.

KU's tremendous comeback led to a another rally. This one, on the Monday morning after the game, produced $160,000 in pledges from students and faculty to construct a new stadium. Memorial Stadium was built in time for the 1921 season.

KU didn't score that many points against Nebraska for another 24 years. But few quickly forgot "the game that built a stadium."

As for Lonborg, he also threw game-winning touchdown passes against Drake and Kansas State in 1920. In the Drake game, a 7-3 KU victory, he also returned 13 punts. (Games of that era often turned into puntfests; even the 20-20 tie with Nebraska featured a total of 21 punts.)

Originally a walk-on who made All-Missouri Valley Conference twice at end, Lonborg was the league's top choice at quarterback in 1920.

Dutch Lonborg's football heroics helped build KU's Memorial Stadium (background).

AN EYE FOR HOOPS
Former KU player, coach loved studying basketball

> *"Dick is one of the most brilliant basketball minds I have ever known."*
>
> – Dean Smith
>   Kansas guard, 1950-53, and North Carolina head coach, 1961-97

Even as a reserve guard at the University of Kansas in the early 1950s, Dean Smith had his eye on coaching.

The man who later won more games than any coach in college basketball history often instructed the Kansas freshman team how to run the offense of KU's varsity opponents.

"He had some of those kids running it better than the teams we played against," says John Keller, who was a year ahead of Smith and a senior forward on KU's 1951-52 NCAA championship team. "He knew the game inside and out."

Keller recalls how Smith, the legendary head coach at North Carolina from 1961 to 1997, mastered teaching the offense of one particular foe.

"Oklahoma had Bruce Drake as a coach, and they called it the 'Bruce Drake shuffle,'" he says. "They ran double and triple screens at times. It was tough getting around it in practice. It was easier to play Oklahoma than it was our own freshmen."

It's obvious now that Smith was a coaching star waiting to shine. But he admits he started too early when he and fellow senior Dean Kelley approached Kansas assistant coach Dick Harp in fall 1952 with a little advice.

Rail-thin B.H. Born had replaced NCAA scoring leader Clyde Lovellette as KU's center at the beginning of the 1952-53 season. Both Smith and Kelley agreed Kansas had little chance of defending its NCAA title if head coach F.C. "Phog" Allen insisted on playing Born instead of Eldon Nicholson.

"We went to Coach Harp and said, 'B.H. is really struggling, maybe you should take a look at Nicholson,'" Smith says. "He said, 'Shut up, Smith and Kelley, we'll do the coaching.'"

Allen and Harp stood by Born and watched him turn into an All-American and Most Valuable Player of the 1953 NCAA Tournament.

"He was showing loyalty to Phog," Smith says of Harp's reaction to his and Kelley's suggestion, "but he also showed us how little we knew."

Throughout his unspectacular college playing career, Smith watched and learned from Harp. At the same time, Harp kept an eye on Smith.

"If I missed a class, I'd hear from Dick," Smith says. "Dick Harp was everything a great coach should be. He certainly was a role model for me."

So much so that Smith had a standing offer for Harp to go to North Carolina as an assistant years after Harp resigned from KU in 1964. He finally accepted in 1986, when he was 68.

"Dean called, and before he hung up, he said, 'You know, you still have a place down here,'" Harp says. "About six-seven days later, we (Harp and his wife, Martha Sue) sold the house. We were looking for something to do. It was a good experience."

Harp, who now lives in Lawrence, spent four years at North Carolina, where he worked alongside current KU coach Roy Williams. The stint capped a basketball career that started when the standout at Rosedale High School in Kansas City, Kan., fulfilled a boyhood dream by entering Kansas to play for Allen in 1936.

Harp's stifling defense quickly caught Allen's eye. Even as a guard, he defended the opposition's pivot player in almost every game.

His brightest moments as a player occurred during KU's march toward the 1940 NCAA Tournament title game. In the Jayhawks' first game of the tournament, Harp hit a long set shot to break a 42-42 tie with about a minute left in overtime against Oklahoma A&M. KU won 45-43.

KU defeated Rice in its next tournament game, setting up a duel with Southern California in what was not yet called "the Final Four."

Harp, team captain, had the assignment of guarding Southern Cal's best player, Ralph Vaughn, who had appeared on the cover of *Life* magazine weeks earlier. Harp outscored the California celebrity 15-6 as KU squeaked out a 43-42 victory.

The Jayhawks lost 60-42 against Indiana in the final, ending Harp's college career. By then, he already had constructed his coaching future, says Howard Engleman, a former All-American and teammate of Harp's who was as proficient at offense as Harp was at defense.

Engleman, whom one newspaper referred to as "a basketball player who never saw a stop sign" after he hit the game-winning shot against USC, says Harp was a valuable scouting resource in the days before game film.

"In those days, we didn't have much in the way of scouting reports," Engleman says. "He would go up to the library and get the Chicago (news)papers and other papers and scout the teams we were going to be playing."

That sort of initiative caused Allen to hire Harp, then the head coach at William Jewell College in Liberty, Mo., as KU's freshman and assistant varsity coach in 1948. The previous year, the Jayhawks had their first losing campaign in 20 seasons.

Allen and Harp directed the program's resurgence. Harp generally receives credit as the coaching brains behind the strong Kansas teams of the early 1950s, but he readily deflects it. He does, however, admit always loving the game's finer points.

"I was taking notes, I scouted players," he says of his role with Allen. "I shared at least that much. I enjoyed playing basketball, and I enjoyed the strategy of basketball."

Players from the early 1950s differ on how much Harp actually handled day-to-day coaching operations, but all agree he was a vital part of their success. Maybe no one describes it better than Gil Reich, a guard on the 1952-53 squad.

"Phog was the motivator," he says. "Dick Harp was the Xs and Os and game strategist. And both were superb in their roles."

Ironically, Harp's once-in-a-lifetime opportunity also was an unenviable task: replacing Allen as head coach. When he did in 1956, he inherited the most dominating player basketball had ever seen, Wilt Chamberlain. Before Harp ever sat on a sideline as a head coach, the Associated Press ranked Kansas No. 1 in its 1956-57 preseason poll.

"He was under a lot of pressure because of taking over for Phog when there were quite a number of people who were not in his corner," says Bob Billings, a guard on Harp's first three KU teams.

DICK HARP

DICK HARP
Basketball,
1937-40
Assistant basketball coach,
1948-56
Head basketball coach,
1956-64

But Billings says Harp, who also worked as an analyst for radio broadcasts of KU football games, handled it admirably.

"Dick was very intense," he says. "But he cared an awful lot about his players. He was extremely interested in what they did off the court as well as what they did on the court.

"Dick really was like a father to me. I have great respect for him."

Harp guided KU to the NCAA title game in 1957, where the Jayhawks lost to North Carolina 54-53 in triple overtime. Some still criticize him for not winning a national championship in two years with Chamberlain. However, he remains only one of five people to both coach and play in an NCAA championship game.

Harp's joy for coaching waned toward the end of his eight years as KU's head coach. Overall, he enjoyed mixed success. His first team won the Big Seven Conference and went to the NCAA final, and he won another conference title in the Big Eight in 1959-60. In his tenure, KU finished second in the conference twice and third two other times.

But Kansas struggled in his last three years, compiling a conference record of only 16-26. After two straight losing seasons, fan and alumni pressure increased dramatically in 1963-64.

By then, Harp was considering leaving for a position with the Fellowship of Christian Athletes. A 70-46 home loss against Kansas State in February 1964, which dropped KU to 10-12 and 5-6 in the conference, helped him decide.

"After we played so badly against Kansas State, it became apparent that for me personally, it would be better to go do that and let someone else do this," he says of coaching Kansas.

Monte Johnson, who played for Harp and was an assistant athletics director at the time he resigned, says Harp's character outshone that of most in his profession.

"He was a quality person," Johnson says. "In some ways, it wasn't surprising that he left coaching to go into the Fellowship of Christian Athletes because he might have been one of the better people who ever coached. He's a very good teacher."

Which is why Smith welcomed Harp to North Carolina more than 20 years after the latter quit coaching – even though Smith jokingly suggests he merely needed Harp's tidy organizational skills.

"He was always organized with his paperwork," says an admittedly disorganized Smith, who got the idea for his famous daily practice plan from Harp. But more than paperwork, Smith wanted Harp for another reason:

"Dick is one of the most brilliant basketball minds I have ever known."

Dick Harp directed the Jayhawks to 121 wins and 82 losses during his eight seasons as head coach.

A COMPLEX MAN

Multifaceted athlete revolutionized basketball, helped change society

Life forever changed for Wilton Chamberlain during a two-month stretch when he was 14 years old.

One of William and Olivia Chamberlain's three sons and six daughters, Wilt always was a tall boy, especially compared with his father and mother, who stood 5 feet 8 1/2 inches and 5 feet 9 inches tall, respectively.

But during those two months, Wilt sprouted another 4 inches to about 6-feet-10.

Four inches. That's what made a relatively inconspicuous life impossible for a complex man with an I.Q. of 127.

Instead, Wilt Chamberlain turned into a flashpoint for changes in basketball and society. Despite self-avowed pleas to be left alone, he opened his soul in a 1973 autobiography and has written subsequent books, including his latest work, *Who's Running the Asylum?* His infrequent public comments – both willingly and unwillingly – still occasionally stoke controversy 25 years after he finished a career as perhaps the best basketball player in the history of the game.

Through it all, he remains one of the most elusive sports characters of the 20th century.

"You really never knew," says Dick Harp, his former coach at the University of Kansas, "what Wilt was thinking."

B.H. Born remembers exactly what he was thinking the first time he played Chamberlain, who had just concluded his junior year of high school. The two met in a summer league game in the resort town of Middleton in New York's Catskill Mountains.

The year was 1954, and Born had just finished a stellar career as a 6-foot-9 center at Kansas, where he made All-America in 1952-53 and was named Most Valuable Player of the 1953 NCAA Tournament. He was considering whether to accept an offer to play for the NBA's Fort Wayne Pistons.

In the game, Chamberlain, who had grown to about 7 feet tall, scored 25 points while holding Born to 10 points.

"He just chewed me up," Born says. "I got to thinking, if I want to make a living at this, I better choose another way."

After watching Chamberlain jump underneath the basket and split his head open on the rim during another game that summer, Born was convinced he was making the right choice. He never played in the NBA. Instead, he played amateur basketball as an employee with Caterpillar Inc., the famous equipment manufacturer in Peoria, Ill.

Chamberlain averaged 37.7 points a game at Philadelphia's Overbrook High School, which lost only three games in the three years he played there. Twice, he scored 90 points in one game, and once in a scrimmage, his high school team defeated Villanova University, ranked No. 2 in the country at the time.

WILT CHAMBERLAIN
Basketball and
track and field,
1956-58

KU first noticed Chamberlain when sports information director Don Pierce saw a photo of him in a newspaper in 1952. But unlike today's long-term recruiting ventures, Kansas coach Phog Allen didn't start recruiting Chamberlain wholeheartedly until February 1955, toward the end of his senior year in high school.

By then, about 200 schools were begging for Chamberlain's services. At a time when blacks across the nation had begun protesting decades of bigotry, Chamberlain wanted to make a statement for his race in college. But also wanted to attend an institution that already had shown progress in race relations.

That desire automatically precluded many schools in the South, where black students weren't admitted in most public universities until the 1960s.

"The first time I went to Kansas, the Missouri coach (Wilbur "Sparky" Stalcup) met me in the airport – he was kind of cutting in – and asked me if I wanted to be the first Negro to play at his school," Chamberlain told famous sportswriter Jimmy Breslin in a December 1956 article that appeared in the *Saturday Evening Post*. "I told him no. Same as I told Oklahoma A&M. And I crossed off a lot of other schools because they never had gone in for colored athletes."

Kansas, on the other hand, was the first team in the Big Seven Conference to start a black basketball player when Maurice King did it in the 1954-55 season. LaVannes Squires was the first black player on KU's varsity roster in the 1951-52 season.

Allen enlisted the help of three prominent blacks to help recruit Chamberlain: Dowdal Davis, editor of the *Kansas City Call*; concert singer Etta Moten, a 1931 Kansas graduate, and Lloyd Kerford, a successful businessman from Atchison whose son and daughter graduated from Kansas.

Davis thought Chamberlain's presence in Lawrence would further enhance race relations in the area as Jim Crow-era segregation laws steadily were disappearing. In the meantime, the NBA's Philadelphia Warriors drafted Chamberlain, even though at that time the league prohibited teams from using players just out of high school.

Eventually, he narrowed his college choices to Indiana and Kansas. After his second visit to Lawrence for the Kansas Relays in April 1955, the track and field lover chose KU.

As Allen had predicted, KU immediately was bombarded by accusations that it paid Chamberlain to come to Lawrence.

"I feel sorry for Stilt when he enters the NBA four years from now," wrote Leonard Lewin, a columnist for the *New York Daily Mirror*. "He'll have to take a cut in salary."

Critics hurled many more barbs at Kansas, especially members of the Eastern media, who weren't Allen's closest friends in the first place. Easterners simply couldn't grasp why Chamberlain traveled all the way to Kansas to attend college.

It's unlikely any school would have escaped unscathed had it landed Chamberlain. Kansas didn't, either. The NCAA, citing a car Chamberlain drove at Kansas as an "inducement to continue his career at the University," placed the school's basketball program on probation for two years in 1960.

Chamberlain contended he bought the car with a loan that he paid back. However, in October 1985, he told New York newspaper reporters that he received about $4,000 from "two or three godfathers" when he played at Kansas. In addition, he said his teammates each had at least one "godfather."

Harp and KU teammates of Chamberlain's, including Gene Elstun, John Parker and Monte Johnson, who was KU's athletics director at the time of the accusations, denied that they were assigned a so-called "godfather." If Chamberlain received excess cash, it would have been difficult for him to hide it from teammates, Elstun told the *Wichita Eagle-Beacon*. Chamberlain's charge that the payments extended to other athletes especially angered his former teammates.

"Wilt was absolutely unique. He was a 19-year-old kid, but he was a 30-year-old person in terms of his experiences to the rest of us. I think Wilt did an absolutely marvelous job of controlling his emotions and controlling his temper where somebody who didn't have that ability would have been in a lot of confrontations."

– Bob Billings, Chamberlain's closest friend at KU

Wilt Chamberlain dominated college basketball for two years with a revolutionary combination of size and ability.

"He's lying," Elstun said. "It's amazing to me that someone can implicate everybody."

***

Chamberlain arrived at Kansas in the fall of 1955. In his autobiography *Wilt*, he recalls how soon he realized Lawrence was not as far along in accepting blacks as he had thought. (The following excerpt appeared in the *Kansas City Star* in 1973:)

"It took me about a week to realize that the whole area around Lawrence, except for one black section in Kansas City, was infested with segregation. I called on a few of the alums who had recruited me and I told them in no uncertain terms what they could do with Kansas if things didn't get straightened out in a hurry. A couple of them told me, 'Look, Wilt, you just go wherever you want. You sit down in those restaurants and don't leave until they serve you.'

"That's exactly what I did ... and when I got through other blacks would follow me. I single-handedly integrated that whole area."

Chamberlain enjoyed an almost cult-like following on campus. Bob Billings, Chamberlain's teammate and closest friend at Kansas, recalls how the 7-foot-1, 285-pound center handled the attention.

"Wilt was absolutely unique," Billings says. "He was a 19-year-old kid, but he was a 30-year-old person in terms of his experiences to the rest of us. I think Wilt did an absolutely marvelous job of controlling his emotions and controlling his temper where somebody who didn't have that ability would have been in a lot of confrontations."

Johnson also regarded Chamberlain, who was featured in magazine articles in *Life*, *Time*, *Look* and *Newsweek* before he turned 21, as a close friend.

"He was just as normal as could be," Johnson says. "He couldn't lead a normal life. He had very little privacy. Wilt was probably one of the nicest gentleman that I have ever met on a college campus. He had absolutely very little pretense about him. A phenomenal athlete, an unbelievable physical specimen, but just about as down to earth as anybody."

Chamberlain's athletic talents weren't limited to basketball. In high school, he ran a 400-yard dash in 48.8 seconds. At age 15, he ran 800 yards in 1:58.6. In 1958, he tied for first in the high jump at Big Eight Conference indoor track meet with a school-record leap of 6 feet, 6 3/4 inches – one day after playing a Friday night basketball game.

He won the conference outdoor high jump title in 1957 with a jump of 6-5, finished third in the triple jump at the Kansas Relays in 1956 and fourth in the triple jump at the Drake Relays in 1957. Also in 1957, he tied for first in the high jump at the Drake Relays and tied for second in the same event at the Kansas Relays.

Chamberlain's speed and agility might have been secondary to his strength. Larry Miller, a former KU baseball pitcher, once told the *New York News* that the only man on campus that Chamberlain couldn't beat arm wrestling was Bill Nieder, KU's Olympic shot-putter who later set world records.

"They'd wrestle to a draw," Miller said.

Nieder is involved in another tale detailing Chamberlain's strength. Shortly after arriving at Kansas, Chamberlain and several other athletes were out one night when he said he probably could throw the shot put 60 feet. Small bets were wagered, and all headed to KU's throwing pit at Memorial Stadium. Chamberlain picked up the shot put and threw it with both hands backward over his shoulder.

Without an official measurement, the throw was said to have measured slightly more than 60 feet. (Chamberlain finished third in the shot put in the conference's freshman indoor and outdoor meets with tosses of 47-2 and 47-5 1/2, respectively.)

After his NBA career ended, Chamberlain started a women's track club in California, where he also seriously considered trying out for the U.S. Olympic volleyball team, even as he approached age 50.

Although Chamberlain enjoyed other sports, basketball was the game he revolutionized. Because of him, offensive goaltending rules went into effect. Opposing schools put nets up to stop inbounds passes from going over the backboard into Chamberlain's waiting hands; later rules prohibited such plays.

Chamberlain also is the main reason the lane was widened, and players no longer can take a running start when shooting free throws. A notoriously poor free throw shooter, Chamberlain simply used to run up to the free throw line, shoot, then dunk his missed shots after leaping over the lane.

Also, player positioning along the lane for rebounds off free throws changed because of Chamberlain. Before him, the two inside positions closest to the basket could be occupied by an offensive player on one side of the lane and a defensive player on the other. Since the mid-1950s, defensive players occupy both inside slots.

In Chamberlain's first game at KU, he led the freshman squad to an 81-71 victory against the varsity, the first time KU's freshmen team accomplished the feat. Chamberlain scored 42 points in front of 14,000 people in Allen Field House.

A year later, on Dec. 3, 1956, Wilt Chamberlain introduced himself to varsity college basketball.

That night, the No.1-ranked Jayhawks faced Northwestern and its All-American candidate at center, Joe Ruklick.

"We all remember that first game against Northwestern," Billings says. "The first two-three times up the floor, Ruklick tried to shoot, and Wilt just slapped it away like a flyswatter."

Ruklick scored 22 points, though, and grabbed five rebounds. But Chamberlain scored 52 points, still a KU record, and had 31 rebounds as KU won 87-69.

About 10 days later, the Jayhawks traveled to Seattle to play Washington. It was Chamberlain's first road game with Kansas.

"On the shoot-around the day before, they had a virtual sellout, standing-room-only crowd to watch him warm up," Billings says. "He was awesome. It was a time that nobody had seen anybody like that."

In two weekend victories the Huskies, Chamberlain scored 67 points and had 44 rebounds.

Kansas didn't lose a game in the 1956-57 season until Jan. 14, when Iowa State incorporated about the only tactic that could stop Chamberlain: the stall. Thirty years before college basketball adopted a shot clock, the Cyclones beat KU 39-37 in Ames.

KU's only other loss before the 1957 NCAA Tournament came at Oklahoma A&M, where the Cowboys passed the ball more than 50 times at one point before

"You were in awe once you saw how he could run, how long his arms are. When people ask me, I still contend Wilt was the greatest center ever to play the game of basketball."

– Eddie Sutton, former Oklahoma A&M guard and current Oklahoma State head coach

Kansas stole it. Still, the slowdown allowed coach Henry Iba's team to prevail 56-54.

Current Oklahoma State coach Eddie Sutton played for the Aggies in that game. He says Iba tried to keep Chamberlain away from the basket by instructing his players to push him above the free throw line.

Sutton remembers how he and his teammates reacted to seeing Chamberlain for the first time. It was not unlike Chamberlain's visits to other arenas.

"You were in awe once you saw how he could run, how long his arms are," Sutton says. "When people ask me, I still contend Wilt was the greatest center ever to play the game of basketball."

Sutton also recalls how big of a deal beating the Jayhawks that day was in Stillwater.

"It was such a big thing, the (school) president called off school," he says.

In the NCAA Tournament, battling a partisan crowd in Dallas that spewed endless racial epithets, the Jayhawks beat Southern Methodist and Oklahoma City on their way to the Final Four in Kansas City, Mo.

There, KU beat San Francisco before losing to undefeated North Carolina, 54-53 in triple overtime. In the three overtimes, North Carolina shot just three times while the Jayhawks attempted only eight field goals. North Carolina coach Frank McGuire, who once told Allen he was "trying to kill basketball" by bringing Chamberlain to the college game, had Tar Heels' center Joe Quigg take Chamberlain outside on defense to reduce his effectiveness. Quigg hit the winning free throws.

When he returned to Lawrence in January 1998 for a ceremony to retire his Kansas jersey, Chamberlain called the game "the most devastating loss of my athletic career." In the years since, he has chided Harp for a lack of coaching ability, particularly in that game. But Chamberlain also has admitted to bitterness that Allen was not his coach. The state's mandatory retirement age forced Allen out after Chamberlain's freshman season.

Harp says he's not bothered by Chamberlain's criticism.

"I really don't know what he expected in terms of the offense, but he had enough opportunity during that year to do what he needed to do," Harp says.

***

Kansas never made it back to the NCAA Tournament with Chamberlain. The Jayhawks finished 18-5 in 1957-58, tying for second in the conference behind Kansas State.

It was Chamberlain's last season at Kansas. Rude road crowds, especially at Oklahoma and at Missouri, which as late as the the late 1940s would not allow even opposing black players to play in Columbia, berated Chamberlain mercilessly.

"Missouri was not a good place to play, it was very, very vicious," Billings said. "Missouri would double- and triple-team him, and he would get very few calls."

In a piece he wrote for *American Heritage*, teammate John Parker recalled the nasty road trips.

"It seemed everywhere we went we heard 'nigger,' 'nigger lover,' and worse," Parker wrote. "Officials would often ignore blatant fouls committed against black players, and opposing schools waved Confederate flags and played 'Dixie.' "

Opposing players did everything they could to stop Chamberlain, even biting him on the shoulders. But mostly, Chamberlain may have left KU because he tired of slow-paced games.

"It got to be boring if people wouldn't run with you, if you were just standing around out there chasing people throwing the basketball back and forth, like we did against a lot of teams," Billings says. "It was not fun basketball. It was exciting, because Wilt was there, but it was not something that would have challenged someone like Wilt."

When teams ran with Kansas and Chamberlain, the Jayhawks ran away with a

"I'm a Jayhawk. There's so much tradition here, so many wonderful things that have helped me here. I'm now very much a part of it – by being up there – and very proud. Rock Chalk, Jayhawk."

– Wilt Chamberlain

victory. Nebraska tried it in Lawrence in February 1958 and lost by 58 points. Two weeks later, the Cornhuskers held the ball in Lincoln and beat KU 43-41.

A shot clock, Johnson says, would have made Chamberlain the most "phenomenal college player ever seen.

"Wilt probably took a bigger beating in most games by the way they tried to guard him and keep him from scoring than anything that was racially related," Johnson says. "But even as hard as they tried, they couldn't have much impact on him. He could do too many things. Talk about a box-in-one – they had a box around him."

So Chamberlain packed his bags after the 1957-58 season for a $65,000 salary with the Harlem Globetrotters. A year later, he began a prolific 14-year career in the NBA.

"When he left school, he came by the house, said goodbye and so forth, and that was it," Harp says. "I think what happened with him was we didn't get things done that really would have pleased him ... perhaps winning the national championship."

Elgin Baylor, the NBA All-Star who played with Chamberlain during the latter's tenure with the Los Angeles Lakers in the early 1970s, once told the Associated Press that Chamberlain had his own set of rules and didn't embrace a team attitude.

"He ate in different places, slept in different hotels and he didn't travel with the team," Baylor said.

Billings acknowledges a similar situation existed at Kansas, and Harp says it made coaching difficult.

"That was not a pleasant chore – having to have Wilt have his way," Harp says. "The players needed him to have his way, too. You're between a rock and a hard place."

Billings, though, says his friend generally has been misunderstood since leaving Philadelphia as a teenager.

"Wilt's a sensitive person, a very caring person," Billings says.

Indeed, Chamberlain rarely receives attention for myriad charitable activities, including taking boys in Harlem on picnics and other outings, donating money and time to churches and civic organizations or donating trophies to telethons.

Constant battering from opponents was one reason Chamberlain left Kansas after his junior year in 1958.

Instead, Chamberlain's infamous comments, such as the one that he slept with 20,000 women, have overshadowed his good deeds in the eyes of some. He made that well-publicized profession in his book, *A View From Above*. During a news conference preceding his KU jersey ceremony, he said the comment constantly is taken out of context, adding he wished he would have phrased it differently.

"I regret that it was misconstrued," he said. "... If you had read the book, you also would know that on the next to the last page, I say that for all you men who think that having 1,000 different women is a cool thing, the really cool thing is having the same woman a thousand different times. That's what life is all about. But no one picked up on that."

Chamberlain's jersey ceremony marked his first trip to Lawrence since 1975. The absence perplexed KU officials, who refused to hang his No. 13 jersey in the field house rafters until he returned.

Chamberlain blamed schedule conflicts for the 23-year delay. Ironically, he also confided that he had hoped to find a wife before coming back to KU.

"I was hoping for the last 12, 13, 14 years I could find a wife to share it with me," he said. "But seriously, this is something I've wanted to do for a long, long while."

At one time, not even Billings knew if Chamberlain, elected to the Basketball Hall of Fame in 1979, ever would return to Kansas.

"Only Wilt would be able to answer that," he said in early 1997. "I hope he will, because I think it would be a wonderful opportunity for the KU family to show their respect and admiration for him."

Billings was right. At halftime of KU's 69-62 victory against Kansas State on Jan. 17, 1998, an overflow crowd at the field house gave Chamberlain a thunderous ovation. Watching his No. 13 unveiled alongside other KU greats, he choked back tears as he told the crowd:

"Forty years ago, I lost what I considered my toughest battle in sports, losing to the North Carolina Tar Heels by one point in triple overtime. It was a devastating thing for me, because I felt I had let the University of Kansas down and my teammates down. But to come here today and feel the appreciation, the love and the warmth …

"Over the years, I've learned that you have to take the bitter with the sweet. And how sweet this is …

"I'm a Jayhawk. There's so much tradition here, so many wonderful things that have helped me here. I'm now very much a part of it – by being up there – and very proud.

"Rock Chalk, Jayhawk."

FUELING THE ECONOMY

A two-time, consensus first-team All-American, Wilt Chamberlain still holds several Kansas basketball records, including single-game records for points (52), rebounds (36), field goals (20) and free throws (18). His 30.1 scoring average in 1957-58 remains a school record, as do his career scoring averages of 29.9 points per game and 18.3 rebounds per game.

But Chamberlain's impact on northeast Kansas transcended basketball or even the societal changes he triggered.

In 1957, Joe Gilmartin, sports editor of the *Wichita Beacon*, estimated Chamberlain was worth $3.89 per mile to the new 236-mile Kansas Turnpike. Gilmartin arrived at his estimate because attendance at Kansas basketball games increased 85,000 in 1956-57, Chamberlain's first season on KU's varsity.

Gilmartin also estimated 51 percent of additional traffic that year at Lawrence turnpike exits occurred because of Chamberlain's presence.

Kansas Governor George Docking, a KU graduate, outraged Kansas alumni when he suggested the state should receive some gate receipts from additional attendance at Allen Field House, which was built with state funds.

"Now that they have Wilt the Stilt, they should be making good money at the gate," Docking said in February 1957.

KU alumni were peeved because Docking made no similar suggestion for Ahearn Field House at Kansas State, which also was built with state funds.

KU's athletics department, as now, did not receive state funding for its operation. Instead, it recirculated revenues to pay for expenses throughout the department.

"This business is by no means as lucrative as it seems," athletics director A.C. "Dutch" Lonborg said at the time, reiterating comments often heard from today's athletics directors, "and I'd like to dispel the idea that we're rolling in wealth, because we certainly are not."

Docking's idea never got past the suggestion stage, and slightly more than a year later, Chamberlain left KU.

TRUE GRIT

Shot-putter overcame
serious injury

"Something can always happen."

Bill Nieder didn't believe it, though. He had just finished fourth in the shot-put competition at the 1960 U.S. Olympic Trials. Only the top three finishers make the team. And here's Stanford University track coach Payton Jordan calling him soon after "the most disappointing day of my whole life" and telling him that "something can always happen." Jordan also asked Nieder to work out with the Olympic team and compete in the three track meets that were scheduled before the team left for Rome.

It wasn't supposed to happen this way. Nieder was an NCAA champion at the University of Kansas in 1955. The next year, he earned a silver medal at the Olympics in Melbourne, Australia. He set world records – indoor and outdoor – a couple of months before the 1960 Trials.

But then, for the umpteenth time, he hurt that knee, this time three weeks before the trials. Fourth place! And now he's being asked to set aside his hurt and keep trying when it's over.

"To my knowledge, nobody has been put on a team where they had three fit people in front of them, regardless of how far you throw," Nieder told Jordan.

Jordan replied, "Well, you can get a lot of your pride back before you hang it up. Your knee is coming along again. Why don't you come down and work out and help the other boys, too?"

So Nieder, a lieutenant in the U.S. Army, played the good soldier. But then the oddest thing happened. At the first track meet in Portland, Ore., he out-threw the U.S. Olympic team by a foot-and-a-half. He won the second meet in Los Angeles. And he broke his own world record with a 65-foot-10-inch heave in warm ups at the final meet in Walnut, Calif.

"Hmmmmm," U.S. Olympic track officials said after Nieder's final showing. "Now-whatta-we-do?"

What they did was unprecedented. They asked Nieder if he was available for Rome. "Absolutely," he replied. Then, unsure of his status, he flew back to The Presidio, his Army base in San Francisco. Meanwhile, the coaching staff, trainers and physicians met long into the night debating their dilemma. At 5 a.m., head coach Larry Snyder called Nieder with their 11th-hour decision: He was on the team, replacing Dave Davies of San Fernando, Calif., who had suffered a wrist injury.

"I said to myself, 'I got this opportunity. When I go this time, I'm coming home with the gold,' " Nieder says.

He was true to his word. After four mediocre throws, he hurled the shot 64-6 3/4 on his fifth and next-to-last try, which won the gold medal. His throw set an Olympic record and was 22 inches longer than that of teammate and bitter rival Parry O'Brien, who took the silver and had won the gold in 1952 and 1956.

"Six weeks ago I was so down in the dumps I vowed I never would try to put the shot again," Nieder said after his victory. "Then, when I saw those three American

"Only a man with an iron determination and a desire to win could or would have stuck it out when time and again, fate seemed to spell certain defeat."

– Bill Easton
on Bill Nieder

flags go up and heard the Star Spangled Banner ring out over Olympic Stadium, I was glad I had changed my mind. It was the happiest, proudest moment of my life. It made it all worthwhile."

In an editorial the day after Nieder's triumph, the *Lawrence Journal-World* noted,

"Bill Nieder, the first Lawrence native ever to win an Olympic gold medal, is a living testimony to what can be accomplished through dedication and hard work ... If ever the values of perseverance and diligence were clear and apparent, they were when Lawrencian Bill Nieder won the Olympic title he worked for so long."

Two weeks after the Olympics, Nieder's knee started hurting again. This time, though, he hadn't done anything to aggravate it. After a two-week hospital stay, when the knee ached so badly that he couldn't stand to have a bedsheet on top of it, Army surgeons told him he had the early stages of traumatic arthritis. The injury forced him to give up throwing the shot.

BILL NIEDER
Track and field,
1954-56

***

"Something can always happen."

Bill Nieder was a hometown boy who wanted to play college football. He was the first football All-American at Lawrence High School and played both ways on the Jayhawks' freshman team.

He started at center in his first varsity college football game, Sept. 19, 1953, against Texas Christian University in Fort Worth, Texas. During the game, Nieder was clipped and his right knee suffered torn muscles, tendons and cartilage.

Soon after he was hospitalized, he complained to a nurse about how badly his knee felt. She told him that when it came to pain, the big guys (Nieder was 6 feet 2 inches, 220 pounds) can't take it. The next morning the doctor came in and told Nieder that his athletics career was over. Then he asked Nieder why he had asked for the nurse so much.

"My knee really hurt," Nieder said. "It is more pain than I've ever been in. But it doesn't hurt anymore. It's the back of my head."

"What do you mean?" the doctor asked.

"Every time my heart beats, it feels like it's coming out of the back of my head," Nieder said.

The doctor pulled the sheet back. Nieder's foot had turned black from the early stages of gangrene. A few hours later, the doctor told Nieder that there was a good chance his foot may need to be amputated.

"I immediately called my dad and said, 'You've got to come and stay with me,

Dad, and make sure they don't give me a knockout pill and go and take my foot off,' " he said.

The crisis passed. Nieder was told later that if another 10 minutes had elapsed, his foot would have been lost. All told, his knee surgery took seven hours, and the gangrene forced doctors to drain almost all of his blood and replace it. He was in a body cast from his shoulder to his toes for five months. In his life, Nieder had his knee drained at least 150 times, underwent three other major surgeries and had a full knee replacement in 1996.

***

"Something can always happen."

Nieder had thrown the shot in high school. He set a state record of 60-9 3/4 as a senior using a 12-pound shot. Bill Easton, KU track and field coach, took notice.

Easton contacted Nieder and asked him to consider track and field. Soon, they started working on rehabilitating Nieder's knee. One room of the track office sported a rack of 2-inch bars that went across the wall. Nieder used the bars to bend his knee further and further. After quite awhile, the knee responded, and he went out for track.

"He was very instrumental in getting me where I am today," Nieder says of Easton. "He was a great supporter who made you feel like a winner at all times. I hurt my knee many, many times at Kansas. He would say, 'You're going to get over this, it's going to get better.' "

Easton was right on both counts. Miles of walking and hours throwing the shot over the beams beneath cold and damp Memorial Stadium with teammate Al Oerter paid off. In 1955, Nieder won the Big Seven Conference indoor championship with a league-record throw of 53-10 5/8. He set that – and future records – using an unorthadox rotation, called the "Nieder bucket," to throw rather than coming up and over his knee because of his injury.

During the outdoor season, he won the Texas, Kansas and Drake Relays. By June, he won the NCAA crown with a put of 57-3. Dissatisfied with that distance, he asked meet officials to stick around after the competition to measure one more toss. That throw sailed 58-11 1/4, an unofficial personal best.

Nieder owned 1956 – almost. He set an NCAA record of 59-9 at the Texas Relays. A week later, he became the first college thrower to clear the 60-foot mark with a throw of 60-3 in a dual meet against Oklahoma A&M in Lawrence. Nieder was the second man to throw this distance; Parry O'Brien, formerly of Southern Cal, was the first. Nieder improved his NCAA record to 60-3 3/4 at the conference outdoor championships in May.

But he slipped a notch at the NCAA outdoor championships and placed second. He took third at the U.S. Olympic trials in July with a throw of 58-1 1/2. At the Olympics, he finished second to O'Brien with a distance of 59-7 3/4.

Easton told the *University Daily Kansan* that no one was more worthy of success than Nieder:

"Only a man with an iron determination and a desire to win could or would have stuck it out when, time and time again, fate seemed to spell certain defeat. This boy's great will to win always kept him fighting and this great moment on the victory stand more than equals his many hours of hard work."

Nieder calls the Melbourne Games "one of the greatest experiences in my life." Still, he was happy but not satisfied. The 1956 Olympics whetted Nieder's appetite for more success.

"What I really didn't catch early in my career was how important the Olympics were, and what a gold medal meant to a person. Even though I got second, it was nothing like getting the gold.

"It's a whole different feeling. You're on top of the world and you stay there."

Bill Nieder turned to track and field after a devastating football injury nearly ended his athletics career.

"Something can always happen."

The view from on top of the world can be dizzying as well as dazzling. After winning the gold in Rome, Nieder had many offers to choose from. His choice was what he called "a fluky thing." He says he was "conned" into signing a movie contract, and he attended acting school at the Desilu Studio in Los Angeles.

"That went just fine, but I could not see myself acting in the movies," Nieder says.

The person with whom he signed the contract kept reneging on the deal, and Nieder saw less and less money. The agent also was a boxing manager, so Nieder took up that sport. He worked out in a gym and felt he was progressing.

The manager arranged for a fight with an established Philadelphia boxer, Jim Wiley. The bout – and Nieder's boxing career – lasted 2 minutes, 10 seconds. While off balance, Nieder was knocked under the bottom rope, out of the ring and into the third row of the crowd.

Finished with boxing, he joined 3M Co. in sales and became the first salesman to promote artificial turf and tartan tracks. Sales were brisk, and he became West Coast sales manager. He asked the company for a franchise but was turned down, so he resigned. Nieder then traveled to Germany to meet with officials of Bayer Chemical, and the two parties struck a deal in which Bayer would sell urethane to Nieder, who would use it to make synthetic surfaces to sell.

As Nieder and Bayer officials celebrated the deal at dinner that night, a German sportswriter approached the group and asked Nieder why he was there. Nieder explained, and the sportswriter wrote a story about the meeting, which ran in the next day's newspaper. By the time Nieder returned to the United States, he had 15 telegrams from 3M, and the company gave him the franchise.

Later, Nieder left 3M and continued selling synthetic surfaces for everything from ship decks to padded walls and floors in jails. He estimates that he has 95 percent of the synthetic surface market in the United States.

Today, Nieder lives the good life, traveling and enjoying time at his 17 houses, all the while aware that *something can always happen* – and chances are, it will be good.

OLYMPIC ICON
Discus dynamo improved with age

All international track and field stars inevitably face three competitors: other athletes, themselves and time. Most, for a while, can defeat the first of these and improve the second. But the third one always catches up. And in the end, it never has lost.

Although he earned his stardom as a powerful thrower, not a swift runner, Al Oerter eluded the final foe with more grace, style and effort than any athlete in the history of modern track and field. The only possible exception is perennial world champion hurdler Edwin Moses.

For that matter, those two also may have cheated time better than Greek athletes in ancient Olympic games. As it is, in 20th century Olympiads, Oerter won four consecutive gold medals in the same event. For four straight Summer Olympic gatherings – 1956 in Melbourne, Australia; 1960 in Rome; 1964 in Tokyo; and 1968 in Mexico City – Oerter overcame a variety of obstacles while maintaining his status as the best discus thrower the world had ever seen.

But he brought something more important to his sport. He was to track and field what Nolan Ryan was to baseball, what George Blanda was to football, what Gordie Howe was to hockey. As his career progressed, others viewed Oerter as a freak of nature not for his astounding ability, which had sufficed in his youth, but for the unprecedented manner in which he stayed on a championship plane with athletes half his age.

Time and distance. They were the hallmarks of Al Oerter's discus-throwing career. He threw long longer than anyone else. His life began Sept. 19, 1936, in New York City. But his international discus-throwing script began after he arrived at the University of Kansas from Hyde Park, N.Y., as a freshman in the fall of 1954.

Here then is that script, given in the order it unfolded and the milestone heaves that highlighted it:

YEAR: 1955   **DISTANCE:** 157 feet, 1 inch

Oerter's farthest throw as an 18-year-old was 70 feet, 10 inches less than the longest toss of his career 25 years later. He also weighed about 100 pounds less than the almost 300 pounds he packed in 1980.

YEAR: 1955   **DISTANCE:** 171 feet, 6 inches

In May, Oerter broke the NCAA record for college freshman at the Big Seven Conference Outdoor Track and Field Championships. The same day he set this record, Oklahoma's Bob Van Dee broke the conference varsity record in the same event with a throw of 165-3 7/8.

After the two concluded throwing, KU shot put All-American Bill Nieder introduced Oerter and Van Dee. Van Dee asked the freshman for a few pointers.

YEAR: 1956   **DISTANCE:** 184 feet, 10 1/2 inches

Oerter, after winning the Kansas, Texas and Drake Relays in his first year of varsity competition at Kansas, exploded onto the international track scene by setting an Olympic record at the Melbourne Games with this throw. He was the first KU track athlete to win a gold medal at the Olympics since Jim Bausch won the decathlon in the 1932 Games in Los Angeles.

Nieder also competed at Melbourne, winning the silver medal. He recalls celebrating with Oerter.

"He was a fantastic guy," Nieder says. "He pretty much kept to himself, but he was fun to be with. We did a lot of crazy things. We tore up the town of Sydney after the Melbourne Games. We had too much beer to drink and it was one great party."

Nieder can't forget another experience with Oerter. One time, Nieder placed his shot put in a case by a heater to warm it up. It rolled out of the case and hit Oerter in the head and the back. But Oerter's head was as tough as his competitive nature: He wasn't hurt.

Nieder had begun his career at KU doubling as a football player, and Kansas coaches begged Oerter to play throughout his time on Mount Oread. But Oerter never cared much for the sport. He often said he liked the singularity of throwing the discus.

In an interview with *Ultrasport* magazine in the early 1980s, Oerter showed somewhat of a disdain for collision sports such as football:

"Discus throwing in our society is never going to be a professional sport. The only way we would draw would be if we were throwing at each other, and someone would be dragged from the arena, bloodied. People would come to see that."

But if determined not to don shoulder pads, Oerter proved relentless in a throwing pit, Nieder says.

"He was probably the finest competitor that had ever been in track and field," Nieder says. "He had lost different track meets from time to time, but when the chips were down and the gold was on the line, he came through."

YEAR: 1958   **DISTANCE:** 202 feet, 6 inches

Track officials disregarded this throw by Oerter at the Arkansas Relays because of the excessive downward gradient of the throwing pit. Nonetheless, it was 8 feet farther than the world record that Fortune Gordien had set five years earlier.

Oerter entered his last outdoor season at Kansas with 36 of the 37 longest discus throws in conference history. Other than the Arkansas Relays toss, his longest throw occurred during his senior year, 188-2 at the Texas Relays.

By the end of the season, he had won his third consecutive triple crown at the Kansas, Texas and Drake Relays, an unprecedented achievement. He also won his second straight title at the NCAA Outdoor Track and Field Championships.

Oerter graduated in 1959 with a bachelor's degree in business administration. In a 1988 questionnaire in which KU's track and field All-Americans detailed their experiences at Kansas, Oerter wrote that he regarded the education he received as "excellent" and listed his greatest moment in sports as, "The first to throw 200 feet officially and winning four Olympic Gold medals – that and running 22.4 (seconds in) 220 yards in Coach (Bill) Easton's track and field class."

But his biggest regret in athletics?

"Wearing pink competition shorts supplied by KU."

YEAR: 1960   **DISTANCE:** 194 feet, 2 inches

Oerter broke his Olympic record in the Rome Games and upset Southern California's Rink Babka and Poland's Ed Piatkowski in the process with a throw almost 10 feet farther than the one that won gold at Melbourne. Only 23, Oerter returned home with his second gold medal.

A year earlier, Oerter foreshadowed his longevity in an interview with the Kansas Sports Information Department.

"I was only 20 when I won at Melbourne," he said then. "Weight men aren't supposed to reach their peak until 27 then stay at it a few years."

YEAR: 1962   **DISTANCE:** 200 feet, 5 1/2 inches

May 18, 1962. That is the date that Oerter officially threw more than 200 feet for the first time. No one before had accomplished the feat, which some regarded as the equivalent of running the mile faster than 4 minutes.

The throw began a string of world records. On July 1, he broke the record with a throw of 204 feet, 10 1/2 inches in Chicago. Then, on April 27, 1963, he threw 205 feet, 5 1/2 inches. His final world record occurred almost a year later, April 25, 1964, when he threw 206 feet, 6 inches. Both of his last two world records occurred at the Mt. San Antonio Relays in Walnut, Calif.

YEAR: 1964   **DISTANCE:** 200 feet, 1 1/2 inches

"He's all heart and guts," U.S. track and field coach Payton Jordan said of Oerter after he won his final Olympic gold medal in 1968.

But no episode clarified the truth of Jordan's statement than Oerter's road to his third consecutive gold medal and Olympic record in the 1964 Tokyo Games.

A week before the Games began, Oerter tore cartilage in his ribs. During the Games, he competed with his ribs heavily taped and the right side of his rib cage frozen to prevent hemorrhaging. He also received two vials of novacaine and oral pain killers, yet still won the event.

YEAR: 1968   **DISTANCE:** 212 feet, 6 1/2 inches

Pick a throw, any throw: this one, 212 feet, 4 inches or 210 feet, 1 inch. Any of Oerter's final three throws at the 1968 Mexico City Olympics would have won gold

"I don't see how winning gold medals enhances a society, makes us better Americans. It interests people, but it doesn't move us forward in any way. If you're going to enhance a society, you have to do it by an example or a deed. Maybe if I were a scientist and had moved us forward in medicine, there would be a real accomplishment. If I'm a hero, I'm a really low-scale hero. A damn discus thrower. That's a hero?"

– Al Oerter

as he again upset longtime-foe Jay Silvester.

Dave Anderson, a well-known sportswriter with the *New York Times*, called Oerter the No. 1 athlete of all time after the 32-year-old thrower completed his four-peat.

"To qualify for four Olympiads is remarkable enough," Anderson wrote. "To have won four gold medals puts him on a pedestal."

Oerter told the Associated Press after winning the competition with a throw that measured more than 5 feet farther than his previous throw entering the 1968 Olympics, "I get fired up for the Olympics. Something happens to me when I get to the Games – the people, the pressure, everything about the Olympics is special to me."

YEAR: 1980   **DISTANCE:** 227 feet, 11 inches

Oerter's longest throw of his career occurred in May 1980, just before the United States boycotted the Olympics in Moscow. Oerter had spent much of the 1970s raising his two daughters and competing when he could, but he regained his status among the elite of his sport at age 43.

YEAR: 1986   **DISTANCE:** 195 feet, 2 inches

His longest throw of the year helped Oerter, a new grandfather three months shy of his 50th birthday, qualify for the finals of the USA-Mobil Outdoor Championships.

"I really have no concept of age," he told AP at the event in Eugene, Ore. "It's something I absolutely do not feel."

But Oerter stopped competing in the amateur open circuit in 1988. He has competed in Master's meets since then, events that use a slightly lighter discus.

Despite his success, he maintains a modest perspective regarding his achievements.

In the 1988 questionnaire, Oerter stated one more clear goal for his discus throwing career: "To be the first 100-year-old to spin in a discus ring without falling down."

Considering his "track" record, don't bet against him.

Al Oerter turned into an international sensation after his sophomore year at Kansas when he won a gold medal at the 1956 Olympic Games in Melbourne, Australia.

UNPARALLED SUCCESS

Easton molded athletes, champions – and men

"We work."

With that simple declaration, Bill Easton explained the secret to the unparalleled success that the University of Kansas track and field team enjoyed under his direction from 1947-65.

And, oh, did they work. It started with Easton himself, whose typical day as coach lasted 18 hours.

"He works harder than any track coach I know of," an unnamed KU sports official told the *Kansas City Star* in 1958. "Some of them go down to the track, look at a stopwatch a little while and call it quits. Easton checks weights and times every day. He watches film like a football coach. No new idea escapes him."

Easton instilled a similar work ethic in his teams.

"We ran if it snowed, we ran if it rained, we ran if it was 110 in the shade," says Herb Semper, 1950 and 1951 NCAA cross country champion and All-American in the two-mile run. "We did everything, and we were in shape. Bill made sure we were in shape."

After all that work, Semper says Easton motivated the team at meets with a simple statement.

"He'd tell us, 'You're ready. These guys aren't ready,' " Semper says.

The Jayhawks almost always were ready. Here is a brief rundown of KU's accomplishments with Easton in command for 18 seasons:

- 16 conference cross country championships;
- 11 conference indoor track championships;
- 12 conference outdoor track championships;
- Eight consecutive conference "grand slams" (cross country, indoor and outdoor championships from 1952-59);
- Two NCAA outdoor championships;
- One NCAA cross country championship; and
- Two second place and two fourth place finishes in the NCAA outdoor championships.

"You can't just give your all in a single race or event," Easton told the *Star* in 1958. "You've got to give your all for hours, most days of the year, so you can achieve that ultimate moment. A boy must want to be the best in high school, in college, in the U.S.A., in the world. He can't flirt with track; he's got to marry it."

But for an athlete to marry his sport, a solid relationship must exist in other facets of his life. That's where Easton excelled. He motivated. He taught. He developed. He helped. He disciplined.

"You had to be a student first, a gentleman and then an athlete. In that order," Semper says. "Everything revolved around Bill."

Easton told the *University Daily Kansan* in 1958 that he looked for three things in a prospective athlete, starting with academic achievement. Next came personality, community involvement, church membership and other activities. He listed athletic ability third.

> "Bill got the very best out of us. He made us!"
>
> – Herb Semper

Easton sought well-rounded athletes, and he wanted them to contribute long after their days in competitive track and field. Distance runner Herald Hadley recalls sitting in Memorial Stadium's bleachers for an early 1960s lecture that Easton delivered to freshman team members.

"He looked at all of us and said, 'You fellas need to understand, you're not just here to run, jump and throw things. When you leave this institution, you can do anything that anyone ever asks you to do,' " Hadley says. "I think that was a really strong statement. He meant that. It wasn't all athletics. He was a real leader."

A leader who helped people, showed them the way but made sure they did the work.

BILL EASTON
Head track and field coach, 1948-65

"As a student, it was up to you to get your way through school," Semper says. "If you needed help, he got you books, he got you a tutor, but he would never interfere with a professor. Because it was your job to graduate."

And with self-reliance comes discipline.

"He was a tremendous disciplinarian," Semper says. "Everybody had to go to church. He didn't care if you were Catholic, Jewish, Christian or whatever, you had to go to church and that was it. And when Monday came around, there's fifty churches in town and fifty different guys, and he knew who didn't go.

"And he'd come out and say, 'Where were you yesterday?'

" 'I was in ch—,' the athlete would answer before getting cut off.

" 'Where were you yesterday?'

" 'Well, coach ...'

" 'Well, what?'

" 'Well, I overslept.'

" 'Well, we won't oversleep again, will we?'

" 'No, we won't coach.' "

Semper recalls another time when Easton discovered that one of KU's track athletes smoked.

"When (Easton) came to practice one night, he had a brand new track suit in his left hand and the guy's favorite cigarettes in his right hand," Semper says. "And he'd just say, 'Now what do you want? Do you want the uniform or the pack of cigarettes? It's one or the other, but not both.' That's how he would do it.

"(The teammate) said, 'I want the uniform, coach.'

"And (Easton) took the cigarettes, threw them in the garbage can, and said, 'We don't have to worry about those anymore, do we?'

"And he said, 'No, we don't.'

"And it didn't happen."

Through hard work, dedication and discipline, Easton extracted extraordinary things from talented, but not always superstar, athletes. Semper notes that very few of his teammates in the early 1950s came to the University as high school state champions.

"But this was Bill's knack," Semper says. "He saw something in a boy, and he made a man out of him. I saw that time and time again."

So did others closely associated with the track team. Again from the *Star* in 1958, one track insider said:

"Bill makes average runners good and good runners great. He comes up to a discouraged, dog-tired boy and says, 'You're getting better. Look at this work sheet for today. Look what you've done. You ran cross country, then you ran three quarters. My gosh, just think of all the work you've done! How can you miss?'

"The boy thinks of all the work he has done, the aching muscles and solitary hours of running. He thinks:

"'Good Lord, he's right. I've killed myself and I'm still alive. How can I miss?' "

They seldom missed. Individually under Easton, the Jayhawks' track and field athletes accomplished these impressive totals:

- 22 earned All-America honors in 38 events;
- 10 won a total of 18 NCAA indoor and outdoor championships;
- Eight appeared in the Olympics, with three winning gold medals (Al Oerter four times, Bill Nieder and Billy Mills one each). Two earned silver medals (Cliff Cushman and Nieder); and
- Four set world records (Mills, Nieder, Oerter and Charlie Tidwell), as did two sprint relay teams.

When he shares his thoughts about his four years at Kansas with Bill Easton, Semper's voice resounds with awe and reverence. The awe stems from achievements, the reverence from the family-like atmosphere in which they were accomplished.

"I think that we all did more than we were literally capable of doing," Semper says. "Bill got the very best out of us. He made us! He worked us hard.

"But on the other hand, Bill was a coach, he was a father, he was a buddy. His wife, Ada, was an absolute sweetheart to all of us. He was like a father to us, and she was like a mother.

"If you were sick, he was there. He was there taking care of you, he was there getting medicine for you. He was there when you needed him.

"That's what made you. You did the work, but you had to be guided."

***

Millard Ellsworth Easton was born Sept. 13, 1904, to Perry and Fannie Culross Easton in Stinesville, Ind. He became known as "Bill" at an early age to end family confusion with his grandfather, Millard.

Bill's father successfully ran real estate and small business ventures and a farm. He also served in the Indiana State Senate.

Easton competed in track as high school student in Sandborn, Ind. He experienced both good and bad times as a young adult. As the *Star* reported in 1958 about his time at Indiana University, where he ran middle distance and distance events for the Hoosiers in the mid-1920s:

"In his first year … Easton had a virtually unlimited checking account and extremely low grades. The next summer most of the family fortunes were lost in the agricultural slump and Bill was facing the hard facts of life. It took him five years to get a degree in business, working part time and borrowing from the banks. But the grades improved substantially and Easton is glad today that he learned to be independent."

Easton worked several jobs after graduating, including a patronage job as a purchasing agent with the Indianapolis sanitary commission. He lost that job when his party lost the election.

He thought about joining the U.S. Army, but friends mentioned that he should try coaching to draw on his enjoyment with track and field. Easton took that advice and coached at four Indiana high schools during a 12-year period from 1928-40. His success in eight years at Hammond High School led him to his first college job, as cross country and track coach at Drake University in Des Moines, Iowa, and as director of the Drake Relays.

At Drake, Easton's cross country teams won three consecutive national championships. He helped turn the Drake Relays into one of the nation's top track and field events. Kansas hired Easton in August 1947, beginning an incredible 18-year era on Mount Oread.

***

All dynasties come to an end, and the Easton dynasty concluded abruptly in 1965. That was the year Easton, as the immovable object, was moved out of office by the irresistable force of second-year athletics director Wade Stinson.

The two men clashed for a year, and the problems came to a head during the Kansas Relays in April 1965. Easton ordered two vaulting boxes, total cost $60, for the annual meet. He said the boxes were needed to comply with NCAA specifications for the pole vault.

Kansas track coach Bill Easton (left) seldom recruited superstar athletes. Wes Santee (right) was an exception.

Stinson wouldn't approve the purchase and returned the vault boxes. Easton learned what happened and intercepted the boxes at a loading platform of a local express office. He then used the boxes at the Relays, and Stinson hit the ceiling.

Stinson fired Easton three days later. Each man told the story differently. Stinson says he made his decision after a series of events that culminated with the vault boxes. He says he called Easton into his office and asked him if he was going to keep disregarding his wishes. Stinson says Easton said he wouldn't change.

Stinson said, "Well, you're fired then." Stinson says Easton replied, "You can't fire me." But Stinson said, yes, he could.

Easton's version, reported by the *Lawrence Journal-World*, had Stinson giving him the choice of resigning or being fired.

"I said, 'Go ahead and fire me,' " Easton told the newspaper.

Regardless of how it happened, Easton's firing caused an uproar on campus. Students protested the firing and hanged Stinson in effigy. The track and field team issued a lengthy statement that detailed how money was – and wasn't – spent on the team.

Meanwhile the change shocked alumni. Former star Wes Santee called the move "incomprehensible."

Easton finished the season with the team. He addressed his final squad the afternoon he was fired. In a breaking voice with tears lining his face, Easton told them, "I hope you've gained something from being associated with this group ... This just means that we're going to have to put out the greatest effort we ever have."

Three days later, KU's four-mile relay team won the Drake Relays in school-record time. "This one was for you, coach," said John Lawson, who ran the third leg of the race.

Later that spring, the Jayhawks won the Big Eight Conference Outdoor championship for the 12th and final time under Easton's direction.

In May 1965, Easton and his wife, Ada, were honored at a testimonial, "This is Your Life" dinner at the Kansas Union. Many former athletes and 350 guests attended the show, in which they presented the Eastons a new Lincoln Continental.

Easton graciously accepted the accolades spoken on his behalf. He told the audience: "I'm completely relieved. The weight is off my back. Lawrence and the state of Kansas have been one of the finest things in my life."

The Rev. Dale Turner, a former minister at the Plymouth Congregational Church in Lawrence, summed up his long-time friend to the audience:

"The real test of Bill's success is the way he had instilled the sense of responsibility and leadership in the young men who have been with him. Nobody can see what he has done along this line and not be inspired."

Easton died Oct. 4, 1997, after a lengthy illness.

MAKING – AND MISSING – HIS MARK

Long jumper rose to the top of the sport but missed Olympics

Years before Bob Beamon and Carl Lewis leaped into the record books, the University of Kansas boasted its own superstar long jumper in Ernie Shelby.

In the late 1950s, less than a dozen men in the world had jumped at least 26 feet, and Shelby, a member of KU's team in 1958 and 1959, was among that elite few.

Shelby might be overlooked by some in the annals of world's greatest long jumpers, but only because he failed to win an Olympic medal. In one correspondence with former KU track coach Bob Timmons, Shelby listed his greatest regret in athletics as missing the Olympics twice, in 1956 and 1960.

Timing wasn't on his side.

Shelby was ranked No. 1 in the world in 1958, the year he won his first long jump title at the NCAA Outdoor Championships. The next year, he won the event again, helping guide the Jayhawks to their first NCAA track and field championship. Shelby was captain of the 1959 squad, the first black who earned that honor at Kansas.

He also claimed a rare triple crown in 1958 by winning the long jump at the Kansas, Drake and Texas Relays. That same year he won four key European meets, including a victory against the Soviet Union. He was a four-time All-American and won three consecutive Amateur Athletic Union long jump titles.

Also a star hurdler, Shelby tied a world record by running 12.4 seconds in the 120-yard low hurdles in a 1958 AAU-sanctioned meet. He made All-America in the 220-yard low hurdles in 1959 by placing third in the event at the NCAA meet.

In his first year at KU in 1958, he set the Big Seven Conference freshman record in the 220 low hurdles with a time of 23.5 seconds.

Former KU star distance runner Billy Mills remembers Shelby for his great athletic achievements and dignity. Shelby joined several KU runners on a recruiting mission to convince Mills, then a student at Haskell Institute in Lawrence, to join the Jayhawks. Mills was flattered such "big names" would be interested in him.

Shelby was a teammate and close friends with Charlie Tidwell and Cliff Cushman, two other NCAA track champions at KU. Mills said that he once tried to room with Shelby and Cushman in Lawrence, but they were denied housing because of their different racial origins.

"I always had tremendous respect for Ernie," Mills says. "He had a beautiful singing voice, a lot like Johnny Mathis."

Shelby's musical and artistic inclinations paid off. Born in Los Angeles, he returned to Southern California after his college years. He earned a bachelor's degree in fine arts from Kansas in 1959 and later became an advertising creative director. He also composed music for several million-selling records, won national design awards and wrote a book.

**ERNIE SHELBY
Track and field,
1958-59**

TRAGIC TURN
Sprinter's star burned out quickly

A trophy case in the atrium of Allen Field House houses the pictures for all to see.

Faces beam with pride on the 1959 and 1960 Kansas outdoor track teams, winners of back-to-back NCAA championships. Smiles convey that relieved-but-confident look that only champions know. Slumped postures denote exhilarated fatigue.

You look closer and study each person. And then you stop when you come to him. There he is, happy, radiant. His black arms are draped around the shoulders of two of his teammates, one of whom is white. Not that there's anything unusual about that, except you remember that the time-frame is a few years before Congress approved the Civil Rights Act. And you remember stories from teammates about separate buses and meals when the team traveled to the Texas Relays.

You look again and study him, but you don't find a clue. There's not a trace of evidence in those or other pictures, or in yellowed clippings heralding him as track's fastest sprinter and hurdler in 1959 and 1960. With four world records to his name at one time, nothing indicates he would be dead in less than 10 years after the team's second championship, a suicide victim – after he murdered his estranged wife.

You ask his teammates about him, and they pause before choosing their words. They say nice things about him, and you believe them. You know they're telling the truth, because their stories are consistent, that Charlie Tidwell was a great athlete, a wonderful teammate and a gentleman. You know it's the truth, because all of the clippings say essentially the same thing.

His teammates' voices trail off when they mention what you already know about his demise. Nobody knows why it happened, and you don't ask.

You just think about him and his wife and those horrible, final moments when hope was an eternity away. And you hope they have found peace.

But you wonder. Everybody does.

***

Charlie Tidwell came to the University of Kansas from Independence, Kan. In high school, he set a national record in the 180-yard low hurdles (18.5 seconds) and a state record in the 100-yard dash (9.8 seconds). He dominated in high school football, too. In a 1959 profile on Tidwell, the *Kansas City Star* reported:

One man who saw Charlie play football chortled as he recalled how Independence fooled so many opponents by having Tidwell take the ball on a wide sweep, while his teammates would delay in the middle of the field. When Charlie apparently was hemmed in at the sideline, he would reverse his field, outrun all his pursuers, pick up his own blockers and scoot across for a touchdown.

Tidwell's athletic dominance continued in college track. He won five NCAA titles, the most of any KU track and field athlete until shot putter Karl Salb won six championships. Tidwell captured his first title as a sophomore in 1958, winning the 220-yard hurdles in 22.7 seconds, a world record.

In 1959, his junior year, Tidwell streaked to the 100-yard dash and 200-meter hurdles NCAA championships, which helped KU win its first outdoor national title. His wind-aided 9.3-second time in the 100-yard dash tied the world record. At the Amateur Athletic Union Outdoor meet that year, Tidwell set a world record in the 200-meter low hurdles with a time of 22.6 seconds.

As a champion on a championship team, Tidwell understood high expectations

"(Tidwell) was just fluid motion."

– Bill Alley

leading into his senior year. The *Star* noted in its feature:

The Jayhawk jet has tremendous desire to achieve even more acclaim for his track feats, but not for the personal glory attached. He explains it modestly but matter-of-factly:

"I just hate to let all these fine people down here in any way. This is the first time they've had anyone in this section get very far in track and they expect me to beat everyone. When I don't, I feel like I'm letting them all down. That bothers me more than the personal disappointment that I have. I want to do well because of the faith and interest they've shown in me."

In 1960, Tidwell won the 100 and 200 hurdles at the NCAA meet, and the Jayhawks repeated as national champions. He also tied a world record of 10.1 seconds in the 100 meters at the Meet of Champions in Houston.

Former teammate Bill Alley says Tidwell looked like anything but a world-record holder off the track.

"I use to call him the 'rubber man,' " Alley says. "He'd walk down to the field house, and you'd think he'd fall apart. If he came across the street, you'd want to help him across.

"But you put him in a set of starting blocks and shoot a gun, and he was just fluid motion. It was unbelievable. He was a neat guy."

Billy Mills, another teammate and Olympic gold medalist, recalls another hurdler on the team getting upset whenever he was put in a heat with Tidwell. The other hurdler wasn't worried about losing, Mills says; rather, he just wanted to watch Tidwell run.

"There was a man who was one of the great, great sprinters of all time," Mills says of Tidwell. "He was a very gentle man, and he was a person of great humility."

***

Here's where the happy ending would go, but there isn't one. Tidwell was injured shortly before the 1960 U.S. Olympic Trials, and his injury prevented him from making the U.S. team. Unlike former KU shot-putter Bill Nieder, who was able to compete after missing the cut at the Trials and literally threw himself onto the team, no provision existed to enable an injured athlete to try out for the team a second time once the injury healed.

So, Tidwell didn't go to the Rome Games, and he missed out on a once-in-a-lifetime chance to become a household name.

"He truly never, never had the opportunity to blossom," Mills said. "He was a great athlete, far greater than any others on the American team."

The United States did not win the 100- or 200-meter dashes in 1960, events in which Tidwell would have competed, but Lee Calhoun successfully defended his gold medal in the 110-meter hurdles.

In 1962, Tidwell signed a contract with the Minnesota Vikings, but he never played in an NFL game. He and his wife, Karen, whom he met at KU, moved to Denver. They had two children, and Charlie worked in the production control department for Honeywell Inc. In 1969, the couple separated, and Karen Tidwell filed for divorce.

On Aug. 28, 1969, Charlie Tidwell visited his estranged wife at her home. They argued. She ran. He chased her to a neighbor's house. He forced her into the neighbor's basement, where he shot her three times, killing her. He then turned the gun on himself.

One family member said afterward how shocked they were from the tragedy.

"You just never would believe that he could do anything like that," the family member said.

No one can. Not then, and not 30 years later.

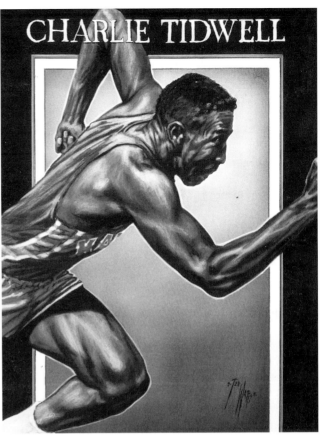

CHARLIE TIDWELL
Track and field,
1958-60

THE SIXTIES
Transition and Triumph

From 1962 to 1964, Gale Sayers (#48) galloped for 2,675 yards, scored 20 touchdowns and was named All-America twice. "The Kansas Comet" then made All-Pro five times in seven seasons with the Chicago Bears. The NFL named him to its 75th Anniversary All-Pro team.

"I DARE YOU!"

Defeat inspired Olympic hurdler to challenge youth

"To watch him perform was to admire him. To compete against him was to learn from him. To know him was to love him."

That's how former University of Kansas distance runner and Olympic gold medalist Billy Mills remembers his track and field teammate, Cliff Cushman. Mills speaks quietly and reverently about Cushman. The above quote, Mills explains, was first used to describe Frank Mt. Pleasant, a supreme Indian athlete and Olympic high jumper and long jumper.

Mills, also a Native American, pauses after recalling Mt. Pleasant and comparing him with his friend.

"That's Cliff Cushman," he says.

Cushman came to Kansas from Grand Forks, N.D., where he won state high school track titles in the long jump, high hurdles and the mile. As a freshman at KU, he competed unattached at the Kansas Relays (freshmen were ineligible to compete at the varsity level) and won the event that became his specialty, the 400-meter hurdles, in a meet-record 51.9 seconds. That race marked his first competitive effort in the event. He also set the Big Seven Conference freshman half-mile record with a time of 1 minute, 54.6 seconds.

As a junior in 1959, Cushman finished second in the 400 hurdles as Kansas won its first NCAA outdoor track and field championship. By then, Mills and Cushman had developed a strong friendship. Mills enjoyed different sides of Cushman's personality.

"Cliff was a very spiritual person," he says. "I think he had incredible, explicit integrity. He also could be a real prankster, a real jokester."

In 1960, Cliff Cushman won an NCAA championship and a silver medal in the Olympics at Rome.

Such as the time when the team found itself in a downpour during a six-mile practice run. During these runs, Mills says, different runners would take the lead and set the pace for the rest of the team. Cushman often pulled some stunt to throw his teammates off in these conditions.

"You could count on Cliff, when he took the lead, he's going to go and sit down (on a curb) and he's going to be up in his armpits in the flowing water," Mills says. "And it's follow the leader; whether or not we wanted to follow and sit down in the flowing water was our choice. Most of the time people didn't, but it was up to Cliff to come up with some concept that was going to break up the monotony of the run."

Cushman's watershed year occurred in 1960: Captain of the Jayhawks' team. Most outstanding performer at the Kansas Relays. National champion in the 400 hurdles, a triumph that helped the Jayhawks successfully defend their NCAA outdoor championship. Olympian.

In the 1960 Olympics at Rome, Cushman kept a flawless 13-step pace and moved to fourth place through the ninth hurdle. At the finish line, he leaned so far forward that he skidded across the track and into second place with a time of 49.6 seconds. His time was just 0.3 seconds behind U.S. teammate Glenn Davis.

**CLIFF CUSHMAN
Track and field,
1958-60**

Mills and Cushman roomed together for a semester after the Olympics. When Cushman left for class ahead of Mills in the morning, Mills occasionally entered Cushman's closet, rubbed the sleeve of Cushman's Olympic uniform and thought to himself, "This guy is the greatest athlete that I know."

The next year, Cushman joined the U.S. Air Force. His training consisted of jet-fighter courses in Alabama and running hurdles, as he sought to return to the 1964 Summer Games in Tokyo.

He entered the 1964 U.S. Olympic Trials as a prohibitive favorite in the 400 hurdles. But he tripped over the fifth hurdle and his Olympic quest ended as he sprawled out on the cinders on the Los Angeles track. His fall prompted an outpouring of public sympathy. Rather than feel sorry for himself, Cushman expressed his thoughts on competition and achievement in his famous "Open Letter to Youth," which has been reprinted many times since 1964 and appears at the end of this story.

Time moved on for Cushman. His wife, Carolyn, gave birth to their only child on Nov. 21, 1965. The new mom and baby came home a few days later on Thanksgiving, the same day Cushman received orders for Vietnam. On Sept. 25, 1966, Carolyn Cushman returned home from church to find Air Force officials waiting for her. They notified her that her husband's plane had been shot down and he was missing in action. Cliff Cushman never was found, and he was listed as dead in 1975.

Later during the war, Carolyn Cushman moved to Omaha, Neb., where she directed the Forgotten Americans Committee and coordinated the National League of Families of American Prisoners in Southeast Asia. In a 1970 interview, she discussed the many speeches she had given in the Omaha area.

"I want people to know about Cliff and the other men and to help," she said. "I can't make 1,600 men real, but I can make one man real."

Through his wife's work and his timeless letter, Cushman's memory remains quite real. The letter serves as a lasting legacy of an athlete and competitor whom Mills described as a "very, very gentle person and a very loyal friend."

AN OPEN LETTER TO YOUTH

"Don't feel sorry for me. I feel sorry for some of you! You may have seen the U.S. Olympic Trials on television Sept. 13. If so, you watched me hit the fifth hurdle, fall and lie on the track in an inglorious heap of skinned elbows, bruised hips, torn knees, and injured pride, unsuccessful in my attempt to make the Olympic team for the second time. In a split second all the many years of training, pain, sweat, blisters and agony of running were simply and irrevocably wiped out. But I tried! I would much rather fail knowing I had put forth an honest effort than never to have tried at all.

"This is not to say that everyone is capable of making the Olympic Team. However, each of you is capable of trying to make your own personal "Olympic Team," whether it be the high school football team, the glee club, the honor roll, or whatever your goal may be. Unless your reach exceeds your grasp, how can you be sure what you can attain? And don't you think there are things better than cigarettes, hot-rod cars, school dropouts, excessive make-up and duck-tail grease-cuts?

"Over 15 years ago I saw a star — first place in the Olympic Games. I literally started to run after it. In 1960 I came within three yards of grabbing it; this year I stumbled, fell and watched it recede four more years away. Certainly, I was very disappointed in falling flat on my face. However, there is nothing I can do about it now but get up, pick the cinders from my wounds, and take one more step followed by one more and one more, until the steps turn into miles and the miles into success.

"I know I may never make it. The odds are against me, but I have something in my favor — desire and faith. Romans 5:3-5 has always had an inspirational meaning to me in this regard. " ... we rejoice in our sufferings, knowing that suffering produces endurance, and endurance produces character, and character produces hope, and hope does not disappoint us ..." At least I am going to try.

"How about you? Would a little extra effort on your part bring up your grade average? Would you have a better chance to make the football team if you stayed an extra 15 minutes after practice and worked on your blocking?

"Let me tell you something about yourselves. You are taller and heavier than any past generation in this country. You are spending more money, enjoying more freedom and driving more cars than ever before, yet many of you are very unhappy. Some of you have never known the satisfaction of doing your best in sports, the joy of excelling in class, the wonderful feeling of completing a job, any job, and looking back on it knowing that you have done your best.

"I dare you to have your hair cut and not wilt under the comments of your so-called friends. I dare you to clean up your language. I dare you to honor your mother and father. I dare you to go to church without having to be compelled to go by your parents. I dare you to unselfishly help someone less fortunate than yourself and enjoy the wonderful feeling that goes with it. I dare you to become physically fit. I dare you to read a book that is not required in school. I dare you to look up at the stars, not down at the mud, and set your sights on one of them that, up to now, you thought was unattainable. There is plenty of room at the top, but no room for anyone to sit down.

"Who knows? You may be surprised at what you can achieve with sincere effort. So get up, pick the cinders out of your wounds and take one more step.

"I dare you!"

Sincerely,

Clifton E. Cushman

BORN TO BOARD
Undersized center had a knack for rebounding

"...when the rebounds went up, he usually was the only person left standing."

– Monte Johnson

Dick Harp had no idea what he was doing when he and a black man went out for dinner in Hobbs, N.M., about 40 years ago.

"Chuck Mather (KU's football coach in 1954-57) had gone to a coaching clinic down there," Harp says. "He told Jerry (Waugh, Harp's assistant men's basketball coach) kind of offhand that he saw a really good basketball player and that we better get off our butts because he was going to go to Kansas State."

That player, Bill Bridges, played for one of the nation's most renowned high school coaches, Ralph Tasker.

"I asked Ralph Tasker if (Bridges') father would be willing to get together for a meal before visiting with Bill," Harp says. "So I flew down there, and his dad and I went to a real nice restaurant. So we were sitting there, and he began to chuckle, and he said, 'You sure don't know what you're doing. Blacks aren't permitted in this restaurant, but here you and I are sitting together.' That might have helped us get him."

Whatever the reason, Bridges attended Kansas, even without a scholarship at first. He waited tables during his freshman year to help make ends meet.

Harp had never watched Bridges play before the latter stepped on campus. His first impression didn't exactly leave Harp awestruck.

"When he came, I watched him before formal practices were going on," Harp says. "I thought, 'My goodness, is that the person we recruited?' But every once in a while, the ball would bounce off the rim, and he would go get it – every time."

With that, Harp for the first time saw perhaps the greatest pure rebounder in the history of Kansas basketball.

A 6-foot-5-inch, 235-pound block of concrete, Bridges claimed KU's center spot in 1958-59 after Wilt Chamberlain joined the Harlem Globetrotters. Still honing raw offensive skills, he nevertheless pronounced his presence.

"The year before, looking at somebody 7-1, then looking at somebody 6-5, it changed the game dramatically," says Bob Billings, a senior guard for the Jayhawks in 1958-59. "But (Bridges) was an awfully good athlete, and he worked hard. He had bad knees all the time; he had to have fluid drained off his knees quite often. He played through pain.

"He was a good jumper, but he had bulk. He had a sense where the ball was going to come off the rim. I don't think there has ever been a rebounder his size as good as he was at any level."

Billings gets no argument from Monte Johnson, a backup center who often battled the quiet, unassuming Bridges in practice.

"He beat me like a drum," Johnson says. "He was one strong person in the middle. He was as easy-going of a person as you could get, but when the rebounds went up, he usually was the only person left standing."

The Jayhawks, playing a tough schedule designed for Chamberlain, finished 11-14 during Bridges' first year. Had Chamberlain stayed for his senior season, Bridges would have played power forward. Billings still contemplates that appealing prospect.

"If Wilt had been here, and Bill could have played forward, that would have been an awesome group," he says.

A year later, Bridges and high-scoring forward Wayne Hightower led Kansas to a share of the Big Eight Conference title. The Jayhawks finished 19-9 and fell a game short of the Final Four, losing to Cincinnati 82-71 in the Midwest Regional final in Manhattan. In that game, future basketball Hall-of-Famer Oscar Robertson scored 43 points for the Bearcats.

In Bridges' senior season, Kansas fell to second in the conference behind Tex Winter's Kansas State squad. But he made all-conference for the third straight season and earned All-America honors.

In three seasons on the Kansas varsity, Bridges averaged 13.7, 13.8 and 14.1 rebounds per game, respectively. Three times he had 24 rebounds or more in one game, including a career-high 30 in the opening game of his junior season against Northwestern. His career average of 13.9 per game is second only at KU to Chamberlain's 18.3 average.

He also averaged 13.2 points per game during his career, becoming the first player in conference history to score 1,000 points and grab 1,000 rebounds.

Whereas some called Bridges a natural-born rebounder, no one ever suggested he was a fantastic shooter. But hours in the gym improved his field goal accuracy from 38.1 percent during his sophomore year to 43.7 percent his senior season. During that time, his free-throw shooting also improved, from 57.4 percent to 71 percent.

"When he came here, he didn't have a lot of skills," Waugh says. "He was a strong kid, very dedicated. He polished those skills. He started from nowhere and did it all himself."

Bridges had a successful professional basketball career, starting with the Kansas City Steers of the American Basketball League. When that league folded, he joined the NBA. In 13 years with the Hawks, 76ers, Lakers and Warriors, he topped the 10,000 mark in both points and rebounds and played in three All-Star games.

After retiring from the NBA in 1975, Bridges briefly attended law school at UCLA and has worked as a business consultant in Los Angeles. Known to battle periods of depression, he recently has lost touch with KU, Waugh says. But those at Kansas who know Bridges haven't forgotten him.

"He was always a very pleasant, polite guy," he says. "There's so many people that care about him."

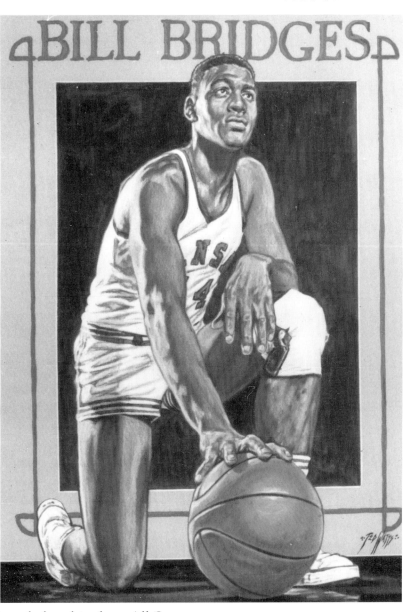

BILL BRIDGES
Basketball,
1958-61

A LASTING FRIENDSHIP

Javelin throwers did everything together, including making the Olympics

Even though Billy Mills ran cross country and track for the University of Kansas, he says he learned a lot from watching Bill Alley and Terry Beucher practice throwing the javelin.

"They were putting in so many hours of work, hours that I was not putting in," Mills says. "I was very thrilled when Al Oerter, Cliff Cushman, Bill Alley and Terry Beucher made the (U.S.) Olympic team in 1960. Here were ordinary people doing extraordinary things.

"I realized I could do this, too. But I realized to be an Olympian, I would have to put in many, many more hours."

Mills, who won an Olympic gold medal in the 10,000-meter run four years later in Tokyo, picked some excellent role models. Oerter won the second of his four gold medals in the discus at Rome in 1960. Cushman lunged to a silver medal in the 400-meter hurdles. And although neither Alley nor Beucher qualified for the finals competition, their work ethic merited Mills' admiration.

Alley grew up in Short Hills, N.J., the son of a self-made landscape architect. His father extolled him to aim high – and far – with sayings such as, "If what you did yesterday seems great, you haven't done much today."

Bill took that lesson to heart and headed off to Syracuse University. But something didn't sit quite right for him there, so he transferred to Kansas.

"I wanted a better education, and I wanted to be part of a good program," Alley says.

He sat out two seasons before he competed for the Jayhawks. He missed the 1957 season because of an arm operation to remove bone chips. Then he relocated to Kansas, which cost him the 1958 season as a transfer student. Competing unattached that year, Alley won seven meets with throws ranging from 229 feet to 246 feet.

By 1959, Alley was rarin' to throw. The Kansas track and field media guide heralded him as the "finest javelin prospect in Kansas history." He quickly lived up to that billing. At an early season meet in Abilene, Texas, he sailed a wind-aided toss of 258 feet, 4 inches, setting an unofficial U.S. record.

A week later at the Texas Relays, Alley wowed the crowd with a throw of 270 feet, 1 inch, which set a U.S. record by 1 inch. The throw also smashed the collegiate record by 13 feet and the Texas Relays record by almost 18 feet.

Alley dominated competition that spring. He won eight other meets and set six meet records with throws ranging from 249 feet to 266 feet. With his sore elbow heavily wrapped to prevent full extension due to continuing bone chip problems, Alley still won the Big Eight Conference championship with a throw of 256 feet, 10 inches.

In June, he captured the NCAA outdoor championship with a sub-par toss of 240 feet, 5 inches.

"That actually was a very painful time with my arm," he says. "I really was on a high roll, things were going well and my distances were getting better. But I had a lot of problems with my elbow, and it got more painful to throw."

More importantly to Alley, the Jayhawks won their first national title at the 1959 NCAA Outdoor Championships. He says he knew the team counted on him to win the javelin, and he encouraged his teammates to do their best in their events.

"It was very exciting. It was a lot of team building, stimulating your teammates, getting them in the right temperament and getting them to relax."

– Bill Alley on KU winning its second straight NCAA Outdoor Championship in 1960

"That's part of the camaraderie that gets built around championship teams," Alley says. "That's the whole thing about the University of Kansas."

***

Besides his track success, the 6-foot-3-inch, 217-pound Alley made quite a name for himself with some unusual training methods. For example, he threw golf balls in the summer, drove spikes into trees with a light sledge hammer, tossed a 12-pound shot with a javelin throwing motion and worked out on a homemade pulley. He also made many of his javelins in a home workshop.

Alley had plenty of time for these exploits in the summer of '59 because he stayed out of competition to rest and treat his arm. He returned in fine form, and 1960 offered more of the same success for Alley and the Jayhawks.

He repeated as a record-setting winner in the Texas-Kansas-Drake grand slam on the Midwest relay circuit. He won the conference championship. At the Meet of Champions a week before the NCAA Outdoor Championships, Alley unleashed a personal-best throw of 273 feet, 10 inches, which also topped the collegiate record.

Then, in Berkeley, Calif., Alley retained his NCAA championship with a toss of 268-9, and the Jayhawks repeated as champions.

"It was very exciting," Alley says of the team championship. "We said, 'Hey, we can put this thing together if we all get together.' It was a lot of team building, stimulating your teammates, getting them in the right temperament and getting them to relax.

"This was a big thing, and a lot of guys get uptight. I thought it was an obligation of those of us who had the experience to help the others relax. And they performed better than they ever had."

BILL ALLEY
Track and field,
1959-60

TERRY BEUCHER
Track and field,
1958-60

Alley placed second at the U.S. Olympic Trials behind Al Cantello. Beucher finished third and joined Alley on the team. Before heading to Rome, Alley gave a monster performance in West Chester, Pa., with five throws exceeding 270 feet and one that sailed 283-8. The last toss was not counted as a world record, however, because of too much ground slope.

Regardless, everything seemed in sync for Rome.

It wasn't. Alley only could manage 221 feet during the Olympics and failed to qualify for the finals, which USSR's Viktor Tsibulenko won. Two weeks after the Olympics, which Alley does not like to discuss, he outdistanced Tsibulenko by 30 feet.

But Alley's achievements far outnumbered his failures. He credits his coach, Bill Easton, and the KU program for his athletic success.

"They gave me all the tools and everything I needed to develop my skills," he says. "(Easton) provided the correct environment, the stimulation, the peers. It just provided me the opportunity to expand on helping me become what I wanted to do, which was be the best in my event."

Alley also sees the parallels between athletic and personal success.

"It was an important part of my building of myself," he says. "It gave me a lot of self-confidence that I carried on through my life and my business career. It gave me the inner feeling to know that if I worked hard enough, I could achieve my objectives and goals."

Today, Alley owns Research Engineering in Morrisville, Vt. The company is involved in product development, architectural construction and robotics for process automation.

**

When Billy Mills thinks back to 1960, he sees Alley and Beucher doing everything together.

"Terry Beucher was Bill Alley's shadow," Mills says, intending his remark as a compliment to both men.

Alley agrees, and he praises Beucher for his hard-working approach to track and field.

"Terry was determined to become good at what he was," Alley says. "He pulled off a third at the (1960) NCAAs and also made the Olympic team. That was a high moment in his life.

"Terry was totally relaxed in the competition and everyone else was tighter than drums. And he was able to do things to the best of his ability."

Beucher graduated from Kansas in 1960. He went from the ROTC program at KU into the U.S. Air Force, and he later won several javelin competitions at military meets.

After the Air Force, Beucher flew as a pilot with Trans World Airlines for 12 years. He also became a lieutenant colonel in the Air Force Reserves and served as commander of the 41st Aerial Port Squadron at Richards-Gebaur Air Force Base in Belton, Mo.

Beucher later worked in quality assurance as an air traffic assistant for the Federal Aviation Administration at the Kansas City Air Route Traffic Control Center in Olathe. He also was serving his fourth term on the Parkville (Mo.) Board of Aldermen when he died of a heart attack Dec. 16, 1984. He was 47.

"He was a neat guy," Alley says. "We had a lot of fun together. We did a lot of things together. After he graduated from KU, we did spend time together and saw each other frequently.

"With your teammates, you spend time with them, you live with them, you share all the experiences with them, the highs and the lows."

And, sadly, even parting at a young age.

JOHNNY VERSATILITY

Hometown hero opened college career with a blast, led KU to its first bowl victory

Lawrence native John Hadl proved an elusive figure on the football field. He almost eluded the University of Kansas as well.

After his senior season at Lawrence High School in 1957, Hadl was leaning heavily toward taking his considerable athletic skills to the University of Oklahoma, coached by the legendary Bud Wilkinson.

"The only reason I was thinking about Oklahoma was because at the time, they had a coaching staff up here (Kansas) that wasn't doing that good," Hadl says.

Enter Jack Mitchell. The newly named Kansas coach made landing Hadl his No. 1 recruiting mission. When it came to recruiting, Mitchell was a master.

"I think basically what he talked about the most was the idea of being from Kansas, being a local player, in the long-term of having graduated from KU, it would be a big advantage," Hadl says. "It's worked out exactly that way, and down deep inside I probably knew it."

Things did work out for Hadl, starting with his first varsity game in 1959. Shortly before halftime against Texas Christian University, Hadl, playing defensive half-back, stepped in front of a short pass near the Kansas goal line and galloped 98 yards for a touchdown. The play marked the longest interception return in school history.

"He probably was one of the best defensive backs we ever had," Mitchell says. "He was a tremendous defensive player."

Hadl was no slouch on kickoff returns, either. The next week, in his second college game, Hadl broke a 97-yard kickoff return for a touchdown against Syracuse. The play stood as a Kansas record until Charles "June" Henley returned a kickoff 100 yards in 1993.

None of Hadl's plays broke the 90-yard mark in his third game, but he was the middle man on a pass-and-lateral play that went for a 49-yard score for Curtis McClinton. Hadl, playing left halfback, later scored on a 14-yard run in the Jayhawks' first victory of the season, a 28-7 decision against Boston University.

All Hadl did in his fourth game was throw a touchdown pass on a fourth-down, double-reverse from the 8-yard line, leading the Jayhawks past Nebraska 10-3. Against Kansas State a week later, he passed an 11-yard touchdown to McClinton, caught a 71-yard touchdown pass and later lateraled to McClinton for another score. Kansas won 33-14.

Hadl used his foot as a weapon in a 7-6 loss against Oklahoma. He kept the Sooners pinned in their territory on eight punts for a 51-yard average. His kicking spree included a 94-yard effort, which remains a school record. Hadl led the nation in

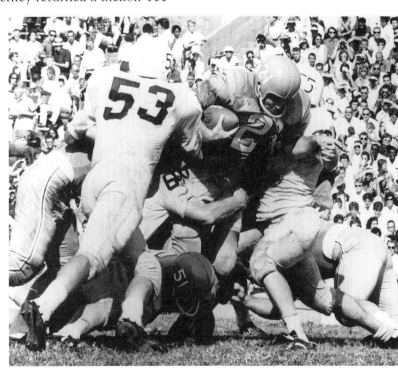

John Hadl (with ball) earned All-America honors at two different positions – halfback and quarterback.

punting that season with a 45.6-yard average, second-highest in KU history.

For the season, Hadl led the Jayhawks in scoring with eight touchdowns. He rushed for 348 yards, averaging 5.1 yards per carry. He also returned kickoffs for an average of 29.6 yards. He was named All-Big Eight Conference at halfback.

Mitchell faced a pleasant problem in the spring of 1960. He had McClinton at one halfback spot and transfer Bert Coan at the other. What about Hadl?

"I thought about him being quarterback from the time I coached him when he got on the varsity," Mitchell says. "But you can't put a guy at quarterback without spring practice that's never been a quarterback. You just don't make a move like that."

So spring practice that year offered Mitchell the opportunity to make a switch. He approached Hadl about moving to quarterback.

"We had the option offense, he had a great throwing arm, he was a great runner and I talked to him about it," Mitchell says. "He said, yes, he would like it."

As Hadl recalls, the team had Curtis McClinton, 6 feet 2 inches and 230 pounds, who ran the 100-yard dash in 9.8 seconds and Bert Coan, 6-3 and 220 pounds, who had 9.6-second speed in the 100.

"I could see that I couldn't outrun either one of those guys," Hadl says. "The position was open and I volunteered to move. In those days, the quarterback position was just another running back, really, because it was options. We threw the ball probably seven or eight times a game."

Hadl stepped right in and performed well. In the '60 season opener, he deftly guided the Jayhawks in a 21-7 upset against TCU. He turned a quarterback sneak into a 52-yard run for the first touchdown of the day and later scored on an 11-yard rollout for the clincher.

JOHN HADL
Football,
1959-61
Assistant football coach,
1978-81, 1988-89
Assistant athletics director,
1990-92
Associate athletics director,
1992 -

Kansas faced three No. 1 teams in 1960 and went 1-2 in those contests. Syracuse rallied to defeat the Jayhawks 14-7 in Lawrence. Four weeks later, the Iowa Hawkeyes stifled KU 21-7 in Iowa City. And in the season finale, Hadl directed a stunning 23-7 upset against Missouri in Columbia.

The Jayhawks went 7-2-1 on the field that season and won their first conference championship since 1930. However, the conference forced Kansas to forfeit victories against Colorado and Missouri based on questions regarding Coan's eligibility.

Hadl earned all-conference honors at quarterback with 566 passing yards and 375 rushing yards. Oddly, the Football Writers Association of America named him All-America – at halfback. Mitchell says that he occasionally inserted Hadl at halfback during his junior and senior years, but that he predominantly played quarterback those two seasons.

Kansas started slowly in 1961, Hadl's senior season. The Jayhawks dropped one-point losses against TCU and Colorado and tied Wyoming. KU finally won against Iowa State, as Hadl engineered scoring drives of 60 and 58 yards in the fourth quarter of a 21-7 victory.

In a 10-0 triumph against Oklahoma, Hadl provided the only touchdown on a 30-

yard pass to Larry Allen. The next week, Hadl passed for two touchdowns and ran for another as Kansas buried Oklahoma State 42-8. The Jayhawks' fourth straight victory occurred the following week as the Jayhawks beat Nebraska 28-6. Hadl ran for one touchdown and threw for another in that victory.

A 44-yard scoring pass from Hadl to McClinton highlighted KU's 34-0 defeat of Kansas State. The Jayhawks pounded California 53-7 for their sixth straight victory. Missouri then ended KU's regular season on a down note as the Tigers edged the Jayhawks 10-7. But at 6-3-1, Kansas was invited to the Bluebonnet Bowl in Houston to take on hometown Rice University.

Hadl earned all-conference and All-America honors at quarterback, passing for 665 yards and rushing for 293. In the bowl game, Hadl's 41-yard breakaway run set up a Ken Coleman touchdown that broke open a tight game as the Jayhawks defeated the Owls 33-7.

After the game, Hadl signed a two-year, $35,000 contract with the San Diego Chargers under a goal post in the rain. He also received a $5,000 signing bonus and a new Ford Thunderbird for going with the upstart American Football League instead of the NFL's Detroit Lions.

"He was probably one of the finest athletes that ever went to the University," Mitchell says. "He could kick, he could throw, he could run. He was a smart player, and he was a dedicated boy. And he was one of the most popular – every place he went he was elected captain."

The Jayhawks went 14-5-2 with Hadl at quarterback, and he led them to their first bowl victory.

"It was just a group of guys in that freshman class who were good players as a whole, and they were all still there," Hadl says. "We didn't lose too many people, which tells you that it was good character, good students and all the things that maintain a four-year period."

Before joining the Chargers, Hadl played in the East-West Shrine game and the College All-Star game, earning most valuable player honors in both contests, the only player ever to accomplish that feat. Kansas retired his No. 21.

Hadl enjoyed a 16-year career in the AFL and NFL. He played for the Chargers from 1962 to 1972 and led the team to the AFL championship in 1963. The Chargers were runners-up in 1964 and 1965. He led the AFL in passing in 1965 with 2,798 yards and 20 touchdowns.

In 1973, he joined the Los Angeles Rams and was named Player of the Year in the National Football Conference. He played another season with the Rams then moved to Green Bay for a year. He retired in 1977 after a two-year stint in Houston. Hadl passed for 33,513 yards in his professional career.

While in San Diego, Hadl was recognized as the NFL "Man of the Year" in 1971. His charity golf tournament there provides a nearby Indian reservation with a mobile dental unit. The program still exists today.

After his pro career ended, Hadl served as an assistant coach at KU to Bud Moore and was Don Fambrough's offensive coordinator in 1979-81. He moved to the pros in 1982 as the quarterback coach for the Los Angeles Rams and later worked as receiver-quarterback coach with the Denver Broncos.

He had his only head coaching job with the Los Angeles Express of the United States Football League in 1984-85 before the league folded. He later returned to KU, where he coached receivers for head coach Glen Mason for two years.

In 1992, Hadl was promoted from KU's assistant athletics director to associate athletics director. He is executive director of the Williams Educational Fund, which oversees the fundraising program for KU athletics. He was elected to the College Football Hall of Fame in 1994.

Hadl considers the University as one of the loves of his life.

"I just love the University and all the people that are involved," he says. "It's fun to come to work everyday. It's happened just like Jack Mitchell said it would happen."

"He was probably one of the finest athletes that ever went to the University. He could kick, he could throw, he could run."

– Jack Mitchell
on John Hadl

THE KANSAS COMET
Star running back succeeded
on and off the field

"He was a great football player, there was no question about that. He had great legs, tremendous speed and he was tough. Sayers was tougher than hell."

– Jack Mitchell

Gale Sayers always looked ahead.

How else can you explain the cuts he made as a ball carrier, leaving defenders grabbing for air and eating his dust?

"He would dig a divot in the turf a foot long and two or three inches deep," says Jack Mitchell, former University of Kansas football coach. "He put so much power on a ninety-degree cut. And he cut on his heels ... at practically top speed."

But more importantly, how else can you explain that Sayers possessed an equally rare commodity, the ability to know football wouldn't last forever (in his case as a professional, less than seven seasons) and that he must use today to plan for tomorrow?

"As you prepare to play, you have to prepare to quit," Sayers says.

Gale Sayers always was prepared.

The Sayers mystique started with his first KU varsity game in 1962. Against Texas Christian, the Omaha, Neb. native rushed a school-record 27 times and gained 114 yards in a 6-3 loss. The Jayhawks won three of their next four games, and Sayers rushed for 112 yards on just 14 carries against Colorado.

Then came the Oklahoma State game on Oct. 27, 1962. The Cowboys led 17-7 at halftime before Sayers and teammates took over the contest. The Jayhawks scored on four of five second-half possessions, including a 96-yard touchdown run by Sayers that made the final score 36-17 in favor of Kansas. For the day, Sayers amassed a then-Big Eight Conference record 283 yards on 22 carries. His 12.9 yards-per-carry average in the game remains a school record.

For the season, Sayers rushed for 1,125 yards on 158 carries, an average of 7.1 yards per carry, a Jayhawks' season record. He recorded five 100-yard games.

As a junior in 1963, Sayers' production dropped to 917 rushing yards and four 100-yard games. But the season offered many exciting runs by Sayers, including a 99-yard touchdown run against Nebraska. Besides the distance, what made the run special was that Sayers performed it in Lincoln, on the soil of his native state.

Mitchell had recruited Sayers away from Nebraska, and the home-state fans didn't forget. The week after the game, Sayers received numerous letters with Nebraska postmarks that decried his disloyalty to the state. Sayers earned All-America honors in 1963.

Despite further statistical slippage, Sayers again received All-America notice as a senior in 1964. That year, he gained 633 yards and provided just two games with more than 100 yards rushing.

But his senior year did offer some high moments. For example, Sayers returned the opening kickoff against Oklahoma 96 yards for a touchdown. Kansas scored on the first and last plays of the game, pulling off a 15-14 upset.

"Give him an inch, and he will take a touchdown," said Gomer Jones, Oklahoma's coach.

During his KU career, Sayers gained 2,675 rushing yards, fourth-highest in school history. He scored 20 touchdowns and led the team in scoring and kickoff returns all three years. As a junior and senior, he led the team in receiving and punt returns. He ranks third at KU with 3,917 all-purpose yards. He was named

Sayers planned for a career after football long before his knee injuries. He became a licensed stockbroker with Paine, Webber, Jackson & Curtis in Chicago in 1966 and wrote his autobiography, "I Am Third," in 1969. He developed the title from a sign that hung in former KU track coach Bill Easton's office that read, "God is first, my friends are second, and I am third."

In 1972, Sayers returned to Kansas as an assistant to the athletics director and later became assistant director of the Williams Educational Fund. He left KU in 1976 to become athletics director at Southern Illinois, a job he had until 1981, when he left to enter private business.

Sayers prefers to talk about himself as a businessman, not a former All-American or All-Pro. He earned two degrees from the University, a bachelor's degree in physical education and a master's degree in education administration.

"My education enabled me to put a different light on Gale Sayers," he says. "I proved that I could be a student and had the smarts to be a success."

His diligent preparation for a business career stems from his athletics experiences.

"I kept doing things to (plan to) retire," he says. "It is very, very difficult to be an entrepreneur. From athletics, I learned about hard work and dedication, and this helped prepare me for owning my own business."

Today, Sayers owns Sayers Computer Source, a service company that distributes hardware and software, performs systems integration and conducts video teleconferencing. The company is based in Mount Prospect, Ill., with offices in Scottsdale, Ariz., and Livermore, Calif.

Gale Sayers' rare combination of speed, power and elusiveness is unparalleled in Kansas football history.

GENERAL JACK
Coach brought KU football back to prominence

Three games into his football coaching career at the University of Kansas, Jack Mitchell knew the Jayhawks were in trouble.

Kansas lost its first three games in 1958 by a combined score of 85-0. Worse, the team didn't seem to care. As sports columnist Bob Hentzen reported in the *Topeka Capital-Journal* in 1966:

"They were laughing and joking about it," Mitchell said at the time. *"They were rushing out of the dressing room to get back to the fraternity houses and their dates."*

Mitchell had seen and heard enough. After the third game, he lit into his players, as Hentzen noted:

"You're nothing," he roared. "A big, fat nothing. You get up in the morning and look in the mirror, and what do you see … nothing, a big, fat nothing. You know what you are? You're a nit. You know what a nit is? A nit is a flea on a gnat. That's the lowest thing there is.

"I'm sick of you, completely sick. We are going to be coaching here for a long time and we're going to have good football teams. You can be remembered as the last of the nits or you can be remembered as the first of the good players."

The players met on their own the next day. Monday they asked for more and rougher scrimmages and more wind sprints. Winning four and tying one of the last seven games, they were indeed the first of the good players.

Good players and good teams served as the hallmarks of Mitchell's nine-year tenure at Kansas in 1958-66. Two-time All-Americans John Hadl and Gale Sayers played for Mitchell's best teams in a six-year span from 1959 to 1964. Those teams won a combined 36 games, lost 22 and tied 3.

Mitchell's best team, the 1960 squad, went 7-2-1 on the field and won the Big Eight Conference title. But the conference forced KU to forfeit two victories, and with them, the league championship. The conference based its ruling on an eligibility dispute involving halfback Bert Coan. The 1961 team finished 7-3-1 and won the Bluebonnet Bowl, KU's first bowl victory.

The Jayhawks' fortunes slid in 1965 and 1966. Kansas won only two games in each season. Mitchell admits that outside business interests consumed more of his time during those years, and it showed on the field. However, he did recruit the nucleus of the 1968 team, including All-Americans Bobby Douglass and John Zook, that shared the conference championship and appeared in the Orange Bowl.

In total, the Jayhawks went 44-42-5 during Mitchell's tenure. Only Glen Mason equaled Mitchell's longevity, and no coach since "General Jack" has left Mount Oread with a winning record.

***

Mitchell grew up playing football in Arkansas City with the Jayhawks on his mind. "I wanted to go to KU," he says. "That's where I always dreamed I would go."

However, Kansas didn't give full-ride football scholarships, but the University of Texas did, including room and board. So, in 1942, Mitchell departed for Austin, Texas. But he didn't stay there long.

"He charmed the porcelain right off your teeth. It was just natural."

– Floyd Temple on Jack Mitchell

After one semester at Texas in the fall of 1942, Mitchell left for World War II. As a lieutenant in the U.S. Army, Mitchell served as a platoon leader in England, France and Germany for about two years.

When he returned from active duty, Mitchell sought a university closer to home. Jim Tatum, the new coach at the University of Oklahoma, sold Mitchell on joining the Sooners. He played for Tatum in 1946 before the coach moved to Maryland, and then he played quarterback on Bud Wilkinson's first two Oklahoma teams in 1947 and 1948.

As a Sooner, Mitchell learned the quarterback-option offense from Tatum and Wilkinson. The two OU coaches had learned the offense themselves as assistants to Don Faurot, the father of the quarterback option at Missouri who guided the highly successful Iowa Pre-Flight teams during World War II. As KU coach, Mitchell enjoyed success with the quarterback option, especially in the John Hadl years.

The Hadl years, 1959-61, provided Mitchell with his best teams at Kansas. The 1960 season entailed a series of ups and downs for the program. In October, the NCAA put the Jayhawks on a one-year probation, which included a ban on postseason play.

The problem stemmed from an August 1959 trip that halfback Bert Coan took to the College All-Star Game in Chicago as the guest of Bud Adams, a KU alumnus. At the time, Coan was transferring from Texas Christian, and the NCAA ruled that Adams' trip was an illegal recruiting inducement, a charge that Coan, Adams, Mitchell and the University denied.

The bowl ban was critical because the Jayhawks were in the midst of their best season in years. Kansas finished 7-2-1, capping off the year with a 23-7 upset against No. 1-ranked Missouri in Columbia. The victory clinched a conference championship for the Jayhawks, their first since 1930. KU would have played in the Orange Bowl after that season except for the NCAA's bowl ban.

A few weeks after the season ended, the conference voted 5-3 that Kansas forfeit its victories against Colorado and Missouri because Coan played in those games. Sports editor Earl Morey of the *Lawrence Journal-World* reported on the decision, which was not one of the conference's finest moments:

JACK MITCHELL
Head football coach,
1958-66

Apparently voting with Kansas at the meeting were Kansas State and Oklahoma State. …Previously, a 6-2 vote was required to pass a measure such as the one that involved KU. But for some unexplained reason, the faculty men at the first order of business changed their policy … to the point where only a simple majority of 5-3 was required in matters of eligibility.

It is understood that when the first vote was called, Missouri figured that Oklahoma would go against Kansas. However, OU apparently didn't do so and it was a 4-4 vote to let Kansas go home free of the charge.

But then a second vote was called for and apparently Oklahoma swung to the Missouri

"He's a very enthusiastic guy, a fun guy to be with. He worked you hard, but it was a good atmosphere on a daily basis."

– John Hadl on Jack Mitchell

side to give the necessary 5-3 vote to convict KU. The big puzzle among KU followers today was why the Big Eight allowed a second vote after KU had escaped the first time around.

"It looks as if they decided to keep voting until they got what they wanted," one man close to the KU scene declared.

Almost 40 years later, Mitchell remains unhappy with the conference ruling.

"Nobody had told us we could not play this boy in two games," he says. "There were two games that we had to forfeit, and it wasn't really necessary for this fellow, Bert Coan, to play in those games. We had to default the games, which was absolutely, completely unfair.

"The people that made the ruling wished they hadn't. They even said that later."

Still stinging from the ruling, Mitchell and the University continued about their business. In March 1961, the University awarded Mitchell with a "lifetime" contract as football coach. Actually, the contract gave the coach a type of permanent status similar to faculty with tenure. The deal called for a 10-year contract with automatic three-year renewals. Though Mitchell was set until at least 1971, he would learn that the life of this lifetime deal would last only six years.

The outgoing Mitchell was regarded as a players' coach, and so even with a half-season of probation left and the loss of its 1960 conference title, the 1961 Jayhawks enthusiastically approached the season. Mitchell sparked that enthusiasm.

"It was a lot of fun," says John Hadl about playing for Mitchell. "He's a very enthusiastic guy, a fun guy to be with. He worked you hard, but it was a good atmosphere on a daily basis. He was a great guy and he had a great staff."

The Jayhawks responded with a 6-3-1 season and earned a Bluebonnet Bowl berth against Rice. KU won the game 33-7 against the hometown team in Houston. When asked about that or other game highlights, Mitchell deflects the questions and focuses instead on his players.

"Your fondest memories are the players that excel and go on in professions and are successful, and we had a large percentage of them," he says.

All-American Gale Sayers certainly fit that description. Sayers says Mitchell helped him as an adviser.

"Jack took me aside and talked to me," Sayers says. "He told me what to do and say to reporters. I was very, very shy coming out of Omaha, and he told me to always say 'thank you' to the linemen.

"Even if I ran 50 or a 100 yards, and I did pretty much on my own, he reminded me that, 'Someone has to block for you.' He said it would come back to me to praise the players who never got any coverage."

Even with players such as Sayers, Mitchell and the Jayhawks could not surpass the success of the 1960 and 1961 teams in the years to come. Frustration started to simmer.

Blessed with central casting good looks and army officer charisma, Jack Mitchell used his brilliant football mind to lead the Jayhawks to 44 victories in nine years.

For example, the Jayhawks lost to Wyoming 17-14 early in the 1964 season. That night, about 300 students hanged Mitchell in effigy. Using his customary wit, Mitchell said, "The way I felt after the loss, if they had called me, I would have helped them."

Another problem occurred when Kansas hired Wade Stinson as athletics director in 1964 to replace A.C. "Dutch" Lonborg. Many people within the athletics department thought that Mitchell would have been ideal to replace the venerable Lonborg.

"At the time they always felt he was going to be athletics director when he finished coaching," says Monte Johnson, an assistant athletics director in the 1960s who later became KU athletics director in the 1980s. "It was promised to him by a previous chancellor. Looking back at it, he might have been one of the best because he could raise money probably better than anybody."

Baseball coach Floyd Temple, who assisted Mitchell with the football team, agrees.

"Jack Mitchell was the biggest salesman, and they made a big mistake when they didn't make him athletics director," Temple says. "I guarantee you, he'd have had that money flowing in here. He could do it all."

Temple elaborates on Mitchell's salesmanship talents.

"He charmed the porcelain right off your teeth," Temple says. "It was just natural. He would tell you stuff, and you knew damn well he was b.s.-ing you, but you *liked* it."

By 1965, Mitchell had entered different private businesses, and he admits the distractions hurt the team. He bought the *Wellington Daily News*, started an insurance company, American Investors, in Topeka and started the University State Bank in Lawrence.

Meanwhile, the Jayhawks suffered back-to-back, two-victory seasons in 1965 and 1966.

"When we had those bad seasons, they were not the result of bad players," Mitchell says. "I got involved in too many activities outside of football. I wasn't able to devote the same amount of time that I had in the past."

In December 1966, Kansas and Mitchell parted company, even though the coach had four more years left on his "lifetime," 10-year contract. The two sides agreed on a partial payoff of $11,000 per year through 1971.

Mitchell stayed in private business and never returned to coaching. Today, he splits time between Wellington and Arizona with his second wife, Peggy. His first wife, Jeanne, died of cancer in 1990. Jackson, his oldest son, runs the newspaper while Judson, his youngest son, operates the local cable TV franchise in Wellington.

WADE STINSON

ALWAYS HIS OWN MAN

Athletics director never strayed from his beliefs

Two years after a night flare nearly blew off his left hand during a military training exercise, Wade Stinson returned to Kansas to attend college. His long recuperation in an El Paso, Texas, Army hospital complete, the former six-man football star from Randall in north-central Kansas sought a good business school and a team willing to take a chance on a back with a mangled hand.

All of Stinson's immediate family and other relatives were "K-State people." Didn't matter. He chose the University of Kansas.

"A lot of them thought I was a turncoat," he says. "It didn't bother me any."

Wade Stinson always made independent, if unpopular, choices. His eight-year mission as KU athletics director displayed a large degree of conservative conformity in a tumultuous time. But his admitted inflexibility on several key issues went against the prevalent grain, inevitably leading to his resignation in November 1972.

He proudly acknowledges making his own decisions throughout a career that started with Equitable Life Assurance, where he served as district manager, and ended with United Missouri Bank, for whom he served as a vice president and later president of banks in Kansas City, Mo., Jefferson City, Mo., and St. Louis. But Stinson thinks he based every choice he ever made, especially controversial ones at Kansas, on sound reasoning and strong ethics.

That includes enrolling at Kansas in 1947. He had always planned on going to college in Manhattan, but his uncle, K-State's director of admissions, told Stinson KU had a better business school. And he told him he was too small to play college football.

Stinson took part of the advice. Equipped with a special glove that protected the three fingers and thumb that remained on his left hand after the training accident, he practiced as a freshman against KU's Orange Bowl team.

WADE STINSON

He developed slowly, but in 1950, he became the first Kansas player to rush for 1,000 yards in a season. A fifth-round draft pick by the NFL's Green Bay Packers, Stinson decided against playing professional football and instead went to work with Equitable. In 1959, the Kansas Alumni Association named him to its board of directors.

***

Five years later, Chancellor Clarke Wescoe chose Stinson as a somewhat surprising successor to A.C. "Dutch" Lonborg as KU's athletics director, a well-liked man who succeeded E.C. Quigley 14 years earlier.

"When I was hired by Clarke Wescoe, he did it himself; he made his own decision," says Stinson, now retired and living in Diamondhead, Miss. "That made a lot of alumni unhappy. A lot of people thought I would be Wescoe's hatchet man."

Most alumni thought football coach Jack Mitchell was the logical choice to replace Lonborg when he retired. In 1965, less than a year after he took the job, Stinson did nothing to warm his cool welcome by firing coach Bill Easton, who had turned KU track and field into a national power.

The controversial firing stunned alumni, but Stinson still defends his decision, pointing to the fact the man he hired to replace Easton, Bob Timmons, continued KU's strong tradition.

WADE STINSON
Football,
1948-50
Athletics director,
1964-72

"Bill had been used to kind of doing as he pleased," Stinson says. "I was a money man, making sure costs were contained, and Bill didn't care for that. I fired him after he had completely challenged me and gone completely against my instructions … the athletic end of things is a strange business. If you're going to run it right, one person has to make the decisions."

Stinson wanted to be that final decision-maker and thought his role consisted of running the day-to-day operations of the department.

"Every time I tried to raise funds, I made somebody mad," he says. "That wasn't my job. The AD has to run the athletic department. If he isn't running it, who is?"

Stinson was the only athletics director at the time who served as a full-time member of the powerful NCAA Council, the organization's top policy body. The NCAA, along with almost every aspect of the so-called establishment, endured increased scrutiny during the protest era of the late 1960s and early 1970s.

Despite that fact, not to mention various NCAA penalties KU athletics endured during his stay, Stinson steadfastly supported the organization's principles, mainly because he shared them. But he says those principles squarely placed him at odds with some influential alumni.

"That's why I left: the alumni pressure," he says. "They wanted to win any way they could, and I didn't believe in that."

But many thought Stinson also should have taken a cue from Ernie Barrett, Kansas State's athletics director at the time, and focused more attention on raising funds, especially because KU's athletics department had started losing money by the early 1970s.

Stinson, though, addressed that issue when announcing his resignation.

"We have financial problems, and in trying to solve those problems, I have encountered roadblocks at every turn," he said, without elaborating.

Monte Johnson, who served as assistant athletics director during Stinson's era and later led the department in the 1980s, says prodding alumni for financial support always made Stinson uncomfortable.

"Most people who give money don't ask for favors, they just support the program," Johnson says. "So philosophically, we might not have agreed on that. But he was a nice enough guy. Other than that, I think Wade during the time he was here made some real contributions."

He certainly did. Stinson hired Pepper Rodgers and Don Fambrough, both of whom took Kansas to bowl games. He also hired Ted Owens, who helped restore men's basketball after a few lean years in the early 1960s.

KU won the Big Eight Conference all-sports award in 1964-65, 1968-69 and 1969-70. As athletics director, Stinson also enjoyed NCAA track and field championships, KU's first conference football championship and Orange Bowl trip in 21 years and, in 1971, the basketball team's first NCAA Final Four appearance in 14 years.

But 25 years after resigning, Stinson, who says he's not at all bitter toward KU, claims his biggest accomplishment was helping Kansas sports programs succeed by "doing it right."

"I don't remember any things I would have done different," he says. "I would have liked to stay longer. I was just disappointed more people didn't stand up for integrity, honesty, and so forth.

"But I enjoyed my days as a student, and I enjoyed my days as AD. Heck, I met my wife at KU, all my kids went to KU. I have no complaints about life at all. I'm very happy."

Although some may dispute his record, few have ever disputed Stinson's integrity. A column appeared in a newspaper in Jewell County, where Stinson grew up, shortly after Wescoe hired him. It indicated how most people there regard him:

"… He has always been an intelligent, determined, honest, courageous and friendly young man … You can be certain the athletic department will be operated honestly and efficiently and that Wade will be in charge."

So he was.

The final version of Stinson's KU experiences cannot be written, though, until after his death. That's when his self-described "epistle," detailing how he viewed his time at Kansas, will be opened.

In the meantime, it sits in the University's archives.

"Every time I tried to raise funds, I made somebody mad. That wasn't my job. The AD has to run the athletic department. If he isn't running it, who is?"

– Wade Stinson

GOLDEN MOMENT

Distance runner overcame much to forge improbable Olympic victory

"I just saw the greatest race of my life. You are the greatest Jayhawker of them all."

– Bill Easton to Billy Mills after Mills won a gold medal in the 1964 Olympics

Heading into the 1964 Summer Olympics, perhaps the only people who thought Billy Mills could win the 10,000-meter race were Mills and his wife, Pat.

Mills, a former University of Kansas distance runner, certainly did believe. But it took him a moment of severe doubt to do so.

A few years earlier, as a junior at Kansas, Mills endured a world of pain. With a half-Native American, half-white ancestry, Mills felt like a person without a people. To the full-blooded Native American world he was an "Eeska" – mixed blood. To the white world, he was a Native American.

"And both worlds broke me," he told a rapt audience in April 1997 at the Kansas Union.

He was alone in a room on the 16th floor of a building when he broke. He approached a window, ready to jump and end his pain.

Then he remembered the secret his father used to tell him: "Life is a gift to you from God. What you do with your life is your gift back to God. Choose your gifts wisely."

Mills realized jumping was not the best gift he could give. He decided on a loftier one. He found a piece of paper, and on it he wrote, "Gold medal, 10,000 meters."

A few days later on campus, Mills was reading a text book in a psychology class. He was startled by what he read at one point: "The subconcious mind cannot tell the difference between reality and imagination. Your mind will respond equally to both."

That's when Mills started dreaming about winning the gold medal in the 10,000. Soon the dream became a heartfelt, hard-and-fast belief. On Oct. 14, 1964, Mills turned his private belief into reality. And all worlds within the world took notice and smiled.

Syndicated sports columnist Red Smith set the stage for the race of Mills' life:

"A dirty, rainy day of sullen skies that brightened only a little in the afternoon when showers ceased and standing water drained off the brick-red track of National Stadium, which was called Nile Kinnick Memorial Field during the American occupation after World War II. Close to 80,000 spectators crouching under umbrellas in the morning, sitting patiently through a two-hour lunch break, folding their bumbershoots as the afternoon weather softens. High overhead, on the rim of the stadium's piebald slopes, the Olympic flame blazing out of a big, black Dixie cup sending oily black smoke up into Tokyo's everlasting smog."

By the three-mile mark, essentially the halfway point of the race, Mills had had enough. His time stood at 13 minutes, 28 seconds, only one second off his fastest time at that mark and exceptional given the soggy track conditions. But he felt that he couldn't continue the pace, so quitting entered his mind.

Before he quit, though, Mills thought again. He decided he wanted to quit while he was ahead, so he planned on running one more lap, taking the lead and then calling it a race.

As he took the lead and prepared to exit the track, Mills spotted his wife in the stands. Pat Mills was crying, and Billy knew why: She shared his pain and his secret.

"She was my positive support system," Mills said. "She empowered me."

Mills kept running. In the final lap, Mills moved along side Australia's Ron Clarke, the world-record holder in the event. Clarke accidentally bumped Mills, and he stumbled into the third lane.

Regaining his footing, Mills again edged alongside Clarke. This time, Mohamed Gammoudi of Tunisia burst through between Clarke and Mills, jostling Mills.

Here's how U.S. radio announcer called the end of the race:

"… Clarke moves out in front, and now here comes Gammoudi of Tunisia, he takes the lead, followed by Clarke of Australia. You can't believe it, they've run almost 10,000 meters, and they are literally shoulder-to-shoulder. Gammoudi of Tunisia is moving now, he's making his move. Clarke is trying to stay with him. Gammoudi is sprinting, he's coming off the curve, they're about to finish the race. There's only 100 meters left …"

At this point, Mills' mind hit full gear as he entered the final curve:

"My thoughts are changing from 'I can win,' to 'One more try, one more try, one more try.' Then I saw the tape stretched across the finish line, my thoughts went back to, 'I won, I won, I won.'

"But I was in third place, and I could see two runners ahead of me. Thirty, 20 yards to go, my thoughts are, 'I won, I won, I …'"

Radio announcer: *"Gammoudi is out in front, no, Clarke is taking him, no Gammoudi is staving off the challenge. Clarke is sprinting. Gammoudi is out in front by a HERE COMES MILLS OF THE U.S.A. MILLS OF THE U.S.A. HE WON! HE WON!"*

Mills' victory is considered one of the biggest upsets in Olympic track history. After the race, sportswriter Jesse Abramson of the *New York Herald-Tribune* put the feat in perspective:

"Of all the improbable happenings in this or any other Olympics since Corebus won the first race on the Plain of Olympia in 776 B.C., this triumph by the darkest of dark horses has to take the prize.

"Who in heaven's name is Mills? was a question voiced in 30 languages when he ran with the leaders throughout, took his turn in forcing the pace and then, when he was knocked about on the sodden track on the next-to-last turn, came on with a storming finish that won the gold medal by three yards in Olympic-record time of 28 minutes, 24.4 seconds …

"The time itself on a track soaked by 24 hours of rain … was almost beyond belief for a 26-year-old veteran who had never won anything more important than the Big Eight Conference title at Kansas, who had never covered the distance faster than 29:10.4 and had run only some six times over this route.

"Billy Mills, running against the world's best this day, was unawed by assignment, confident in his own fitness and mental readiness. In as dramatic a struggle as ever enlivened an Olympic scene – and I have covered them all since 1928 – (Mills) … left some of the greatest names in track strewn in his wake.

"Coming back from a violent straight-arm by an equally unknown Tunisian named Mohamed Gammoudi that by all rights should have finished him, Mills, from third place eight yards away, gathered himself anew, called on the sprint reserve he had been husbanding and collared Clarke, the world 10,000-meter recordholder, then Gammoudi 30 yards from the tape."

Mills is the only U.S. athlete to win the 10,000 meters in the Olympics. After Mills' victory at Tokyo, former Kansas teammate Cliff Cushman wrote to him:

BILLY MILLS
Cross country and
track and field,
1958-61

"When I saw you race on television, I cried. Not because of what you accomplished, but because of where you had to begin."

***

Where Mills "began" was the Pine Ridge, S.D., reservation. He was born June 30, 1938. His mother, Grace, was one-fourth Sioux and three-fourths French. She died of cancer when Billy was 7. His father, Sidney, was three-fourths Sioux and one-fourth English.

Sidney implored his son to pursue athletics as a way off the reservation. A former prizefighter, Sidney taught Billy how to box. Billy preferred running to punching, but tragically, Sidney Mills would not live to see his son blossom as an athlete. He died when Billy was 12.

In 1953, Billy, all 4 feet 9 inches and 97 pounds of him, left the impoverished reservation life for Haskell Institute (a high school at the time, now it's known as Haskell Indian Nations University, a four-year college) in Lawrence. He went out for the track team and showed determination and progress. As a sophomore in high school, he won a two-mile cross country race in 9:28.1, a time that broke Wes Santee's state record by 30 seconds.

In his senior year, Mills set a Haskell (both high school and junior college) record with a 4:22.8 mile. That time also eclipsed Glenn Cunningham's state high school record.

Through his running, Mills enjoyed popularity at Haskell, where he was student council president and an honor roll student. Highly recruited for college, Mills decided to stay in town and attend KU beginning in 1957.

Mills did not experience the same highs at KU as he did at Haskell. He was one of five Native Americans on campus. He tried fraternity rush only to be shown the door because of his heritage. His teammates, unknowing of the pain they caused him, often called him "chief."

He performed inconsistently in track, usually succeeding in cross country and the winter indoor track season and then faltering in spring outdoor competition. Nonetheless, Mills still finished fifth, sixth and fifth in the NCAA Cross Country championships and won the 1960 Big Eight Conference Cross Country Championship as a senior. In the spring of 1961, he won the two-mile run in the conference indoor (9:17.4) and outdoor (9:31.4).

Mills thought highly of Kansas track and field coach Bill Easton, yet he endured difficult times with him, too.

"I put a lot of trust in Bill Easton, and he put trust in me," Mills says. "He was counting on me, and expecting me to deliver while I was at the University of Kansas. I didn't.

"He basically said, 'Trust me, you've got the potential, I can help you become great.' I put that trust in him, I went overboard with my trust in him, I put my whole life in him.

"The anger, the frustration and the disappointment that I faced at KU from a time in society when society was not ready to address racial issues – and they existed – I put that burden on Bill Easton: 'Why is society this way?' And Bill was in no position to answer that. He was in no position to change society. But I expected him to.

"So, we had this conflict. He expected me to perform to the best of my ability. I expected him to change society for me so I could perform to the best of my ability. That did not happen here.

While at KU, Billy Mills enjoyed success in cross country, but he often struggled in outdoor track. Later, a physical exam revealed he needed more protein. Correcting this problem helped Mills win a gold medal in the 1964 Olympics.

"However, I continued having the faith in Coach Easton, and he continued to have the faith in me as an athlete."

That faith was tested to its foundation when Mills dropped out of his last race at the NCAA Outdoor Championships.

"One of the reasons for dropping out was I put all of this responsibility on Coach Easton," Mills says. "I never had the maturity to say, 'Coach, here are all of the things that are bothering me.' I just expected him to know."

Mills returned to the reservation in 1961. There, he rediscovered the pleasure of running and the despair of his people. He returned to KU when two friends died after drinking antifreeze.

***

The year 1962 marked several turning points in Mills' life. He married Pat Harris of Coffeyville that year. The two met at KU on a blind date. He graduated with a degree in education. He joined the U.S. Marine Corps and completed officer candidate school.

While in the Marines, Mills began training for the Olympics, but his body kept breaking down, just as it had in the outdoor seasons at KU. A battery of tests revealed that his diet needed more food with protein and a protein supplement. He changed his diet and noticed an improved performance in three months.

"Then I was able to take the performances I had in cross country and carry them year-round," Mills says.

He also reconciled with Easton. The coach told him he had the capability to be a great runner and complimented him on his maturity as a Marine. As usual, Easton knew talent and ability, and Mills proved him correct by winning the gold.

Mills stayed with his track career for a year after Tokyo. In 1965, he set a world record in the six-mile run with a time of 27:11.6. That same year, the men in Mills' Marine unit with six or more months left in their commission were shipped to Vietnam. Mills had only five-and-a-half months left, so he stayed home. His unit suffered 38 percent casualties in Vietnam, and Mills was devastated. He retired from running.

"I could not do a sport with friends and people in my unit getting killed in Vietnam," Mills says.

In 1968, Mills tried a comeback for the U.S. Olympic team but finished fourth at the trials.

A 1983 movie, "Running Brave," reviewed his life. The critically acclaimed film, starring Robby Benson as Billy, covers Mills' challenges, time at KU and Olympic triumph.

Mills enjoyed a successful career selling insurance, and today he runs Billy Mills Enterprises, which includes a promotion arm for ventures such as the movie and commercial endorsements; a speaker's bureau (Mills gives about 70 speeches a year); and charitable work. He also serves as national spokesman for Christian Relief Services.

Billy Mills has succeeded well past the 1964 Olympics, and he gives back whenever and however he can.

After Mills' epic race, Easton wrote him a short note that read: "I just saw the greatest race of my life. Congratulations. You are the greatest Jayhawker of them all. Love, Bill Easton."

The letter, Mills says, was "so meaningful to me. In retrospect, it was a great moment, realizing that he and I did not give up on one another."

And for Billy Mills, it meant not giving up on himself, either.

SWEET HITTING, SOUTHERN LAUGHS

KU fell short in 1964 despite efforts of two All-Americans

The 1964 Kansas baseball team featured a collection of talent unmatched to that point in the history of the program. With future major-league pitchers Chuck Dobson and Steve Renko Jr., a great hitter in Steve McGreevy and a highly touted second baseman in junior-college transfer Sterling Coward, many thought the Jayhawks would challenge for their first Big Eight Conference title in 15 years.

Renko, despite sitting out part of the season, finished the year with an earned run average of 0.99, still the best in KU history. Dobson won six games and struck out 90 batters in 66 2/3 innings pitched. And McGreevy and Coward both were named All-Americans, the first KU players to receive that honor since John Trombold a decade earlier.

But the Jayhawks finished only 16-11, 11-10 in the conference. Fourth place.

"We were picked to a do a whole lot and probably didn't do as much as we should have," McGreevy says. "But you were always fighting the weather during three-game series. Missouri really had a top-notch team, and the Oklahoma schools always had really good teams."

It was, in many ways, the golden era of Big Eight baseball. Even Colorado, which no longer fields a team, had a fine squad.

The Jayhawks went into their final two series of the 1964 season with a 15-6 record and still had an outside shot at the conference championship. At Colorado, KU won the opener before losing twice. Then, Missouri beat KU 2-1, 2-0 and 4-3, sweeping a three-game series in Lawrence.

Losing to Missouri, though, hardly was shameful. The Tigers won their third straight conference title, went undefeated in 19 conference games and lost in the finals of the 1964 College World Series.

In nine career games McGreevy played against Missouri from 1963 through 1965, KU won just one. But rarely could anyone fault McGreevy, an outfielder and first baseman from Paola, for KU's shortcomings.

"Probably the sweetest little hitter that I've ever seen," is how former Kansas baseball coach Floyd Temple describes McGreevy. "For a college hitter, he was as good as I ever had. He'd take it to all fields, but not for very much power. An outstanding young man; it's a shame that he didn't have more

STEVE McGREEVY
Baseball,
1963-65

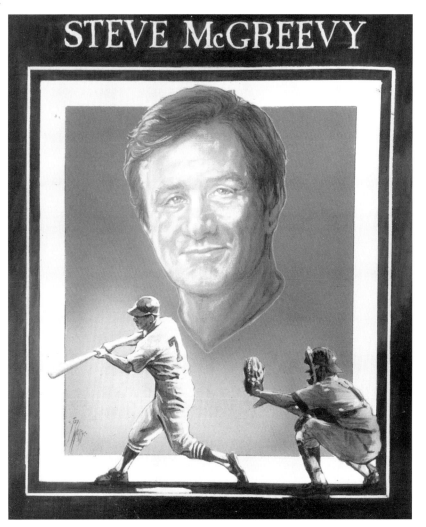

STEVE McGREEVY

STERLING COWARD
Baseball,
1964

size or wasn't right-handed so he could play the infield."

Renko, who later was McGreevy's roommate for a time in the Los Angles Dodgers' minor-league farm system, says McGreevy was a "Wade Boggs type of hitter," referring to the All-Star third baseman with the Tampa Bay Devil Rays.

"I remember Steve being on base a lot," Renko says. "He swung the bat well. He used the whole field."

In three seasons with the Jayhawks, McGreevy compiled a batting average of .366. He hit .400 in 1964, leading the conference with a .421 average in league games, and hit .379 in 1965. During his junior and senior seasons, he led the conference in hits, and his nine doubles in 1965 league games led all players in that category.

McGreevy recalls how he inexplicably found his stroke after struggling a little in 1963, his sophomore season.

"Everything just seemed to come together in 1964," he says.

That's the year that Coward arrived at Kansas. A lanky Southern lad who defied the traditional scrappy, hard-nosed stereotype of most second basemen, he stayed just one year before signing a professional contract with the Dodgers only weeks before the 1965 season began.

"He was real smooth," McGreevy says. "I hadn't seen anybody come in who was that good. He had great range, and a lot of pop in his bat."

Temple recalls finding Coward at the National Junior College World Series in Grand Junction, Colo.

"Sterling was a GOOD second baseman," he says. "Turned the double play, a good hitter. Just an all-around good kid. He had all the tools."

McGreevy generally led off or hit third in the batting order for the 1964 Jayhawks, and Coward hit second or fifth. Somewhat of a jokester, Coward led the team in runs scored with 26.

"He had a bit of a Southern-boy prankster mentality," McGreevy says. "He was a tall, skinny guy, but real fluid. Just a great all-around ballplayer."

After Coward and Dobson left, the 1965 Jayhawks won 12 and lost 13, finishing sixth in the conference. But after McGreevy and Renko left, the 1966 Jayhawks dipped to last place in the league.

McGreevy was chosen in major-league baseball's first free-agent draft in 1965. He played four seasons in the Dodgers' minor-league chain. He returned to the Kansas City area, where he stayed until 1976.

Now, McGreevy and his family live just outside of Providence, R.I., where he owns and operates three retail businesses. He says he doesn't miss his playing days one bit, especially losing to Missouri. But he's glad he had the opportunity.

"I did it," he says, "and it was absolutely wonderful."

POSITIVELY A WINNER

Cross country champion inspired by example

As John Lawson passed the four-mile mark and approached a hill at the 1965 NCAA Cross Country Championships, one thought entered the mind of University of Kansas distance runner: "If he can go faster, he can have it."

"He" was Doug Brown, a heralded runner from the University of Montana who set a blistering pace from the start of the race to the incline of the hill. The same Doug Brown who edged Lawson in a photo finish for first place in the two-mile run five months earlier at the NCAA Outdoor Track and Field Championships.

Now Brown had Lawson – who read Norman Vincent Peale's "The Power of Positive Thinking" before each race – doubting himself: *"If he can go faster, he can have it."*

Brown had the race won, or so Lawson thought.

"And that's when Brown fell off," Lawson says. "He was thinking the same thing."

Lawson took the hill and the race. Many positives came out of his championship.

For Bob Timmons, the victory meant the Jayhawks' coach was positively right when he assessed Lawson.

"I don't think I ever doubted that he would be the national champion," Timmons says. "He had all the mental plusses that he needed to be a champion."

For teammate Herald Hadley, the race was positively the gutsiest effort he had seen.

"What a race! That was a real performance," he says. "It looked to me like he was running flat out that entire race."

As for Lawson, well, he was positively sick to his stomach all afternoon.

"I had never had an effort like that," he says.

On a more positive note, the race earned Lawson some geographical immortality. Lawrence played host to Lawson's triumphant run, the first time the NCAA Championship race occurred outside of East Lansing, Mich. Timmons named the spot where Lawson took command of the race as "Lawson Hill."

Although the University's west campus has usurped the original course that featured Lawson Hill, which sits west of the KU Endowment Association building, the name lives on at Timmons' Rim Rock Farm. The former coach has developed some of his own land into another cross country course (site of the 1998 NCAA Championships) and a hill there bears Lawson's name.

And there's the positive sense of accomplishment that comes with winning a championship.

"I look back and think, 'I was the best cross country runner in college in 1965,' " Lawson says. "I think there were more talented individuals in the race, but I was just inspired to give it my all."

Lawson drew inspiration from Peale's book, one of the early self-motivational tomes.

"It changed my life at that time," Lawson said. "I got a lot of inspiration from it. I think it was truly a spiritual book that puts you in touch with your own feelings and your own capabilities.

"Leading up to big meets, there's a lot of pressure. It somehow settled me down, made me concentrate on my own strengths (and) don't worry about the next person.

"And that applies today. You can look around and see a Bill Gates with $38 billion and feel pretty insignificant, but you can go to skid row and see people who are a lot worse off. I think it's kept me in touch with my own self throughout my lifetime."

"I look back and think, 'I was the best cross country runner in college in 1965.' I think there were more talented individuals in the race, but I was just inspired to give it my all."

– John Lawson

JOHN LAWSON

JOHN LAWSON
Cross country and
track and field,
1963-66

Before he read Peale's book, several sources inspired Lawson. His father, Lester, served as his earliest inspiration. The elder Lawson had won a regional race for Wyandotte High School in Kansas City, Kan., as a junior. But Lester, the oldest of eight children, left school before he graduated so he could help support the family during the Depression.

Next for John Lawson came KU.

"I always wanted to go to the best college in the nation for distance runners," he says.

And with Kansas track and field came Bill Easton.

"He had an ability to spot when a person was ready to move to the next level," Lawson says.

After Easton was fired in 1965, former assistant coach Timmons led the Jayhawks.

"My senior year (1965-66) with Timmons, he took me to the next level, training-wise," Lawson says.

That year also marked Jim Ryun's first year at Kansas. Lawson appreciated running with the first U.S. high schooler to run a sub-4-minute mile.

"Training with someone of his stature brought me along," Lawson says.

Don't get the idea that Lawson only sought inspiration. He provided plenty of his own.

"He was a real gutty performer," Hadley said. "He was always tough. He didn't have real tremendous speed, but you could bet that he would put everything he had on the line."

Lawson followed his championship with second-place finishes in the two-mile run at the 1966 NCAA Indoor Championships and in the three-mile race later that spring in the NCAA Outdoor Championships. In the 1966 Big Eight Conference Indoor Championships, Lawson won both the mile and two-mile races. He also won the two-mile race at the 1964 conference indoor meet.

Timmons calls Lawson a very, very dedicated athlete.

"He lived in Templin (Hall), on the seventh floor," Timmons says. "I don't think he ever rode the elevator. That was against his ideals.

"He was a great leader for the team. He was happy, enthusiastic, always up, always encouraging."

Timmons remains impressed how Lawson took Peale's lessons to heart.

"That was how he conducted his leadership, the power of positive thinking," he says.

Lawson's positive approach also helped smooth the way for Timmons to take over the Kansas track program from the popular Easton.

"For me coming into (that) situation, I couldn't have had a better captain," Timmons says. "He was a marvelous leader."

Today, Lawson works in human resources for Seagate Technology, the largest computer disk-drive manufacturer in the world. He lives in Lake Forest, Calif.

Of his KU days, Lawson says he still pinches himself when he thinks about running for the same university that produced Glenn Cunningham, Wes Santee, Al Oerter, Bill Nieder, Billy Mills and Ryun.

"I probably appreciate it more now than I did then, although I appreciated it then, because I wanted to be with the best," he says.

Lawson gets nostalgic when he thinks of his college days. As he told the *Kansas City Star* in 1994:

"I like being outside and the individuality of cross country. But the team camaraderie among athletes – I miss that. College is such a short segment in your life, yet it looms so large. Four years is nothing, but it means so much."

TWO-MILE SURPRISE

Change in events led runner to an NCAA championship

It never hurts to ask. Just ask Herald Hadley.

Hadley, a distance runner for the University of Kansas track and field team of the mid-1960s, had qualified for the 1965 NCAA Indoor Championships in the 1,000-yard and mile runs. The trouble was, he preferred longer runs, such as the two-mile.

So Hadley found coach Bill Easton. The coach asked Hadley what event (of the two for which he had qualified) he would prefer to run at the championships in Detroit.

"I said, 'Coach, you and I both know I'm not a real speedster when it comes to that short stuff. I really would like to run that two-mile,' " Hadley says. "He said, 'Oh, well, let me call them (NCAA meet officials) up and see what they say.' He called them up right then. And all they said was, 'You're coach Easton, and if you say your boy can run the two-mile, he can run the two-mile.' "

And Hadley proved he could run the two-mile. The race was run on a short track where 11 laps equaled a mile. Hadley, a senior at the time, recalls the race coming down to him and Bill Smith of Purdue.

"For the last five curves, he kept trying to pass me," Hadley says. "I could see his knees in my peripheral vison. I think I got him by about five yards on the last curve and straight-away."

What's also unusual about the race and its circumstances is that Hadley hadn't run a competitive two-mile since his sophomore year. At that time, he was the surprise winner of the 1963 Big Eight Conference Indoor Championships in 9 minutes, 25.2 seconds.

Hadley arrived at KU from tiny Shallow Water in western Kansas. He graduated from high school with nine other class-mates. He wasn't too sure whether he'd like Lawrence and KU until his recruiting visit, when Easton won him over.

"Coach Easton was a very positive individual," Hadley says. "I probably baited him a little bit with a couple of questions about some other schools. All he would say was, 'That's a fine institution.' And he'd get right back and talk about KU and the program they had, not only in athletics but in the academic end."

No one knew it at the time, but Hadley was Easton's last champion. The long-time coach was fired that April in what Hadley describes as "a political deal."

Despite that turbulent ending to both of their track and field careers, Hadley looks back fondly at his KU years.

"I felt privileged when it was all over," he says. "Especially after graduation and looking back, that was really a lucky decision on my part to go there. I could have gone anywhere, but that was the best place."

Hadley now owns a lighting company in Spokane, Wash. He says he liked the hilly, green Pacific Northwest after traveling to Oregon for a national track meet.

"There's another reason for going to KU," he says. "I know I wouldn't be out here if it wasn't for that trip in college."

HERALD HADLEY
Cross country and track and field, 1962-65

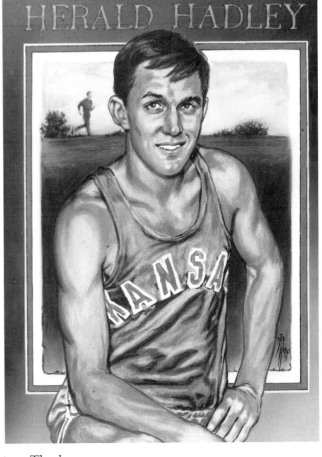

WONDERFUL WALT
Center refined his game through extra work

When practice ended for the University of Kansas basketball team, work was just beginning for Walt Wesley.

That's when the 6-foot-11-inch center went one-on-one against the "iron defender." Coach Ted Owens and assistant coach Sam Miranda wanted to break Wesley of his habit of shooting the ball on the way down from his jump. After Miranda saw a magazine piece on the iron defender, a contraption that could be set at different heights, Owens enlisted the help of maintenance man "Skinny" Replogle to build one for them.

"We had it built at the level that if (Walter) didn't shoot at the height of his extension, he would throw it right into the iron defender," Owens says. "So every day, when everybody else had gone in, I said, 'OK, Walter, you've got to hit 150 turnaround-jump shots before you can go.'

"He'd grumble and all that, but I said, 'You said you wanted to be an All-American when you came here, and this is what it's going to take.' And he became an unbelievable shooter on that turnaround jump shot."

Wesley's jump shot wasn't all that needed work when he arrived in Lawrence from Dunbar High School in Fort Myers, Fla. Although he could run the court well, Owens said Wesley lacked some basketball fundamentals.

"He had two bad habits when he got here: He didn't bend his knees, and he didn't carry his arms above his waist when he played, which are two basic fundamentals of basketball," Owens said. "He just had to be retrained."

It worked. Shooting over the iron defender and attention to other skills paid off by Wesley's junior year, 1964-65. He averaged 23.5 points and 8.8 rebounds that season, Owens' first as head coach. His 26.9-point average in conference play led the Big Eight. During Wesley's senior year in 1965-66, he averaged 20.7 points and 9.2 rebounds for the conference-champion Jayhawks and earned All-America honors.

After winning the regular season conference title, the Jayhawks were 22-3 entering the 1966 NCAA Tournament. In its first game, Kansas edged Southern Methodist 76-70, setting up a showdown with Texas Western.

In a classic struggle, the Miners defeated the Jayhawks 81-80 in double overtime. Kansas appeared to have won at the end of the first overtime period when Jo Jo White hit a long jump shot as the clock ran out. But officials ruled White stepped out of bounds and nullified the basket. More than 30 years later, Wesley, who scored a game-high 24 points, still cringes at the mention of that game.

"That's one I try to forget," he says. "It hurts. It's a memory, but it's not a fond memory."

Instead, Wesley chooses to recall his sophomore year, when KU defeated Cincinnati, snapping the Bearcats' 91-game home-court winning streak. He also savors the conference championship his senior year. He finished his KU career with 1,315 points, which ranks him 16th on the Jayhawks' all-time scorers list entering the 1998-99 season.

Wesley enjoyed a 10-year career in the NBA. He was a first-round draft pick of the Cincinnati Royals and later played for seven other teams. In 1976, he retired from the NBA and returned to KU to finish a bachelor's degree. During his return, Wesley helped Owens coach the Jayhawks on a part-time basis.

"It was a good experience," Wesley says. "I learned a lot from the coaching aspect of the game."

Owens and Wesley went through a lot together as coach and player and coach and coach. But the two experienced one ordeal together before Wesley committed to Kansas in 1962.

Owens first learned of Wesley while scouting the National Negro High School Tournament in Nashville, Tenn. The tournament included top black high school teams from 16 Southern states that still were segregated in the early 1960s.

At the tournament, Owens introduced himself to Wilts Alexander, executive secretary of the Florida Negro High School Association. Owens questioned Alexander about college prospects in Florida, and Alexander told him about Wesley. So Owens flew to Florida to talk to the Wesley family.

"Back then you could entertain people, take them out to dinner, which you can't do anymore," Owens says. "I said to the Wesleys, 'Why don't we go out and get something to eat?' And they laughed, and they said, 'Coach, there's no place all of us can go eat here.' It just hit me right in the face, because Kansas was one of the early states as far as the Civil Rights opportunities.

"And then Mr. Wesley said, 'That's not quite true. Howard Johnson announced a national policy that their restaurants are open to people of all races.' They said, 'Are you willing to try?' And I said, 'Sure.'

"We went to eat, and I'll never forget, we walked in and a Florida trooper was sitting at the counter. He unbuckled his holster, and the whole time we were there, he glared at us and kept rubbing his .45 the whole time, just to try to intimidate us."

After earning a degree, Wesley took his coaching experience and became a full-time college coach. He assisted at Western Michigan and the United States Military Academy through the 1989-90 season. Today, he is the executive director of the Police Athletic League in his hometown of Fort Myers.

Owens is pleased that Wesley returned to school. And he's even happier that he got to know Wesley as a person as well as a player.

"He is just one of the really nice people in the whole world," Owens says.

WALTER WESLEY
Basketball,
1963-66

SKILLS PLUS

Jumper competed in several events – and football

Versatility defines some athletes who possess enough raw talent to excel at almost any endeavor they choose.

Gary Ard personified versatility at the University of Kansas. His speed, strength and adaptability helped him perform his best when posed with a new obstacle, a new goal, a new opportunity.

During his two-year career as a Jayhawk in 1966 and 1967, Ard established himself as one of the finest long jumpers in school history. He was swift enough to lead off a KU sprint medley relay team that set a world-record time of 3 minutes, 15.2 seconds at the 1967 Texas Relays, establishing a mark that lasted nine years. And he was tough enough to earn a letter in football as a flanker on the 1967 KU team that finished second in the Big Eight Conference.

"Gary was very versatile," says former KU track and field coach Bob Timmons. "He was very, very fast, and that's an important factor for a long jumper."

Timmons had a tough sell to get Ard, a Modesto, Calif., native, to Kansas. The two met while Ard was competing for Modesto Junior College in an indoor track meet in San Francisco. Ard told Timmons he was bound for the University of Southern California.

GARY ARD
Track and field
and football,
1966-67

But during a recruiting trip to Lawrence, Ard was drawn to Kansas by a flickering light he had never seen before.

"We came back here (to my house), and we chased lightning bugs all over the backyard," Timmons says. "He was fascinated with those lightning bugs. It was out of this world."

So Ard committed to Kansas but almost changed his mind when he arrived on a bitterly cold day in January 1966. But challenges intrigued him, so he leapt from the California coastlines to the Great Plains of Kansas.

At KU, Ard competed in the long jump, triple jump, high jump and 100-, 220- and 440-yard dashes. In 1966, Ard helped Kansas claim the NCAA indoor title by finishing third in the long jump at 24 feet, 1 1/2 inches.

"Winning the team championship was big to me," Ard says. "I was mostly a team player. I did a lot of events, so it was more rewarding to win a team championship."

Besides the world-record relay effort, another shining moment came at the 1967 NCAA Outdoor Championships, when he captured the long jump title with a leap of 25-9. That same year, he placed second in that event at the NCAA Indoor Championships.

His personal records were 26-1 in the long jump and 50-8 in the triple jump. Ard often won both jumps in the same meet. He did so at the conference outdoor championships in 1966, as well as at the 1966 Southwestern Relays and the '66 and '67 Kansas Relays.

Ard earned a bachelor's degree in art education from Kansas

GARY ARD

in 1967. He later returned to KU to get a master's degree in physical education. After college and a two-year stint in the U.S. Army, he returned to his hometown to teach at Modesto Junior College. He coached track and field for 23 years and later became the school's golf coach, guiding his team to a 1997 conference title.

Even after college, his athletic prowess and versatility remained his hallmark. He took up golf and soon was shooting more pars than bogeys. He crafted a one-handicap game good enough to play with the likes of Jack Nicklaus and Arnold Palmer in the 1996 U.S. Senior Open, in which he missed the final cut by two strokes.

Today, when asked if he regrets not pursuing a golfing career early in life rather than track and field, Ard barely pauses to answer.

"It's certainly a lot easier on my body," he says.

'TIMMIE'
Coach set lofty goals, and most were achieved

Bob Timmons looks out his patio window and sees Gary Ard chasing fireflies on his recruiting trip, Theo Hamilton glancing backward on a career that almost never happened and Jim Ryun realizing a dream as a world-champion miler.

But most of all, Timmons sees 23 years of practices as University of Kansas track and field athletes strived to be their best.

"I enjoyed practice more than anything," says the former KU track and field coach about his 1965-88 tenure. "Just the relationships, working with the guys. I looked forward to the conference and national championships. The other meets weren't that important to me, they were just meets."

The practices didn't make KU teams perfect, but they came close. They did give Timmons a good reason to look forward to the Big Eight Conference and NCAA indoor and outdoor track and field championships. Consider that the Jayhawks with Timmons as coach:

- won three NCAA indoor championships: 1966, 1969 and 1970;
- tied for the 1970 NCAA Outdoor Championship;
- finished second in the 1975 NCAA Indoors and tied for second in 1973;
- placed third, fourth or fifth in the NCAA indoors six other times;
- finished second in the 1969 NCAA Outdoors;
- placed fifth in three different NCAA outdoor meets;
- won 12 conference indoor championships;
- won 13 conference outdoor championships, including 10 consecutive titles from 1967 to 1976; and
- developed 11 NCAA champion athletes, including six-time champion Karl Salb and five-time titlist Jim Ryun, plus three champion relay teams.

Through all of this success, Timmons deflected the spotlight and shared the credit for these milestone accomplishments.

"There was never any doubt that we just capitalized on the great record of Bill Easton," Timmons says of his predecessor.

Easton coached Kansas from 1947 to 1965. He directed the Jayhawks to two

"He is KU track and field."

– Theo Hamilton on Bob Timmons

NCAA outdoor championships and an eight-year stretch in which KU won conference titles in cross country, indoor and outdoor competitions.

"We tried to recruit the best athletes in the United States," Timmons says. "I had good assistants in John Mitchell (now head coach at Georgia), Harvey Greer, Gary Pepin (current head coach at Nebraska) and Roger Bowen. They were four of the most successful recruiters around."

***

Timmons grew up in Pittsburg, Kan., where he played high school tennis, ran track and convinced his parents to let him play football in his senior year. His mother opposed football because her son stood only 5 feet 2 inches and weighed just 115 pounds as a senior.

As with many students in the mid-1940s, World War II interrupted Timmons' college years at KU. He joined the Marines and fought in the South Pacific and China.

After the war, Timmons took classes at Pittsburg State in the summer and returned to Lawrence in the fall. By his senior year, Timmons faced another sales job with his parents. He wanted to abandon his engineering studies and become a coach.

"It wasn't a very popular decision with my parents," he says. "I was going to be quite a bit older when I got out."

Older and wiser, Timmons landed his first coaching job in Caldwell, Kan. He served as an assistant football coach and head basketball coach.

"My basketball career was disastrous," Timmons says.

Caldwell lost its first 11 games, and opponents sometimes doubled or tripled the score on the team. But Timmons rallied his players, and Caldwell won five of its last seven games in what the coach calls "a great experience."

From Caldwell, Timmons moved to Emporia High School for a year, Wichita East for a season, then across town to Wichita West for two years before returning to East for eight highly successful years in cross country, swimming and track and field.

During his second stint at East, Timmons coached at least one state championship team every year. In total, his teams won 16 of a possible 24 state championships from 1956 to 1964.

Timmons instilled goal-setting among his athletes, and he credits that as a big step for developing champions.

"Each one of my athletes was asked to establish season goals and intermediate goals during the year in all of the sports that I had," he says. "We had high goals."

Timmons set the highest of the goals for a gangling runner named Jim Ryun, who competed at East from 1962 to 1965. As Ryun improved his times in the mile as a sophomore, Timmons saw the potential the young runner possessed. Ryun enjoyed remarkable improvement as a junior and made the U.S. Olympic team in the 1,500

BOB TIMMONS
Head cross country and track and field coach, 1965-88

meters in 1964, the summer between his junior and senior seasons. He later became the first high school miler to break the 4-minute barrier.

The year 1964 also marked a big move in Timmons' life. He left East for an assistant coaching position with Easton at Kansas. Timmons the goal-setter had notched a big achievement by joining the staff of one of the top college track and field programs in the country. What no one could know, however, was how tumultuous the spring of 1965 would prove for Timmons, Easton, the University – and Ryun.

Toward the end of his first year at Kansas, Timmons accepted the head coaching job at Oregon State. Ryun, then a senior at East, committed to Oregon State so he could run for his former coach.

Timmons and his family barely had reached Corvallis, Ore., when he learned that KU athletics director Wade Stinson had fired Easton after a long-simmering dispute between the two boiled over. Stinson called Timmons and offered him the job.

These moves left Timmons stuck in the middle. He called Easton and Easton told him that he would like to be reinstated as coach, which would leave Timmons in Oregon. Stinson stayed in touch with Timmons and fine-tuned his coaching offer.

"I was in Corvallis for about a week and I never got off the phone," he says. "I wouldn't come back until the athletics director told me that there was no possible way that Bill Easton would be reinstated. Under those conditions, I decided to come back."

Now Ryun was caught in the middle. His commitment to Oregon State was not binding because Kansas did not have a mutual letter-of-intent agreement with OSU. Within a month, the Oregon State athletics department decided not to stand in Ryun's way and allowed him to be reunited with Timmons at KU.

***

The Easton legacy, Ryun, Salb and Timmons' relentless pursuit of excellence kept KU at or near the top of college track for years. In Timmons' first year, the Jayhawks won the 1966 NCAA Indoor Championships without Ryun's help. Ryun was a freshman and ineligible to compete with the varsity.

From 1967 through 1971, the Jayhawks won both the conference indoor and outdoor championships and finished in the top six at both NCAA meets except for the 1968 Outdoor Championships.

As with Easton before him, Timmons emphasized hard work, clean living and academics. These values succeeded with his early teams but were tested by some athletes in 1969-70.

"(Timmons) was really a fair guy," says Gary Ard, an All-American long jumper in 1967, Timmons' second year as coach. "He treated everybody the same. There were no favorites. If you broke the rules, you got punished. If you went along with his rules, you were one of the guys."

Jim Neihouse, who ran the opening leg on the two-mile relay team that set a world record in 1970, attests to the work ethic that Timmons instilled in the team.

"I still remember going out on those long runs," Neihouse says. "He had to take us out in the pickup, (and) we had to ride in the back. During the cold weather, we'd have our sweats all bundled up, socks on our hands and our hooded tops all closed up so you could barely see out of the hole there.

"We'd get in the back of the pickup and he had a tarp. We'd pull that tarp down over us, and he'd drive us out in the country, anywhere from 16 to 20 miles, drop us off and let us run back to town."

Shot-putter and discus-thrower Doug Knop, who competed in 1968-70, says Timmons was popular with athletes.

"Everybody that I knew on the team really, really liked Coach Timmons," Knop says. "Hardly ever did we call him 'coach.' We called him 'Timmie' because he was a real friend, and he really helped us a lot."

Still, times were changing during those years as Vietnam War protests and racial issues started tearing the KU campus apart. Timmons, an ex-Marine and defender of

"Everybody that I knew on the team really, really liked Coach Timmons. Hardly ever did we call him 'coach.' We called him 'Timmie' because he was a real friend, and he really helped us a lot."

– Doug Knop

the status quo, was bothered by what he saw.

"It was difficult for a person who believes in discipline and has strong beliefs in things our country stands for to watch the burning of buildings on campus and shootings during those years," he told the *University Daily Kansan* a decade later in 1979.

The changes also permeated the Kansas track team.

"Most of the people on our team had good attitudes," he says. "But there were a great many of them who were influenced from the outside.

"In '69, we were having tremendous problems. We cut people from the team for having long hair and mustaches. People came on campus involved in disrupting athletic programs. The drug thing was coming on strong."

Timmons realized he had to change some of his approach to stay in coaching.

"I had to become more receptive to ideas, be more tolerant of different points of view," he said.

***

With those adjustments came longevity. Timmons remained as coach until he retired in 1988. His last few years were not as successful as his earlier teams. The number of scholarships decreased from 25 when he started in 1965 to 17 at the end of his career. Today, track and field is allotted 12.6 scholarships at Kansas.

Timmons also did not recruit foreign athletes, which most universities did to enhance their track programs. Timmons says he thought U.S. athletes should get the scarce number of scholarships.

"I was a flag waver," he says.

He also has been a banner-carrier for student-athletes. After the NCAA declared star sprinter Cliff Wiley ineligible in the late 1970s for taking money from his Basic Educational Opportunity Grant (now known as Pell Grants) on top of his scholarship, Timmons moved to the forefront of this cause. He has testified before Congress on his student-athletes' bill of rights that tackles myriad NCAA rules. He admits that he may not get far with his proposal, but he continues on with it because he thinks it is worth fighting for.

When Timmons retired from KU, he brought his considerable energy to new sources. He and his wife, Pat, traveled to Africa and Europe. Church missions took them to China and Mexico.

Community service also has kept him busy. He has worked with a youth center in Topeka and also assists the American Red Cross Disaster Program. He spent time in Puerto Rico after Hurricane Hugo struck the island in 1989.

Sports also factor into his life. He coached various sports at the junior and senior high schools in Baldwin City, and he has built a championship-level cross country course at his Rim Rock Farm north of Lawrence. The course played host to the last Big Eight Cross Country Championship and is the site of the 1998 NCAA Cross Country Championship.

Rim Rock offers a covered bridge, and several features are named after former KU distance runners. There's the Jim Ryun Skyline Bend, John Lawson Hill, the Billy Mills Ascent and the Glenn Cunningham Finish Line.

Even in retirement, Timmons touches the University. Theo Hamilton, an All-American long jumper from 1975 and current KU assistant track coach, says he is indebted to Timmons for taking him back on the team in 1974. Hamilton was a transfer student from Jefferson State Junior College in Birmingham, Ala., who had to return home for a semester to finish class work so he could enroll at KU.

Hamilton frequently sees Timmons at Allen Field House while Hamilton is working and Timmons is working out. The former student says of his former teacher:

"I always felt good when I talked to him, because I felt I had been listened to. He would come up with positive solutions for you. He is KU track and field."

"Each one of my athletes was asked to establish season goals and intermediate goals during the year... we had high goals."

– Bob Timmons

PEOPLE'S CHAMPION

Miler transcended sport even before reaching KU

Before there was Tiger Woods, there was Jim Ryun.

As an athlete who transcended sport, as Woods has done in golf, as Michael Jordan did in basketball and as Chris Evert did in tennis in the 1970s, so, too, did Ryun in track and field in the mid-to-late 1960s.

By the time Ryun enrolled at the University of Kansas in the fall of 1965, he had:
- run the first sub-4-minute mile by a high school runner (3:58.3 on May 15, 1965, in Wichita);
- competed in the 1964 Tokyo Olympics;
- dealt with pressure from the media and from fans, such as the 6,500 people who attended the 1964 Kansas High School State Championship track meet and the 30,000 spectators at the U.S. Olympic Trials that same year; and
- become a household name.

"He's mild in manner, but that just hides an intense competitive spirit," said Bob Timmons, his high school coach at Wichita East and later his coach at KU, to the *Kansas City Star* in 1964. "He never shows his emotions, and I can't tell what he is thinking."

Timmons was the coach who saw something in Ryun that even Ryun and his family did not see – that Ryun possessed the talent, skill and potential to be the first high school runner to break the 4-minute barrier. As an unheralded sophomore in 1963, Ryun ran a 4:26.4 mile in his second competitive race.

That's when the prescient Timmons stepped in and told Ryun that he could be a 4-minute miler. Ryun ran a 4:21.7 mile in his next race. His times kept decreasing that year and the next, which led to the sub-4-minute mile as a senior.

Timmons had left East by Ryun's senior year. He became an assistant coach for Bill Easton at Kansas in 1964. In the spring of 1965, Oregon State named Timmons as its new head track and field coach. Ryun, who had roomed with two University of Oregon athletes – Bill Dellinger and Dyrol Burleson – at the Olympics, decided to follow Timmons to the Emerald State.

But before Timmons could get settled in Corvallis, Ore., Kansas fired track and field coach Bill Easton and asked Timmons to return to KU as head coach. Timmons agreed, and a month later, Ryun changed his mind and picked KU as his school.

Freshmen still were ineligible for varsity competition in 1965-66, but that didn't stop Ryun from competing "unattached" and quickly becoming a drawing card at college track meets.

At the 1966 Big Eight Conference Indoor Championships, the 6-foot-2-inch, 160-pound Ryun, whom the *Star* described as "a human greyhound – long-limbed, small-boned and slender" thrilled 4,600 fans by running a 3:59.6 mile on the 12-lap board track at Municipal Auditorium in Kansas City, Mo.

Bill Mayer of the *Lawrence Journal-World* described Ryun's mile that day:

"He runs with that smooth, easy grace that minimizes lost motion. He treats the time clock as though it is a strong, fresh opponent running on his right shoulder on the curve …

"They're part of a portfolio of experiences that affect my life today, in which I can look back and truly thank God for the memory."

– Jim Ryun on his world record times in the mile run

JIM RYUN
Track and field
and cross country,
1966-69

The crowd of 4,600 started cheering as the gun signalled the start of the race and the noise built steadily for nearly four minutes ... He lapped virtually the full field of frosh competitors. As the lithe Wichitan crossed the finish line, the clock, which generally lags a little bit struck 4:00 and the crowd almost blew the roof off the hall."

Ryun's early showing previewed how special 1966 would be for him. In April, he won the mile run at the Kansas Relays in 3:55.8. In May, he defeated Kenyan distance star Kip Keino in a two-mile race in Los Angeles in which he set a U.S. record with a time of 8:25.2. A few weeks later, he almost set a world record in the mile with a 3:53.7 time in Compton, Calif. In June, he established a world record in the 880-yard run with a time of 1:44.9.

Then, Sunday, July 17, 1966, two events occurred that altered Ryun's life forever. He set a world record in the mile with a time of 3:51.3 at the University of California's Edwards Stadium in Berkeley. Michel Jazy of France had set the previous record, 3:53.6, in 1965.

"Well, 1966 was a particularly sweet memory because it was after that race ... I had an experience that changed my life and is still with me," Ryun says. "After I walked off the track, after signing autographs and talking to the media, I discovered that some-one had stolen my equipment.

"As I was jogging across the field, this young, attractive girl came up and asked for an autograph. I told her at that time I was busy, it had been a long day, thank you, and no thank you. She, if you will, was what you might say the image is in your mind of a Heisman. Later, she became a blind date at Thanksgiving of 1966, and she's my wife today. Anne has been a marvelous asset and a wonderful wife.

"I remember 1966, too, because it was a world record at Berkeley and the first time that an American would hold that world record since Glenn Cunningham in the 1930s. It meant, to a certain extent, the ending of one pressure; there were always those who said I would never achieve that. And entering into another pressure that said I couldn't continue on."

The media gave Ryun many athlete of the year awards. Among his honors included the Sullivan Award, which goes to the nation's top amateur athlete, and *Sports Illustrated*'s "Sportsman of the Year" award.

By the end of 1966, Jim Ryun was 19 years old and had yet to run competitively for KU's track and field team. He continued to rewrite history in 1967, but the following two years offered disappointment.

***

Ryun added to his world record list in 1967. The first new mark that year was a 1:48.3 time in the indoor 880 in a dual meet against Oklahoma State in Lawrence.

Although it was only a Kansas Relays record, Ryun excited the home crowd of 23,700 by winning the mile in 3:54.7 in April. He also had won the mile at the 1967 NCAA Indoor Championships and then claimed that same title later at the NCAA outdoor meet.

At the Amateur Athletic Union Outdoor Championships on June 23, 1967, Ryun broke his own world record in the mile at 3:51.1. He says that race in Bakersfield, Calif., offered a unique experience for him.

"I hadn't planned on a world record, whereas 1966 was a planned race," Ryun says. "But 1967 was one that developed as the race went along. I've often thought that given better circumstances, it might have been even faster. Because without a doubt, it was one of the easiest races that I ever ran, and yet it was a new world record."

In July, Ryun set a world record in the outdoor 1,500 meters with a time of 3:33.1, 2.5 seconds faster than the previous record. Although Ryun set an indoor mile record in 1971, the 1,500 triumph marked the last of his world records while he attended college.

Thirty years after both outdoor mile records, Ryun speaks modestly about what his accomplishments mean to him.

"They're part of a portfolio of experiences that affect my life today, in which I can look back on and truly thank God for the memory," he says. "And yet out of each one of those, I have a new experience that has taught me something new in life."

The year 1968 should have belonged to Ryun. He improved as a runner in 1967, but illness and injuries afflicted him in 1968, an Olympic year. Mononucleosis and a slight hamstring pull slowed him in the early part of the year after he won the NCAA indoor in the mile and the two-mile.

Another problem at that time existed between Ryun and Timmons. The student-coach combination, in its sixth year, became strained concerning how Ryun should train for the Olympics in high-altitude (7,415 feet) Mexico City. Timmons thinks that high-altitude experts advised Ryun in "negative" terms about training at altitude. Timmons says he offered a more "positive" approach, but Ryun didn't always agree with his coach.

Ryun ran a terrific race in the 1,500 in Mexico City. He finished in 3:37.7, the fastest high-altitude time ever run by a runner who grew up near sea level. Unfortunately, Keino defeated Ryun by 20 meters with a time of 3:34.9.

"I couldn't have run a better race as far as I'm concerned," he said at the time.

***

Ryun was right, but the race took its toll on him. The following track season, he walked off the track during races at the Drake Relays, the NCAA outdoors and the national AAU meet in Miami.

"We felt sorry for him with all the pressure he was under," says teammate Ron Jessie, an All-American long jumper in 1969.

When Ryun pulled out of the NCAA meet in the three-mile run, his decision cost the Jayhawks a national championship, and they finished second. He had run the mile earlier in the day and finished second to Villanova's Marty Liquori.

By the time Ryun left the track at Miami, he had damaged his reputation. He says he learned a lot during that trying year.

"I learned that when you are a self-made man, or you've had a lot of success as a young man, (if) you don't have a foundation on which to fall when things are difficult, you can find that life can be pretty disappointing," Ryun says. "And it was for me in that year – a difficult year – because I had some pretty high expectations, but I happened to finish second in the Olympic games, which in our country is difficult to deal with. And yet at the same time, I felt that I had a pretty good year.

As a KU freshman in 1966, Jim Ryun came from behind to defeat Kip Keino (1) in a two-mile race in Los Angeles. Two years later, Keino defeated Ryun in the 1,500 meters at the Mexico City Olympics.

"I look back at it now, and I realize I made a terrible mistake by stepping off the track in Miami. Because to walk away from something without dealing with it is not healthy for the future. I would sum up all of this by simply saying, that when it came time to test me, so to speak, and to see what I was really made of, I found that I wasn't made of what I really wanted to be made of. And so that was part of the process for me in terms of becoming a Christian, because that was a reality check that caused me to realize ... who was I?"

The year 1969 marked Ryun's last at KU. He married Anne Snider in January that year. And he "retired" from racing for awhile.

Time heals all wounds, though, and Ryun and Timmons reconciled.

"I consider Bob Timmons a gift from God to me," Ryun says. "I say that because he was a man with a vision who knew how to implement it and helped me realize some wonderful goals in my life. He took me from nowhere, on not being able to make an athletic team to becoming a world-record holder.

"I thank God for the talent, but I also thank God for the fact that Bob Timmons was there. He had the ability to dream a dream but to put the mechanics in place to see it realized."

Ryun also made a stirring comeback for the 1972 Olympics. But he was bumped in a qualifying heat for the 1,500 and fell down. Olympic officials rebuffed the many appeals that Ryun and Timmons sought to allow Ryun to run in the finals.

Despite that enormous setback, Ryun found himself in a much better position to deal with it than he had with the silver medal in Mexico City. He had committed himself to Christianity before the Olympics, and he found solace in the Bible.

"That particular decision is one of the reasons that I'm in Congress now," Ryun says about his 1996 election to the U.S. House of Representatives. The conservative Republican represents Kansas' 2nd District in the eastern part of the state. "It turned me from thinking I was the center of the universe into understanding that to be involved in leadership, you've got to serve others and to have more of a 'How can I help you attitude?' instead of 'What's in it for me?' "

In speeches during his campaign, Ryun recalled his "very valuable times" as a track athlete with Kansas.

"I often tell people, (that) they watched me grow up in Kansas before their eyes, with the visibility I had as a runner, then with the media's interest," he says. "They got to see when I did well, and when I made mistakes. It was a growing time."

FUN AND GAMES
Witty football coach gave Kansas its second Orange Bowl berth

As two-a-day drills wound down for the 1967 University of Kansas football team, new coach Pepper Rodgers called a meeting.

He asked assistant coach Doug Weaver to assemble the team. So, Weaver gathered the team in a large meeting room. But Rodgers was missing.

"They're all sitting there, scared to death that I was going to raise hell with them," Rodgers says.

Suddenly, there's a knock on the meeting-room door.

Weaver asks, "Who's there?"

The voice on the other side hollers, "I wanna go out for football."

Weaver says, "Come on in."

So in walks a character in shorts, sandals, sunglasses and a turtleneck sweater. Oh, and a wig. Can't forget the bushy wig.

It was Rodgers, doing his best to have fun.

"I had just come from UCLA, and I looked like a real hippie," he says of his outfit.

Then came the song that Rodgers sang to the team. Thirty years later, Rodgers still can carry a tune:

> "I wanted to go out for ball, but Rodgers, he wasn't fair,
> I told him, I'd climb or crawl up a wall, but I would not cut my hair.
> He told me it was lots of fun, but I would not cut my curls,
> so you keep your jocks, I'll keep my locks, and I'll end up with the girls."

"That was a fun time for me," Rodgers says of the four years, 1967-70, that he coached the Jayhawks. "But life has always been a fun time for me. Woody Allen said in a movie, 'God put me down on Earth to be different.' And I figure that God put me down to be different from most of the coaches."

Different in approach, yes. But the same competitiveness burned within him as with all other successful players and coaches.

***

Franklin Cullen Rodgers was born in 1931. He was nicknamed "Pepper" after colorful second baseman Pepper Martin of the St. Louis Cardinals' "Gashouse Gang" of the 1930s. Rodgers achieved tremendous success as a quarterback for Georgia Tech in 1951-53. Coach Bobby Dodd and Rodgers directed the Yellow Jackets to a 30-2-1 mark in those three seasons, including a victory in the 1952 Orange Bowl and victories in the 1953 and 1954 Sugar Bowls.

After a stint in the Air Force, which included two years as a player-coach at a base in Hamilton, Calif., he worked as an assistant coach at the U.S. Air Force Academy in 1958-59. Rodgers then moved to the University of Florida as an offensive assistant from 1960 to 1964. While on the Gators' staff, Rodgers helped develop quarterback Steve Spurrier, who won the Heisman Trophy in 1966 and coached Florida to the No. 1 spot in the final 1996 Associated Press poll.

In Rodgers' last assistant's job before leading Kansas, he served as Tommy Prothro's top offensive assistant for UCLA in 1965 and 1966. Rodgers helped

"Life has always been a fun time for me. Woody Allen said in a movie, 'God put me down on Earth to be different.' And I figure that God put me down to be different from most coaches."

– Pepper Rodgers

develop Bruins' quarterback Gary Beban, who won the 1967 Heisman Trophy.

At Kansas, Rodgers succeeded Jack Mitchell, whose last team went 2-7-1 and was winless in its last seven games. Rodgers said he was attracted to Kansas because athletes such as John Hadl and Gale Sayers had played there. The Jayhawks' basketball success also factored into his decision.

"I knew they were interested in sports," Rodgers says. "I knew (the selection committee) was committed to try to win. It was a nice fit for me. I liked Lawrence, Kansas, a lot and I liked the University very much."

**PEPPER RODGERS
Head football coach,
1967-70**

The 1967 Jayhawks suffered an inauspicious beginning to the Rodgers era, losing their first three games. The fourth game that year, Nebraska in Lawrence, didn't appear as one in which the Jayhawks would rebound. But KU surprised the Cornhuskers 10-0, which Rodgers calls one of his most special moments as coach of the Jayhawks.

Kansas then defeated Oklahoma State, Iowa State and Kansas State before losing to Colorado and Oklahoma. So the Jayhawks entered the season finale against Missouri with a 4-5 record. Kansas had not beaten Missouri since 1960. As the Jayhawks prepared to take the field, defensive end John Zook suggested that Rodgers lead them to the bench.

"We had always taught our players when they got on the field to hit the ground and do a forward roll," Rodgers says. "I come out of the locker room, leading the team across the field running full speed. By the time I got to the bench, I thought 'What the hell,' and I did a forward roll.

"And all my assistant coaches did forward rolls. And obviously, the team did, because we taught them to. That was such a special moment, and then we won the ball game (17-6).

"But then the legend grows, and by today it's a double somersault."

***

The Jayhawks entered the 1968 season with forward momentum after winning five of their last seven games in 1967. Rodgers says he knew the 1968 Jayhawks would be good because of strength at quarterback (Bobby Douglass), fullback (John Riggins) and Zook's ability to rush the passer. But he admits he did not expect the great season that occurred.

An extremely talented coaching staff assisted Rodgers. Most of the assistants became head coaches, including John Cooper (Tulsa, Arizona State and Ohio State), Terry Donahue (UCLA), Dick Tomey (Arizona), the late Dave McLain (Wisconsin) and Sandy Buda (Nebraska-Omaha). Weaver was hired after Kansas State fired him. Rodgers also retained other assistants from Mitchell's staff, Don Fambrough and Floyd Temple. Fambrough succeeded Rodgers after the 1970 season and coached KU in two separate four-year periods, 1971-74 and 1979-82.

Kansas won its first seven games in 1968. Nebraska served as the fourth victim that season, as the Jayhawks won 23-13 in Lincoln. Nebraska has not lost to the Jayhawks since.

Temple, Rodgers' roommate on the road, remembers that day not for its historical significance but for a stunt the head coach pulled in their room that morning.

"The motel had brought us a bowl of fruit to eat," Temple says. "Pepper says, 'I tell you what, we're gonna kick their ass,' and he took a grapefruit and threw it hard up against the wall – POW! You should have seen that room, the grapefruit just exploded. Scared the hell out of me."

With Douglass directing the offense, the Jayhawks averaged 38 points a game and finished 9-1 in the regular season. As Big Eight Conference co-champion, Kansas received a trip to the Orange Bowl against Penn State.

In two years, Rodgers had turned the Kansas football program completely around and had fun doing it. But KU achieved the turnaround through discipline and hard work, Rodgers' occasional antics not withstanding.

"He was so tough his first couple of years," says Monte Johnson, an assistant athletics director at the time. "Players couldn't ever, ever enter the football field without their helmet on. He changed things so much; part of it was to make sure they all stayed focused."

Peers also heralded Rodgers for his strategic savvy.

"He might have been one of the brightest offensive coaches I've ever met in football," Johnson says. "If you told Pepper he couldn't score against you, he'd figure out a way to score against you."

The Jayhawks foundered in 1969 and finished 1-9 under Rodgers. Kansas seemed to right its course in 1970, opening 5-2. But the Jayhawks lost their last four games and then lost Rodgers, as he took the UCLA head coaching job after the season. He won 20 games and lost 22 in his four years with the Jayhawks, a time he calls "very meaningful."

He later coached at Georgia Tech and for the Memphis, Tenn., franchise in the United States Football League in the 1980s. Today, Rodgers lives in Memphis, where he works as a vice president, Memphis operations, for the Tennessee Oilers.

Pepper Rodgers enjoys football, its players and life. He summarized his feelings by recounting the time his UCLA team trounced Stanford and amassed more than 600 rushing yards. He was stunned when the first question in the post-game media conference noted that the Bruins had not passed much in the game.

"I go, 'Look, boys, lemme give you my philosophy,' " he says. " 'The four most important things in life are fast backs, big linemen, beautiful women and good music. At two in the afternoon for me, it's fast backs and big linemen. At six in the evening, it's beautiful women and good music.

" 'And damned if it ain't past six.' "

ONE TOO MANY

Thirty years later, longtime KU fans still wince when they remember the 1969 Orange Bowl. On one hand, the game represented the pinnacle of Kansas' resurgence in football. The game itself offered fans a classic: two evenly matched teams, a close score, bursts of offense and oppressing defense.

Unfortunately, the Jayhawks lost in a bizarre finish that took a lot of the fun out of KU's wonderful season.

Kansas led 14-7 when it punted with 1:16 left in the game. Penn State partially blocked the kick, and the Nittany Lions took over at midfield. On first down, Penn State quarterback Chuck Burkhart threw a long pass that Kansas almost intercepted. But the pass was completed to the Jayhawks' 3-yard line.

Two ensuing plays produced no yardage, but on third down, with 15 seconds to play, Burkhart ran 3 yards for the touch-down. The Jayhawks broke up his pass on a two-point conversion attempt, and it appeared that Kansas won the game.

But the officials ruled that Kansas had 12 men on the field during the extra-point play (actually, KU had 12 men on the field for a few plays before the extra-point attempt). Penn State converted its second two-point attempt and won the game 15-14.

"It was one of the most memorable (Orange Bowl) games ever," Rodgers says. "Nobody has ever forgotten the game."

Case in point: Rodgers attended an Orange Bowl Hall-of-Fame induction a few years back in which Penn State running back Charlie Pittman was honored.

"He got up to the podium and said, 'I want to thank my mama, I want to thank my daddy, I want to thank (Penn State) coach (Joe) Paterno, but most of all, I want to thank coach Pepper Rodgers for having

those 12 guys in the game," says Rodgers, laughing at the recollection.

"Having the 12th guy in the game is something that happens to every football team. What happened, we sent in a big ol' lineman to replace a linebacker when they got down to the 3. And he was so damn slow, he got there just about the time that they came out of the huddle, and he just sort of flopped down and never told anybody. So (Penn State) never went in a huddle because time was running out, and nobody ever saw him.

"Anyway, though, that game in the Orange Bowl was a wonderful thing for the University of Kansas."

Kansas finished the season ranked No. 6 in the United Press International poll and No. 7 in the Associated Press poll. The Jayhawks didn't experience another top-10 finish until 1995.

ALL-AMERICAN COMPETITOR

Orange Bowl quarterback known for toughness, spirited play

Mention Bobby Douglass to former University of Kansas football teammates and coaches and a word association game with variations of the same answer develops.

"What a competitor he was," says John Zook, an All-American defensive end and Douglass' teammate from 1966 to 1968. "He was very talented, tough and highly competitive. Just an excellent athlete and a dream competitor."

Jack Mitchell, Douglass' first head coach at KU, appreciated his versatility.

"Bobby was a tremendous athlete," Mitchell says. "Physically, Bobby Douglass could play tackle, guard, center, end. He would have made All-America at end. He could play anywhere, because he'd knock your ass off."

BOBBY DOUGLASS
Football,
1966-68

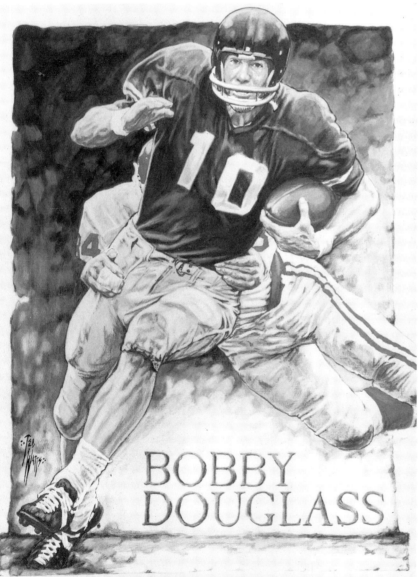

BOBBY DOUGLASS

Pepper Rodgers, who succeeded Mitchell and tailored the Jayhawks' offense to suit Douglass' running ability, says the 6-foot-3-inch, 212-pound El Dorado native was a great leader for KU.

"All you have to do is look at any film on Bobby and know he was one of the toughest guys who ever played," he says.

Douglass played sporadically during his sophomore season in 1966. An injury to starting quarterback Bobby Skahan forced Mitchell to rotate his signal callers during that disappointing 2-7-1 campaign, Mitchell's last at Kansas.

"I started him against Arizona, and he wasn't ready," Mitchell said of the Jayhawks' second game that year, a 35-13 KU victory. "I hadn't had enough time to spend with him. I didn't have the whole spring practice, because I was working with Skahan."

Though third-string quarterback Dave Bouda led the Jayhawks to that victory, Douglass did get significant playing time during the year – but not always at quarterback.

"He was a hell of a good athlete, and we needed a fullback," Mitchell says. "So I moved him to fullback. I probably would have been better off staying with him (at quarterback) and suffering through it."

For the season, Douglass completed 17 of 38 passes for 175 yards and rushed for 105 yards in 72 attempts.

Change swept through the Kansas football program after the 1966 season. Rodgers replaced Mitchell as coach. Rodgers also changed how the Jayhawks approached football.

"There's no doubt (Rodgers) brought us a winning attitude," Douglass said in a 1988 interview. "He started by working us harder as a team than in previous years. We did things (off-season weight program) the good schools were doing – with enthusiasm."

At first, the changes didn't seem effective. Kansas, with Douglass firmly in command as quarterback, sputtered in Rodgers' first three games as coach. The Jayhawks lost two road games, a one-point setback against Stanford and a three-point defeat against Indiana. And in the home opener, the University of Ohio embarrassed the Jayhawks in a soggy 30-15 defeat.

By then, the 0-3 Jayhawks could have called it a year. But the offense got in synch, the defense rallied and the coaches made the players believe they were better than their record. In its next game, Kansas defeated Nebraska 10-0 for the Jayhawks' first triumph.

KU won three more in a row. Douglass used his laser-like left arm to pass for a season-high 204 yards against Iowa State in KU's third victory. The next week, he relied on his running skills to gain 122 rushing yards in a 17-16 victory against Kansas State.

Kansas then lost two in a row to Colorado and Oklahoma. But the Jayhawks defeated Missouri in the season finale.

Sportswriters named Douglass as "back-of-the-year" in the Big Eight Conference. He gained more than 200 yards in total offense in four straight games, the first back in league history to do so. For the season, Douglass passed for 1,326 yards and seven touchdowns and rushed for a team-high 415 yards and scored seven touchdowns.

***

After a strong finish, and with most starters returning, KU eagerly awaited the 1968 season. Douglass made sure the Jayhawks didn't disappoint themselves.

The year 1968 belonged to Kansas football. The Jayhawks won their first seven games, lost to Oklahoma and then beat arch-rivals Kansas State and Missouri for a 9-1 season, a share of the conference title and a trip to the Orange Bowl. And Douglass led the team every step of the way.

In the season opener at Illinois, he threw touchdown passes of 44 and 45 yards and ran for another score in the 47-7 victory. The next week against Indiana at home, Douglass scored on two unusual plays, one a pass reception on an option play, the other on a third-down-and-one quarterback sneak that turned into a 71-yard romp. KU won 38-20. In their final non-conference game, the Jayhawks dominated New Mexico 68-7. Douglass threw two scoring passes and ran for two other touchdowns in the rout.

Kansas faced Nebraska in the season's fourth game, and the contest proved pivotal to the Jayhawks' success. Playing at home, Nebraska led KU 13-9 with less than 10 minutes left in the game. After the Cornhuskers had scored to take the lead, Douglass led Kansas on a 14-play, 73-yard drive, which he culminated with a one-yard touchdown run.

Holding a 16-13 lead, the Jayhawks defense held Nebraska on downs and took possession of the ball on the Cornhuskers' 26-yard line. Douglass clinched the victory with a 10-yard scoring run around left end as Kansas won 23-13, its last triumph in the series entering 1998.

The Jayhawks continued their offensive onslaught the next three weeks. Douglass rushed for 93 yards, ran for a touchdown and passed for two more, including a 50-yarder, as Kansas cruised past Oklahoma State 49-14. Against Iowa State, the Jayhawks struck for four touchdowns in a 4-and-a-half minute span, defeating the Cyclones 46-25. Douglass accounted for two touchdown passes and a rushing score.

"He went from being an average quarterback under a different system to being a great quarterback under the system that allowed him to run and throw and use his athletic skills."

– Pepper Rodgers on Bobby Douglass

Bobby Douglass used a strong left arm to lead Kansas to the 1969 Orange Bowl against Penn State.

In a 27-14 defeat of Colorado, Douglass ran for 108 yards and the team rushed for 428 yards.

Oklahoma handed the Jayhawks a 27-23 defeat the following week as Douglass played valiantly. He threw for a career-high 240 yards, including a 75-yard touchdown pass to George McGowan. After the Sooners took the final lead, Douglass directed the Jayhawks from their 20-yard line to the OU 26 in seven plays. But Douglass and the Jayhawks could go no farther that day as four pass plays were unsuccessful.

The Jayhawks regained their footing the next week against Kansas State in Manhattan. Douglass ran for three short touchdowns and passed for another, propelling KU past the Wildcats 38-29. In the season finale, a 21-19 victory against Missouri, Douglass accumulated 186 total yards.

For the 1968 season, Douglass passed for 1,316 yards and 12 touchdowns and ran for 495 yards and 12 touchdowns. The Jayhawks averaged 401.8 yards per game in total offense, second-highest in school history. The team's 34.5-point-scoring average remains a school record.

"He went from being an average quarterback under a different system to being a great quarterback under the system that allowed him to run and to throw and use his athletic skills," Rodgers says.

In the infamous 1969 Orange Bowl, Penn State rallied to defeat Kansas 15-14 when officials penalized the Jayhawks for having too many men on the field for the Nittany Lions' failed two-point conversion attempt. Penn State converted its second try after the penalty to win the game.

Although the loss devastated the Jayhawks, Douglass put the game and season in proper perspective in a 1988 interview.

"It was so enjoyable to get to the Orange Bowl and have the last two years go so well," he said.

Including the bowl game, he gained 3,832 yards in total offense for his career, a school record at that time. Today, he ranks seventh on Kansas' career total offense list and sixth in career passing with 2,817 yards.

Douglass played 12 years in the NFL, including six years with the Chicago Bears. Today, he lives in Lake Forest, Ill. Rodgers marvels at Douglass' toughness as a pro.

"Bobby's the guy who went to the Chicago Bears, and when he wasn't playing quarterback he asked to cover kickoffs," he says. "Anybody who wanted to test his courage was making a mistake."

FULL SPEED AHEAD
Defensive end went all-out
on every play

Being chosen an All-America football player is special, but remember, almost 30 players are picked every year.

But making the Deaner's list as Dean Nesmith's favorite athlete is really special, because you're the one that the longtime University of Kansas trainer admired most for toughness.

"I guess John Zook was probably his favorite," says Don Fambrough, former KU football coach and an assistant when Zook played for the Jayhawks in 1966-68. "John wouldn't let you put a piece of tape on him if his foot was hanging by a thread. And Dean always used him as an example. He loved those kids who could play hurt and had great attitudes."

Zook, a stellar defensive end, shrugs off such high praise, much as he did offensive linemen.

"Maybe I was a favorite because I didn't spend much time in the training room," he says with a typical understatement.

Zook was born Sept. 24, 1947, in Garden City. He grew up on the family farm near Larned and filled out his 6-foot-4-inch frame with 230 pounds. Head coach Jack Mitchell recruited Zook, an all-state defensive lineman and fullback, in 1964. A standout high school basketball player as well, Zook chose KU because he wanted to stay in state and he enjoyed his recruiting trip, which involved a Jayhawks' basketball game.

"He was a helluva football player, no question about it," says Mitchell, who coached Zook during his sophomore season in 1966, Mitchell's last year at Kansas. "He was a good, strong, dedicated boy. He comes from a very fine family, and he was raised right. He's just a first-class boy all the way."

Pepper Rodgers replaced Mitchell for the 1967 season. The Jayhawks lost their first three games that year before facing Nebraska in Lawrence. In an inspired performance, Kansas shut out the Cornhuskers 10-0. Zook made 15 tackles in the game, and the Associated Press named him national lineman of the week.

"We never blocked him last season, and we didn't block him today," Nebraska coach Bob Devaney said after the game.

For the season, Zook tallied 80 tackles, third-highest on the Jayhawks. He made the all-Big Eight Conference team. But ask Zook about

JOHN ZOOK
Football,
1966-68

memorable moments of the season, and all he'll say is how he enjoyed Rodgers turning a somersault as he led the Jayhawks on the field against Missouri.

The Jayhawks, Zook included, were encouraged by a strong finish in 1967. KU finished 5-5 but won five of its last seven games. With Bobby Douglass at quarterback and Donnie Shanklin and John Riggins in the backfield, Zook thought the Jayhawks were "great" on offense and "good" on defense.

He underestimated the defense, which he anchored, but called the offense just right. Kansas won nine, lost one and shared the conference championship in 1968.

The Jayhawks went to the Orange Bowl, where they lost 15-14 to Penn State in the unforgettable "12th man" game. Kansas lost the game in the final seconds after officials spotted 12 Jayhawks on the field following Penn State's unsuccessful attempt for a two-point conversion. Given a reprieve, Penn State converted on its second attempt for two points, thus writing a painful ending to KU's storybook season.

"I'd kind of like to forget that game," Zook says. "I thought we had the game won when they went for the two points late. That was a super disappointment."

The game marked Zook's last as a Jayhawk. He gained all-conference and All-America honors in 1968 and finished his career with 202 tackles.

"He never played but full speed from snap one to snap hundred," Rodgers says. "He was the most full-speed player on every snap that you could ever imagine. I loved John."

Zook played 11 seasons in the NFL, seven with the Atlanta Falcons from 1969 to 1975 and four with the St. Louis Cardinals from 1976 to 1979.

Pro scouts amazed Rodgers when they told him they didn't think Zook was fast enough to play defensive end in the NFL. The scouts based their assessment on Zook's 4.8-second time in the 40-yard dash, one of the league's favorite measuring sticks. Rodgers disagreed with the scouts and told them so.

"John Zook might run 4.8 in the first quarter, and there might be someone else who runs 4.6 in the first quarter," Rodgers says. "But when they're running five-flat in the fourth quarter, John Zook is still running 4.8."

Today, Zook lives in suburban Atlanta and covers a 72-county territory for Safeco Inc., selling occupational, health and safety equipment to industrial accounts such as Ford, General Motors and Georgia Pacific.

"He never played but full speed from snap one to snap hundred. He was the most full-speed player on every snap that you could ever imagine. I loved John."

– Pepper Rodgers

LOOK OUT BELOW!

John Zook's hobby in college differed from most players: He belonged to the Parachute Club of America and was a member in good standing.

"I jumped 54 times over at Forbes Air Force Base in Topeka," he says. "It's just one of those things, it's just a thrill. I really enjoyed it. It was really a lot of fun."

Zook jumped well enough to perform 30-, 45- and 60-second releases, which means waiting those durations after jumping before deploying the parachute. He used an altimeter and a stopwatch to calibrate the jumps.

All good things must come to an end, however. Zook let it slip during an interview with the Big Eight Skywriters about his hobby, which the 1967 Kansas football media guide reported "caused consternation among last year's coaching staff." He sold his parachutes and jumping gear in the spring of 1968.

The former All-American defensive end denies that the Jayhawks' coaches forced him to stop jumping. Besides, Zook says, "I didn't jump during the season."

Alas, he never regained the urge to jump after college.

"I haven't done it since, and I probably won't," Zook says. "I'm at the point in my life where I probably won't be jumping out of any perfectly good airplanes."

A RECORD SHARED, A RECORD BROKEN

Trio of hurdlers set world mark during college careers

A college high hurdle stands 42 inches tall – or chest high next to University of Kansas world-record hurdler George Byers, who is "not quite" 5 feet 10 inches tall.

"I never ran against an athlete who was shorter than me," Byers says. "Coach (Bob Timmons) was going to make me an intermediate hurdler because he thought I was too short. But I didn't want that."

Competing at KU in 1965-69, Byers became the Big Eight Conference's fastest hurdler to that date by running 13.6 seconds in the 120-yard high hurdles in 1968. He placed fourth in the same event in the 1969 NCAA Outdoor Championships.

Yet his greatest claim to fame is a world record he shared – and later broke – in the late 1960s with KU teammates Lee Adams and J.W. Johnson.

As only a freshman, Byers ran 6.7 seconds in the 60-yard low hurdles, tying the indoor world record.

"He was one of the quickest people over the hurdles I've ever seen – a beautiful hurdler," Timmons says of Byers.

The next season, Adams, a junior transfer from Bakersfield (Calif.) Junior College, and KU freshman Johnson broke the 60-yard hurdle record in the same race. Each ran 6.6 seconds in a 1967 Kansas Federation meet in Lawrence.

"J.W. had a blazing start, but I caught him off the last hurdle and beat him in a photo finish," Adams says.

But Byers wasn't through. The world mark set by Adams and Johnson lasted just one year. Byers tied their record and then broke it with a 6.5-second race in 1968.

Not only were Byers and Adams linked on the track, they were roommates and close friends off the track. Both cherish their friendship.

"To meet other people from other regions of the country was a very enlightening and maturing process," says Adams, who was heavily recruited at Bakersfield, where he was an All-American hurdler and a member of two record-setting relays.

Adams learned of KU's rich athletics tradition by reading clips about Gale Sayers, Wilt Chamberlain and Charlie Tidwell and listening to his junior college coach, Bob Covey, a KU graduate who once set the freshman quarter-mile record.

"I remember (1968 Olympians) Tommie Smith and Lee Evans called me and tried to convince me to come to San Jose State," Adams says. "But KU's tradition was impressive. When I visited KU, it was so picturesque. I came home rippin' and roarin' about wanting to attend Kansas."

Adams capped off his KU career by winning a conference indoor title in the 60-yard high hurdles and participating in an NCAA record-setting, 480-yard shuttle hurdle relay.

After college, he returned to California. Today, Adams works as an associate dean in admissions and special programs at California State University in Bakersfield.

Byers, who grew up in Kansas City, Mo., and attended Central High, followed his

GEORGE BYERS · LEE ADAMS
J.W. JOHNSON

dream to become a teacher. He coaches football and track at Southeast High
School in Kansas City, Mo.

Adams and Byers were sorry to see Johnson quit school after his freshman year.
He had come to KU as a heralded sprinter from Wichita East High School, where
Timmons previously coached. But apparently Johnson's heart wasn't into being a
student-athlete.

"We had to wake J.W. up every morning just to get him to English class," Adams
says.

BETTER LATE THAN NEVER

Jumper's tardiness enlivened track meets for coach

Bob Timmons sensed doom at the 1969 NCAA Indoor Track and Field Championships.

The University of Kansas coach saw the Jayhawks' chance for the team's second national championship in four years slipping away. Long jumper Ron Jessie couldn't find his mark along the curb of the runway leading up to the jumping board.

Jessie and teammate Stan Whitley had made their marks the night before at Cobo Hall in Detroit.

"I checked down there, and they repainted the curbings along the track and along the runways, so those marks that we measured the day before were gone," Timmons says.

With the championships about to start, the marks weren't the only things missing. Jessie and Whitley were late, a common occurrence in Jessie's case.

"I'm frantic," Timmons says. "You don't have a chance to win a national championship every time."

Jessie and Whitley eventually showed – barely in time – as Timmons remeasured the runway. The perturbed coach spotted the jumpers.

"You guys gotta get warmed up," Timmons says.

Jessie replies, "I'm ready, coach."

"But we don't have your mark down."

"I'll take that one."

At this point, 30 years later, Timmons gets annoyed all over again.

"It's like a pole vaulter saying, 'I'll use that pole over there,' " he says. "That's absurd! (Jessie) didn't know the stride of that guy or anything."

Timmons finished measuring, retired to the stands and relayed the bad news to assistant coach John Mitchell.

"I said, 'John, we've lost this national championship because of these two kids' carelessness and lackadaisical attitudes. We're not going to score any points in the long jump,' " Timmons says.

But Jessie and Whitley did score some points.

"They went one-and-two. One-and-two!" Timmons says. "Oh, boy. I could have killed those guys."

Timmons restrained himself, however, and the Jayhawks won the team championship. Jessie jumped 25 feet, 7 inches for his title.

Jessie recalls he was mad before he won the long-jump championship. Not because paint covered his mark, even though he thinks "someone was trying to sabotage me."

No, what upset Jessie was that he thought he had qualified

**RON JESSIE
Track and field
and football,
1969-70**

for the high-hurdles finals. But meet officials ruled that Jessie did not qualify for the last spot based on a photo finish. Jessie disagreed and sought his coach.

"So, I'm grabbing Timmie and I say, 'Come on, man, you gotta look at the picture, because I think I beat the guy,' " Jessie says. "We went up and looked at the picture, and it was inconclusive. Still to this day, I think I should have qualified for the finals in the high hurdles."

But he recovered for the long jump, mark or no mark.

"I just used Stan's mark," Jessie says with a laugh. "It came out well. I was a little bit behind the board, but it was enough to win."

***

Jessie says the championship jump means a lot to him for a not-so-obvious reason.

"I never practiced," he says about his track conditioning. "I got my practice on the long jump at Robinson Gym. I used to go over there and play basketball with the basketball players, Jo Jo White, Bud Stallworth. It used to be football players against basketball players.

"That's where I did my conditioning. Because Timmie had a rule that you really didn't have to come to practice. So, that's how I stayed in shape for track. I went out there and chased Jo Jo White all around the court all the time."

In those pick-up games, Jessie played with the football players because he also played halfback and flanker for KU in 1969 and 1970.

"He was a fabulous athlete," says Pepper Rodgers, former KU football coach. "When he touched the ball, he was really a b-a-a-a-d guy. He was terrific."

Football enticed Jessie, a native of Yuma, Ariz., to the University. Kansas was the only school recruiting Jessie that would allow him to run track and play football. So Jessie signed with the Jayhawks after three semesters at Imperial Valley Junior College in El Centro, Calif.

Jessie says he appreciated Timmons for taking an interest in him.

"He'd always ask, 'Ron, what are you going to do?' " Jessie says, doing a dead-on imitation of Timmons. "I'd say, 'I'm going to play some pro football.' And he'd say, 'Well, what if that doesn't happen?' He was always staying on me to get my education. He's a good guy, always concerned."

Jessie did play pro football. He spent four years as a wide receiver with the Detroit Lions, five years with the Los Angeles Rams (he missed the 1980 Super Bowl with a broken leg) and two seasons with the Buffalo Bills. Today, he works as an investigator for a lawyer and lives in Huntington Beach, Calif.

Probably for his aggravation, Timmons should get the last words on Jessie. The former coach tells about Jessie showing up late – of course – at the Big Eight Conference Indoor meet at Kansas City's Municipal Auditorium.

After hearing a brief lecture on responsibility, a repentant Jessie told Timmons he couldn't run that night for lack of an athletic supporter. Timmons tore around the arena and found a jock strap for Jessie, who won his race.

Another time, the Jayhawks were leaving their motel after competing in the Drake Relays in Des Moines, Iowa. The bus was loaded, ready to go.

No Jessie.

The bus took the Jayhawks to the cafeteria where they dined every year.

No Jessie.

Timmons and crew looked every place.

No Jessie.

So they returned to the motel. Timmons checked Jessie's room. The windows were flung open. Curtains danced in the strong breeze. There's Jessie, sprawled in bed, with no sheet on, no clothes on, not a care in the world, fast asleep.

"And then," Timmons says, with a hint of awe in his voice, "Ron gets on the bus, and within two minutes he's sound asleep again.

"Ron Jessie was a great character, and maybe one of the finest athletes of all the athletes we've had."

A COMPLETE PLAYER

Smooth guard could do whatever it took to win

The pass, says Ted Owens, is a great communicator.

Get the ball to the open man, the former University of Kansas basketball coach says, and he understands his teammates have confidence in him. Ignore the open man, and he thinks his teammates don't believe in him. A pass can speak volumes.

And in guard Jo Jo White, Kansas possessed one of the premier basketball orators of the late 1960s.

"One of Jo's great qualities, one of the things we liked about him best, he would get the ball to the open man," Owens says. "Jo was a guy like Bird, like Magic, like Kareem – their strength was they made their teammates better players.

"He could score three points, if that's all that we needed, or he could get 30 points if that's what you needed. He didn't seem to mind either way. He was a very unselfish player."

White gave Kansas two great full seasons and two great partial seasons. He graduated at mid-term in the 1964-65 school year from McKinley High School in St. Louis. Kansas, through assistant coach Sam Miranda, won a spirited recruiting battle against more than 60 universities to sign White.

"I'm not sure a lot of people knew he was graduating," Owens says. "He graduated one day, waited one day and was at the University of Kansas the next day. And in two days, he started in a freshman game."

He dominated freshman play. White had improved his game through daily play while growing up in St. Louis. In the summer, pickup games on the playground meant playing against college players and even an established pro named Lenny Wilkens.

"I found I could hold my own," White told the *Topeka Daily Journal* in 1966.

So White played with the Kansas freshmen in the second half of the 1964-65 season and the first half of the 1965-66 season. He continued to improve, and by early 1966 he started dominating the Jayhawks' varsity guards in practice.

Now Owens and his coaching staff faced a decision. The Jayhawks were a good team without White, and were only a half-game behind Nebraska in the Big Eight Conference standings. But with White, the

JO JO WHITE
Basketball,
1966-69

Jayhawks could become a great team, perhaps national champions. And in the days when the NCAA Tournament consisted of a 22-team field, winning the regular-season conference championship was almost mandatory to make the tournament.

Owens and his assistants debated their decision at length. Bringing White in would improve the team. But it also would disrupt the starting lineup, and it would mean that he could not play a full season with the Jayhawks as a senior.

"We really thought for a long time about holding him out," Owens says. "But we thought we had the chance for the national championship."

Owens also involved the team in the decision. He sought one of the captains, Riney Lochmann, for consultation.

"I said, 'Riney, we think we have a real shot at the national championship,' " Owens says. " 'The coaches think that Jo Jo can help us to win it. And Jo Jo wants to play now.

" 'But we have one problem. If he did (play), he'd probably would start for you. And it's important for me that you know about that.' "

Lochmann didn't hesitate with his answer, Owens recalls.

"He said, 'Coach, we all want to win the national championship. Don't you worry about whether I start or not. We want Jo Jo to play now, and if that means giving up my starting spot, so be it.'

"I'll never forget that."

Owens also won't forget preparing for White's first game. The Jayhawks, 15-3, played Oklahoma State on Feb. 12 in Lawrence. A self-conscious Owens was trying to get Jo Jo to relax before his first game. He need not have bothered.

"I avoided saying anything in my pre-game talk about 'Don't be nervous,' " Owens says. "I didn't even bring his name up except as a starter. He walked by me on the way to the court, slapped me on the leg and said, 'I'm OK, coach, don't worry.'

"So, we get the tip, he goes down and shoots in the first shot he takes."

The new-look Jayhawks won that game and six others in conference play, winning the league title with a 13-1 mark. With White in the lineup, the Jayhawks raised their team scoring average from 74 points to almost 84 points a game during the regular season.

"Jo was cool and smooth ... a great ballplayer," says former KU teammate Walt Wesley, an All-American in 1965-66. "I wish Jo could have been with us for a full year. He would have been a tremendous asset with the likes of Al Lopes at the other guard and Del Lewis, Ron Franz and Riney Lochmann.

"And he did, at the time, make us a lot more versatile."

***

Owens' decision to play White seemed prescient as the Jayhawks entered the NCAA Tournament. In its first game in Lubbock, Texas, KU subdued Southern Methodist University 76-70. The victory put Kansas, 23-3, into the regional finals against Texas Western, (now known as the University of Texas-El Paso), 25-1. The next night – March 12, 1966 – will live forever in Jayhawk infamy.

The Jayhawks and Miners waged war that night. Both teams lost leads, both teams fought back and both teams fouled each other. A lot. Officials called 25 fouls on KU and 21 on Texas Western. The game was tied at 69 at the end of regulation after White scored a three-point play with 38 seconds left.

Through cautious play and fatigue, both teams had scored only two points each in the first 4 minutes, 53 seconds of the 5-minute overtime period. With 7 seconds remaining, the Miners were called for charging under KU's basket.

The Jayhawks inbounded the ball to White, playing in only his ninth college game. He took the ball, dribbled two-thirds of the length of the court along the left sideline. With 1 second left, White let fly a beautiful 35-foot arc that landed true to its mark. The Jayhawks were headed to the Final Four.

But official Rudy Marich saw things differently. He ruled White's foot brushed the

---

"It takes a whole village for a person to be successful, and Kansas was my village."

– Jo Jo White

out-of-bounds line, which nullified the basket. The game headed to a second over-time.

Disheartened and running out of players – three starters had fouled out – the Jayhawks fell behind 81-75 in the second overtime. A late rally brought KU within one, but the Jayhawks ran out of miracles and time. Texas Western won 81-80. A week later, the Miners defeated Kentucky for the NCAA championship.

Thirty-one years later, White is attending his induction into the Kansas Sports Hall of Fame in Abilene when the question comes up for at least the zillionth time: Were you out of bounds?

"It showed clearly – *it showed clearly* – that I was not on the out-of-bounds line," White told the *Topeka Capital-Journal* about the game replays.

White showed the conference what he could do with a full season in 1966-67. He made all-conference and directed the Jayhawks to their second straight league crown, again with a 13-1 record, and another NCAA Tournament appearance.

Again, Kansas seemed primed to make the Final Four. The Jayhawks played host to the Midwest Regional, opening against the University of Houston. But the Jayhawks never could get untracked against Elvin Hayes, Don Chaney and the rest of the Cougars, losing 66-53. A victory in a meaningless consolation game against Louisville gave Kansas its second straight 23-4 season.

That summer, White led the U.S. national team to championships in the Pan American Games and the World University Games.

In 1967-68, White averaged 15.3 points per game and was named All-America. The Jayhawks slipped to 10-4 in conference play and settled for the National Invitational Tournament. Kansas won three straight games at Madison Square Garden before losing to the University of Dayton 61-48 in the championship game.

At this point in his college career, White had established himself as one of the best players in the United States. And one of the most frustrated. Texas Western. Houston. Dayton. Three great seasons, three tough season-ending losses.

Because he joined the Jayhawks one game into the second semester of the 1965-66 season, White only could play 18 games, or one game into the second semester of the 1968-69 season. So he entered his senior year knowing he could never be an NCAA champion.

***

As bleak as that prospect was, White did have one more shot at a championship – an Olympic championship. He earned a spot on the 1968 U.S. team coached by Henry Iba of Oklahoma State. The United States had never lost in Olympic basketball competition, dating to the sport's debut in 1936.

But this U.S. team seemed vulnerable. Several top black players passed up the team as part of a boycott attempt to draw attention to racial issues in the United States. White had looked forward to playing in the Olympics since he was a child, and his dream went undeterred. He was second in scoring, behind Spencer Haywood, and the United States won the gold medal. At last, White was a

Jo Jo White was the second-leading scorer on the U.S. men's basketball team that won the gold medal at the 1968 Olympics.

champion, and he called the championship his biggest thrill in basketball at the time.

Owens calls the Olympics one of the greatest honors that an athlete can experience. He was thrilled that White made the team and excelled.

"That was a team that was not well thought of, and it was a great achievement to win it that year," he says.

Iba gave credit where it was due.

"He probably is as complete a ballplayer as you would want to run into in a university class," he said of White.

Although abbreviated, White's senior year was a memorable one. He averaged 18.1 points a game and again was named All-America. The Jayhawks were 15-3 after his last game, an 80-70 defeat of Colorado on Feb. 1, 1969. Playing in front of his parents, White scored a career-high 30 points. He finished his career with 1,286 points, 17th on the all-time Kansas scoring list heading into the 1998-99 season. Kansas won 68 of 84 games in which White played.

A few days before the Colorado game, Dick Russell of the *Topeka Capital-Journal* summarized White as follows:

"For three years now, he has floated through pressure defenses like an evasive helium balloon. Perhaps you could hold him momentarily, but at the precise moment of release, he was gone – synchronizing his way downcourt with the precision and grace of a Balanchine dancer.

"For three years, he has been the adhesive tape of the Kansas defense. He made the spectacular seem almost commonplace, stealing passes so often that his mere presence provided psychological traumas to opposing guards.

" ... he became the type of guard that coaches only dream about – a staunch defender, devastating outside shooter and soloist on breaking down the opposition."

The Boston Celtics drafted White, the ninth player selected overall, in the 1969 NBA draft. He starred for the Celtics from 1969-70 through 1977-78 and helped the team to NBA championships in 1973-74 and 1975-76. He was named the most valuable player of the 1976 championship series against Phoenix. White finished his career with the Kansas City Kings in 1981 after two years with Golden State. The Celtics retired his No. 10 jersey to honor his success.

Today, White is the manager of the continuing education program for the NBA and the NBA Players' Association at Northeastern University in Boston.

During his acceptance speech at the Kansas Sports Hall of Fame ceremony, Joseph Henry White, a St. Louis native who played on the world stage as an Olympian and found fame in Boston, sounded a familiar theme when he reflected on his time in the Sunflower State:

"It takes a whole village for a person to be successful, and Kansas was my village."

THE SEVENTIES
Loyalty
Perseveres

Don Fambrough (waving) has come to symbolize University of Kansas football. During separate stints as head coach in the 1970s and early '80s, he led the Jayhawks to two bowl games. Former players and fans honored him at halftime of the 1995 Kansas-Missouri game in Lawrence, a 42-23 KU victory.

'A TEAM WITHIN A TEAM'

Trio controlled college shot put competition for two years

**DOUG KNOP, KARL SALB
and STEVE WILHELM
Track and field
and football,
1968-71**

Barriers meant little to Karl Salb, Doug Knop and Steve Wilhelm.

Take, for instance, an indoor track and field meet in 1969 at Michigan State University. The University of Kansas shot putters were scheduled to throw in the last flight of the 40-man field.

Knop recalls that most throws that day landed in the 50- to 53-foot range. Track officials had placed a barrier at the 55-foot mark to stop the shot from rolling onto the track. The 60-foot mark fell in the first lane of the track.

Then came the Jayhawks' turn. Knop tried to explain to an official that the barrier should be moved back.

"When I get up there, I say, 'Look, I'm the worst thrower of the three of us, and I can throw over your barrier,' " Knop says. " 'And our best thrower can hit the last lane of your track.' And the guy just laughed at me. So, I say, 'No problem.' "

No problem indeed. Knop threw the shot over the barrier. Meet officials moved the barrier back. Then Salb threw over the relocated barrier.

"They had to stop the meet while we threw," Knop says.

The trio won, of course. They always did. Salb won six consecutive NCAA championships in the national indoor and outdoor meets from 1969-71. At the 1969 and 1970 NCAA Indoor Championships, Wilhelm finished second and Knop finished third both years.

Knop, who graduated in 1970, won the Big Eight Conference discus championship three consecutive years, 1968-70. He placed fourth in the discus at the NCAA Outdoor Championships in 1970.

Salb also threw the discus and placed third at the NCAA Outdoor Championships in 1970 and fourth in 1971. Wilhelm, who competed with Salb during the 1969-71 stretch, finished third in the shot put at the 1971 NCAA Indoor Championships.

During the 1969 and 1970 seasons, when all three performed together, the Jayhawks won the Big Eight Indoor and Outdoor and the NCAA Indoor Championships. Kansas also

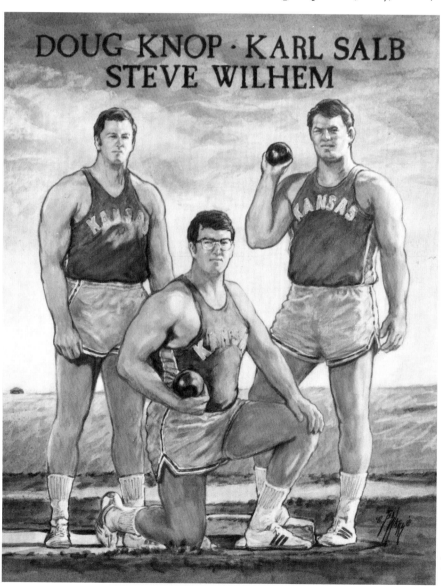

finished second at the 1969 NCAA Outdoor Championships and tied for first in 1970. When Knop departed, the Jayhawks continued to win conference meets in 1971 but tied for fourth at the NCAA Indoor and finished fifth at the NCAA Outdoor.

"Those three guys became a fantastic team within a team," says Bob Timmons, former KU track and field coach.

The "team within a team" trained by themselves, Knop says, underneath the west side of Memorial Stadium.

"We called it the pump room," he says of their weightlifting area. "When we went in there, it was just the three of us, we locked the door and nobody came in until we were finished."

It's doubtful anybody would have wanted to invade their space.

"Their weightlifting practice was sometimes like a football game," Timmons says. "I mean they'd get fired up, and they'd really go."

The three of them also brought intensity to practice.

"Every single practice we had was a competition," Knop says. "And you think about it, we competed against the best three guys in the nation as our routine.

"We didn't talk to each other ever during the meet. But prior to that time or during practice, we always encouraged and helped each other."

Their reputation and achievements often "psyched out" the competition before a meet, Knop says.

"Karl would stand in the front of the ring and throw way, way, way farther than everybody else," Knop says. "A lot of times, I saw people just put their shots away as he would warm up."

The trio was fortunate not to be a duo at NCAA championship meets. An old NCAA rule did not allow a school to enter three athletes in the same event at the national level. Timmons petitioned the NCAA to change the rule, which it did.

"We told them (the NCAA) about their distances," Timmons says. "We promised them that there would be no embarrassment over it, because we thought the three guys would do rather well."

Timmons calls their double one-two-three finishes in the two NCAA indoor meets "an absolutely unheard-of situation."

One time, Don Cannon, the NCAA indoor meet director, told Salb that his shot was illegal and couldn't be used.

Cannon told Timmons the shots the KU athletes used were bouncing unusually high in the air after landing and that the field announcer was worried about getting killed from a bouncing shot.

Timmons prevailed again, and he explains that KU's shots met weight specifications but were slightly smaller and harder than the shots used by other competitors. The next year, Cannon had the team use a newly styled shot that was softer and wouldn't bounce.

Timmons recruited Salb from Crossett, Ark., where he was an all-state football player and the national high school champion in the shot.

"Wilhelm found out we were recruiting (Salb)," Timmons says. "And Wilhelm was a great competitor. He wanted to compete with Karl. That was important to him.

"Wilhelm had a great background in lifting, which Karl did not have, nor did Doug."

Knop always wanted to come to KU and wear a letter sweater. The Olathe native came to KU to play quarterback but changed his mind and quit the team after red-shirting his sophomore year. He returned to football late in his college career as a defensive lineman and suffered a knee injury. Wilhelm, from Los Altos, Calif., also played football as a lineman.

Salb enjoyed the most successful football career of the three. Along with John Zook, he helped anchor the defensive line of the 1968 Big Eight Conference co-champions.

That season, Salb missed making the U.S. Olympic track and field team and

"I was never beaten by anybody but my own teammates, I was the worst (of the three) and we'd still beat everybody by 5 feet."

– Doug Knop

reported to football practice four days before the season opener. He played so well with such little preparation in that game against Illinois that coach Pepper Rodgers said, "He'll set coaching back 100 years."

Today, Salb owns and operates a hunting resort in Buckner, Ark. Knop runs an insurance business and works as a tax representative in Olathe. Wilhelm is an attorney in California.

Knop relishes the Kansas track dominance of his era.

"We had a team of outstanding, hard-working, dedicated individuals who really enjoyed each other considering the vast differences between each other," he says. "I always remembered the lessons learned and the rewards obtained from continuous dedication to the single cause of being the best."

As one-third of the "team within a team," Knop offers this final perspective:

"I was never beaten by anybody but my own teammates," he says. "I was the worst (of the three) and we'd still beat everybody by five feet."

KATHOL / McELROY / STEWART / NEIHOUSE

A BIG VICTORY
Relay team's world record clinched a championship for Kansas

On the second and final day of the 1970 NCAA Indoor Track and Field Championships, Bob Timmons huddled with his University of Kansas team and assessed their chances for repeating as national champions.

"He said that the two-mile relay team had a chance to win it, and if we would win it, then we had a real good chance to win the national championship," says Jim Neihouse, who ran the first leg of that relay. "So we were all pretty pumped."

Of course, national championships don't come easy. An assorted cast of athletes would determine whether Kansas would win. Marty Liquori, Villanova's premier miler, presented a threat. Although he was not entered in the two-mile relay, how well he fared in the mile also would determine if Villanova could overtake Kansas and claim the title.

Then Dennis Stewart, who ran the second leg of the race for KU, posed a problem. No one but Stewart knew that he had pulled a muscle two days before the race. No one knew because Stewart kept his injury a secret so he could run in a championship race.

And for direct competition in the two-mile relay, Kansas State – of all teams – stood in the Jayhawks' way. The K-State runners had defeated the Jayhawks a couple of times during the season, and Timmons and the team were concerned whether they could beat their arch-rivals.

Kansas caught a big break when Liquori finished second in the mile.

"We knew that if we won (the two-mile relay), we had a good chance to win it (all) then," Neihouse says.

About that time, though, Stewart started to panic. Fearing he would let his teammates down if the leg injury proved worse than he'd thought, Stewart decided Mike Solomon, his alternate, should run in his place.

"I thought, 'My god, there are 10,000 people here, and we're going for a national championship. I can't screw up,' " Stewart says. "So I started jogging around the track to find Mike. But I never found him. I had to run."

Neihouse, a Salina native who picked Kansas over K-State, opened the race for KU and fought his way through a tightly packed field to finish his 880 yards in 1 minute, 50 seconds, good for second place when he handed off to Stewart.

Somehow, Stewart gathered himself to run 1:53.6. Roger Kathol, a highly recruited half-miler from Kapaun High School in Wichita, took the third leg in 1:52.4. He handed off to Brian McElroy for the anchor leg. McElroy was running against K-State's Ken Swenson for the championship.

"We knew Swenson had a great kick," Niehouse said. "So if he was close, he was pretty tough. Of course, Brian had a real good kick, too."

An excellent kick, it turned out. McElroy brought the baton home in 1:49.7. The Jayhawks won the race in a world-record time of 7:25 and won the national championship by 1.5 points over Villanova.

"As they came around the last turn, I knew that Swenson wasn't going to catch (McElroy)," Neihouse says. "All the way from the last turn to the finish line, I was just jumping up and down, running around, hopping up and down, yelling and screaming. I remember seeing a couple of the officials look at me like, 'Whoa.' I was pretty excited."

Stewart sought solitude afterward.

"I remember I was finding a nice, private place to throw up when (Coach Bob Timmons) ran up to me and said, 'How does it feel to get a world record?' " Stewart says. "I couldn't believe it. Without Brian McElroy, there's no way we'd have done it. He almost (set) a world record in the individual half mile."

Neihouse and Stewart became teachers after college. Neihouse teaches physical education, biology, health and driver's education at Downs (Kan.) High School. He also coaches boys and girls cross country and boys track. Stewart teaches advanced biology at William Chrisman High School in Independence, Mo.

His leg injury notwithstanding, Stewart was lucky to make the team, let alone be part of a world record and national championship. A walk-on, Stewart admits he "lied all through my application" to join the KU track team in 1967. The application asked questions such as how many records he had set and his fastest times in each event.

But Stewart didn't have any "real" times or records to report. His high school didn't have a track team.

"I put down everything I thought I could run," Stewart says. "When I had my interview, Bob Timmons looked at my application sheet and said, 'These times aren't any good. But you seem real sincere.' So he gave me a two-week trial."

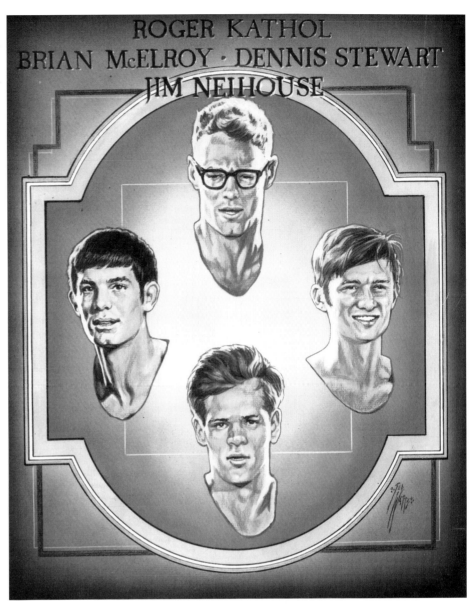

ROGER KATHOL, BRIAN McELROY, DENNIS STEWART and JIM NEIHOUSE, Track and field two-mile relay team, 1970

Kathol, "the most brilliant kid on the team," in Stewart's opinion, runs a medical psychiatry program for the University of Iowa hospitals in Iowa City, Iowa, where he lives with his wife and three children. He recently began his own consulting firm, Cartesian Solutions, to train other doctors how to integrate care for people suffering from emotional and physical problems.

"I look back on my track days as a tremendous character builder," Kathol says. "It was a great thrill to get a world record, win an NCAA championship and become an All-American in one fell swoop."

McElroy transferred to Villanova after that season.

"He was a star that we lost," Timmons says of the Massapequa, N.Y., native. "He reminded me a lot of Jim (Ryun). He was a beautiful runner, effortless. He could accelerate anytime he wanted to."

Neihouse recalls that each runner gave the race his best effort. He says, with pride, that their world record stood until 1982, when the meet moved from Detroit's Cobo Hall and its short track (11 laps for a mile) to Syracuse, N.Y., and the eight-lap track at the Carrier Dome.

Neihouse also holds one final memory from the race.

"We got up on the awards stand for first place," he says, "and laying on the floor in front was Marty Liquori."

JAN JOHNSON

HIGH HOPES
Vaulter sailed to NCAA championship

**JAN JOHNSON
Track and field,
1970**

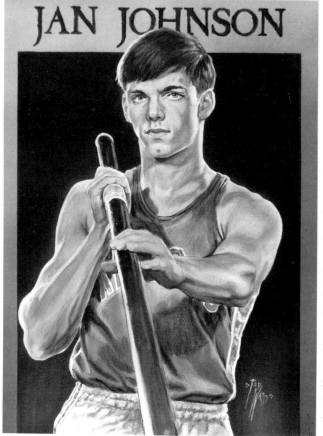

Mankind had yet to walk on the moon in 1968, Jan Johnson's senior year in high school.

And no pole vaulter in the world had cleared 18 feet. Johnson wanted to become the first – sort of a Neil Armstrong of his sport.

The former University of Kansas pole vaulter nearly achieved that lofty goal during his second year at Kansas when he soared to victory in the 1970 NCAA Outdoor Championships. That feat made him KU's first outdoor All-American in the pole vault.

Johnson cleared an astonishing 17 feet, 7 inches, one foot higher than his previous best, and won the national title. Meet officials then raised the bar to 18 feet, where no vaulter had gone before. On his third and final attempt, Johnson's body barely struck the bar on his way down.

"I made it by three or four inches, but in my excitement I jerked my arms back and my chest hit (the bar) coming down," he told the *University Daily Kansan* in 1970. "Eighteen feet really surprised me. I had dreamed about it the night before."

Johnson actually won an NCAA outdoor title while competing indoors.

"It rained so bad they had to move the competition indoors," says Bob Timmons, former KU track and field coach. "At the time, 17-7 was a world (indoor) record. He was a fantastic vaulter with incredible courage."

Only two years before, Johnson regularly was clearing 15 feet in high school. He won both the indoor and outdoor Illinois state pole vault championships in 1968.

He also ran sprints and competed in the long jump for Bloom Township High School in the Chicago suburb of Arlington Heights, Ill. He once ran the 100-yard dash in less than 10 seconds.

"One of his greatest assets was natural speed," says John Mitchell, who recruited Johnson out of high school and coached him at KU and the University of Alabama. "He could have been a world-class decathlete."

At Kansas, Johnson was a quick study and made steady progress. He also was a student of his sport and reportedly kept a list of 32 items to think about for each jump.

"There are so many athletes who are more physically capable. Yet they don't have the right mental attitude," Johnson said.

Mitchell served as an assistant at Kansas from 1965 to 1969 and then became head track coach at Alabama. Johnson followed him, transferring from KU to Alabama after the 1970 season.

Johnson realized his Olympic dream in 1972, when he qualified for the U.S. team. He won a bronze medal at the Munich Games. Johnson finished just behind pole vaulting legend Bob Seagren, his teammate and the silver medalist.

Johnson also competed in the 1976 Olympics in Montreal, but he did not win a medal. He eventually became a pole vaulting camp director in Atascadero, Calif.

DAVE ROBISCH

CLUTCH SOUTHPAW

Forward was at his best with game on the line

Ted Owens laughs when he recalls recruiting Dave Robisch.

"I met with him and his parents and had a good visit," says the former University of Kansas basketball coach about his January 1967 meeting with the Robisch family at their Springfield, Ill., home. "When 10 o'clock came, his dad brought my top coat and my hat, handed them to me, and said, 'We've enjoyed the visit, coach, it's time for David to go to bed.' "

At the time, Owens didn't think that was too funny. He was confused and thought he may have lost the 6-foot-9-inch, left-handed forward.

"I go away thinking, 'Did I say something wrong?' " Owens says. "But that was the way Mr. Robisch was. He was direct."

Time passed, and Owens saw Dave play and stayed in touch. After Robisch dominated the Illinois high school playoffs with 152 points in four games, Owens called to congratulate him. He also talked to Dave's father, an engineer-turned-Lutheran minister, and asked if he could return to Springfield for a visit.

"Reverend Robisch said, 'Coach, we'd like you to be here this Thursday at three o'clock.' I'll never forget that," Owens says with a laugh. "I was there, you can

DAVE ROBISCH

DAVE ROBISCH
Basketball,
1968-71
Baseball,
1969-70

believe that, and signed him that night. Reverend Robisch felt that Kansas was a really good place for Dave, and he did not play around with all that recruiting."

Dave Robisch remembers things a little differently. He told the *Lawrence Journal-World* in 1997: "After coach Owens arrived, he sat down, and I asked my dad if he'd go in the other room with me. I told my dad I really wanted to go to Kansas, so we went back in and I told coach Owens I was going to KU.

"He about fell out of his chair. He said, 'I haven't even given you my best pitch yet.'"

Regardless how he got to Kansas, Robisch stayed, liked it and succeeded. He led the Jayhawks in scoring in each of his three seasons (freshmen weren't eligible then) and finished his career with 1,754 points, which is sixth on the Jayhawks' all-time scoring list.

Despite his scoring success, Robisch put the team first. As a junior in a game at Iowa State, he scored 39 points and collected 26 rebounds. Yet the Jayhawks lost 91-89 in overtime, and Robisch has expunged the memory of that game from his mind.

"I look at that junior year, and individually, I had some really great numbers, but I wasn't satisfied because we didn't win the conference and go to the NCAA," he says. "I learned a lot from that season and worked even harder."

KU went 17-9 that season but rebounded the next year to have one of the finest years in school history. Robisch, naturally, played a big part in that success.

"He might have been the greatest clutch shooter in the second half of a game when the game was on the line," Owens said. "The guy could get it in the hole."

Good thing for the Jayhawks Robisch possessed that skill. In his senior year, KU played in seven games against Big Eight Conference teams that were decided by five points or less, including three overtime contests. The Jayhawks won all those games; in fact, they went undefeated in conference play.

"We had a lot of close games, and we had a lot of old arenas to play at Missouri, at Colorado, at Kansas State," Robisch says. "I think it was tougher to win in those places than it is today. The closeness of the fans, and it's just tougher to win in those old buildings."

The Jayhawks were 25-1 entering the 1971 NCAA Tournament in Wichita. There, KU defeated Houston 78-77 and Drake 73-71 in two heart-stoppers and advanced to the Final Four. Robisch scored team highs of 29 points against Houston and 27 points against Drake.

"For back-to-back games, and for what was on the line, those were probably the two best games I ever played at Kansas," Robisch says. "That's what it was all about. That was my goal when I went to Kansas, was to go to the NCAA and play for the national championship."

Next up was the Final Four against UCLA in the Houston Astrodome.

"It was the first time that it was played in a dome," he says. "The court was put out in the middle of the Astrodome, not like how they do it today where they put it at one end. The floor was elevated, and the lighting – you struggled from certain angles shooting because you looked right up in the lights. So the atmosphere was unusual, and you had about 35,000 people there."

Robisch's other memory isn't as pleasant. But his tone of voice signals more disbelief than bitterness.

"We made a run in the second half, and we got within one," he says. "I take a shot that I've taken – over the course of my college and pro career – hundreds of times. I hit a jump shot on the wing that would have put us ahead. It would have changed the momentum of the game. And the ref called me for traveling.

"I'm not saying one play makes the difference in the game, but we never got the momentum back after that. If I traveled that time, to me I must have traveled 200 or 300 times."

KU lost 68-61 and lost the consolation game against Western Kentucky, finishing 27-3.

Robisch continued playing basketball in the American Basketball Association and then the NBA. He played for five teams, including the Larry Brown-coached Denver Nuggets of the mid-1970s.

Today, Robisch is back in Springfield with the Illinois Secretary of State's office as a youth education coordinator. He and his wife, Lou, have a daughter, Stacey, and two sons, Brett and Scott. Brett completed his eligibility with Oklahoma State's basketball team in 1998, while Scott still plays for the Cowboys.

> *"He might have been the greatest clutch shooter in the second half of a game when the game was on the line."*
>
> – Ted Owens on
> Dave Robisch

LONG SHADOW FROM THE MOUND

Dave Robisch was ahead of his time.

In the late 1990s, pitcher Randy Johnson is all the rage in major league baseball. The left-handed Johnson has a blazing fastball, and his 6-foot-10-inch presence casts a big shadow from the mound.

But in 1969 and 1970, Robisch did for the University of Kansas baseball team what Johnson does today: pitch, dominate and intimidate.

"He could throw that baseball through a wall," says former KU baseball coach Floyd Temple. "They were kind of standing on eggshells when hitting in there."

Robisch's fast ball was clocked in the 95-98 miles-per-hour range. He had a winning record as a Jayhawks' hurler and posted a 2.66 earned run average in 1969 and 1970 as an all-Big Eight Conference selection.

"Floyd only had a few scholarships, so he kind of relied on picking up a few players," Robisch says. "John and Junior Riggins came off the football team and played. It was a unique experience playing with those guys. It was kind of fun."

Fun but not too serious, at least not for Robisch.

"I didn't play my senior year because I wanted to get ready for the (basketball) draft," Robisch says. "Floyd really wanted me to play that last year because he knew I would have been drafted and signed for a reasonable bonus. But I thought it would have been awful tough to play two sports at the professional level."

Temple says he talked to several scouts who indicated Robisch could have received a bonus from $30,000 to $50,000. Temple pointed out that Gene Conley had played both sports, pitching for the Milwaukee Braves and playing for the Boston Celtics in the early 1960s.

"I told him, 'Robo, you need to try baseball.' And he wouldn't," Temple says. "I told him '(Conley) did it, you do it. Go get the money, and if you don't make it, they're giving it to you. You might like it. Pitching every fifth day is a lot better than playing about four basketball games a week.

"I think he would have been a major league player."

STRING MUSIC

Trumpet player-turned-recruit was a maestro at shooting the basketball

Music brought Isaac F. "Bud" Stallworth Jr. to Kansas, and through basketball he left there as a student on a high note.

In the summer of 1967, Stallworth attended band camp at the University of Kansas. The trumpet player was the second member of his family to come to KU for musical instruction. His older sister, Harriett, had attended the camp a few years earlier at the suggestion of her piano instructor. Harriett enjoyed her experiences so much that she later attended the University and earned a degree in mathematics.

But back to Bud. During his off-hours from the camp, he wandered across the street to Robinson Gymnasium to play basketball. A sharp-shooting guard from Hartselle, Ala., Stallworth held his own against the Robinson crowd. He didn't know it at first, but his competition included some players named Wesley, White, Vanoy and Franz, among others.

The word spread about Stallworth. Jo Jo White, KU's star guard, walked over to Allen Field House to see head coach Ted Owens and assistant Sam Miranda.

"Coach, there's a good player over at Robinson, and he's here for music camp," Owens recalls White telling him.

The next thing Stallworth knew, his counselor called him at the residence hall where he was staying. As he walked to the counselor's office, Stallworth wondered if he was in trouble for one of the pranks that summer camps seem to spawn.

Instead, the counselor asked him if he had heard of Ted Owens.

Stallworth was clueless. For all he knew, Ted Owens was some camper he had roughhoused with who had squealed on him.

Not quite, the counselor said. He told Bud that Owens had called for him a few times and would appreciate hearing back from him.

So Stallworth called Owens and learned that Hartselle, Ala., didn't register a blip on KU's national recruiting radar.

"I gave him a call, and he said, 'Bud Stallworth, some of my players tell me that you're a pretty good basketball player, and we've never heard of you,'" Stallworth says.

Owens asked Stallworth for some background information. Stallworth obliged and then asked the coach not to tell his parents that he had been playing basketball. Bud's father had forbidden him to play ball at camp, lest an errant elbow fatten his lip and keep him from practicing the trumpet.

Owens did Stallworth one better.

"Based on what these guys are telling us," the coach told the erstwhile musician, "if you will send us a schedule, we'll come and see you play, and we'll offer you a full scholarship."

Stallworth liked that offer enough to go home and tell on himself. A year later, he arrived back at Kansas to stay for four years.

***

Stallworth learned lessons quick and well. At age 7, he started shooting basketball, and his father taught him proper fundamentals.

"He showed me the form, the right kind of extension," Bud says.

From television, Stallworth studied Jerry West and Oscar Robertson. He noted

> *"I think the ball going through the net was like a soothing sound."*
>
> – Bud Stallworth

BUD STALLWORTH

their techniques and how they always squared their bodies when they shot. Stallworth combined that knowledge with his father's teachings and developed into a good shooter.

"I think the ball going through the net was like a soothing sound," Stallworth says. "It just turned me on. I used to shoot all the time."

He's not exaggerating. Stallworth used to shoot at his school gym for three to four hours at a time. His parents, a little concerned about his obsession, never had to worry where he was.

"They knew if I wasn't at home or in the backyard shooting, I was down at the gym," he says.

Both of Stallworth's parents were teachers, and his father also was the high school principal. Academics came first in the Stallworth household, and Bud graduated as class valedictorian. As if he had a choice.

"If I didn't have all A's, basketball was out," Stallworth says. "Even if I did bad on a test, or didn't do what they felt I should be doing on my reports, the first thing gone was that ball. I think my father knew that was the carrot."

So when the 6-foot-5-inch Stallworth played his first college game as a sophomore (freshmen still were ineligible then), he knew how to shoot and he knew the value of hard work. And he showed everyone how well he learned his lessons by scoring 27 points in his debut.

He matched that amount one other time, topped 20 points two other times and scored in double figures in 19 out of 26 games in 1969-70.

Things fell more into place for Stallworth and the Jayhawks in 1970-71. He raised his scoring average to 16.9 points per game and earned All-Big Eight Conference honors with Dave Robisch, who was named All-America. Kansas went undefeated in conference play and earned a trip to the Final Four.

"With Bud, we complemented each other so well, especially that last year when we went to the Final Four," Robisch says. "He was a great shooter, a great offensive player. If teams sagged in on me, then he would be able to be out there and take that pressure off me by hitting those shots."

As a senior in 1971-72, Stallworth didn't have a complementary player on the team to take the pressure off him. Robisch and Pierre Russell had graduated. Leonard Gray transferred to Long Beach State. Randy Canfield suffered a collapsed lung.

"I ended up put in a position where I had to do scoring and rebounding, and we were not a very good basketball team," Stallworth says. "We struggled. Our team manager started a game for us. He wasn't bad, but when you have to go that deep into the roster, it was just one of those situations."

Despite the 11-15 season, Stallworth and the Jayhawks always will have Missouri. On Feb. 26, 1972, in his last home game, Stallworth torched the Tigers for 50 points in a 93-80 KU victory.

Missouri coach Norm Stewart's comments before the game inspired Stallworth. Stewart was promoting his star, John Brown, for conference player of the year. Stewart acknowledged that Stallworth was having a great season (a league-leading 25.3 scoring average), but the Jayhawks as a team were struggling.

"I took that personally," Stallworth says.

Most definitely. With his mother in attendance, Stallworth was ready to show the league who its best player was. Roommate Aubrey Nash promised to get Stallworth the ball if he was open. Stallworth assured Nash that he would indeed be open.

"The first couple of shots felt like we were going to do this thing," Stallworth says. "It was just one of those days that was made to explode."

Owens recalls the aura surrounding the day.

"It was a great game," he says. "Missouri tried about everyone on him that day. That day, we were honoring the national championship team of 1952, and they were there.

"When you have the great teams back, the great players of the past back, it's so important. The players want to play so well to make a good impression on them. So it was an absolutely perfect day."

Stallworth hit 19 field goals and 12 of 13 free throws to reach 50 points. Another roommate, Wilson Barrow, commited a lane violation that cost Stallworth a point. Stallworth still likes to kid Barrow that he cost him a shot at Wilt Chamberlain's school scoring record of 52 points.

After the season, the Seattle Supersonics chose Stallworth with the seventh pick in the first round of the NBA draft. In two years with Seattle, Stallworth averaged 6.3 points both seasons in 15 minutes of playing time per game. Left unprotected in the 1974 expansion draft, the New Orleans Jazz plucked him from the Sonics, which surprised Stallworth. He played three seasons for the Jazz before suffering a career-ending back injury in a car accident.

Stallworth returned to the KU campus in 1996 as assistant director for design and construction management. He manages the $44 million "Crumbling Classroom" project that will provide improvements to more than 60 buildings.

"I feel that I am giving something back," Stallworth says. "This program will help take the University into the next century."

A PASSING FANCY

Quarterback set a multitude of school records in early '70s

Never underestimate the power of Kansas basketball when it comes to recruiting. Football recruiting, that is.

In the case of David Jaynes, the last All-American quarterback for the University of Kansas, a trip to Allen Field House in 1970 convinced him that Lawrence was where he should go to school and play football. That development isn't so unusual.

But colleges across the country wanted him to be their quarterback, and the native of nearby Bonner Springs was interested in leaving Kansas. As he tells it:

"When I was coming out of high school, I didn't have a sense of KU. The first KU football game I ever saw was when they were recruiting me. I just didn't go to college football games; I just watched everything on TV.

"I watched Alabama on TV. That's really where I wanted to go. Back in those days you signed a conference letter-of-intent. Thirty days later, you signed a national letter-of-intent. When all the recruiting was done, I decided Alabama was the place for me. When you have 'Bear' Bryant recruiting you, it's a pretty awesome experience."

So, Jaynes signed a conference letter with Alabama, a letter he fully intended to honor. The recruiting "went away," he says, which gave him time to think. That's when Terry Donahue, an assistant on head coach Pepper Rodgers' staff, invited him to a KU-Kansas State basketball game, the season finale at Allen Field House.

"I go up and watched the game on a Saturday night," he says. "Allen Field House had such a huge impact on me, the fans and that whole thing."

Jaynes rethought his college decision.

"KU was always in the running, there's no doubt about that," he says. "At that point, I decided that it makes sense to stay right here."

The 6-foot-2-inch, 212-pound Jaynes never played for Rodgers and Donahue. Freshmen were ineligible for varsity competition in 1970, and Rodgers left Kansas for UCLA after that season. Donahue followed as Rodgers' assistant and eventually was head coach of the Bruins from 1976 to 1995.

But Jaynes stayed in Lawrence for new

DAVID JAYNES
Football,
1971-73

coach Don Fambrough, played for three years and was the full-time starter his junior and senior years. As a junior in 1972, Jaynes threw for 2,253 yards and 15 touchdowns. In his first game that year, Jaynes bombed Washington State for 401 yards, but KU lost 18-17. The team finished 4-7 that season.

The Jayhawks, behind Jaynes, started 3-0 in 1973. KU finished its non-conference schedule that year against Tennessee in Knoxville. Jaynes staged a record-breaking performance with 35 completions in 58 attempts. Both the completion and attempts stand as school records, and the 35 completions broke a Big Eight Conference record. Unfortunately, the Volunteers defeated the Jayhawks 28-27. A late KU two-point conversion attempt failed when a receiver fell in the end zone and Jaynes was tackled.

"I have never seen a quarterback have a better day in his life," Fambrough says of Jaynes' 394-yard performance. "I never will forget the performance he put on there, and I mean against a helluva good football team."

Jaynes calls the game bittersweet.

"In terms of my performance, it was probably the most 'on' I've ever been in my career," he says. "If we had won the game, it would just jump out, it would just stand there, and I'd go, 'Boy, this was pinnacle of my career, right here.' But we lost, and it kind of diminishes any individual effort."

The close Tennessee game set the tone for the Jayhawks' conference play. KU rebounded the next week and defeated Kansas State 25-18 in a come-from-behind victory. Except for a four-touchdown loss to Oklahoma, the rest of the Jayhawks' league games were decided by two points or less. Kansas defeated Iowa State and Colorado by two points, edged Missouri by a point, lost to Nebraska by a point and tied Oklahoma State.

Jaynes finished the regular season with 172 completions in 330 attempts, 13 touchdowns and 2,131 yards passing. He finished fourth in the Heisman Trophy balloting behind running back John Cappelletti of Penn State, lineman John Hicks of Ohio State and running back Roosevelt Leaks of Texas.

At the time, Jaynes' career yardage mark of 5,132 put him first in the Jayhawks' all-time passing department. Frank Seurer later established a new mark, 6,410 yards, and Kelly Donohoe now is second with 5,382 yards. Jaynes' 35 career touchdown passes still stand as a school record.

By finishing 7-3-1, the 1973 Jayhawks earned a Liberty Bowl berth against North Carolina State. The Wolfpack, coached by Lou Holtz, defeated KU 31-18 in chilly conditions. Jaynes threw for 165 yards, a touchdown and a two-point conversion in his final college game.

"I don't remember anything about the game," he says. "People would probably say, 'You played that way, too.'"

Jaynes says he enjoyed his time at Kansas, but time has dulled his memory on game specifics.

"There comes a time when you can't dwell on all of this," he says. "I think it's counter-productive to keep your head back there."

A third-round pick of Kansas City in the 1974 NFL draft, Jaynes played a season for the Chiefs before his brief professional career ended. Today, he splits time between his home in Los Angeles and Texas, where he handles real estate investments.

Although he maintains a "don't look back" philosophy, Jaynes credits his time at the University for broadening his horizons.

"It moved me from being a small-town kid in Kansas to someone who could function in a pretty significant environment (with) people from all over the country, which basically gives you the opportunity to really grow," he says.

WALKING TALL

Southern transplant tackled problems, controversies head on

"A cold-blooded businessman."

That's what sports columnist Chuck Woodling of the *Lawrence Journal-World* called Clyde Walker upon the latter's May 1978 resignation as athletics director at the University of Kansas.

An appropriate label? Certainly. A derogatory one? Depends whom you ask.

Legions of Don Fambrough supporters and students from the mid-1970s might still consider Walker's name a dirty word. But athletics administrators who watched him progress, as well Kansas alumni and fans who benefited from improvements to the program's physical structures, might beg to differ.

He was an outsider who grew up, attended college and coached high school football in North Carolina, never visiting the Kansas campus before interviewing for the AD position.

But Walker's experience in the University of North Carolina's athletics department, including one year as assistant athletics director, impressed KU Chancellor Archie Dykes and others at Kansas, which was groping for direction after athletics director Wade Stinson resigned in November 1972.

Walker also came highly recommended by a certain successful Kansas alumnus who worked with him at North Carolina. Dykes chose him over three other finalists, including Tom Butters, later an effective athletics director at Duke University and chairman of the NCAA Men's Basketball Committee.

"I feel Clyde Walker is an excellent choice," Fambrough, KU's head football coach, said the day Walker accepted the position, July 10, 1973. "I've had several conversations with Bill Dooley (North Carolina football coach) and Dean Smith (that certain KU alum) as well as other football coaches in that area, and all are very high on him."

A year-and-a-half later, after a 4-7 season and six straight losses in 1974, Fambrough resigned after Walker announced he wouldn't renew the coach's contract past 1975. Instead, Walker went back to familiar Southern territory and hired Bud Moore, which provided a short-term fix. Moore left, however, after a 1-10 season in 1978.

Walker also forced men's basketball coach Ted Owens to reorganize his staff. Meanwhile, he turned down overtures to return to North Carolina as athletics director in 1976. But he returned to his home state to take the same position at upstart North Carolina-Charlotte days after resigning from KU.

During his reign at Kansas, Walker fought. He fought student government, which more than once charged him with using student activity fees for frivolous purposes.

"I think sometimes you have to spend money to make money," he once told the *University Daily Kansan.*

He fought the Kansas Board of Regents, which actually suggested only months after he arrived that financial pressures might force KU and other regents institutions out of their respective athletics conferences.

He also fought Title IX, the federal statute designed to end discrimination against women in college programs. Walker reasoned Title IX could have the unintended effect of downgrading men's athletics programs.

"Ninety percent of those who contribute to our program could care less about

women's athletics," Walker told the *Kansan* in 1974. "There aren't women who can compete with men, and they readily admit it."

But Title IX survived, and by the time he left Kansas, Walker had arranged for KU's women's teams to share sports and training facilities with men's teams. He also had developed a plan to provide as much as $150,000 in scholarships for women's athletics.

Walker inherited a debt-ridden athletics department facing an operating deficit of $250,000. When he left KU, the department was turning a profit. In addition, he directed renovations of both Allen Field House and Memorial Stadium, tripled the annual size of the Williams Fund, which provides money for athletics scholarships, and doubled the number of athletics administrators.

He also envisioned and developed the basis for this book, the University of Kansas Athletics Hall of Fame.

"You better believe Walker is leaving the athletic corporation in better shape than it was when he came here," Woodling wrote – shortly before dubbing him a "duck out of water in Kansas."

Walker wouldn't disagree, yet he remained proud of his time at KU.

"Whoever comes in here will probably have a much easier time than I did," he told the *Journal-World* shortly after leaving. "At least I would hope somebody would have an easier time than I did."

COMPETITOR, BENEFACTOR, SURVIVOR
Former millionaire rebuilds life, rearranges priorities after prison term

When Jim Hershberger competed in any sport, he gave his all.

When Jim Hershberger gave money to the University of Kansas, he gave his all, too.

And when Jim Hershberger paid his debt to society, he about gave up all he had. But he survived the five-year, three-month ordeal and has found faith, humility and himself.

After first attending the University of Oklahoma on a wrestling scholarship, Hershberger transferred to KU and ran track for the Jayhawks in the early 1950s. He performed best in the 220- and 440-yard dashes. His time of 20.9 seconds in the 220 ranked second in the world at that time.

Hershberger graduated in 1953 but kept competing in different sports. He won 20 national championships at various indoor and outdoor track meets in races from sprints to marathons. He also earned awards in 15 other sports.

In 1958, he played 180 holes of golf in slightly less than 13 hours. Hershberger averaged 88 strokes per round and played the last five rounds with torn knee cartilage. He performed this strenuous stunt, running from shot to shot, to win a bet.

On his 50th birthday in 1981, Hershberger competed against famous athletes one-on-one in 18 events during a 14.5-hour span that started at 5 a.m.

In 1985, the NCAA named an award in his honor. It is given annually to the outstanding college track and field athlete as voted by coaches. And in 1986, his picture appeared on Wheaties cereal boxes as an example of the nation's top amateur athlete.

Hershberger took this drive into business and built two successful oil companies. His business success allowed him to pay back the University he loved, and he did so in a big, big way.

In 1969, Hershberger donated $125,000 to KU for an all-weather track at Memorial Stadium. To show its appreciation, the University named it the Jim Hershberger Track. In a 20-year period, he donated about $750,000 to the University. The money went for renovation of the original track, four track and field scholarships (annually) and championship rings for KU athletes.

"He was a great fan of KU athletics, not only track," says Bob Timmons, former KU track and field coach whose program received the bulk of Hershberger's gifts. "He followed all the other sports, too. He was very helpful to me. I remember once he took me up in his Lear jet and we went on a recruiting mission."

Apparently, the money came with no strings attached.

"With all this financial help that he gave our track department, I never felt that he interfered, he never did tell me how to run the team," Timmons says. "It was just always encouragement."

In time, Hershberger would need every bit of that encouragement back. In 1990, he was convicted of 25 fraud-related charges connected with his business, Petroleum Energy Inc. Prosecutors contended Hershberger schemed to defraud investors and banks.

Hershberger maintains his innocence and blames a business partner for the charges. But he was sentenced to prison for nine years and nine months, and he served five years and three months before being paroled Oct. 2, 1995.

During his imprisonment, Hershberger maintained a six-hour-a-day exercise regimen and kept a journal to fend off boredom. Monte Johnson, former KU athletics director, visited Hershberger 190 times at the Federal Prison Camp in Leavenworth. Timmons was another frequent visitor.

But no one supported Hershberger as did his wife, Sally. She drove from Wichita to Leavenworth with great frequency and eventually moved to Lawrence to be closer to him.

"I think one of the most impressive things about the whole thing of prison is that Sally's and Jim's love for one another has been really amazing," Timmons says. "It never diminished a bit, and she continued to visit him, and she always loved and admired him and has been his biggest backer. I don't see any difference in their relationship now and before all of this happened, and I think it's wonderful."

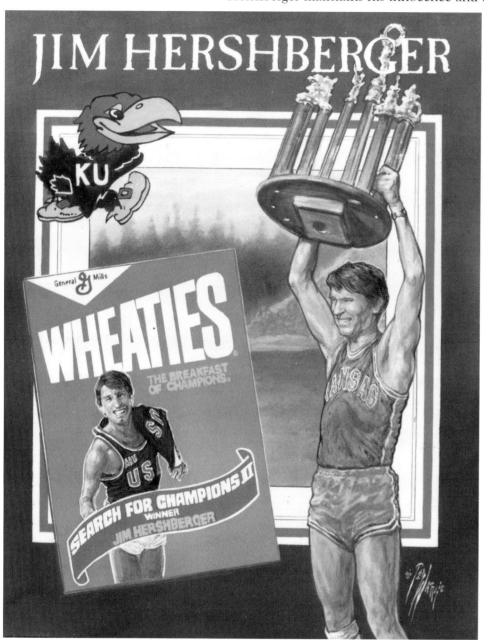

JIM HERSHBERGER
Track and field and
longtime benefactor

The Hershbergers live in Lawrence today and lead quiet lives without the trappings of success that they once enjoyed. Sally Hershberger wrote a book, "Fame, Fortune, Framed, Freed," that details their tribulations. But mostly they work and keep to themselves.

Timmons is struck by how Jim Hershberger emerged from prison.

"I think prison certainly strengthened his relationship with the Lord," Timmons says. "He came out of there a much stronger person than when he went in."

PERFORMANCE AND DEDICATION

"Deaner" was synonymous with KU athletics

Four hundred ten days.

That's how much unused paid sick leave Dean Nesmith had accrued when he retired from the University of Kansas in the summer of 1984. As KU's head athletics trainer for 46 years, he also never missed a football game. He worked 475 straight, including one in 1982 when a severe bladder infection had hospitalized him. That time, he left the hospital for the game and returned when it ended.

In fact, during his career at KU, Nesmith only missed two football *practices*, one for a wedding and one for a funeral.

But remarkable attendance merely is one indication of Nesmith's hard-working, loyal nature. His resourcefulness and innovations made him one of the world's elite sports trainers; his toughness and adoration of KU are legendary.

How tough was Nesmith? Listen to some of the former athletes he taped and treated, a student trainer he taught and the coach who stayed at KU almost as long as he did.

First, Cliff McDonald, a KU running back in the late 1940s:

"Dean was well-liked by the squad," McDonald said in *Deaner*, a biography of Nesmith and his years at Kansas written by Mike Fisher, another former KU football player. "But don't think he wasn't tough. I remember running a punt back against Oklahoma for a long gain. I called a time out to try to catch my breath. We had on wool, long-sleeved jerseys in 100-degree heat.

"Dean came running out on the field and wanted to know who called time out. When I owned up, he told me that I needed some extra running the next week to get in shape."

Tim Friess, a KU defensive end and co-captain who played toward the end of Nesmith's career, says, "If you came in there with an injury, you damned well better be hurt. Because if you came in there for sympathy, you weren't going to get it. When I hurt my shoulder, he worked my butt off. He never once gave me a break, but he always cared about what you were doing.

"Deaner was always mad at the coaching staff for letting some of these guys spend their whole week icing and heating during practice, walking around with the red cross on, then go out on Saturday and play full speed. Deaner was livid when that stuff happened.

"He always used to tell the story about, 'Hell, Nolan Cromwell (KU's wishbone quarterback of the mid-1970s) used to play with broken ribs, why the hell can't you play with a little pinky finger broken?'"

Lynn Bott, Nesmith's full-time assistant for eight years and the only person since he retired to serve as KU's director of sports medicine, says Nesmith took the same approach to sports training as he did as a Kansas lineman in 1933-35.

"He was rough and gruff," Bott says. "He was tough on me. He expected a lot. But he was always very, very good to me.

"Yes, he was tough on kids. (But) in his own way, he loved every kid who came in

"There's never been a person on the face of this earth more loyal to the University of Kansas than Dean Nesmith."

– Don Fambrough

there. He motivated them by his actions or by sitting them down and telling them what he thought. He was always 'for' the student-athlete."

Don Fambrough, who requested Nesmith's counsel every morning as KU's head football coach during separate stints in the 1970s and early '80s, remembers the famous trainer enjoying kids who practiced hard.

"He loved those kids who could play hurt and had great attitudes," Fambrough says. "He had no time for the kid that was trying to pull the wool over his eyes. I tell you what, kids couldn't fool him, and they knew they couldn't fool him. He just had an instinct about people, he really did. A kid could come in there, and Dean could tell right then whether that kid was really hurt or if he was trying to dog it."

And Otto Schnellbacher, an All-America end when Nesmith doubled as trainer and assistant line coach during and shortly after World War II, says Nesmith's approach served a definite purpose.

DEAN NESMITH
Football,
1933-35
Head athletics trainer,
1938-84

"Dean knew the toughness you had to have to win," Schnellbacher says.

Nesmith's toughness often overshadowed his ingenuity. When athletics trainers started hearing about the benefits of whirlpool therapy in the late 1940s, KU couldn't afford one. So he rigged a hose to a locker room shower and ran it through a hole in the bottom of an empty 35-gallon barrel, creating a "jet stream," as he called it.

Nesmith loved his job – his work attendance attested to that. When he was inducted into the KU Hall of Fame in March 1984, he told the crowd at the halftime of a men's basketball game:

"I'm the luckiest man in the world because through all these years there was never a day I didn't look forward to going to work. I was going to a job I thoroughly loved and enjoyed. How can you be luckier than that?"

***

Actually, it was KU's good fortune to have someone so entirely devoted to the University.

Nesmith arrived at KU in 1932, when the Chi Omega fountain still marked the west edge of campus and little more than washboard dirt roads dotted the territory beyond it. A product of the Depression, Nesmith came to Lawrence from his hometown of Belleville, Kan.

"All the time I was in high school, I worked for the telephone company," he told the *University Daily Kansan* in November 1983. "I always thought I'd make a career out of it. But the Depression came along. I saw the handwriting on the wall."

After that, he called Lawrence home the rest of his life. The only exception occurred in 1936, when he joined his brother Ole with the NFL's New York Yankees. But he returned to KU the next year to finish a degree in education. A year later, after trainer Elwyn Dees left for Oklahoma A&M, Nesmith took the job he kept until he retired.

As much as he loved his job, he might have loved the University more.

"I'll never leave KU for money," he once said when asked why he didn't accept more lucrative offers elsewhere.

Wade Stinson, a former athletics director who questions few moves he made during his nine years at the head of the department, says he does think he made a mistake with Nesmith.

"I think I always underpaid Dean," Stinson says. "He was a tremendous guy."

Nesmith took the job in 1938 for $140 per month, a salary that didn't change until he received his first pay raise in 1942. But it's clear working as a trainer for KU meant more to Nesmith than money could provide.

"To me, whether it's an assistant coach or an athletic director, number one is the loyalty to the University," says Fambrough, who exhibited similar love for Kansas during his lengthy coaching career. "And there's never been a person on the face of this earth more loyal to the University of Kansas than Dean Nesmith."

Nesmith made trip arrangements, planned meals and played psychologist for Fambrough, F.C. "Phog" Allen and other KU coaches during his career. He also served as an unofficial liaison in the days when coaches couldn't speak to players during timeouts. Only trainers were allowed on the field or court to give players water or check an injury, and they weren't supposed to relay instructions.

"Doc (Allen) would tell him something to say, and he would relay it," says 1940s football and basketball All-American Ray Evans, mimicking Nesmith talking under his breath to a squad: " 'You guys are loafing! Get off your ass!' "

But above all, Nesmith is an invaluable part of sports training history.

"He was one of the founding fathers of athletics training," Bott says.

Nesmith – who winced when people called him "Nay-smith," as if he were the inventor of basketball – saw many changes in injury treatments during his career. For instance, heat applications and liniments were a popular treatment when he began in the late 1930s.

Years later, not one bottle of liniment made his treatment repertoire. In addition, his promotion of ice as a treatment alternative to heat helped him gain a position as chairman of the National Collegiate Trainers Association in 1952-53. His reputation also earned him a trip to Rome as the trainer for the 1960 U.S Olympic basketball team.

But Nesmith received perhaps his greatest honor in 1971, when the Helms Foundation elected him to its Hall of Fame, one of the few athletics trainers accorded the honor.

The twilight of Nesmith's career coincided with increased attention on women's athletics. Bott admits Nesmith might have had a tough time adjusting to treating women but says Nesmith's record proves he would have changed with the times.

Besides his job as trainer, Nesmith was actively involved with the K-Club, the school's alumni organization for athletes who earned varsity letters. He cherished a unique ring the K-Club gave him that depicted Memorial Stadium, the Campanile, the KU Seal, the Olympic rings and three words: "Performance and Dedication."

Those three words also appear on a plaque honoring Nesmith in KU's new athletics training facility, which is named after him.

Fisher's 1986 biography details Nesmith's life from the time he arrived at KU until he died of cancer Sept. 25, 1985, at age 71. His death occurred during only the third Kansas football season in the past 54 of which he wasn't a part.

"Dean really defies description," says Fisher, who knew Nesmith well as KU's academic counselor in the late 1970s and early 1980s and now is an English instructor at Arizona's Pima Community College. "He's almost an enigma. He held (somewhat) of a journeyman's position in the athletics department for 46 years. But he held a great deal of influence over athletes, coaches, administration and alumni.

"He was a man of immense courage, sincerity and warmth. To many of us, he was KU. He is the embodiment of the University of Kansas athletics department, with all its faults and frailties. He's a reflection of the state of Kansas itself."

NO FAIR-WEATHER CHAMPION

Straddle jumper reveled in inclement conditions

Gene Kelly enjoyed singing in the rain. Randy Smith loved jumping in it.

Ask the former University of Kansas high jumper his fondest memory from college, and his answer will surprise you.

It's not the NCAA outdoor championship he won in 1974 with a personal-record leap of 7 feet, 2 inches, although that's pretty close.

It's not the day that same year he claimed a U.S. Track & Field Federation victory by out jumping world-record holder Dwight Stones.

No, Smith prefers to talk about the time he defended his high-jump title in the 1974 Kansas Relays – in the pouring rain.

"I was always good in the rain because mental toughness was my strength," he says, recalling that he begged KU Relays officials not to call off the event before he cleared 6-11 to win it. "I got the trophy, and there was absolutely nobody in the stands. It was the worst conditions I'd ever seen."

Worse yet, the *University Daily Kansan* reported that the high jump had been canceled because of the weather. Smith knew he'd won, but no one else did.

Besides mental toughness, the 1975 KU graduate owned another distinguishing trait: his jumping style. He remained one of the few high jumpers in the 1970s who still used the straddle technique. Most had copied 1968 U.S. Olympic champion Dick Fosbury, who popularized his new style, the backward "flop."

Smith taught himself to high jump as a little boy by jumping over an old bamboo pole in his backyard. At first, he cleared the bar with a scissors jump. Then a boy who straddled defeated him in a Junior Olympics meet. Smith quickly learned to straddle.

By the time he was winning three consecutive state meets in the high jump for McPherson High School, including a record 6-9 leap his junior year, it was too late for Smith to be a flopper.

"By the time of my senior year in high school, probably 75 percent of the high jumpers I knew were floppers, and there were very few straddlers when I got to college," he says.

One famous flopper was Stones, who competed against Smith in several big meets during the mid-'70s.

Former KU track coach Bob Timmons remembers a USTFF meet in Oklahoma City where he says Stones received preferential treatment because of his jumping style and his world-class status.

RANDY SMITH
Track and field,
1972-75

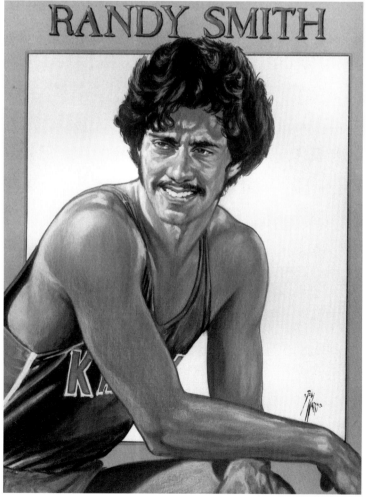

RANDY SMITH

Meet officials wanted to see a world record that day, so they set up a long approach for Stones, Timmons says. Smith didn't get the same courtesy, and he had to run over the track as part of his approach. Stones prevailed in that meeting.

"It always bothered me that Randy got shabby treatment there," Timmons says. "A lot of guys, it would have blown their minds. It didn't Randy. That's just the way he was – a great attitude. He never complained."

Smith admits he wasn't bothered.

"When you're a world-record holder, you can pull some strings," he says.

After college, Smith competed at the 1976 U.S. Olympic Trials, but didn't make the finals. He admits to being "mentally burned out." Shortly after, he quit the sport.

"Even today, I don't miss it at all," says Smith, who teaches in the health and physical education department at Moorhead State University in Moorhead, Minn. "I reached my potential."

ADAPTABILITY
Pole vaulter could adjust to any situation

TERRY PORTER
Track and field,
1973-74

Terry Porter always could adapt to circumstances.

Take the 1976 U.S. Olympic Trials in Eugene, Ore. The former University of Kansas pole vaulter was preparing to warm up when he realized something terrible: his pole was missing.

KU coach Bob Timmons remembers feeling near panic when he approached Porter. But Porter wasn't sweating. He told Timmons, "That's all right, coach. I'll borrow a pole."

"He did," Timmons says. "He borrowed a pole and qualified for the Olympic team."

That was vintage Porter.

From 1973 to 1976, he ranked among the best vaulters in the United States. In 1973, as a KU junior, Porter won the NCAA Indoor Championships by clearing 17 feet. He took third the same season at the NCAA outdoor meet, also at 17-0.

Porter placed 13th at the 1976 Olympics in Montreal. He is one of three former KU pole vaulters who have competed in the Olympics, joining Jan Johnson and Scott Huffman.

"Terry Porter was a character," Timmons says. "He was one of those vaulters who could always get up in the air. Some vaulters, if their step is off, they're not going to charge it. He could adjust to anything."

Timmons remembers another meet, a U.S. Track & Field Federation event in Wichita. Porter contended he had submitted his entry, although meet officials didn't have any record of it. Porter talked his way in, but the event already

had started, and the bar was placed at 18 feet.

"He clears it," Timmons says, noting the height was a personal high for Porter.

Porter grew up in Azle, Texas, and transferred to KU before the 1973 season from Ranger (Texas) Junior College, where he was the first junior college vaulter to clear 17-0.

Porter won the national junior college championship in 1972. That same season he also jumped 16-11 3/4 at the Kansas Relays.

By his senior year in 1974, Porter ranked as one of the top three vaulters in the nation. His career high to that date was 17-4 3/4 at the 1973 World University Games in Moscow.

Porter was as an eccentric, his former teammates say.

"I saw him one time at practice in his boxer underwear, running up and down the runway in his boxers," says Theo Hamilton, an assistant track and field coach at KU and a former Kansas All-American. "But he was one of the best pole vaulters I've ever been around."

Porter's life has taken a downward turn in recent years, though. As of 1998, he was incarcerated in a Texas Department of Corrections prison on a burglary conviction.

SAM COLSON

FORCED PARTICIPATION

High school rule leads to college championship

When Sam Colson played football with Mankato (Kan.) High School in the late 1960s, his coach had one steadfast rule: Any starter on the football team must compete in another sport during the spring.

That rule proved instrumental in the birth of an NCAA champion javelin thrower for the University of Kansas who almost won a medal at the 1976 Summer Olympics.

A star football and basketball player in high school, Colson recalls the day when he contemplated going out for track and field, a spring sport. But which would it be: track or field?

"I saw people on the track throwing up, and I saw people up on the field throwing things," he says.

Colson decided to throw things. It proved a wise choice. Colleges came calling, but most pursued him as a football or basketball player. His lifelong wish was to attend Kansas, but the KU football team didn't recruit him. Colson also had concerns about injuries in football.

As a basketball player, he described himself as "a big, lumbering 6-5 center" in high school.

"The Kansas guards at the time were 6-5, and they weren't lumbering," Colson says. "So I chose to walk on the track team."

By 1973, his senior year at KU, Colson had won three Big Eight Conference titles in the javelin, three U.S. Track & Field Federation championships and an NCAA outdoor title his senior year. He finished fourth in the NCAA as a sophomore and third as a junior.

"I should have won the NCAA as a sophomore and a junior, and I finally won it as a senior," he says.

Colson "expected" to win, an attitude he says was prevalent on the track team.

"The attitude fostered by Timmie (KU coach Bob Timmons) was that you were expected to be the best," he says. "The KU team at that time was so good. Everyone was committed to get better and win."

Colson's throw of 272 feet, 5 inches at the 1972 USTFF Championships was the longest ever, to that date, by a U.S. left-hander.

He would have set the U.S. record and perhaps a world mark at a 1973 dual meet at Alabama, if not for officials deeming the field illegal because it was slightly downhill and short.

That day, he heaved the javelin a personal record 291-10. Timmons recalls hearing shouts coming from the javelin competition during the Alabama meet.

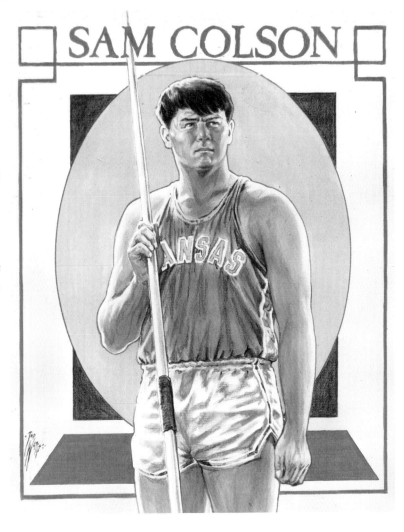

**SAM COLSON
Track and field,
1971-73**

"Somebody comes to get me. He said, 'Sam has almost thrown the javelin off Bear Bryant's practice field,' " says Timmons, who proceeded to investigate. "I went clear down at the end of the field. There were some bushes just in front of their chainlink fence. The javelin was in the bushes there."

Colson, who grew up on a wheat and hog farm, said his rural upbringing blessed him with a tremendous work ethic. Still, he needed to strengthen certain parts of his body. He suffered a back injury in 1974, a year after college graduation, that nearly ended his career.

By the 1976 Olympics, he had healed well enough to qualify for the Summer Games in Montreal. But he was not at full strength. Colson placed fifth in the Olympics, his final competition. The second through eighth-place finishers all came within five feet of each other.

"I was less than 1 1/2 feet from a silver medal," Colson says. "It was an absolutely wonderful experience."

One experience he'd like to forget happened a week before the 1972 Olympic Trials. Colson had recorded one of the longest javelin throws in the world that year and was among the favorites to win Olympic gold.

But while he and former KU shot-putter Karl Salb were training, the two decided to run 40-yard sprints for time. Salb won the first race. Colson pulled a quadriceps muscle in the second heat, which hindered his performance in the Olympic Trials.

"I yanked it pretty good," Colson says. "I should have made the Olympics in '72. It was a disappointment."

After his track career ended in 1976, he taught and coached track and field at Clemson University. Colson now lives with his wife and two children in Plymouth, Wis., where he is vice president of sales for Sargento Cheese Co.

BLAZE TO GLORY
Sprint relay team boasted gifted collection of athletes

One sprinted from the University of Kansas campus to the 1976 Olympics.

Two darted from college to NFL playing fields.

Three capped their KU careers with a bang by winning an NCAA championship as seniors.

Four composed the 440-yard relay team that won it all in 1974.

KU seniors Mark Lutz, Emmett Edwards and Tom Scavuzzo and sophomore Eddie Lewis blazed to glory at the 1974 NCAA Outdoor Championships by winning the 440-yard relay in 39.5 seconds. The foursome was one of the most gifted collection of sprinters in school history.

"For me, Tom and Emmett, that was our last relay together," says Lutz, who later became an Olympian. "It was a fitting finish that we went out as national champions."

Theo Hamilton, a KU coach who competed for the Jayhawks in the mid-1970s, fondly remembers the sprinters because their victory happened at his first NCAA outdoor meet. Their speed and athleticism impressed him.

Edwards and Lewis also played football for Kansas. Both had brief NFL careers.

"For those guys to play football and do track and field, I thought that was great," Hamilton says. "(Lewis) was the first one at practice, every day. He wasn't even on a track and field scholarship."

Lutz arguably was the swiftest of the four. As a KU sophomore in 1972, he placed second in the 200-yard dash at NCAA outdoor meet and was part of KU's fourth-place 440 relay. He was Big Eight Conference outdoor champion in the 100- and 220-yard dashes as both a junior and a senior. He set KU's school record in the 220 (20.5 seconds) and ran a personal-record 20.41 in the 200, his favorite event. His 200-meter time ranked third in the world in 1976.

"(Lutz) was a blazer," former KU head track coach Bob Timmons says. "I remember in the NCAA championships, he came off the curve way back, and he just exploded. He was way back with 50 meters to go, and boom, he ends up in second place."

Lutz advanced to the 1976 Olympics in Montreal by placing third in the 200 in the U.S. Olympic Trials, but not without a price. He strained a hamstring in the qualifying race and barely could run in the weeks leading up to the Summer Olympics. He limped into the Games and was eliminated in the first round.

"It was bittersweet because I'd worked my whole life to reach that point," Lutz says. "I got there, but I wasn't able to do what I wanted."

He also remembers a dark cloud hanging over the 1976 Olympics because of tight security measures enforced to prevent a repeat of the terrorism at the 1972 Munich Games.

"We were treated almost like a prison camp," Lutz says. "The dorms had barbed wire fences, there were spotlights, and you had to show passes everywhere you went."

On the football field, Edwards and Lewis enjoyed additional success for the Jayhawks. Edwards led the KU football team in receiving in 1973 and 1974 and made all-conference both years. He ranks third in career receiving (105 catches, 1,808 yards) at KU and went on to play for the NFL's Houston Oilers in 1975 and Buffalo Bills in 1976.

MARK LUTZ · EMMETT EDWARDS
TOM SCAVUZZO · EDDIE LEWIS

**MARK LUTZ,
EMMETT EDWARDS,
TOM SCAVUZZO
and EDDIE LEWIS
Track and field
440-yard relay team,
1974**

"He had great speed and great hands, also," says former KU quarterback David Jaynes. "He made catches that were unbelievable."

Lewis, a defensive back, led the Jayhawks in kickoff returns in 1974 and continued his career with the San Francisco 49ers in 1976-78 and the Detroit Lions in 1979.

"(Lewis) was a great competitor in football and that kind of competitor in track," Timmons says. "Not necessarily the fastest guy on the team but a solid competitor."

Scavuzzo played high school football and ran track in Littleton, Colo., but concentrated on track at KU. As a junior, he won the 440 in a personal-record 49.5 seconds at the conference indoor championships.

"He was a wonderful leadoff runner," Timmons says of Scavuzzo. "And on a little track, boy, he was a demon."

Lutz grew up in Rochester, Minn., and moved back to his hometown after college. He always wanted to be a trucker, and he hauls fuel for a local cooperative.

"The reason I went to KU was they had one of the best track teams in the country," says Lutz, who helped Kansas win consecutive conference outdoor titles from 1971 to 1974. "At first, my folks wanted me to go to Minnesota, and I wanted to go to UCLA. We compromised on KU."

THE THRILL OF
IT ALL

Coach who guided Jayhawks to two Final Fours revels in KU tradition

It wasn't the games for Ted Owens, even though he won 348 of them.

And it wasn't the success, even though he enjoyed plenty of it: two Final Fours, seven NCAA Tournament appearances, a second-place finish in the National Invitational Tournament, six regular-season Big Eight Conference championships and eight seasons with 20 or more victories.

No, what Owens enjoyed the most as head basketball coach at the University of Kansas may seem mundane at first.

"I suppose the biggest thrill that I ever had was when you ran out on the court with your team through the tunnel coming from the dressing room," he says. "That was a thrill to be a part of a great tradition. I am proud that I had a chance to be a part of that."

Owens was "a part of that" as an assistant coach from 1960 to 1964 and then as head coach from 1964 to 1983. He is one of seven men to coach the Jayhawks (more men have walked on the moon – 12 – than have coached KU basketball), and he's well aware of what it means.

"It's a great honor to be, and to have been, a part of that," Owens says of Kansas basketball. "At the same time, there's a tremendous amount of pressure. Not so much from the outside, but from within yourself, not wanting to disappoint the great following you have there.

"Kansas basketball plays a very important role in the spirit and history of the university. So, you feel a huge responsibility that you're successful and that you measure up to the past. That's overwhelming sometimes.

"It's like, (current Kansas coach) Roy (Williams) had an incredible year (in 1996-97). And yet, I could see the agony on his face, he wanted so much – not just for himself – but for his team and for the people who follow the program. You just don't want to let them down."

Even though he was fired in 1983 after back-to-back losing seasons, including matching 4-10 records in conference play, Owens and his family remain big fans of the Jayhawks. The former coach recalls how his then 15-year-old son, Teddy, mowed "KU" into the lawn of their Tampa, Fla., home as the 1997 NCAA Tournament began.

"When (Kansas) lost, he said, 'Dad, we're not cutting it down,' " the elder Owens says with a laugh. "He wanted me to take a picture and send it to Coach Williams to let him know that even though we lost, he was proud of them."

They would have, too, except that the homeowners' association intervened and asked the Owens' family to "mow the KU down."

***

When it came to mowing things down, Owens sat in the driver's seat and watched the basketball machine he helped create chew up opponents, especially in his first 10 seasons. From 1964-65 to 1973-74, he directed the Jayhawks to two Final Fours, four conference championships, six 20-victory seasons and a 191-83 record.

The two Final Four teams, 1970-71 and 1973-74, remain "close to my heart," Owens says. The 1970-71 Jayhawks went undefeated in conference play, eked out two close games to advance to the Final Four but then lost to a UCLA team on its way to its fifth of seven straight national championships. The Jayhawks, led by All-American Dave Robisch, finished 27-3, Owens' most victorious team.

The 1973-74 team featured balance and a strong bench in reaching the Final Four. No starter averaged more than 12.4 points per game for the 13-1 conference champions. The Jayhawks again won two close games in the regionals, including a 93-90 overtime victory against Oral Roberts University on its home floor in Tulsa, Okla. Marquette eliminated KU in the national semifinals, and after a consolation game loss to UCLA, the Jayhawks finished 23-7.

TED OWENS
Assistant basketball coach,
1960-64
Head basketball coach,
1964-83

But Owens also enjoys talking about some of the other teams that enriched his career. For example, the 1964-65 team, his first as head coach.

Owens helped re-establish KU as a basketball force in his first season. The Jayhawks played Kansas State in the semifinals of the old conference holiday tournament. The Wildcats ruled the conference at that time and had played in the Final Four the previous season. Kansas defeated the Wildcats 54-52 and beat Colorado the next night, winning the tournament.

"We felt that was a major breakthrough for us in getting the program really going again," Owens says.

Kansas finished 17-8 in 1964-65 and placed second in the conference.

The next season, KU returned to national prominence with a 13-1 mark in league play and a 23-4 record overall. The 1965-66 team remains one of Owens' favorites.

"There's nothing like your first championship," he says. "That was a great team. I'm not sure there was a better team in Kansas history."

Certainly, of Kansas' top teams that didn't make the Final Four, the 1965-66 edition is near the top of the list. The team featured All-American Walt Wesley at center, Ron Franz at forward, and the three-guard offense of Del Lewis, Al Lopes and a future All-American, Jo Jo White, who joined the team in the second semester.

In the 1966 NCAA Tournament, the Jayhawks lost an 81-80, double-overtime heartbreaker to Texas Western (now known as the University of Texas-El Paso). What made the loss even more difficult to take was that it appeared White had hit a game-winning shot at the end of the first overtime, but an official ruled he had stepped out of bounds. Texas Western won the national championship a week later by defeating Kentucky.

The next season featured identical 13-1 conference and 23-4 overall records. Owens expresses fondness for the 1966-67 team, which also made a surprise early exit from the NCAA Tournament. That year, Kansas played host to the Midwest Regional and faced Houston. In the other bracket, Southern Methodist played Louisville.

The Jayhawks got caught looking one game ahead and expected to play Louisville for the right to go to the Final Four. When SMU upset Louisville in the first game, the Jayhawks really thought the Final Four was a cinch. But Houston, with future Basketball Hall-of-Famer Elvin Hayes and star guard Don Chaney, derailed the Jayhawks' plans in a 66-53 defeat.

"We lost to a great team, but in those days it was almost a lay-down that we were going to win in Allen Field House," Owens says. "But that's the fun of sport. If everything was totally predictable, it wouldn't be fun."

***

If everything was totally predictable, Ted Owens likely would have pursued football rather than basketball. Born in Hollis, Okla., he grew up poor but happy during the Depression and World War II. When *Basketball Weekly* honored him as its 1977-78 National Coach of the Year, Owens told writer Bob Hentzen of the *Topeka Capital-Journal* how his upbringing shaped his values:

"I don't think there is any question that that background of really not having any luxuries – it makes you appreciate the good things that happen to you. We didn't have very much – until I went away to college, I'd never had indoor plumbing. But we had strong love in our family. We had plenty to eat. That's a good thing about farm life. We worked hard, but we lived in an environment of love."

Owens picked the University of Oklahoma for his school because his friend, Leon Heath, went there to play football. Owens also dreamed of playing football for Bud Wilkinson's Sooners. Instead, he was a non-scholarship end who worked part-time in a grocery store and slept in a fire station.

Occasionally, Owens shot baskets at OU's fieldhouse. A two-handed set-shot specialist, he caught the eye of an assistant basketball coach and eventually earned a scholarship. Owens played three years, 1948-49 to 1950-51, for coach Bruce Drake and then became his graduate assistant for a year.

He joined the U.S. Army in 1952 and was shipped to South Korea. After his two-year military duty ended, Owens played a season for the Ada (Okla.) Oilers of the National Industrial Basketball League. In 1956, Owens became head coach at Cameron College in Lawton, Okla. He compiled four seasons with 20 or more victories and an overall mark of 93-24.

In 1960, KU basketball coach Dick Harp hired Owens as an assistant to replace Jerry Waugh. Four years later, athletics director Wade Stinson promoted Owens to head coach after Harp resigned.

***

Sometimes the past you have to measure up to is your own. Owens encountered his own shadow several times after the 1974 Final Four. In 1977, after two fourth-place conference finishes, Kansas alumni and fans turned restless. Athletics director Clyde Walker quelled the problem and gave Owens a vote of confidence.

Two of Owens' assistants resigned, and Owens filled one of the vacancies with Wichita Heights High School coach Lafayette Norwood. With Norwood came guard Darnell Valentine, a high school All-American. Valentine's play breathed life into the Jayhawks, and the team won the conference and finished 24-5 in 1977-78.

Then the Jayhawks slipped to 18-11 in 1978-79 and 15-14 in 1979-80. After the 1980 season, KU athletics director Bob Marcum took Walker's cue and expressed confidence in Owens to improve the team.

Owens and the Jayhawks rewarded that confidence with a 24-8 season in 1980-81, Valentine's last season. Kansas won the conference postseason tournament and won two games in the NCAA Tournament before losing to Wichita State by a

"Kansas basketball plays a very important role in the spirit and history of the University. So you feel a huge responsibility that you're successful and that you measure up to the past."

– Ted Owens

point in the regional semifinals.

Then came back-to-back losing seasons and a new athletics director, Monte Johnson. Owens was upbeat after the 1982-83 season because of returning sophomores Ron Kellogg and Calvin Thompson. Wichita State transfer Greg Dreiling also would be eligible as a sophomore in 1983-84.

But Johnson saw things differently. He expressed concern about the Jayhawks' recent pattern of one highly successful year followed by two average seasons. A 3,500-fan dropoff in average attendance that season didn't help Owens, either.

Johnson fired Owens in March 1983.

Owens remained upbeat after his dismissal and handled it with class. At the team's annual banquet a few weeks after his firing, the *Lawrence Journal-World* reported the conclusion of his speech to the crowd of 250 people:

"I won't say there's been no anger and bitterness – honestly, it comes and goes, but there is so much to be grateful for. I have four wonderful children and a wife who supports me. That's what really matters.

"Only history will determine what kind of job we did here, but I know this … no one loves this place more than I do."

Robisch expresses disappointment that Owens wasn't treated better in 1983.

"I don't really feel that he got his reward for the success that he had," says the former All-American. "Yeah, he had a couple of bad years, but he took a number of teams to the Final Four and had great success. When you're there for 19 years, and you have the tradition that Kansas has, somehow I just felt … that he hasn't gotten the justice he deserves."

Owens has done himself justice since leaving Kansas. He became an investment counselor and in two years built a substantial client base and seemed set for life.

Then basketball called. He took the head coaching job at Oral Roberts, and Owens followed his own advice on surviving his firing. As he told the *Topeka Capital-Journal* in 1985:

"I don't know how many speeches I've made about getting back up when you get knocked down, dealing with adversity, overcoming obstacles. I said to myself, 'Life goes on, and we're not going to sit around and lick our wounds. No matter how unfair it seems, it's not going to change.' "

After two years at ORU, he left to become coach and general manager of the Fresno, Calif., team in the World Basketball League, a professional league for players 6 feet 5 inches and shorter. However, the league folded before it started, and Owens was jobless again.

But not for long. He landed a coaching job with Maccabi Tel Aviv in the European League for three years. After that time overseas, he and his family returned to Tulsa, where he served as basketball coach and director of development for Metro Christian Academy.

Today, Owens works as athletics director for St. Leo's College, a Division II university in suburban Tampa, Fla. He says he is enjoying the challenge of improving the school's athletics programs, which have not won a championship in any sport during their 21 years in the Sunshine Conference.

In the years after his firing, Owens has adapted to several jobs and homes. He also reconciled with the University. While Owens and family visited KU in October 1992, current KU coach Roy Williams and assistant Matt Doherty gave them a tour of Allen Field House. Owens told the *Kansas City Star* in 1993:

"They made us feel really good. And Roy made our children feel like their dad was something special. That meant a lot to me."

A STRONG START
Coach took Kansas to bowl game in first year

When the University of Kansas named Bud Moore as its football coach, he knew he needed to instill a winning attitude in the Jayhawks.

So before the 1975 season, Moore scrawled the names of the starters at Alabama, where he had served legendary coach Paul "Bear" Bryant as offensive coordinator, on one side of a chalkboard. On the other side, he wrote the names of the Jayhawks' starters.

The Jayhawks' players listened intently as their new mentor discussed skill levels on both sides of the board. Alabama was Alabama after all, and the Crimson Tide was coming off a season when it almost finished No. 1.

"I said the winning tradition and knowing how to pay the price goes to Alabama, but the talent is on our side," Moore says. "The biggest change from Alabama was convincing the alums and the players what it took to maintain a winner and compete on a national level. For the players, it was a matter of convincing them they could succeed."

And succeed they did, at least at the outset.

In Moore's first season, the Jayhawks enjoyed a 7-4 regular season. One of those victories, a 23-3 defeat of Oklahoma in Norman, broke the Sooners' 37-game unbeaten streak. Moore, a disciplinarian who installed the wishbone offense into the Jayhawks' attack, was named Big Eight Conference Coach of the Year. The Jayhawks capped the season with an invitation to the Sun Bowl in El Paso, Texas, where KU lost to the Tony Dorsett-led Pittsburgh Panthers 33-19. The next year, Pitt went undefeated and finished No. 1 in the final Associated Press poll.

In 1976, Kansas started 4-1. On Moore's 37th birthday, Oct. 16, 1976, the Jayhawks faced Oklahoma in Lawrence. Star quarterback Nolan Cromwell suffered a torn knee ligament in the game and was lost for the season. That game, a 28-10 loss, marked the start of a downhill slide for the Jayhawks and Moore. Kansas finished 6-5 that year, then slipped to 3-7-1 in 1977 and 1-10 in 1978.

Moore, with an overall record of 17-27-1, was fired with one game to go in the 1978 season. His four KU seasons were his last in college football.

He retired from coaching and started his own businesses. He owns a beer distributorship in Pensacola, Fla., and also raises cattle, catfish and walking horses in Catherine, Ala.

Moore carries fond memories of Kansas and former Jayhawks such as Cromwell, Terry Beeson, Mike Butler, Kurt Knoff and Laverne Smith. He calls Cromwell the best athlete he ever coached.

"Most of his passes looked more like kickoffs," Moore says of the Ransom Rambler, "but he could sure run."

Clyde Walker, KU's athletics director in the mid-'70s, convinced Moore to come to KU. The two had been football assistants together to Bill Dooley at the University of North Carolina. Besides coaching at the University of Alabama in the early '70s, Moore played end and tackle for the Crimson Tide in 1958-61. He was a member of coach Bryant's first Alabama team.

Moore says he knew bringing football success to Kansas would be an uphill climb.

BUD MOORE

"The schedule was awfully tough, and KU lacked the facilities," he says. "The only place we had for winter conditioning was the upstairs corridors in Allen Field House."

Moore recalls the only big improvement KU made during his years was a new football dressing room.

"My last year, we had (numerous) starters go down to injury at one time or another, and some of that could have been prevented with the right off-season conditioning to improve strength and quickness," he says.

But Moore also accepts his share of the blame.

"I didn't do as good of a job at recruiting as I would have liked," he says.

After KU, he decided to leave coaching and return to his old stomping grounds. He was born in Jasper, Ala., and grew up in Birmingham, Ala.

Moore says he turned down the head coaching job at the University of Miami at one point and also declined an offer to join Bud Wilkinson's staff with the NFL's St. Louis Cardinals. His early years at Kansas remain a bright spot in his coaching career.

"It gave me an opportunity to meet a lot of special people," he says.

Moore says he didn't think anyone in Kansas would remember him, but the victory against Oklahoma on Nov. 8, 1975, ensured that Jayhawks' fans never will forget Robert W. "Bud" Moore.

THE BEST AND BRIGHTEST

Relay team spawned three attorneys, one executive

One of the swiftest mile-relay teams in University of Kansas history may well have been the smartest.

Three sprinters on the 1977 NCAA Indoor champion mile-relay team – David Blutcher, Cliff Wiley and Jay Wagner – became attorneys. The fourth, Kevin Newell, became a marketing executive for fast-food giant McDonald's Corp.

Together, the relay partners defined the term "student-athletes."

Yet, only a year before they won the NCAA championship, two members of this dream team experienced one of their worst nightmares. In 1976, the NCAA declared Wiley and Newell ineligible for accepting Basic Equal Opportunity Grants, now known as Pell Grants, on top of their athletic scholarships. The grants generally are given to students from low-income families.

The NCAA told Wiley that he must repay the grant money, which amounted to several thousand dollars, to retain his eligibility. Wiley, one of 10 children from a low-income family in Baltimore, thought he needed the money to stay in school. He sued the NCAA concerning its ruling, and the legal action inspired him to pursue a law degree.

"I had a lot of athletes saying, 'What are they doing to you? I got this money, too,' " Wiley says. "I was scared. The NCAA puts this specter over you that they're going to ruin your life."

Wiley got a restraining order to compete, but he almost left Kansas. Yet he persevered, and the legal proceedings ground on long enough for him to graduate and enter KU law school by the time a federal court threw out the case without ruling on the merits of the claim. The court decided the case wasn't under federal jurisdiction. The Supreme Court also denied to hear it.

"It was a terrible experience, but I learned a valuable lesson: that life is not a bunch of jellybeans," says Wiley, who practices investment law in Kansas City, Mo.

Eventually, the NCAA allowed scholarship athletes to accept Pell Grants. Wiley's case helped pave the way.

Kansas lost a pair of Big Eight Conference track titles from the ordeal, although Wiley never had to pay back any money, nor did he return any medals. And he won plenty of them for finishing in the top six at the NCAA championship level: three at indoor meets and nine at the outdoor meets from 1975-78. KU finished in the top five at the NCAA Indoor Championships three of Wiley's four years.

"There was a certain, quiet confidence about the program at KU," Wiley says. "It's like you're a gunslinger who walks into town and everybody freezes."

Blutcher, who owns a private law practice in Chicago, carries fond memories of when KU's mile-relay team lined up for the NCAA indoor meet at Detroit. He ran the second leg and handed off to Wiley.

"The most amazing thing was I gave the stick off, kneeled down by the track, and then I looked up and Cliff was passing me again," Blutcher says. "I thought, 'He's

"Going to Kansas, I learned something different about people, being around Midwestern values. I never felt any anxiety, and people did not look at you differently because of the color of your skin. That was refreshing."

– David Blutcher

really flying.' "

Newell recalls, "We just ran away from everyone. We were supposed to be in the also-ran heat, and they had stacked the other heat because they thought the winner would be Villanova. We shocked everyone but ourselves."

The foursome came to the KU campus from the North (Newell, Chicago), South (Blutcher, Birmingham, Ala.), East (Wiley, Baltimore) and Midwest (Wagner, Bennington, Kan.). Wagner grew up on a wheat farm near Salina.

As with the other three runners, colleges heavily recruited Newell, whose Lane Technical High School team set a national mile-relay record in 1974. He chose Kansas for its academic focus and coach Bob Timmons.

"I lived in a pretty rough neighborhood, and he was the only coach who paid me a home visit," Newell says. "I remember he took an FBI agent, a friend of his, with him to my home. I flew to KU in the winter and fell in love with the campus.

"All the other schools showed me their athletic facilities first. When I got to KU, the field house was the last thing I saw. I had dinner with the dean of the business school. That told me where the focus was – academics first and athletics second. You didn't get the sense you were a free agent – legs for hire."

Newell, a 1979 graduate, became McDonald's lead director of marketing for special sites. He married Adrian Mitchell, who played for the KU women's basketball team in the 1970s.

Blutcher and Newell both live in Chicago, where Blutcher specializes in civil law at his practice on the southwest side. He grew up in Birmingham, Ala., during the height of the Civil Rights movement. Blutcher attended a black school several miles away from his home, which was located a block from a white school.

One reason he turned to sports was the integration that had occurred on the field. Attending KU also offered a pleasant surprise.

"Going to Kansas, I learned something different about people, being around Midwestern values," Blutcher says. "I never felt any anxiety, and people did not look at you differently because of the color of your skin. That was refreshing."

Timmons carries fond memories of the relay team and their competitiveness. Wagner, for example, sat out the 1976 season because he didn't think he would get a legitimate shot of making the mile-relay team. His perception changed in 1977.

"He was absolutely determined that no one was going to keep him off the mile-relay team," Timmons says. "And they didn't."

The coach admired Wagner for his courage. Wagner's right leg was shorter than his left, and an arthritic back plagued him.

"He kind of ran a little bit sideways," Timmons says. "He didn't have the free-wheeling that you like to see in a runner, but he was a fantastic competitor, I mean all out."

Wagner attended Kansas on a Summerfield academic scholarship and was the Big Eight's Academic Athlete of the Year in 1977. He was nominated for a Rhodes Scholarship but withdrew from competition after deciding not to continue studies in his undergraduate field

"There was a certain, quiet confidence about the program at KU. It's like you're a gunslinger who walks into town and everybody freezes."

– Cliff Wiley

KEVIN NEWELL, DAVID BLUTCHER, JAY WAGNER and CLIFFORD WILEY Track and field mile-relay team, 1977

KEVIN NEWELL · DAVID BLUTCHER
JAY WAGNER · CLIFFORD WILEY

(natural sciences) as required by the Rhodes committee. Instead, he attended law school at the University of Virginia.

Wagner practiced law briefly but then returned to farming full time. He farms 2,500 acres of wheat, soybeans and other crops near Bennington.

Of the four sprinters, Wiley attained the highest stature on the track. Besides earning a dozen All-America honors, he set a world record in the 300-yard dash at 29.48 seconds and ran on a 400-meter relay team that also established a world record. Both record-setting races occurred in 1977.

Wiley also qualified for the 1980 U.S. Olympic Team. But another bittersweet moment in his career occurred when president Jimmy Carter ordered a U.S. boycott of the Summer Olympics in Moscow because the Soviet Union refused to withdraw troops from Afghanistan.

Wiley emerged as the nation's top quarter-miler after winning the U.S. championships in 1981 and 1982. But he strained a hamstring in 1983, and he couldn't shake the injury. Wiley failed to qualify for the 1984 Olympics, even though he was a favorite.

THEO HAMILTON

A SECOND CHANCE
Long jumper persevered, returned to Kansas and became a champion

A leap of faith brought Theo Hamilton to the University of Kansas.

The leap part is easy to figure. Hamilton was an excellent long- and triple-jumper at Jefferson State Junior College in Birmingham, Ala. As for the faith, it looked as if he didn't have a prayer of making the Jayhawks when he had to return home to finish some coursework after arriving at Lawrence in fall 1973.

"We brought him up here as a junior college athlete, and we were so excited about him," says Bob Timmons, former KU track and field coach. "Then we found out that he was missing some courses. So he had to go back to junior college, finish those up and then transfer here.

"When he went home, I'll always remember him looking back in that bus. I thought, 'He's never coming back,' and I almost had tears in my eyes. But he did come back."

Timmons didn't know that Hamilton's mother made sure he was coming back to Lawrence.

"I went home, and my mother told me straight up, 'You are going back to Kansas,' " Hamilton says. "I didn't question it at all. I went back to juco, took some courses and probably had the one of the best quarters I had there at school.

"My mother has a really good feel for things. She's a very religious lady. She prays a lot, and she prayed on this deal. She saw me at the University of Kansas."

When Hamilton returned to Lawrence in the spring semester of 1974, he realized that he was a stronger person from the ordeal. He also believes it was his destiny.

"For me coming back, what that tells me, it was meant for me to go to KU," he says.

Hamilton made the most of his second chance. He won the U.S. Track & Field

Federation National outdoor long jump championship in 1974. The next year he triumphed in the same event at the NCAA Indoor Championships at Cobo Hall in Detroit.

But Hamilton hardly got off to a flying start at the meet.

"I was running really good on the runway, but my first time ... I hit the board, and I went 19 feet," he says. "What happened, I hit a dead spot in the runway, and I couldn't get the lift I wanted to get, which made (assistant) coach (Gary) Pepin furious. He yelled, 'Theo, what's the problem?' I said, 'I got it, I got it, I got it, no problem.' "

No problem indeed. Hamilton redeemed himself in his next four attempts. He jumped 25 feet, 9 inches, then 25-10, then a 26-footer and finally, his winning jump of 26-7 1/4 inches. Hamilton became the first – and only – KU long jumper to reach 26 feet indoors.

"Everything just went from there," he says of his efforts that day. "I had some really, really good jumps out there. I just felt like I was ready to go and it was time for me to win."

Later that season, Hamilton set a Big Eight Conference record in the long jump as he won the conference outdoor title.

"He was a wonderful athlete," Timmons says. "Great coordination for a tall, slender athlete. An easy-going guy with a pleasant personality. Another very humble person who never talked about himself."

***

How far is a quarter-of-an-inch? Depending on the size of type that you're reading in this book, a quarter-of-an-inch may be as long as the word "jump." But for Theo Hamilton, in 1976, a quarter-of-an-inch might as well have been a mile. That's because he finished fourth by that margin at the U.S. Olympic Trials in Eugene, Ore. Only the top three finishers qualify for the Olympics, which took place in Montreal that year.

"Afterwards, I thought about that thing, and I felt really, really bad," he said. "I felt like I should have made that team."

Instead, Hamilton joined the Jayhawks' coaching staff in 1976 and assisted Timmons through the 1983 season. He also served a three-year stint as the Jayhawks' head women's cross country and distance coach. Hamilton then assisted the University of Virginia's track team in 1983-85 and moved to Knoxville, Tenn., to assist the University of Tennessee's track program in 1985-88. He returned to Lawrence as a KU assistant in 1988 when Gary Schwartz replaced the retiring Timmons.

All told, Hamilton has spent 20 years with the Jayhawks' track program, a pretty amazing tenure for someone who made it to Lawrence – the second time – on the wings of his feet and a prayer.

THEO HAMILTON
Track and field,
1974-75

EXPECTATIONS FULFILLED

Sprinter was first KU woman to win a national championship

From 1974 to 1997, KU women captured seven gold medals in the 100- and 200-meter dashes at the Big Eight Conference Outdoor Track and Field Championships. All-American Sheila Calmese Wesson claimed four of them.

Calmese Wesson, a 1978 national champion, displayed one of her greatest performances during the '78 conference outdoor championships in Norman, Okla., where she won four times.

She dashed to victory in the 100 in 11.86 seconds and the 200 in 24.17. Then she led two relays – the sprint medley and 400 – to first-place finishes.

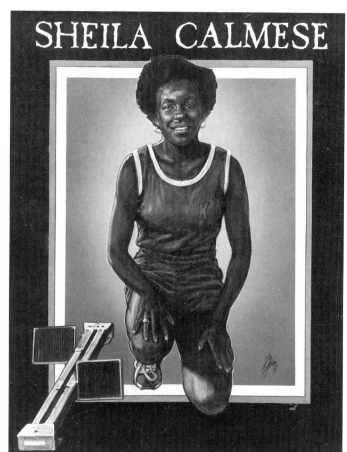

SHEILA CALMESE
Track and field,
1976-79

"She is one of the toughest girls I've ever seen run," says KU assistant coach Theo Hamilton, who coached KU's women sprinters at the time.

Calmese (pronounced CAL-mees) Wesson recalls that Hamilton always pushed her to succeed.

"I remember Theo yelling at me a lot," she says, half-joking. "He had high expectations."

Calmese Wesson rose to those high expectations and became recognized as one of the school's greatest women sprinters. Setting a U.S. record, Calmese Wesson won the 300-yard dash in 35.26 seconds at the 1978 nationals, known as the Association of Intercollegiate Athletics for Women Indoor Championships. She also placed second in the 60-yard dash.

Later that year, she placed third in the 100 meters in 11.75 seconds at the AIAW Outdoor Championships.

She came to KU in 1976 from St. Louis, where she grew up and ran track for the Amateur Athletic Union Royal Knights. Her AAU coach, Mike Carr, played an instrumental role in directing Calmese Wesson to Kansas.

Her arrival marked the start of KU's rise in women's track and field. Kansas took second in the 1978 conference indoor championships and third in the outdoor championships the same year.

"We had some good teams back then – that's what I remember most," she says. "We were all very supportive. It was like having a second family with Theo, the coaching staff and the rest of the team."

To recognize Calmese Wesson, the women's 100 at the Kansas Relays carries her name: The Sheila Calmese 100 meters.

"It's quite an honor," she says.

Calmese Wesson holds one school record and shares another. She set the 55-meter indoor record with a time of 6.81 seconds at the Missouri National Invitational in 1978. Calmese Wesson and Natasha Shafer share a KU-record outdoor time of 11.44 seconds in the 100. Calmese Wesson first set the record at the 1978 Arkansas Relays.

She competed her senior year in 1979 but was hindered by injury.

Calmese Wesson currently works as a registered nurse and is studying for a master's degree to become a family nurse practitioner. She lives with her husband and their six children in Dallas.

SHARON DRYSDALE / BOB STANCLIFT

BUILDING A PROGRAM

Two coaches were instrumental in early success of Kansas softball

So here's how women athletics were treated at the collegiate level in the early 1970s:

At the University of Washington, where 41.4 percent of the student body consisted of women, the athletics department spent about $2 million a year on sports. Of that amount, women athletics received $18,000 – 0.9 percent. A *Sports Illustrated* report found the school spent about $700,000 a year on men's basketball and football, two sports that at least produced revenue on their own. But men's sports not producing revenue still received about $1.3 million.

Few women actually received scholarships to play sports. Astonishingly, the Association of Intercollegiate Athletics for Women, established in 1971, initially prohibited scholarship athletes from competing in its events. And because the NCAA governed only men's sports until 1982, the AIAW, which operated on $24,000-a-year budget and had just two employees, was the only organized venue for women's college sports in the 1970s.

At the University of Kansas, women's sports were so far down on the importance list that season-by-season softball records are not available from the first year of the program in 1969 through 1972. And some game results are not available from 1969 through 1977.

That's a shame, because the Kansas softball team played in six consecutive AIAW World Series from 1972 to 1977 and appeared again in 1979. In all, the Jayhawks made seven series appearances in the first nine years the AIAW existed.

Coach Deb Artman led KU to its first appearance in 1972. But the two coaches credited with putting KU softball on a solid foundation, Sharon Drysdale and Bob Stanclift, guided the Jayhawks to the other six.

In fact, no team Drysdale coached ever failed to go to the Series. As coach in 1973-76, her teams had a combined record of 68-20.

Stanclift took over in 1977 for the next 11 seasons. His squads averaged 33 victories and 16 losses a season, and his combined record totaled 360-174. During his tenure, Kansas produced two Big Eight Conference championships, seven players who

A HERITAGE OF ATHLETIC ACHIEVEMENT / 247

SHARON DRYSDALE
Head softball coach,
1973-76

BOB STANCLIFT
Head volleyball coach,
1976-78
Head softball coach,
1977-87

received All-America honors of some sort and 26 all-conference selections.

Stanclift, who also coached KU's volleyball team from 1976 to 1978, says attracting attention for KU's softball squad often proved difficult.

"Early on, the media attention wasn't there," he says, recalling how KU's World Series appearance in 1977 received three sentences in the *Lawrence Journal-World.* "They didn't get the type of recognition they deserved."

But Title IX federal anti-discrimination regulations forced colleges to address inadequacies in women's sports programs. That statute, combined with the support of athletics director Monte Johnson in the mid-1980s, are the biggest reasons KU's softball program gained more status inside and outside the KU athletics department, Stanclift says.

"During his time there, budget-wise and acceptance-wise, there was a lot more unity in the athletic department between men and women," says Stanclift, who guided KU to seven top-20 seasons.

Stanclift now is the adult sports supervisor with Lawrence's parks and recreation department. He says his induction into KU's Athletics Hall of Fame was rewarding because it finally recognized the outstanding KU softball teams of the 1970s.

"It's long overdue," he says.

A LESSON LEARNED

Baseball coach succeeded
within limitations

Floyd Temple didn't have to wait long for his defining moment as a coach.

The year was 1955, his second as head baseball coach at the University of Kansas. Frustrated during one of KU's 16 losses that season, the 29-year-old Temple was angry. Angry at losing. Frustrated at having only three scholarships to give his team, about one-fourth the amount of those given by the Big Seven Conference's elite programs, making almost any playing field that the Jayhawks stepped on an uneven one. Angry enough to snap at his non-scholarship shortstop, whose playing ability put the word "student" in student-athlete.

"I lost my temper with him in a game, and I jumped all over him," Temple says. "The kid had tears in his eyes. I went home that night, and I got up and went to the bathroom, and I looked in the mirror.

"I said, 'You SOB. Here's a kid who comes out of the student body, and he's the

FLOYD TEMPLE
Baseball and football,
1949-50
Assistant football coach,
1958-77
Head baseball coach,
1954-81
Assistant athletics director,
1981-92

best you got. There's not anybody any better. And you go out there and get on him like that. He's probably giving you everything he has.'

"I said, 'You're going to have to change your outlook or get out of this sport.' "

The conversation completed, Temple resolved to change.

"From that day on, I made up my mind that I would work as hard as I possibly could to get each player to be as good as he can be," he says.

"From that day on" lasted another 26 seasons. When he retired in 1981, the Jayhawks under his direction had won 438 games and lost 396. In his last six seasons, when KU's baseball team received a full complement of 13 scholarships, the Jayhawks went 171-100, a .631 winning percentage.

"It was amazing that as soon as I got more scholarships, I became a better coach," Temple is fond of saying.

Don't let him kid you. Floyd Temple could coach.

"I learned as I was coaching," he says. "Every guy I ever had, every scout, we talked baseball. I got a great rapport with scouts."

And the scouts helped Temple find players. During most of his 28-year

baseball coaching career, Temple also served as an assistant football coach for the Jayhawks. Those duties often conflicted with his baseball recruiting, so the scouts would call Temple about prospects. One such conversation with Los Angeles Dodgers scout Bert Wells led the Jayhawks to pitcher Terry Sutcliffe, whose older brother, Rick, was a Cy Young-award winner with the Chicago Cubs.

That Temple made it to KU to talk with players, scouts or himself in the bathroom mirror is itself a story. A Coffeyville native, he joined the Marines after graduating from high school during World War II. He fought in the last part of the Guam campaign and participated in the invasion of Iwo Jima.

"You'll always remember," he says, pausing, "how so many people can get killed in such a short period of time on such a tiny island."

After the war, Temple returned home and played football and baseball at Coffeyville Junior College. As he told the *Lawrence Journal-World* in 1992, he planned to play football at Kansas State. He also planned to get married before arriving in Manhattan. But Wildcats' coach Ralph Graham told Temple he didn't have a place for the couple to live and that Temple would stay in a dormitory with the team. Temple said no thanks, or words to that effect, and found a more sympathetic coach in J.V. Sikes at KU.

Temple, a 5-foot-9-inch, 165-pound fullback, didn't play much for the Jayhawks' football team. But he did star as a third baseman for the baseball team, and he was a member of Kansas' last conference champion in 1949.

After giving professional baseball a try, Temple taught high school in Paola and managed the Class D minor league Iola Indians in the summer. The University called him during the middle of the season about a job as an assistant athletics director and baseball coach. Temple took the $4,900-a-year job and moved his family to Lawrence, where he's been ever since.

As a coach, Temple relied on the discipline he learned as a Marine. His players viewed him as demanding and tough. Former All-American Matt Gundelfinger remembers attempting to play catcher soon after arriving at KU. A pitch glanced off his mitt underneath his mask and hit him in the mouth, and he wandered toward the mound spitting broken teeth and blood as he went. Temple took exception.

"He said, 'Gundelfinger, what are you doing? Get back behind the plate,' " Gundelfinger says. "So I got back behind the plate and later had about $700 worth of work done on my mouth.

"That was Floyd Temple to a 'T'. He was a crusty old guy, but he grew on you."

And, despite scholarship limitations, he grew some pretty good ballplayers. Gundelfinger was one of four All-America selections. Seven of his players made it to the major leagues, including Bob Allison, the late slugging outfielder of the Minnesota Twins.

Regardless if they were student-athletes or major leaguers, Temple said he appreciated watching players progress during their time in college.

"That's the great thing about coaching," he says. "To remember that kid, when he was here, and four or five years later, you look at him, and he's a man. Not only the physical make-up but the mental make-up, too."

Temple knows. He survived war. He competed. He taught. And he reined himself in early as a coach because he listened and learned when he was tested. Temple believed KU basketball coach F.C. "Phog" Allen when Allen told him: "You're young. Good players make good coaches. Great players make great coaches. You can't create them. The best coach in the world can't make something out of something that isn't there."

Temple said Allen's words were some of the best advice he received.

But never discount the good counsel of a bathroom mirror.

"It was amazing that as soon as I got more scholarships, I became a better coach."

– Floyd Temple

Much attention is given today to two-sport stars such as Deion Sanders, Bo Jackson and Charlie Ward.

Floyd Temple received limited attention in his career as a two-sport coach. But from the start of the Jack Mitchell era until the mid-1970s, Temple assisted the Jayhawks football team in the fall and juggled that job plus his head-coaching duties for the baseball team in the spring. He seldom lacked anything to do.

"I just did whatever the coaches needed," Temple said.

His duties included coaching weak-side tackles for Pepper Rodgers and defensive backs for Mitchell. Temple used his baseball signals to call plays from the sidelines. And he recruited, which can be a full-time job in itself.

Temple is grateful for those experiences, but he admits they took their toll.

"You get into a career and you look back," Temple said. "I have two children, a son and a daughter. And the only thing I regret about what I did, (is) the time that I missed in those developing years in those children.

"You have to have a great wife (Beverly). Without her, it would not have been possible."

After Bud Moore became head football coach, he decided he didn't need Temple's help. Temple calls it the best move he made because it allowed him to get into administration work with the athletics department. In 1981, he resigned as baseball coach and became assistant athletics director.

And when Temple retired from that job in 1992, his 40-year tenure in the athletics department trailed only that of basketball coach F.C. "Phog" Allen and trainer Dean Nesmith in longevity.

Floyd Temple directed KU to a 438-396 record from 1954 to 1981.

MATT GUNDELFINGER

"YOU JUST NEVER KNOW"

Speed paved way for KU's all-time home run leader

Matt Gundelfinger, a former high school tennis player, proved he could run fast while trying out for the Kansas baseball team as a freshman walk-on in fall 1977.

It's a good thing. The 6-foot-4-inch graduate of Shawnee Mission North High in Overland Park didn't prove much else.

At the time, Floyd Temple was KU's head baseball coach and also an assistant football coach. He recalls the first conversation he had about Gundelfinger with Russ Sehon, a baseball scout who ran KU's fall baseball program while Temple concentrated on football.

"We'd meet about every other night and go over everything," Temple says. "He'd had them running wind-sprints, timing them. I said, 'Did you get some guys who can run?' He said, 'I have one guy out there, I had to put the clock on him twice.' "

Temple listened to Sehon rave about Gundelfinger's speed. Then he asked another question.

"He could KILL that baseball . . . I tell you one thing, he could flat swing the bat."

– Floyd Temple

MATT GUNDELFINGER
Baseball,
1978-80

"I said, 'What's he look like swinging?' " Temple says. "He said, 'Oh, it's the god-awfullest-looking sight you have ever seen.' "

But Temple instructed Sehon to keep Gundelfinger solely for his speed. By the end of fall practice, the two spoke again about walk-ons who should make the team. Sehon had prepared a list.

"I said, 'You don't have Gundelfinger down there,' " Temple says. "He says, 'No.' And I said, 'Well, I think we ought to keep him ... a big guy like that. Hell, we can use him for a pinch runner or something.' He said, 'Well, that's all he can do is run. He can't throw a lick.' And he couldn't. It looked like he was serving a tennis ball. Damndest thing I've ever seen in my life."

But Temple kept Gundelfinger and worked with him in the batting cage all winter. The next spring, in 1978, Gundelfinger hit his first home run for KU. It was a shot so prodigious, the baseball rolled onto Naismith Drive beyond the left field fence at KU's Quigley Field (now Hoglund-Maupin Stadium).

The blast was the first of Gundelfinger's 27 career home runs in a KU uniform. He still holds the school record in that category, even though he left to pursue professional baseball after his junior season.

"An amazing story," Temple says. "A tennis player, never played high school baseball. You just never know.

"He could just *kill* that baseball. I tried him at first base, but he couldn't throw from first to home. He just did not have any arm. I put him in left field and tried to protect him. But I tell you one thing: He could flat swing the bat."

Mostly, Temple put Gundelfinger, who had played American Legion baseball before walking on, at designated hitter. He played sporadically his freshman season, but he hammered opposing pitchers for strong KU teams in 1979 and 1980.

Gundelfinger attracted hordes of professional scouts in 1980, when he hit .409 with 16 home runs and 50 runs batted in. Before him, no KU player had hit as many as 10 home runs in a season. Gundelfinger did it twice. In addition, his 1980 RBI total smashed the KU record of 37 set by Lee Ice two years earlier. Gundelfinger led the Big Eight Conference in 1980 with eight home runs and 26 RBI in league games.

Temple says Gundelfinger knew scouts were watching his progress in 1980. He laughs while thinking of the time the poor-throwing fielder told him between games of a doubleheader that his arm was hurting. About 15 scouts were present.

"He was just bruising the ball," he says. "I played him in left field and at DH. He came up after the first game – he had DH'd; he knew he was going to be playing left field – he came up and said, 'Coach, coach: My arm is burning up.'

"I said, 'Gundelfinger, get your ass out there in left field! Those scouts know you can't throw a lick. You think that they don't know it? By *now?*'

"Boy, I mean his face got red as a beet. He was trying to hide it."

In spite of his throwing deficiency, the California Angels took a chance on Gundelfinger in the fourth round of the 1980 major league draft, and he gave up his senior season to turn professional.

Injuries mounted for him, though, and he didn't have a good minor league season until 1983. By that time, he was playing for the St. Louis Cardinals' Class A club in Springfield, Ill. He hit .300 with 28 home runs that season, but injuries suffered in a serious car accident ended his baseball career by the mid-1980s.

Today, Gundelfinger runs a small advertising agency in Dallas, where he says he's content despite never making it to the major leagues.

"You can't go through your life looking back," he says. "As I get older, I look back on my overall experience very positively. I was fortunate to play in a sport that I enjoyed for as much time as I put in."

Whenever Gundelfinger sees any of his former teammates, the years since KU quickly fade.

"I look back at the friendships and the camaraderie," he says. "The players I played with in college who I haven't seen in years ... it's like no time has gone by."

As for Temple, Gundelfinger always will appreciate the opportunities his former coach gave him.

"If he hadn't decided to keep some gangling kid," he says, "my life truly would have been different."

BOB MARCUM

"A VERY SPECIAL PLACE"

Former athletics director relishes memories of brief stay

Shortly after accepting the position of athletics director at the University of Kansas on Aug. 1, 1978, Bob Marcum had little trouble identifying the primary problem within the school's athletics department.

He replaced Clyde Walker, who, despite genteel Southern mannerisms, commanded a domineering presence within the department. Arriving at Kansas after seven years as an associate AD at Iowa State, Marcum brought a more cozy, open atmosphere.

"I thought at the time, people in the athletic department needed to have enough freedom so that their personalities could surface," says Marcum, athletics director at Massachusetts since 1993. "We needed to feel good again about being a part of KU athletics."

Feeling good was difficult, though, when whispers about a troubled football program echoed throughout campus. While the Jayhawks suffered a 1-10 season during Marcum's first four months on the job, the whispers grew to screams demanding change.

"The football situation had really deteriorated," says Marcum, a key recruiter for football coach Woody Hayes at Ohio State in the late 1960s, the last time as of 1998 that the Buckeyes finished No. 1 in the final Associated Press poll. "That needed immediate attention."

So Marcum fired Bud Moore, Walker's hand-picked choice after Don Fambrough resigned under pressure four years earlier. And whom did Marcum hire to replace Moore?

Why Fambrough, of course.

"There were some other good candidates, one in particular," he says, referring to Bo Rein, then the head coach at North Carolina State. "But I was thinking if there was so much division among alums, I was thinking we needed to go through a process to get the alums back on track.

"I told (Fambrough) what we really need is someone who loves the University

BOB MARCUM
Athletics director,
1978-82

and can renew support. He said, 'I agree, who can we get?' And I said, 'You.'

"He told me, 'Are you nuts?'"

Some Kansas alumni and members of the area's sports media wondered the same thing. Sure, Fambrough loved KU, but he was in his late 50s. A few surmised he would take the job for four years before turning it over to former KU quarterback and NFL star John Hadl. But that was never the deal, Marcum says.

"(Chancellor) Archie Dykes said he was never in favor of getting rid of Fambrough in the first place," he says.

By 1981, the hiring made Marcum look like a genius. Fambrough led the Jayhawks to an 8-3 regular season record and a trip to the Hall of Fame Bowl, where they lost 10-0 to Mississippi State.

Fambrough credits Marcum for allowing him to succeed during his second stint as KU's head coach.

"He was a coach's athletic director," Fambrough says. "He did everything he could to make his coaches successful and cared nothing about any credit for himself."

But just as the most publicized move he ever made at Kansas began paying off, Marcum left. South Carolina had courted him at the Hall of Fame Bowl, and thinking that school had more overall sports potential than Kansas because of its supreme devotion to football, Marcum accepted the position as the Gamecocks' AD in January 1982.

If hiring Fambrough was Marcum's most publicized move in his 3 1/2 years at Kansas, his handling of women's sports carries the most significance 20 years later. He guided the merger of KU's men's and women's athletics programs and was a force behind the Big Eight Conference's decision to open its doors to women's sports.

"Not all people were buying into it," Marcum says, adding those people included some women who thought their programs would founder if they shared a revenue base with men's programs. "(But) most people in women's sports today would agree it was the best thing for women's sports."

Indeed, women's athletics continue to grow at Kansas, as does the Williams Educational Fund. The fund, which provides scholarships to student athletes, doubled during Marcum's stay, even though many thought no more room existed for additional Kansas sports fund raising.

Marcum stayed at South Carolina until 1988, when he was fired for allegedly mishandling a drug-testing program. The firing came after *Sports Illustrated* uncovered widespread steroid use among South Carolina football players.

But Marcum successfully sued the school for wrongful dismissal, salvaging his reputation. Later, he served as vice president of the Charlotte, N.C., and Atlanta motor speedways before Massachusetts hired him as its athletics director.

Wherever he is, though, Marcum remembers his days at KU fondly.

"Just being a part of KU is a highlight for my career," he says. "The tremendous loyalty alums have for KU ... they have an attitude of 'can do,' not 'won't do.'

"KU gave Bob Marcum more than I gave that program. I still have an awful lot of friends there."

Typical, Marcum says, is a marble bench that sits in the shade on the northeast side of Allen Field House. KU's athletics department employees erected the bench to commemorate Marcum's wife, Cecile, who died of leukemia in 1994.

"That really doesn't surprise me about KU people," he says. "It's a very special place."

MR. KANSAS FOOTBALL

Almost four decades spanned program's highs & lows

The gunshot pop of helmets striking helmets splits the drizzly April air as Don Fambrough strolls the east sideline of Memorial Stadium.

It's the first day of full-contact drills at spring football practice under another new coaching regime at the University of Kansas. This time, Kansas has entrusted Terry Allen to find the winning consistency that has eluded so many before him.

Fambrough straddles the edge of the north goal line as he watches football's answer to boot camp for trench warfare: a series of head-to-head drills between the offensive and defensive lines.

"They certainly seem like they're excited," says a nearby observer.

Fambrough replies as he zeros in on Allen, whom he hopes can find Kansas football's holy grail.

"Yeah, but they shore ah gonna be sore in the mawnin' " he says, his distinctive east Texas drawl accompanied by a small grin. "Then they probably won't be so excited."

This is Don Fambrough in his element. Name a great moment in Kansas football from World War II to the early 1980s, then try to find a way Fambrough didn't influence it.

On the other hand, review some of the most controversial or forgettable seasons during that time. Not identifying him with them also is virtually impossible.

For good or bad, even now, Fambrough symbolizes Kansas football. During most of a 37-year stretch, the program's peaks and valleys mirrored those of his playing and coaching career. Whether participating in KU's last three conference championships or enduring several disappointing seasons, Fambrough, as the cliché goes, has seen it all in KU football.

"I never wanted to go anyplace else," he says. "This is the place I always wanted to coach. A lot of my coaching friends thought I shouldn't talk like that. They said, 'Even if you feel that way, you should keep it to yourself, because nobody else will want to hire you.'

"And I said, 'That's fine with me because I don't want to coach anyplace else.' And that's the truth. I never did want to coach anyplace but the University of Kansas."

So he didn't, except for the dark four-year stretch in the mid-1950s when Chuck Mather was KU's head coach. He also spent Bud Moore's four-year tenure as an assistant director of the Williams Educational Fund, the school's athletics scholarship endowment.

Otherwise, in one capacity or another, he directly affected the fortunes of KU football during eight presidential administrations, spanning Harry S Truman's to Ronald Reagan's.

Fambrough's first coaching experience came in 1948, shortly after he turned down a $7,000 annual salary to play guard and middle linebacker with the San Francisco 49ers. After the most successful two-year period in the history of Kansas football, coach George Sauer had left for the same job at the U.S. Naval Academy.

DON FAMBROUGH

DON FAMBROUGH
Football,
1946-47
Assistant football coach,
1948-53 & 1958-70
Head football coach,
1971-74 & 1979-82
Assistant athletics director,
1975-78

J.V. Sikes took Sauer's job at Kansas. When Fambrough told him about San Francisco's offer, Sikes, a fellow Southerner, countered with his own.

"He looked up and said, 'How would you like to be my freshman football coach?'" Fambrough says. "I thought I'd died and gone to heaven, and I forgot all about the 49ers."

Fambrough assisted Sikes at Kansas, then followed him to East Texas State after KU fired Sikes in 1953.

During their six seasons together at KU, Sikes and Fambrough produced entertaining teams that went 35-25. And most of KU's stars during that era got their first taste of Kansas football from Fambrough.

"Don was super," says George Mrkonic, a freshman in 1949 who made All-America as an offensive lineman two years later. "He was like a brother or a dad, and I still consider him that. He was certainly a guy you looked up to."

***

Going to East Texas State returned Fambrough to his roots. He grew up in Longview, Texas, and originally attended the University of Texas. There he played football for legendary coach Dana X. Bible before World War II.

But by the 1950s, Fambrough apparently was too entrenched in Lawrence to return home permanently. After three years as an East Texas State assistant and one year at Wichita University, he found his way back to KU in 1958 as an assistant to new football coach Jack Mitchell.

For nine years, Mitchell guided the Jayhawks. Gale Sayers, John Hadl, Curtis McClinton, Doyle Schick and Elvin "Crash 'Em" Basham were just a few of the strong recruits Mitchell lured to Kansas.

"Not enough has been said about some of the great individual football players we've had," Fambrough says. "Unfortunately, so many years we didn't have enough of them."

Mitchell and his staff quickly turned a feeble program into one of the best in the Big Eight Conference. KU won its first bowl game in 1961, beating Rice 33-7 in the Bluebonnet Bowl.

But by 1966, the program once again had declined. A 3-3 tie with lowly Kansas State, which had won only five conference games in the previous seven seasons and hadn't scored against Kansas since 1959, sealed Mitchell's fate.

But Fambrough stayed. Only two years later, with Fambrough as an assistant to the quirky Pepper Rodgers, the Jayhawks won their first conference championship since the former's days as a pulling guard. But two years after that, Rodgers left for UCLA after back-to-back losing seasons, including a 1-9 debacle just one year after KU lost a heartbreaker to Penn State in the Orange Bowl.

By then, Fambrough had to make a decision. Would he follow Rodgers to Los Angeles, a prospect that didn't necessarily appeal to him? Or would he get out of football if a new KU coach didn't hire him as an assistant?

Athletics director Wade Stinson made the choice for him. Fambrough had thought he was ready for a head coaching position when Stinson hired Rodgers. In 1971, Stinson gave him the chance.

"When Pepper left, Wade came in one day – this is the way he was – and he said, 'Don, you're the next head football coach at the University of Kansas,' " Fambrough says. "Then he turned and walked out."

Fambrough immediately turned his attention toward recruiting, probably his best coaching asset. Months later, he enjoyed an auspicious start to his head coaching career as the Jayhawks beat Washington State and Baylor by a combined score of 56-0 in the first two games of the 1971 season.

KU won only two more games all season, but those victories came against Kansas State and Missouri.

Just three weeks before the 1972 season began, the NCAA put the KU football program on a one-year probation for recruiting violations discovered by the conference two years earlier. The Jayhawks, banned from any bowl games following the season, again went 4-7.

But in 1973, behind the strong arm of All-American quarterback David Jaynes, Kansas went 7-3-1 in the regular season, giving Fambrough his first bowl trip as a head coach. The Jayhawks, who earlier lost road games to Tennessee and Nebraska by one point apiece, lost to North Carolina State 31-18 in the Liberty Bowl.

Expectations were high as the Jayhawks began the 1974 season. The Jayhawks defeated Washington State, Florida State, No. 5 Texas A&M and K-State, opening the season 4-1.

But in a season eerily similar to Glen Mason's last year at Kansas in 1996, the Jayhawks lost their last six games. The wheels first fell off with a 56-0 loss at home against the Cornhuskers.

Stinson had resigned by that time, and Clyde Walker was running KU athletics. He refused to extend Fambrough's contract past the 1975 season, so Fambrough resigned. So unpopular was Walker's decision, KU's Student Senate drafted a resolution asking Fambrough to reconsider.

He said thanks but no thanks.

"I have to feel good the way I'm leaving ... because I feel we have some outstanding young talent on this football team," Fambrough said at the time. "We are real close to having a real good program here."

Closer than anyone thought. The next season, Moore's first as coach, the Jayhawks stunned No. 1 Oklahoma 23-3 at Norman en route to a 7-5 season and another bowl trip.

Three years later, fate intervened again when athletics director Bob Marcum fired Moore and rehired Fambrough.

Again, Fambrough needed just three years to get Kansas back in a bowl game. In 1981, KU lost 10-0 to Mississippi State in the Hall of Fame Bowl and finished 8-4. The successful season gave Fambrough one of his fondest memories.

"I can't tell you the score of hardly any game we played," he says. "But I can remember we had to beat Missouri to get to the Hall of Fame Bowl. Boy, we were in bad shape, we were really hurting. David Lawrence, one of my captains, tore up his knee, just tore it all to pieces.

"He came into the office the week before the Missouri game and said, "Coach, I believe I can play.' I laughed at him and said, 'No, David, I wouldn't let my own son go out there with a knee like that, and I'm not going to let you.' "

But Lawrence, an all-conference offensive lineman, begged Fambrough. The coach finally relented, telling Lawrence he could play if he received permission from team doctors.

"I never did want to coach anyplace but the University of Kansas."

– Don Fambrough

Doctors determined Lawrence couldn't damage the knee any further and constructed a heavy brace so he could play.

"You could hardly pick it up off the ground," Fambrough says. "And he went out there and he played – I can see him now, dragging that darn thing.

"Things like that, to me that's what I coached for. That's why I loved the game. You can't believe what that did to our kids that day. We had no business winning that football game. They were *better* than we were, but we won the damned football game."

KU won 19-11, finishing in a tie for third in the conference.

"He was a great motivator," says former KU All-American kicker Bruce Kallmeyer. "Plus, he was excited. You could just feel his enthusiasm, especially when we played Missouri. Just his tone of voice – the players just really liked him. That's what a head coach should be like."

Tim Friess, an undersized defensive end and a captain of Fambrough's 1982 team, recalls how Fambrough always prepared KU players for season-ending clashes with Missouri by reliving William Quantrill's raid on Lawrence. (In 1863, as the Civil War and the Kansas-Missouri border war raged, Quantrill and his Confederate guerrillas from Missouri burned Lawrence and killed about 150 men and boys.)

"He's going nuts about Quantrill's raid," Friess says. "He says, 'A hundred years ago they came over here and burned the damned town down! Are you going to let them do it again? Are you going to let them bandits come in here and try to win a game on your turf?'

"You wanted to laugh, but he had that serious look ... He's a story-teller deluxe, but it was just great. He had a way of getting you going."

Friess, who played one year for Moore, noticed distinct differences between the two.

"Comparatively, Fambrough had so much more," he says. "He was just a man who cared about you. He could rip you just as good as Moore could or anybody else, but he was just as quick to praise you.

"I don't know who you could find that would say something bad about him, even guys that didn't get a chance to play."

Again, though, 1981's success proved fleeting, and Fambrough's grip on the program slipped. Allegations of numerous severe recruiting violations by assistant coaches surfaced, and KU finished 2-7-2 in 1982 amid an NCAA investigation.

In December 1982, just one week after KU hired new athletics director Monte Johnson, he fired Fambrough, ending his coaching career for good. A year later, the NCAA again slapped KU with probation.

Fambrough briefly served as a state field representative for former Kansas Sen. Bob Dole in the mid-1980s before retiring. Since then, he's maintained close ties to KU football, and more than 400 people attended a reunion of his former players before the Jayhawks' game against Missouri in 1995.

Athletics director Bob Frederick has said the warmth of that reunion is what spurred him to hire a coach like Allen, who has a reputation for openly communicating with players.

Fambrough, meanwhile, will watch Allen's progress with much anticipation as he continues reflecting on his passionate loyalty to Kansas.

"There were some individuals who I felt like weren't fair with me, but there have been at least three times when I had been knocked down and each time, the University of Kansas came around and picked me up," he says. "It's kind of hard to explain to somebody from the outside who really didn't know how I felt about the school.

"I've had too many great kids, been around too many great alums, too many great people here at the University to let something that was a little bit unpleasant overshadow all the good things that happened."

He recalls the 1979 game at Iowa State when a bus hauling the KU band broke down several times traveling to Ames. Finally, the band walked the last mile to the

"You could just feel his enthusiasm, especially when we played Missouri. Just his tone of voice – the players just really liked him. That's what a head coach should be like."

– Bruce Kallmeyer
on Don Fambrough

stadium. Motivated by the band's effort, KU beat heavily favored Iowa State 24-7, and Fambrough gave the game ball to the band.

The next day, band director Bob Foster and several dozen band members showed up at Fambrough's house. Having signed the game ball, they gave it back to him. It sits on a mantle in his Lawrence home, about a half-mile west of Memorial Stadium.

"I've had so many thrills, I've had my share, I'll tell you," he says. "Like I say, I've had some tough times, but that probably made me appreciate the good times even more. I have absolutely nothing but fond thoughts about my career as a player and a coach."

FEROCIOUS FAMBROUGH

Looking for the source of Don Fambrough's passion for KU? Start with Ray Evans.

A teammate of Fambrough's on the Second Air Force squad during World War II, Evans convinced Fambrough to take a visit to the KU campus after the war.

Fambrough, a fullback for the powerful 1942 Texas team that won the Cotton Bowl and finished 9-2, had planned to return to the Longhorns after the war.

"I came up with no intentions at all of coming to the University of Kansas, mainly just to visit Ray," he says. "But once I got up here, everything just fell into place. To be perfectly honest, I was a farm kid from down in east Texas, and the University of Texas was way too big for me.

"I just fell in love with KU – all the people, the size, everything about it. I decided I wanted to come to school here. I talked to Del (his wife), and she was really floored."

But she relented. Fambrough started at offensive guard and middle linebacker on KU's Big Six Conference championship teams of 1946-47, making all-conference as a senior and receiving KU's Most Valuable Lineman award.

"Don was a tenacious, ferocious, active player," says Otto Schnellbacher, KU's All-American end in 1947. "He was all heart. Somehow we knew that if we had to have it done, Don was going to do it."

Fambrough thinks players today miss what he and his teammates experienced.

"We had so much fun playing in those days," he says. "We weren't on TV, thank goodness. I'd hate to have to wait and stand out there for those darn commercials.

"I don't think I could play football like these people do now. I think we had more fun maybe than kids do today. We weren't thinking about the pros, we were playing football and going to school to get our

degree and go from there."

Fambrough and four other KU athletes were the focus of an eligibility controversy in 1948. After spring practice, other conference schools decided that an NCAA rule giving some war veterans four years of varsity eligibility didn't apply to Fambrough, football players Marvin Small, Gene Sherwood and Tom Scott and basketball player Jack Eskridge.

KU Chancellor Deane Malott, with the backing of the Kansas Board of Regents, prepared to defy the ruling. Other conference schools then threatened not to schedule football games with Kansas, which effectively would force the University out of the conference.

A similar dispute had occurred 18 years

earlier when conference schools questioned the eligibility of Jim Bausch, KU's famous football and track and field star.

In 1948, neither KU nor other conference schools were willing to budge. So the five athletes declared they would withdraw from further collegiate competition. Their sacrifice allowed KU to alleviate an impossible position with the conference, as well as end the threat that Kansas athletes wouldn't have a chance to compete against conference foes.

"I always thought that my friends over there at Missouri instigated that business," `. "That's one reason I love them so much."

Blocking, tackling, kicking: Don Fambrough (No. 22) did it all for the Jayhawks in 1946-47.

Rebuilding Yields Sweet Rewards

Perhaps Danny Manning's most forgettable performance at Kansas occurred the only time he donned a red game jersey. KU lost 71-67 to Duke in that 1986 Final Four semifinal. But two years later, Manning scored 25 points as the Jayhawks, on their way to an NCAA title, defeated the Blue Devils in a Final Four rematch.

DRIVING FORCE
Point guard served as heart of KU hoops for four years

Darnell Valentine's arrival at the University of Kansas campus in 1977 signified a big transition period in KU basketball.

For starters, it showed Ted Owens still could land a big recruit, as he had with earlier All-Americans such as Jo Jo White, Dave Robisch and Bud Stallworth. Valentine also proved significant because unlike White, Robisch and Stallworth, he was a Kansan and probably the best in-state prospect since Kansas City's Pierre Russell 10 years earlier.

At the same time, though, Owens finished recruiting Valentine without long-time assistant Sam Miranda at his side. Miranda resigned that spring, ostensibly bowing to alumni pressure after Kansas suffered two sub-par seasons out of three following the 1974 Final Four team. Owens hired Lafayette Norwood, Valentine's high school coach at Wichita Heights, to replace Miranda.

Meanwhile, the game was changing. Nationally, more teams were playing up-tempo basketball and succeeding with it. The Big Eight Conference experimented with a 30-second shot clock in 1977-78, which also altered strategy.

So, expectations soared with a blue-chip recruit running the team in 1977-78. Valentine didn't disappoint, either, leading KU to a regular season league championship with a 13-1 conference record. He led the team in assists, steals and in scoring with 13.5 points a game.

Valentine's leadership breathed new life into the Jayhawks that year. Besides his scoring touch, Valentine was a deft passer and a felonious defender. His steals triggered fast breaks and his assists added aplomb to the transition game.

"He was an enormous worker who played both ends of the floor well," Owens says. "He was a tremendous competitor."

That competitiveness helped the Jayhawks zoom past most opponents during Valentine's freshman year. The team's scoring average jumped to 81.6 points per game, nine points better than the previous season and 18 points ahead of the 1975-76 season. KU averaged a 15.2-point margin of victory in 1977-78, an amount that has been surpassed only five times since.

But the season ended in disappointing fashion. KU lost to Kansas State in the semifinals of the conference postseason tournament. The loss bumped the Jayhawks out of a favorable Midwest Regional slot in the NCAA Tournament and sent them packing to Eugene, Ore., to play a strong UCLA team. The Bruins defeated the Jayhawks 83-76. Kansas finished the season 24-5 and ranked in the top 10.

The 6-foot-2-inch Valentine was named conference newcomer of the year and made honorable mention All-America. Only Michigan State's Earvin Johnson brought more magic to the court among that year's freshman class.

Coach Ted Owens advises Darnell Valentine, his coach on the floor for four years.

"It was a nice honor, but it was nothing to be overwhelmed about," Valentine said in a 1978 interview. "I feel it's a matter of how much basketball you play, not your age. A freshman may have more experience than a senior."

The next two years proved trying for Valentine and the Jayhawks. He continued to lead the team in scoring, assists and steals, but the Jayhawks stumbled to 18-11 in 1978-79 and 15-14 in 1979-80. The team did not advance to postseason play in either year.

But the magic returned for Valentine's senior year in 1980-81. Kansas tied for second in the conference with a 9-5 league record and went 19-7 in the regular season, including a 10-game winning streak. The Jayhawks marched through the conference post-season tournament, defeating Oklahoma State, Missouri and Kansas State.

This time, the Jayhawks received a more favorable draw in the NCAA Tournament. Kansas traveled to Wichita, and Valentine delighted his hometown fans by leading KU past Mississippi 69-66 and Arizona State 88-71. The Sun Devils boasted a pretty fair guard in Byron Scott, but he and his team were no match for KU.

The two victories set up a Kansas-Wichita State matchup in the Midwest Regional semifinals in New Orleans. Wichita State's lineup included Antoine Carr, Valentine's former high school teammate.

As grudge matches go – the two teams had not played against each other in almost 26 years – the game was tight and physical. Wichita State won at the end 66-65 when Valentine was roughed up on an inbounds play but did not get the foul call.

Valentine finished the season as the Jayhawks' second-leading scorer with a 15.6 points per game average, just 0.2 points behind Tony Guy. Valentine also led the team in assists and steals, as he did in all four of his seasons at Kansas.

Valentine received all-conference honors for the fourth year in a row, making him the first Big Eight athlete to earn that distinction. He earned All-America honors, and he made the academic All-America team for the third straight year.

"He was a good student," Owens says. "He had it all, including a wonderful mother, Rose."

Valentine was the last of five All-Americans to play for Owens. The coach saw a common thread that ran from Walt Wesley to White to Robisch to Stallworth to Valentine.

"With all of these guys, you can point to a good mother, father or coach that makes a tremendous difference in their lives," Owens says.

For his career, Valentine ranks fourth on KU's scoring chart with 1,821 points and third in assists with 609. He leads all Jayhawks with 334 steals during his four years.

In 1980, Valentine made the U.S. Olympic basketball team. But he and the team never made the Moscow Games because of the U.S. boycott. Valentine, who

DARNELL VALENTINE
Basketball,
1977-81

played extensively against NBA All-Stars in a series of exhibition games with the Olympic team, took the setback in stride.

"I don't know about the other guys on the team, considering the mood about the Olympics, but the whole thing was a tremendous thrill for me," he said in a 1981 interview.

The Portland Trail Blazers selected Valentine as the 16th overall pick in the first round of the 1981 NBA draft. He played four-and-a-half seasons for the Trail Blazers before getting traded to the Los Angeles Clippers, where he spent two-and-a-half years. He ended his NBA career in 1991 after two years with the Cleveland Cavaliers. He averaged 8.7 points, 5 assists and 1.5 steals per game in nine NBA seasons.

Today, Valentine lives in Portland, Ore., and works for the NBA Players Association as a counselor. He advises players for most of the West Coast teams about handling their finances and adjusting to extensive travel.

In July 1997, Valentine suffered an abdominal aneurysm. He required a lengthy rehabilitation following surgery to repair internal bleeding.

"He must be very careful," Norwood said at the time. "He has to slow down, which is going to be hard on him."

Especially for someone who brought action back to Kansas basketball at blur speed.

JILL LARSON

TOILING IN THE SHADOWS

Lack of amenities didn't dampen softball player's enthusiasm

Jill (Larson) Bradney played softball at the University of Kansas during the dark ages of women's amateur athletics – even though less than 20 years have passed since her collegiate career ended.

Now, women's college basketball players sign six-figure professional contracts. Former college softball players, such as three-time Kansas All-American Camille Spitaleri, barnstorm with women's pro baseball teams. And *Sports Illustrated* introduces a magazine devoted entirely to women's sports.

Then, a wobbly chainlink fence enclosing a dank corner in the recesses of Allen Field House housed the softball team's weight room. Players maintained KU's off-campus home field at Holcom Sports Complex in west Lawrence and warmed their hands during cold spring games by starting fires in large trash cans.

Not exactly a picture postcard of NCAA glory. Then again, women didn't compete in the NCAA until after Bradney's KU career ended. During her era, when women's pro sports were a far-fetched dream, collegiate women competed in the bygone Association of Intercollegiate Athletics for Women (AIAW).

"They have a lot more opportunities than we did," Bradney says of today's female athletes. "We had to 'make do' a lot."

She remembers the time the entire Kansas team spent the day before an important Nebraska series raking the muddy Holcom Complex field.

JILL LARSON
Softball,
1978-81

"We all had blisters on our hands from the rakes," Bradney says. "We literally carried water in buckets off the field."

Bradney is anything but bitter. On the contrary, she thinks toiling in the shadows while playing college softball was more than worth it.

"I think it made us appreciate our success more," she says. "We had real good team cohesiveness."

Bradney enjoyed a stellar career from 1978 to 1981. The third baseman from Wichita totaled 188 hits for a .341 career batting average, the fifth-highest in school history.

More importantly to Bradney, teams on which she played compiled a 134-63 record. She also remains the only KU softball player to hit .400 during a season. She ended the 1979 season at exactly .400, leading the Jayhawks to the AIAW College World Series.

Two years later, she became the first All-American in the brief history of KU softball.

"My parents have a lot to do with my successes," she says. "I'm real proud of my All-America honors because I know it makes my parents proud."

These days, Bradney works as a health instructor in the Perry-Lecompton school district, where she started the girls high school softball program. She had coached basketball and softball at Baker University after graduating from KU.

She played fast-pitch softball for eight years after leaving KU, but coaching is Bradney's only contact with the game now. Although she has no regrets, she admits wondering what it would be like playing for KU today.

"I loved playing softball," she says. "I like their facility. I'm a little jealous I didn't get to play on it."

SANYA OWOLABI

DISCOVERING KANSAS
Prep star jumped west for college

As a triple jumper for Sleepy Hollow High School in North Tarrytown, N.Y., Sanya Owolabi jumped from oblivion into the track and field spotlight by winning a state championship as a sophomore.

"One minute I'm nobody, and the next minute I'm state champion," says Owolabi, a KU triple jumper from 1979 to 1983.

He stayed a state champion through high school. By his senior year in 1978, Owolabi became the second legend of Sleepy Hollow. He won state indoor titles in the long and triple jumps. He claimed triple jump titles in a series of national and international meets: the Golden West Invitational, the International Prep Invitational, the junior Amateur Athletic Union meet, a triangular with the United States, Great Britain and West Germany, and the U.S.-U.S.S.R. junior dual in the former Soviet Union, where he broke the U.S. high school record with a leap of 53 feet, 4 1/4 inches.

For the season, almost all of Owolabi's winning triple jumps exceeded 50 feet. *Track & Field News* voted him as its 1978 male prep athlete of the year.

Then came the biggest leap in his life to that point: Where would he attend college? In Owolabi's mind, Kansas stood far beyond a hop, step and a jump in the recruiting picture until he became acquainted with Kansas people and the school's tradition. One influential figure was KU alumnus Chet Vanatta, who lived in New York at the time.

"I had my pick of any school," says Owolabi, who almost became a teammate of Carl Lewis at the University of Houston. "I remember when I first saw a portrait of the Jayhawk. It caught my attention. I received a lot of literature from the (Kansas) coaches about the heritage of the track and field program. I had no idea about KU's tradition."

SANYA OWOLABI
Track and field,
1979-81 & 1983

The triple jumper joined a KU tradition of national track and field champions when he won the 1980 NCAA Indoor Championship, the same year he finished second in the NCAA Outdoor meet. In 1981, he was runner-up at the NCAA Indoor.

"He was one of the most talented athletes that we've ever had," said Bob Timmons, former KU track coach. "He had good speed and great coordination."

Injuries cut short Owolabi's career at Kansas. A nerve problem in his right leg prevented him from achieving even greater success. An injury redshirt in 1982, he ended his KU career with a personal best of 55-7 3/4. He retired at age 24 after failing to qualify for the Olympics during the 1984 U.S. Trials.

Reflecting on the injuries, Owolabi says he's thankful for receiving a solid education. He earned a business degree and worked for Brown & Williamson, a cigarette manufacturer in Louisville, Ky.

He and his wife, Janice, have two children: Deji and Jaye, both named for their Nigerian tradition. Owolabi's father, a doctor, came from Nigeria, and Sanya lived there for eight years as a young boy.

Life at KU, he says, taught him the importance of individual responsibility, discipline and professionalism.

"I met some really great people at KU, including my wife," Owolabi says.

He jokes that one reason he chose Kansas was to focus on academics, "because there's nothing else there to do."

His advice to today's high school athletes considering different colleges: "You have to go because of the school and the people, or you find yourself lost. The things learned in athletics carry on afterward. Don't blame others for shortcomings. Take responsibility. Bounce back from the low points and enjoy the great moments."

PURE SPEED
Sprinter set KU standard in early 1980s

Few track athletes are fortunate enough to win one individual national title. Michael Ricks did it twice.

The University of Kansas sprinter known for his sleek running style and explosive speed became a two-time national champion in consecutive years by winning the 600-yard dash at both the NCAA and junior college levels.

In 1980, Ricks won the NCAA Indoor Championships in his first season at Kansas, running the 600 in 1 minute, 10.06 seconds.

Only a year earlier, competing for Hutchinson Community Junior College, he dashed to victory in the National Junior College Indoor Championships with a time of 1:10.94.

"(Ricks) was a splendid indoor runner," says Bob Timmons, former KU track and field coach. "He could negotiate turns and handle himself really well indoors."

In 1979, Ricks transferred to KU from Hutchinson, where he also had placed fifth at outdoor nationals in the 400-meter dash in 1978. He attended high school in Newport News, Va. His older brother, Wayne Ricks, played football for the Jayhawks.

At Kansas, Ricks achieved instant success. He ran a school-record 1:08.9 in the 600, winning the 1980 Big Eight Conference Indoor Championships only two weeks before his NCAA victory. His conference time proved the fastest clocking on a 220-yard flat track that year in the world.

He also excelled at shorter distances such as the 300-meter, 400- and 440-yard dashes.

At the 1980 NCAA Outdoor Championships, Ricks covered his 400 leg in just 45.4 seconds, which helped KU's 1,600-meter relay team set a school record and place second. He also took seventh individually in the 400 at the national outdoor meet, with a personal-best mark of 46.2 seconds. That time ranked him fifth on the school's all-time list at that distance.

Ricks also recorded the sixth-fastest time in school history in the 400 intermediate hurdles by running 51.87 seconds at the 1980 Kansas Relays.

Teammate Sanya Owolabi, a world-class triple jumper, remembers the 1980 Kansas Relays as one of the team's greatest performances. That's because so many individuals turned in record times and distances.

"That was an excellent day for all of us," Owolabi says.

Ricks seemed to rise to the occasion on his home turf. He ran the fastest 440 ever inside Allen Field House with a time of 47.52 seconds during a 1980 dual meet against Colorado.

MICHAEL RICKS
Track and field,
1980-81

MICHAEL RICKS

COURAGE PERSONIFIED

Timmons says vaulter was his toughest competitor

Pole vaulter Jeff Buckingham soared through his track and field career at the University of Kansas like a real-life profile in courage, says Bob Timmons, his former coach.

"If I were in combat, and I had my choice of any guy whoever competed for KU to protect my backside, it'd be Jeff Buckingham," Timmons says.

That assessment is strong praise indeed, coming from an ex-Marine who served three years in World War II and later coached Kansas for 23 years.

The feeling is mutual on Buckingham's part.

"He's one guy I would cover with my life because I really like him," Buckingham says of Timmons. "He's one of a kind."

That Buckingham ever made it to the University to push the 19-foot vaulter's envelope is a testament to his toughness. When he was 7, Jeff and his younger brother, George, were camping with a friend in the backyard when a fire started in their tent. Jeff suffered third-degree burns on 65 percent of his body.

"My heart stopped twice," Jeff says of the fateful day.

Buckingham not only survived the ordeal, including 18 months in a Galveston, Texas, burn unit, but he prospered. He started vaulting after getting cut from his school's seventh-grade basketball team. His father, Charles, was a pole vaulter at Wyandotte High School in Kansas City, Kan., and he built a vaulting pit in their backyard in Gardner, located in southern Johnson County.

Jeff Buckingham used his home pit to his advantage and developed into the No. 2-ranked prep vaulter in the country. During high school, he won two state 3A indoor vault titles and three outdoor vault championships. He also triumphed at the 1977 National Junior Olympics and the 1978 Golden West Invitational. And he set a state high school record with a vault of 17 feet, 3/4 inches at the U.S.-U.S.S.R. dual meet in the former Soviet Union.

As a freshman at Kansas, Buckingham made an indelible impression on his team. He won the Big Eight Conference Indoor pole vault at 17-4, then took second at the 1979 NCAA Indoor Championships by scaling 17-3. He also won the conference outdoor championship with a 16-2 vault. That summer, he set a Kansas school record with a 17-9 vault.

**JEFF BUCKINGHAM
Track and field,
1979-80, 1982-83**

In 1980 as a sophomore, Buckingham again won both conference vaulting crowns, but his overall season was not as strong as his inaugural campaign. He then missed the 1981 season as an injury redshirt but returned strong in 1982. That year, he set another school record with a vault of 17-10 1/4 in a dual meet against Nebraska.

Buckingham excelled his senior year. He set school records indoors (18-7 1/4) and outdoors (18-10 3/4) in 1983. The latter mark still stands. And he finished fourth in both the NCAA indoor and outdoor championships. Buckingham was looking like an Olympian at that point, but things didn't work out.

"In '84, I was the best vaulter in the U.S., but I hurt my leg when I missed the pit prior to the (Olympic) Trials," Buckingham says. "I've been battling injuries ever since."

He never vaulted in the Olympics, yet he came extremely close. He qualified for the Olympic Trials in 1988 and made it to the finals four years later. But setbacks such as a cracked heel and Achilles injuries kept hindering his progress.

One disappointment for Buckingham is that the Jayhawks didn't win an NCAA track title during his career.

"We had good teams for the conference championships, but none of us got it together at the national level," he says.

Buckingham still vaults occasionally, though he mostly keeps busy with a quick print business, Gardner Printing, that he runs with his father. He's also the parent of three children. One son, Jeff Jr., has started vaulting. And Jeff Sr. proudly announces that his son already has cleared 7 feet in the backyard pit.

LYNETTE WOODARD

UNLIMITED IMPACT
Basketball star touches lives wherever she goes

Like one of her spin moves in the lane, Lynette Woodard's life came full circle with the advent of the Women's NBA in 1997.

Woodard, the best women's basketball player in the history of the University of Kansas, almost was born too soon to play professionally in the United States. Twenty years spanned the time she entered the University in 1977 and the WNBA's inception.

No matter. Woodard always possessed the desire and talent. She earned All-America honors all four years she played at Kansas, from 1977-78 to 1980-81, one of only three players to do so. She scored 3,649 points, the most ever in women's college basketball. (KU's fourth- and sixth-ranked men's leading scorers, Darnell Valentine and Dave Robisch, scored a combined 3,575 points).

Woodard received the Margaret Wade Trophy as the nation's top women's basketball player in 1981. She was named academic All-America twice, and she graduated with a bachelor's degree in speech communications.

In 1980, Woodard earned a spot with the U.S. Olympic women's basketball team. But the team did not get to play in the Olympics because of the U.S. boycott of the Moscow Games. Four years later, she was named captain of the U.S. Olympic team. That team won the gold medal at the 1984 Summer Games in Los Angeles.

A year later, Woodard made history as the first woman to play for the Harlem Globetrotters. She played for the Globetrotters for two years. Lynette Woodard

LYNETTE WOODARD

LYNETTE WOODARD
Basketball,
1977-81

became a household name around the world.

"It's really important that we don't limit Lynette's impact," says Marian Washington, KU's women's basketball coach and Woodard's mentor and friend. "Lynette impacted our program. But Lynette was a pioneer for all college women, and she became a pioneer for all professional women's basketball players.

"She has impacted the university and the state, but she is much bigger than that. She continues to be such a positive ambassador for young men and certainly, for young girls.

"She has excelled in so many ways."

***

A tragic event helped lead Woodard to basketball. In 1965, a U.S. Air Force tanker crashed across the street from her house in Wichita. Twenty-nine people were killed, and the one-square block crash site stood vacant for five years. Eventually, the city built Piatt Park on the crash site, a park that featured basketball goals.

Woodard became a fixture at the park, playing there until after 9 p.m. on school nights and then burning the midnight oil there during the summer. She even scored the first basket at the park, as she told the *Kansas City Star* in 1981:

"I remember we were all standing there while this steamroller finished the basketball court. They were telling everybody to get back. But I just couldn't wait. The man barely pulled off the asphalt when I ran out and sank one.
"I can't tell you why. The game just grabbed me."

It never let go, either. Woodard led Wichita North High School to state titles in 1975 as a sophomore and 1977 as a senior. Her last-second shot in the 1977 championship game clinched the title for North.

She brought her game to Kansas and succeeded instantly. She averaged 25.2 points as a freshman in 1977-78 and followed that performance with a sensational sophomore year. In 1978-79, she scored 1,177 points (an average of 31 points per game) and grabbed 545 rebounds (14.3 per game). The Jayhawks went 30-8 that season, the most victories in school history.

As a junior and senior, Woodard's scoring average dropped but her game improved. She averaged 23.8 points as a junior and 24.5 points as a senior. For her career, Woodard averaged 26.3 points and 12.4 rebounds, and the Jayhawks went 108-32 during her scintillating stay.

"Lynette does it all," Washington told the *Kansas City Star* in 1980. "She has played every position, and she plays them all well. She's an excellent passer and a very intelligent player. She is a beautiful player to watch."

Woodard attracted national attention as a senior in the 1980-81 season. Al McGuire, college basketball announcer with NBC, came to town for an interview and an eight-point game of one-on-one. Final: Woodard 8, McGuire 0.

Then came the Hanover Christmas Tournament at Madison Square Garden in New York City. Woodard staged a dunking exhibition outside of the famed arena to promote the tournament. Bryant Gumbel interviewed her on the "Today" show.

And on Jan. 6, 1981, Woodard's 12-foot jumper in the lane against Stephen F. Austin broke Cindy Brogdon's college scoring record of 3,204 career points. Brogdon played for Tennessee and graduated in 1979.

Woodard finished her career with 3,649 points. But the NCAA doesn't recognize her totals because she compiled them under the jurisdiction of the Association of Intercollegiate Athletics for Women, a judgment that bothers Washington to no end.

Still, a record is a record. The AIAW's basketball rules were the same as the NCAA's rules. And Woodard accomplished her feat during the era of the larger basketball and without benefit of the three-point line. When Woodard played, the women's basketball was the same size as the men's. Today, women use a slightly smaller ball.

Besides her fourth All-America honor and Wade Trophy, Woodard also earned

"Lynette does it all, she has played every position, and she plays them all well. She's an excellent passer and a very intelligent player. She is a beautiful player to watch."

– Marian E. Washington

the Broderick Cup and was the first woman to receive the NCAA Top Five Award.

"For girls like Lynette to succeed is important for all women," Washington told *Sports Illustrated* in 1981. "It means that whatever their blessed gift is, it has the right to be developed and can be. And it's important, in particular, for black girls.

"We've always had role models in sports, but most of them have been white. Now we can have both."

***

Kids from everywhere like Lynette Woodard.

For example, Francis Garmon, coach of Delta (Miss.) State, told the *Star* in 1981: "I coached Lynette in the World Games on an Asian Tour (1978). In Japan and China, little kids would just naturally flock up to her. That's the kind of person you hope gets the Wade Trophy." And a photo accompanying a 1996 feature in the *Lawrence Journal-World* shows a smiling Woodard surrounded by kids at Washington's summer basketball camp.

Then there's Washington recalling how she found film of an interview that occurred when the Jayhawks went to Madison Square Garden. The interviewer mentioned to Washington how many KU fans came out and watched Darnell Valentine play for the men's team but how few did the same for Woodard's games.

"I was quoted as saying that it was really sad, because here was a young person who happened to be a woman, who was making history almost every time she stepped on the floor," Washington says.

Sad but true. Woodard lacked an audience. Women's professional basketball didn't exist in the United States in 1981. So she played overseas, in Italy and Japan. She also played for the United States in two different World University Games. Scattered in between were two stints as an assistant coach to Washington, the 1984 Olympics and her two-year stay with the Globetrotters.

She competed two seasons with that team, from 1985 to 1987. Woodard grew up following the Globetrotters' stylish play because her cousin, "Geese" Ausbie, played for the team for 24 years and later became the coach.

While in Japan from 1990 to 1993, Woodard played for the Daiwa Securities team and became interested in the financial industry. But after she returned to the United States in 1993, the Kansas City (Mo.) School District hired her as athletics director.

During her 18 months at that job, she met Pat Winans, owner of Magna Securities, New York, at a benefit golf tournament. The two became friends, and Winans suggested that Woodard become a stockbroker, which she did. Today, Woodard is a vice president with the firm.

Woodard apparently was set for awhile on Wall Street, but she heard the basketball siren song one more time. In February 1997, the Cleveland Rockers picked her 10th overall in the WNBA's "elite draft." She returned to basketball (averaging 7.8 points, 2.4 assists and 4.1 rebounds per game) but not at the expense of her stockbroker's job.

Today, she is armed with a strong game, a cellular phone, laptop computer, pager and fax machine for the brokerage business. At age 38, she is starting with a new team, the Detroit Shock, after getting picked in the WNBA's 1998 expansion draft.

"It's not really tough because I love both," Woodard said in a 1997 television interview about her dual careers. "If I do feel myself being pinched, I'll think of those times that I used to take 18 or 20 hours in college."

Woodard quickly emerged as one of the league's marquee names. Fellow WNBA players call her a "class act."

"It's great to see her compete in a league that she helped create," says Tamecka Dixon, a former Jayhawk who plays for the WNBA's Los Angeles Sparks. "She's definitely a role model for me."

Count Washington among the many people cheering for Woodard's latest opportunity.

"She really is one of the greatest athletes I've ever seen," Washington says. "I'm really happy to see that she's got a chance to play for another couple of years. I only hope that there will be some people that will understand what she has accomplished."

rules that restricted college recruiting.

"The AIAW really wanted to avoid some of the pitfalls of men's athletics," Washington says. "They really kept recruiting to a minimum. We could call, but we could not pay for the athletes to come here and visit, we could not pay for anything once they were on campus (and) we could not go into the home to visit."

Fortunately for Washington, Woodard had visited Lawrence as a sophomore when her high school, Wichita North, won the Kansas State 5A High School tournament at Allen Field House. Washington saw her play and awarded Woodard her championship medal.

Other than that incidental contact, the AIAW's rules stymied Washington from getting to know Woodard and other prospective players. Not many outlets existed for recruits to learn about women's college basketball, either. Washington notes that recruits could read about the Jayhawks women's team in most newspapers if they

Twenty-four hours.

That's how much time Lynette Woodard gave women's basketball coach Marian Washington to sell her on the University of Kansas.

Washington faced another constraint besides Woodard's time limit: Association of Intercollegiate Athletics for Women's

remembered to check the women's society page - rather than the sports page - for the score.

Anyway, Woodard took a bus from Wichita to Lawrence for her 24-hour recruiting visit. Then Washington went to work - with a soft-sell approach.

"I talked to her basically about our academics here," Washington says.

From Lawrence, Woodard headed to a "Texas school" for a 48-hour recruiting trip.

"They wined and dined her," Washington says. "Even Tom Landry, the Dallas Cowboys coach, was involved in recruiting her. So, it was really tough.

"But I think I was very fortunate that Lynette was as mature as she was and she understood when I tried to explain that education was absolutely critical. It just so happened that when she went to visit the other institution that there was very little said about academics. And she was serious about her academics."

TAMMY THOMAS / RON NEUGENT

TWO ROADS CONVERGED ON MOUNT OREAD

Record breakers exhibited different backgrounds, similar dedication

One, a long-distance specialist, came highly touted with the trappings of a U.S. champion.

The other, a sprint artist, arrived relatively unknown before bursting into national prominence four years later.

Two decidedly different paths converged in the early 1980s at the University of Kansas, where Ron Neugent and Tammy (Thomas) Ammons left memorable marks not only on the Kansas swimming program, but on the rest of the University, the Big Eight Conference and the entire U.S. swimming establishment.

"Their whole history contrasted one another," says Gary Kempf, women's swimming coach at Kansas since 1976 and the men's coach since 1981. "Ron was a great athlete coming of high school, a highly-recruited athlete.

"Tammy came from a completely different background. Not many people had heard about her."

Arguably, Neugent's star had peaked by the time he enrolled in 1981, whereas Ammons had yet to experience widespread recognition. However, that changed by the time their senior years concluded in 1983, when Ammons stunned the amateur sports world by turning the NCAA Championships into her own record-setting extravaganza.

For six years, Jill Sterkel of Texas had the dominating role as premier women's sprinter in U.S. swimming. In 22.17 seconds, Ammons stole a portion of the part, and claimed the remainder in 48.40 seconds two days later.

That's how long – or how quickly – it took Ammons to win the 50-yard and 100-yard freestyles, respectively, at the 1983 NCAA meet. Both times, she upset Sterkel. Both times, she set U.S. records. Both races made her an instant favorite for the 1984 Olympics in Los Angeles.

Those victories started a whirlwind publicity ride for an unsuspecting Ammons, who broke her 50-yard record about a month after setting it. From national magazine writers to local grade-school children who wrote letters congratulating her, people yearned to hear her story. Suddenly, she was the 1983 Big Eight Women's Athlete of the Year.

"Everybody was saying, 'Who is this?' " Ammons says. "I had goals that I had set. That's what I was going for. It's nice all the recognition came with it."

She deserved it, Kempf says.

"Tammy had to overcome a lot of things," he says. "Tammy had to overcome people not believing in her ability. I mean, they just felt like she was a fluke."

Doubting Ammons, it seems, came easy because she hadn't blossomed on the national swimming scene in her teens. Sterkel, Tracy Caulkins and other swimmers often rise to fame before they turn 20.

The daughter of a career Army officer, Ammons was born in Fort Knox, Ky., and moved often before attending high school in Lawton, Okla. She was a high school All-American, even though she swam with the men's team as a freshman because no women's team existed.

Despite recruitment by a few high-profile swimming programs such as Florida, Michigan and Texas A&M, her skills were, as Kempf remembers, "raw" when she arrived at Kansas. Her development, he says, is a credit to her work ethic.

"Basically, through every step of her college career, she improved," he says. "She learned how to work, she learned how to train."

Training taught Ammons how to harness the power in her 6-foot-1-inch frame.

"She was one of the strongest young ladies I've ever seen," Kempf says. "She was very, very aggressive in the weight room and just really worked hard to perfect her strength. She was weak in the lower body; most great sprinters in the sport of swimming are great kickers. When Tammy came here, she was anything but a great kicker.

"But she was probably the most explosive athlete off the blocks I have ever seen."

Ammons, though, fell short of the '84 Olympics, a missed goal that doesn't bother her today.

"I believe to be an Olympic athlete, you have to have that

TAMMY THOMAS
Swimming,
1979-83

RON NEUGENT
Swimming,
1980-83

dream from a young age," she says. "I never had that dream."

Ammons can look back on a wonderful career at Kansas, where the women's team continued a string of 10 straight conference championships during her stay. The U.S. records she set remain school records, as does her 53.54-second time in the 100 butterfly. She remains the only Kansas swimmer, men's or women's, to win an individual NCAA championship event.

***

Olympic dreams drove Neugent for a long time. A nationally recognized swimmer at Wichita East High School, he attended Southern Methodist University during his freshman year before sitting out a year to train for the 1980 Olympics in Moscow.

He never fully realized his dream, though, even after making the Olympic squad. The United States boycotted the 1980 Games because of the Soviet Union's invasion of Afghanistan. It's still a sticking point with Neugent.

"The press said most of the athletes were in favor of the boycott," he says. "That's not true. I would estimate about 90 percent of the athletes were not in favor of the boycott. You don't like to see government mix with athletics."

After the Olympic disappointment, Neugent transferred to Kansas, where his coach from ages 12-17, Bill Spahn, had taken over for former coach Dick Reamon in 1978.

After sitting out another year because of NCAA transfer rules, Neugent was ready to swim for his old coach – until reading in a newspaper one morning that Spahn had resigned to take a similar position at New Mexico, near his original home.

"I was very disappointed," says Neugent, whose older brother, Roger, and younger brother, Todd, also swam at KU.

Neugent nevertheless attended Kansas. At the beginning of his senior year at KU, he broke the U.S. record in the 1,500-meter freestyle in 15:01.77. He set five school records, two conference records and won two conference titles during his two years on a team that wasn't as dominant as its women's counterpart.

"If we were in a tough meet, and we needed a win, Ron was who we went to," Kempf says. "Ron had tremendous versatility. I could look at a team's lineup, say, 'Ron, this is their top guy, I need you to go after him.' And he had the ability and character to do that."

Neugent says he relished that responsibility.

"When I swam, I put my heart into the race," he says. "I didn't want to let my teammates down."

Neugent's career at KU, though, didn't match the hype of being a former Olympic team member. In his signature event, the 1,650 freestyle, he never won an NCAA title as he battled pneumonia his junior year and finished 11th his senior season. But he and Ammons led KU to third place at the U.S. Swimming Nationals during their senior year, and he was the first KU men's swimmer to earn All-America honors in 12 years.

"I would have liked to done more," he says. "I would have liked to have done better at the NCAAs. But I'm very proud of the records I had at KU, and I'm proud of things our team accomplished."

Accomplishments for Neugent and Ammons didn't end at Kansas. Neugent served on the athlete's advisory council of the U.S. Olympic Committee in 1984-92 and served on that organization's board of directors in 1988-92. He is an orthodontist in Wichita.

Meanwhile, Ammons has opened her own landscaping business in suburban Houston, where she lives with her husband and son.

"They were team leaders from the word go," Kempf says. "Both had everybody's respect because of their work ethic, because of their attitude and because of how they cared about their teammates.

"I guess the great thing is, no matter how long you coach, you're not going to get a lot of kids at that caliber. They don't come along very often – and I'm talking anywhere in the country – as good as Ron and Tammy."

"They were team leaders from the word go. Both had everybody's respect because of their work ethic, because of their attitude and because of how they cared about their teammates."

– Gary Kempf,
Kansas swimming coach

COOL, CALM & COLLECTED HONORS

Kicker keyed several Kansas victories

The Kansas Jayhawks had not appeared on a network college football telecast in six years. But the Jayhawks attracted some attention with a 3-0 start in 1981, so ABC decided to televise KU's Oct. 3 game against Arkansas State in Lawrence on a regional basis. The nation's heartland would have a chance to rediscover Kansas football.

Having already beaten Tulsa, Oregon and Kentucky, KU figured to buoy its bowl hopes with a convincing defeat of what appeared to be the weakest team in the non-conference portion of its schedule.

The Jayhawks figured wrong. On a wet, dreary day that threatened to wash away any bowl visions, the Jayhawks trailed 16-14 with just seconds remaining. Their only hope: a 38-yard field goal attempt as wind whipped rain into kicker Bruce Kallmeyer's face.

"It was a driving rain," Kallmeyer says. "That was a tough one because whenever the carpet is wet like that, you kind of have to adjust your style so you don't slip. You don't plant as hard."

He adjusted well. The Jayhawks won.

"That one really stands out," says Kallmeyer, who made 53 field goals for KU from 1980 to 1983. "Had we lost that game, we may not have gone to a bowl game."

Kansas also may not have advanced to the 1981 Hall of Fame Bowl had Kallmeyer not booted a 28-yard field goal with 1:33 left in a 17-14 victory against Kansas State three weeks later. That field goal atoned for a 43-yard miss with 4:26 left.

"Bruce had the perfect personality," says Don Fambrough, KU's head coach during Kallmeyer's first three seasons who also had kicked for the Jayhawks more than 30 years earlier. "He was a cool, calm, collected type of kid. I never will forget up at Nebraska when he kicked five field goals (in a 31-15 loss in 1981)."

Kallmeyer says of his pressure kicks, "I didn't really get nervous. Fortunately, I never had a situation when I missed one of those types of kicks where it meant the difference between winning and losing. I was very lucky. That would have bothered me had it happened."

The former high school safety didn't miss many kicks, period. During his four years after replacing another fine kicker, Mike Hubach, Kallmeyer made 78 percent of his field goal attempts, including 24 of 29 during his All-America senior season in 1983.

His 57-yard field goal against Iowa State in 1983 remained a school record until Dan Eichloff topped it twice in the early 1990s. With 98 points in 1983, Kallmeyer set a Big Eight Conference record for a kicker and a school record for points; 21 of those came in a 57-6 blowout of Wichita State.

"1983 was purely a reflection of our offense," he says. "I've always said that if we could have had the defense of 1981 with the offense of 1983, we would have won the national championship. That's how good they were. I had more attempts my senior year than I had my first two years."

BRUCE KALLMEYER
Football,
1980-83

Kallmeyer only missed three field goals of less than 40 yards while at KU and twice had strings of nine consecutive field goals made. But he remembers specifics more than statistics. As with the game-winning kicks his sophomore year, he fondly remembers KU's upset of Southern California in Los Angeles in 1983. And he won't forget a 54-yarder in a 37-27 upset of top 20-ranked Missouri when it visited Lawrence for his final game with the Jayhawks in 1983.

"(Coach Mike) Gottfried asked me on the sideline, 'Do you have a shot at this?' " Kallmeyer recalls. "And I said, 'Yeah, basically if I hit it just right, I think I can do it.'

"I hit it against the wind just perfectly. Had I hit it any lower or any higher, it wouldn't have made it."

Kallmeyer thinks that kick clinched his All-America status, which wouldn't have transpired had Gottfried not reinstated him after kicking him off the team the previous February.

Gottfried had just taken over as coach, and he dismissed Kallmeyer for missing team workouts to attend his brother's wedding and catch up on his engineering coursework.

"It was just one of those things where he was coming in trying to be an authoritarian," Kallmeyer says. "I think I had had a good tenure at KU up to that point. I did my job."

The two eventually worked out their differences, and Kallmeyer's standout senior year gave him a shot at the NFL. But injuries cut short stints with New England and Chicago, so Kallmeyer turned to a career as a stockbroker. He since has opened an insurance agency concentrating on long-term health care plans in the Kansas City area.

Although he hasn't kicked in years, it's apparent Kallmeyer carries the same attitude toward his career as he did football.

"If you do the best job you can, sure you're going to make most of them, but sometimes, you're going to miss," he says. "That's just a fact of life: winning versus losing."

MONTE JOHNSON

BUSINESS ACUMEN
No-nonsense approach stabilized troubled program

Monte Johnson apparently has no problem fulfilling friendly requests. At least he didn't when he accepted the job as athletics director at the University of Kansas.

Only a year-and-a-half after leaving a job as a bank executive in Wichita, Johnson had a comfortable life in late 1982. He was president of a Lawrence land development and investment firm owned by his good friend and former college basketball teammate, Bob Billings, and shared a nice home with his family in a town he loves.

But Johnson, a former KU basketball player, watched intently as the school's athletics program began to unravel.

Early in 1982, KU athletics director Bob Marcum took the same job at South Carolina. Then the men's basketball team finished next-to-last in the Big Eight Conference, its worst finish in 20 years. Finally, the KU football team finished 2-7-2 in 1982 after going to the Hall of Fame Bowl just a season earlier.

Worst of all, an ongoing NCAA investigation into substantial football recruiting violations cast a pall over the campus.

"I really felt there were things that needed to be done," Johnson says. "It was a combination of things. The facilities were in terrible shape, football and basketball were as bad as they had been in a long time, and financially, they weren't in very good shape. A couple of friends asked me if I'd get involved."

Did he ever.

A former KU assistant athletics director from 1961 to 1970, Johnson returned to the program. This time, a search committee and KU Chancellor Gene Budig chose him over 85 other applicants as the successor to athletics director Jim Lessig, who bolted for a job as commissioner of the Mid-American Conference five months after replacing Marcum.

A "KU person" hadn't run the department since Wade Stinson resigned 10 years before. So Johnson's professed love for the school – "he bleeds blue for KU," Billings says – made him an attractive choice.

He moved swiftly to restore KU's lost prominence. About a week after KU announced his hiring Nov. 28, 1982, Johnson fired football coach Don Fambrough. Three months later, he fired Ted Owens, men's basketball coach for 19 years, after a second consecutive seventh-place conference finish.

"He really considered those decisions because he's a (KU) traditionalist, he's a loyalist," Billings says. "But our fortunes were going down rapidly, and there just had to be a change made. It's unfortunate two very good people were there in a period when things weren't going very well."

Johnson knew he would take heat for firing two well-liked coaches four months into his new job. But he says the decisions were difficult only because he considered both Owens and Fambrough as friends.

"I guess I looked at it as what's best for the University, and those changes aren't difficult when you look at it that way," he says. "We had (basketball) games on Saturday when there were only 3,000 people there. And I was watching those games and hearing people say, 'You should never play games on Saturday because the fans don't come out.'

"Now we could play Tuesday morning, Sunday morning, Wednesday morning ... it doesn't matter. When you're a good basketball team, they come when you're playing, when the ball goes up."

Attendance at Allen Field House averaged only 9,500 during Owens' last season, and Johnson knew probation lay ahead for the football program. Still, some alumni

MONTE JOHNSON
Basketball,
1956-59
Assistant athletics director,
1961-70
Athletics director,
1982-87

balked at the way he cleaned house. He even sold the rights for KU football and basketball broadcasts to an independent network. That decision cost Tom Hedrick his job as "Voice of the Jayhawks" but created an additional revenue source.

A week after he fired Owens, Johnson participated in a reunion of players from KU and North Carolina who played in the classic 1957 NCAA Championship final, a triple-overtime victory for the Tar Heels. The players were honored guests of the NCAA Midwest Regional in Kansas City, but fans booed loudly when Johnson was introduced.

"I got a lot of letters, and I answered every one of them," he says. "I didn't ever look at those as being personal."

Criticism turned to praise by 1986, though, when Johnson's choice to succeed Owens, Larry Brown, led KU to its first Final Four in 12 years.

A stickler for separating emotions from business, Johnson approached KU athletics the same way: as a business.

"It's a very big business," he says. "I think the difference is most people who get involved talking about athletics wouldn't run their own business the way they'd like to see you run an athletic program. I just like the idea of seeing a business make money."

***

Johnson shaped his no-nonsense attitude growing up in Kansas City, Kan. He attended Wyandotte High School and was a walk-on at KU during F.C. "Phog" Allen's last year as head coach, 1955-56.

"Basketball was a means to an end," he says. "I couldn't afford to go to college. It gave me a chance to walk-on as a freshman, and they said if I made the starting five (on the freshman team) at the end of the year, I'd get a scholarship. And I did."

A year later, Dick Harp took over for Allen, who retired. He recalls Johnson's biggest asset.

"Hustle," he says. "Otherwise, Monte couldn't have been there at all. Monte had a lot of pride. He was helpful to us."

Billings, a starting guard, compares Johnson, a 6-foot-5-inch reserve, with a recent KU player who built a reputation on extraordinary effort.

"He was a little bit like Jerod Haase," he says, referring to the KU guard of the mid-1990s. "He was always on the floor, diving for balls, skinning his knees and elbows. He would sacrifice himself totally for the team. His statistics would not indicate nearly his contribution to the team."

But as athletics director, one statistic clearly defined his contribution. The Williams Educational Fund, the department's scholarship fund for student-athletes, doubled from $1.2 million to $2.4 million annually during his regime.

Johnson regards that as his one of his biggest accomplishments, along with placing the department on solid financial ground. In his first six months, the department turned a projected $100,000 budget shortfall into a $100,000 profit. It never lost money again in his tenure, and Johnson helped create a cash reserve of $598,000 by the time he left.

But after four-and-a-half years in the position, and after years of going to work at 6:15 every morning, Johnson cited burnout and impatience with university decision-making when he resigned in March 1987.

At that time, he also faced the prospect of rebuilding the football program. Mike Gottfried, whom Johnson hired to replace Fambrough, had moderate success but left for the University of Pittsburgh after only three years. Johnson hired Bob Valesente to replace him, but the Jayhawks finished just 3-8 in his first season, 1986, and lost every conference game.

A rift also had developed between the athletics department and faculty members as a result of overall poor academic performance by athletes, something Johnson struggled to comprehend.

"I'd be less than honest if I didn't say the last three years on the academic problem have been as difficult for me to take as anyone," he told the *Topeka Capital-Journal* when he resigned. "I could understand a one-year problem, a two-year problem, but three years is hard to understand."

Nevertheless, Budig's comments after receiving Johnson's resignation portray how the latter affected Kansas athletics.

"In a short period of time, Monte has established an enviable record of success," Budig said. "He has given the University a return to national recognition in men's basketball. Monte has laid a solid foundation with improved facilities and support for football, basketball, baseball and track."

As for Johnson's oft-scrutinized commitment to academics, he and his family contributed $100,000 in January 1997 to establish a new scholarship for KU basketball walk-ons.

Johnson is semi-retired but still occasionally works as a consultant, which often allows him to reflect on his time with KU.

"It was," he says, smiling, "a labor of love."

TRACY BUNGE / SHEILA CONNOLLY

TWO FOR THE RECORD BOOKS
Good memories last for KU softball coach, former teammate

One was a walk-on. Doctors once told the other she would never pitch again. Together, they formed the backbone of some of the best teams in University of Kansas softball history.

Sheila Connolly and Tracy Bunge: A shy, unassuming centerfielder and a fiery team leader who currently heads the KU softball program. Both arrived at Kansas in fall 1982. During the three years they played together (Connolly didn't play as a redshirt in 1984 after knee surgery), Kansas went to an NCAA regional each season (1983-85-86) and won 115 of 157 games.

Both made All-America, and their names still dot the KU record book in various categories. Bunge hit 15 home runs with KU, nine of which came in 1986. Those represented career and season records intact as the 1998 season began.

As a pitcher, Bunge is second behind Stephani Williams on KU's all-time strikeout list with 642 and shutouts with 44. But she's tied with Williams as KU's career leader in lowest earned run average with a mind-boggling 0.68. She owns the single-season ERA record of 0.55 in 1986, when she won 24 of KU's 44 victories. Fifteen of those 24 were shutouts.

Connolly hit for a .391 batting average in 1987, KU's second-highest, single-season mark behind Jill Larson's .400 average in 1979. She's in the top 10 on KU's all-time hits list, fourth on KU's runs scored list and was a first-team academic All-American.

Bunge, though, remembers Connolly's defense more distinctly than her hitting.

"Sheila was the best centerfielder I've ever had the chance to play with," says Bunge, who played with on the nation's top amateur team, the Raybesto Brakettes, after graduating with business degree.

Connolly was so good with her glove, Coach Bob Stanclift moved her to shortstop to shore up KU's middle infield defense halfway through her final year, 1987.

TRACY BUNGE
Softball, 1983-86
Head softball coach,
1997 -

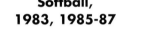

SHEILA CONNOLLY
Softball,
1983, 1985-87

Stanclift's reasoning for the move is clear in a letter he wrote that spring to the Big Eight Conference recommending Connolly for the league's Women's Athlete-of-the-Year award.

"I have coached for eleven years and have been around the sport for twenty," he wrote. "Sheila Connolly is the *best* female athlete and the best softball player I have ever coached."

Bunge wasn't far behind. The daughter of a former men's basketball All-American at Maryland and the sister of an all-Southwest Conference basketball player at Arkansas, Bunge's pedigree had "athlete" written all over it.

But she didn't pitch during her senior year of high school in Bartlesville, Okla., after severely injuring her pitching elbow. Doctors said her pitching career was finished.

Naturally, colleges backed off recruiting her somewhat, but she still attended Kansas the following fall. That's when she met Connolly, who started playing softball as a sixth-grader in Germany, where her father was stationed in the U.S. military.

Connolly's family, though, also lived in northeast Kansas for a time when her father was stationed at Fort Leavenworth. As a result, she and her four siblings, including her twin brother, Michael, all attended KU.

"I never really even thought about scholarships," says Connolly, who came to KU from high school in Fort Sheridan, Ill. "I really didn't know if I wanted to play. I'm kind of a shy person; walking on kind of intimidated me."

Bunge, though, proved immune to intimidation. She made an immediate impact during her freshman season. Take, for instance, the time she pitched 18 innings in a 1-0 victory against Missouri, then pitched 14 innings the next day in another 1-0 victory against the Tigers. Both victories were against Missouri's All-American pitcher, Teresa Wilson.

By Bunge's junior and senior years, she was KU's emotional leader, Connolly says. "She was intimidating," Connolly says, contemplating the advantages and disadvantages of having a great pitcher. "It's bad from the standpoint you're not going to get many balls hit to you! But it's a great mental advantage."

In 1986 Bunge, Connolly, catcher Kelly Downs and outfielder Ann Brent led Kansas to a ranking as high as No. 3 during one point in the season. But the Jayhawks lost two 1-0 games to Texas A&M in the NCAA regional tournament.

The second loss occurred after international tie-breaking rules went into effect. The Aggies scored their run against Bunge after the rules placed a Texas A&M runner on second at the beginning of the 10th inning. Two sacrifice hits later, the Aggies won.

"It was one of the best games I ever pitched," says Bunge, who also lost two NCAA regional games to Texas A&M during her freshman season.

For Connolly, failing to beat Nebraska in the conference tournament, which the Cornhuskers won from 1984 to 1988, is a sore memory. In 1985, the Jayhawks were a strike away from beating Nebraska in the conference final before losing. Days later, in an NCAA regional for the right to go to the College World Series, KU lost two of three to the Cornhuskers.

"They were our nemesis," she says. "We could not get over the hump. But time fades the disappointment and magnifies the accomplishments."

Bunge agrees. "I exceeded my own expectations as far as what I was able to do personally," she says. "I loved playing for KU, I loved the campus. I loved going to school here."

While playing for the Brakettes, Bunge found time to work as an assistant coach for Iowa State and Yale. She then became head coach at Ohio University, where she led the Bobcats to their first NCAA regional in 1995 and was named Mid-American Conference Coach of the Year.

She returned as KU's head coach in 1997 and promptly led the Jayhawks to a top-20 ranking and an NCAA regional final.

"It's a dream come true to return to your alma mater," Bunge says.

Connolly, now a pharmacist in Lawrence, often watches her former teammate lead the program to which they both contributed considerably as players.

"I see her encouraging her players," Connolly says, "and it's the same old Tracy."

SCOTT HUFFMAN

A QUANTUM LEAP
Vaulter made huge strides to make Olympics

**SCOTT HUFFMAN
Track and field,
1985-88**

The 1997 Kansas Relays were drawing to a close. Shadows from Memorial Stadium angled across the southwest corner of the track. A lone figure emerged from those shadows around the corner of the stadium, wheeling an old, manually operated scoreboard that listed the pole vault participants and the heights they had cleared.

It was Scott Huffman, star vaulter for the University of Kansas track and field team. He had competed earlier in the afternoon and had not fared exceptionally well. Still sweaty from his performance, he nonetheless was refreshed. He seemed fatigued but gregarious, greeting a well-wisher with a smile and kind word. Just nine months earlier, he had vaulted for the U.S. Olympic team in Atlanta, and here he was gladly cleaning up after himself at his old stomping grounds.

But that's Huffman: aware of his lofty status as one of the world's best vaulters yet well-grounded enough from his small-town upbringing to pitch in and help at his old school.

Huffman entered Kansas more on potential than ability as a walk-on in 1983. He had attended a track camp at KU before his senior year at Quinter (Kan.) High School and made a one-foot improvement in his vaults, from 13 feet to 14 feet, during his stay in Lawrence. KU assistant coach Roger Bowen noticed and set the recruiting process in motion.

A late bloomer, Huffman added an inch to his height and 15 pounds to his frame to become a muscular 5-foot-9-inch, 155-pound freshman. The muscle provided more speed, and the combination propelled him from vaults of 14-5 to 16-6 that season.

As a redshirt freshman, Huffman was guided by new assistant coach Rick Attig, who helped take the vaulter to the next level. Attig taught Huffman more about harnessing his speed and strength, how to sprint on the runway and more technical aspects about the vault. The result was a quantum leap for Huffman, from 16-6 to 18-5.

Huffman explains that making a champion vaulter doesn't just occur on the field. He and Attig spent many hours watching film and discussing vaulting theory.

"Pole vaulting is all about physics," Huffman said. "He explained the objectives to me in a biomechanical sense."

Improvement also includes getting physical. Huffman trained rigorously in the off-season by running the steps at Memorial Stadium for an hour at a time, concentrating on weight training, running and, of course, sprinting and vaulting.

"There's a lot more that goes into being fast for 45 yards and jumping than people would think," he says. "You have to be explosive, strong in the legs. You have to be a sprinter, because speed is everything in the vault. Then you have to be a long jumper, so you have to train for the long jump take-off. Then you turn into a gymnast.

"So you really have to blend three different types of activities. And you have to put it all together in a two-and-a-half second span."

Huffman won the Big Eight Outdoor Championships in 1986. By his senior year in 1988, Huffman put everything together to reach 18-6 1/2. He won the Big Eight Indoor and placed second in the NCAA Indoor that year. But he faltered at the U.S. Olympic Trials and placed 10th, far out of the running for a trip to Seoul. Four years later, he entered the trials as a favorite but again finished 10th.

Still, Huffman persevered and improved. He won the U.S. Track and Field Federation vaulting championships for three straight years in 1993-95. At the 1994 U.S. Championships, he set a national record with a vault of 19-7. The 1996 Summer Games in Atlanta loomed as his next goal.

Huffman realized that lifelong goal when he made the 1996 U.S. Olympic team. But he did not achieve without tribulation. He beat Pat Manson, his friend and former KU vaulter, for the third and final spot on the team. And Huffman was bothered by a nagging groin injury that kept him from a peak performance. He finished 13th in Atlanta.

"The Olympic experience itself was probably one of the worst competitions of my life," Huffman says. "The last two world championships, I had placed in the top six each time. I felt like I should be able to at least do that and probably get a medal in the Olympics.

"But I just had one of those bad, bad days on the day of the Olympic finals, and the actual final was a disappointment."

Still, he keeps his accomplishment in perspective.

"Once you're out of college athletics, people don't really recognize what you do anymore," Huffman says. "So making the Olympic team finally made me legitimate in other people's eyes. It's reaching the pinnacle of your sport. If I had to quit today, I would probably feel pretty fulfilled knowing I had made the Olympic team."

For now, Huffman competes in international meets and jets home to Lawrence to be with his wife and two children. Fulfilled by making one Olympic team, he now has his sights set on making another.

"I'd be happy to go to 2000; I'll be 35 years old," Huffman says. "Making another Olympic team would be my ultimate goal."

LEARNING TO LEAD
Maturity caught up with superstar's extraordinary skills

Bob Hill, a former assistant basketball coach at the University of Kansas and a former head coach in the NBA, probably would have liked to retract this comment he made to the *Kansas City Star* in early February 1988:

"Danny is a great basketball player, but he doesn't have the personality to take a team on his shoulders and lead it. He's more of a blend player."

At the time, however, Hill's assessment of Danny Manning's role with the Jayhawks seemed harsh but true, primarily because KU was struggling merely to secure a berth in the NCAA Tournament.

Two months later, then-Oklahoma coach Billy Tubbs watched Manning control both ends of the court when the Jayhawks beat the Sooners in the 1988 NCAA Tournament championship game.

"I don't think any team went out and stopped Danny," says Tubbs, now the head coach at Texas Christian. "Danny might have stopped Danny, but no team ever did."

It's no secret Manning, an admittedly private person who dodges publicity when he can, reluctantly assumed a leadership role with the KU basketball team. He realized soon after arriving at KU that he wasn't assertive enough on the court.

"I don't know why," he told the *Los Angeles Times* in 1985 as his sophomore season at Kansas approached. "I don't know what it is. I just have to keep telling myself, 'you have to be a leader,' then go out and do it."

It took him awhile, almost too long. But once he did, he supplied the missing piece to the previously unsolvable puzzle that was KU's 1987-88 season. Meanwhile, his detractors turned silent.

***

The four years Danny Manning rewrote Big Eight Conference records didn't signify the evolution of a basketball player as much as they did an individual personality.

It's not that Manning didn't improve as a player during his Kansas career. His scoring and rebounding averages and shooting percentage all improved between his freshman and senior seasons, despite additional attention from defenders each year.

"His senior year, he reached the point where he was a man among boys," says Mark Turgeon, a KU guard during Manning's first three seasons and a graduate assistant coach in 1987-88.

It's just that anything less than All-America honors and scoring records for Manning would have shocked the basketball world. Before he stepped on the Allen Field House court for the first time as a freshman, college basketball observers already considered him a prototype for the 21st century.

They compared him with Magic Johnson. He can lead or finish a fast break, they said, dish like a point guard, pound with centers in the paint, defend like a lion and shoot like a lamb.

Before arriving at KU, Manning was a Lion – for one year at Lawrence High School. He moved to Lawrence from Greensboro, N.C., for the 1983-84 school year, shortly after the new Kansas coach, Larry Brown, hired his father, Ed, as an assistant.

Brown's controversial hiring of a truck driver whose son happened to be the

DANNY MANNING

DANNY MANNING
Basketball,
1984-88

nation's best high school basketball player drew waves of media attention before Danny's first game at Lawrence High. *Sports Illustrated* and *The Sporting News* broached the issue. Even "The CBS Evening News" ran a feature.

Naturally, Brown defended his decision, which eventually worked out well for all involved.

"When you get the best player in the country, it's a pretty amazing thing for your program," Brown says. "Not only to get the best player, but to get his dad, who was a great friend and coach."

It's not as if Ed Manning didn't have a basketball background. He was a former professional player for Brown in the American Basketball Association and a former college assistant coach. Danny Manning told *USA Today* in March 1986 that watching his father play professional basketball actually spawned his own versatility and team-first attitude.

"He wasn't a great offensive player," said Danny Manning, who averaged 20.1 points per game in 147 games at KU, still the most career games in which a conference player has appeared. "But he played good defense, and he rebounded well. He was a great complementary player."

Maybe that's why the younger Manning, despite his obvious scoring skills, often said he enjoyed passing more than shooting. Maybe that's why it took Brown so long to convince him to demand the ball.

Turgeon says another coach may never have convinced Manning to fully unleash his scoring skills while assuming team leadership.

"The best thing that happened for Danny, I think, was to play for Coach Brown, because he was always challenging him," he says.

During the first two seasons after he was named Most Valuable Player of the 1984 McDonald's High School All-Star game, Manning relied on KU's upperclassmen to provide leadership while he simply played his game. Kansas also didn't rely on him to score too often, even though he averaged 14.6 points per game as a freshman and led KU with 16.7 points an outing as a sophomore, when he was named conference player of the year for the first time.

"I think Danny as a sophomore felt like it was Ron (Kellogg), Calvin (Thompson) and Greg's (Dreiling) team," says Turgeon, speaking of the 1985-86 KU squad that finished 35-4, went to the Final Four and ended the regular season ranked No. 2 in the Associated Press poll.

That season ended with a disappointing 71-67 loss against Duke in the NCAA semifinals. Manning scored only four points before fouling out. He later called it one of his worst experiences.

Kellogg, an all-conference forward who recalls Manning contributing to "great team chemistry," says Manning took the Duke loss hard.

"He was pretty upset about it because he didn't get a chance to get involved in the game," Kellogg says.

The loss, though, made Manning more determined. With Kellogg, Thompson and Dreiling gone, his scoring average soared to 23.9 points per game in 1986-87. He was named first-team All-America for the first time and nine times scored 30 points or more in a game. He led KU with 42 points in a 67-63 victory against Southwest Missouri State in the second round of the NCAA Tournament.

"That year, we needed Danny to score almost every time down the court, it seemed," says Turgeon, now the head coach at Jacksonville State (Ala.).

But Manning didn't fine-tune his role as a team leader until the last half of the 1987-88 season. His teammates noticed the subtle but important change once he realized leadership and team play could go hand-in-hand.

"Danny was the type of player who made everybody around him twice as good," says Chris Piper, the defensive-minded forward who played alongside Manning on KU's front line. "He was a phenomenal passer. He probably loved to pass more than anything. He had no ego on the floor. He was sometimes too unselfish. But he

"Danny was the type of player who made everybody around him twice as good. He was a phenomenal passer. He probably loved to pass more than anything. He had no ego on the floor. He was sometimes too unselfish. But he wanted to do whatever it took to win."

– Chris Piper

wanted to do whatever it took to win."

By the end of the year, Manning was a near-consensus choice as the best college player in the nation. But his talent went beyond the 24.8 points and nine rebounds he averaged each game that season. Even his teammates admitted marveling at how he could dominate games.

"I was a victim out there," Kevin Pritchard, KU's point guard, once said after one of Manning's stellar performances. "I was just watching him. Nobody can guard him man-to-man. He's the best in the nation."

Brown, though, says Manning's ability to add the leadership role to his wonderful skills allowed him to take his game – and KU – to another level.

"Danny had the whole package," Brown says. "He was a great kid, he was a team player, and that is something that is really important to me. When your best player is a great kid and a team player, it puts your program right there where you want it. I wanted to have good kids. When your best player exemplifies all the good qualities, you're pretty fortunate."

Manning, who spends summers in Lawrence, entered the NBA as the league's No. 1 draft pick with the Los Angeles Clippers. Injury-free throughout college, he suffered a season-ending knee injury early in his rookie season. Knee injuries also cut short his 1994-95 and 1997-98 seasons with the Phoenix Suns.

When he's managed to stay healthy, he has been a two-time All-Star and, as he was in college, one of the league's most versatile players.

Meanwhile, his immense legacy at Kansas may never be matched. He scored 2,951 points with the Jayhawks, the most in the history of the conference. He was conference player of the year three times, and members of the media named him as the league's player of the decade for the 1980s. He left KU with 16 individual conference records.

Tubbs, who says the toughest thing about preparing for Manning were the mismatches he posed for opposing defenses, contends his legacy goes beyond Kansas. Few disagree.

"I thought they were the two guys who elevated the Big Eight more than anybody," Tubbs says, referring to Manning and Wayman Tisdale, a three-time All-American at Oklahoma in 1982-85. "I thought they took it to a new level. They really brought TV cameras to the Big Eight.

"Those guys deserve a tremendous amount of credit."

REFLECTIONS ON A NATIONAL CHAMPIONSHIP

"A testament to determination, to hard work, lots and lots of hard work, to pride, to teamwork and the courage to dream."

That's how President Ronald Reagan referred to the 1987-88 Kansas Jayhawks when members of the men's basketball team met him at a White House ceremony honoring the team's NCAA championship.

A week earlier, April 4, the Jayhawks had accomplished what many thought impossible, beating Oklahoma 83-79 in the NCAA title game at Kemper Arena in Kansas City, Mo.

But when practice began six months earlier, few thought a national championship for KU was unreasonable.

Danny Manning, a first-team All-

American and the best player in college basketball, had turned down the chance to go to the NBA for another shot at a national title. His presence was the main reason that the Associated Press had Kansas ranked No. 7 before the season started. *The Sporting News* ranked Kansas No. 2, and *Basketball Times* picked the Jayhawks to win it all.

Few media types remembered those lofty rankings when coining terms such as "Danny and the Miracles" during KU's march to – and through – the Final Four.

Larry Brown didn't remember them, either, while a series of problems rocked the team at midseason, ending the KU careers of players on whom the Jayhawks

had counted.

"We lost (center Mike) Masucci, we lost Marvin Branch, a couple of our junior college kids didn't work out, and we lost Archie (forward Archie Marshall)," Brown says. "There were a lot of problems that year, there were a lot of things that affected the team."

The height of despair probably came Jan. 30, 1988. That day, Kansas State's Mitch Richmond scorched the Jayhawks for 35 points as the Wildcats ended KU's 55-game home winning streak, then a Big Eight Conference record, with a 72-61 victory.

Chris Piper, KU's defensive specialist at forward, remembers the postgame locker room scene. It was KU's third straight loss and fourth in five games. But Brown, a notoriously demanding coach, stayed calm.

"He was upbeat," Piper says. "He laid off us a lot toward the end of the year, which really wasn't his style."

Brown says, "I told those guys during those five games (KU lost its next game, as well, against the Sooners at home) we were making progress. I remember after those games, I told the guys we were getting better and we were going to be damn good."

By the time the Jayhawks played the Wildcats three weeks later at Ahearn Field House in Manhattan, their upswing had begun. A 64-63 victory, sparked by sophomore point guard Kevin Pritchard's three-pointer with 29 seconds left, gave the Jayhawks more momentum.

"We won a real critical game at K-State," Brown says. "That kind of turned it around. We had a lot of people step up. Milt Newton took over for Archie and was phenomenal, we moved (Jeff) Gueldner into the lineup and Scooter, Chris Piper, Pritchard and a lot of guys complemented Danny."

KU lost its next game, at home against Duke, 74-70 in overtime. Even so, Piper says the team had regained confidence. More importantly, Manning had taken over as its leader.

"Coach Brown had always wanted Danny to be more vocal," he says. "That wasn't Danny's way. But toward the end of 1988, he started being more selfish – in a good way."

Former KU guard Mark Turgeon's first season as a student assistant coach with the Jayhawks was 1987-88. He says Brown made great mid-season adjustments.

"He almost changed his whole approach to practice," Turgeon says, "and the team got better defensively. It was really hard for teams to score against our starting five."

The Jayhawks were 21-11 when the NCAA Tournament started but had lost their last game, a 69-54 defeat to K-State in the semifinals of the conference tournament. Pritchard, suffering a sprained right knee, didn't play in that game.

With Pritchard ailing but scheduled to start, Kansas, unranked and a No. 6 seed, opened the tournament against Xavier in Lincoln, Neb.

"I was really worried about the first game

because a lot of people didn't realize how good Xavier was," Brown says.

But Pritchard set the tone for the game and possibly the entire tournament. In the first few seconds, he took a long pass that broke the Musketeers' full-court press and finished with a two-handed dunk. The play sparked the Jayhawks to an 85-72 victory.

During the next three weeks, KU rolled through the tournament, squeaking past Murray State, pounding Vanderbilt and avenging losses to K-State and Duke.

That set up the final against the swaggering Sooners. Their ultra-confidence was understandable, what with their 35-3 record and three starters who later played extensively in the NBA. They also had defeated Kansas twice during the season.

But the Jayhawks, Piper says, entered the game emotionally prepared.

"That tournament was a loose, laid-back atmosphere," he says. "We practiced hard, but (Brown) was more concerned with Xs and Os."

Hours before the game, Brown says, the Jayhawks got an extra dose of confidence.

"I remember sitting there up at our pre-game meal, and ESPN had our game on in its entirety," he says of KU's 95-87 loss at Oklahoma earlier in the season. "And we watched it, and as were were watching it, everybody kind of knew, 'Hey, we can beat this team.' There was a sense in that room ..."

Brown often has received credit for giving the Jayhawks the freedom to play Oklahoma's tempo in the first half, then tightening the reins in the low-scoring second half. But he says it wasn't entirely by design.

"I didn't want to sit back and not try to attack their press," he says. "I thought that would be a real disaster. But I didn't want to go up and down. But they were making their shots, and we were making shots, and we just had to play that way.

"I had a feeling that if we started to hurt their press – in the past, (Oklahoma coach) Billy Tubbs always came out of it. I thought there was a time when we could get control of the tempo, and I kept telling the team 'Just get to the last five minutes, because we'll find a way to win: We have the best player.'"

And so they did. At halftime, Brown says he recalls thinking how the 50-50 score on the 50th anniversary of the Final Four – and how his college coach at North Carolina, Frank McGuire, had won the 1957 NCAA title in Kansas City against KU – all were good omens.

They probably were, Tubbs says.

"They shot really, really well that night," he says. "The thing about that night, I've always thought ... you know a lot of times, you lose and you say, 'Well, we didn't play that well.' But we played pretty well. It wasn't like we played a lousy game. They made the plays at the end of the game that allowed them to win."

Manning finished the game with 31 points, 18 rebounds, five steals, two assists and two blocked shots. His two free throws sealed the 83-79 victory with five seconds left. Tubbs, though, says the key to the game might have been Oklahoma star Stacey King's inability to handle Manning during the Sooners' full-court press.

Whatever the key, Brown was just glad Manning returned for his senior year.

"I didn't expect him to come back," Brown says. "We had a lot of things happen that year, but as a result of all the problems we had, all the injuries and the academic problems, it really did more for Danny than any other year he had. He really had to step up."

Piper, though, says he never thought Manning would turn professional early.

"He wanted to win a national championship," Piper says.

But he wouldn't have had KU's unheralded supporting cast not found its niche.

"We had Danny, and we had a lot of guys on our team that in their roles were very, very underrated and very productive players," Brown says. "That was the most unique team I think I've ever been around in terms of guys doing their roles and allowing a great player to play the way he was capable of playing.

"It was pretty neat."

KANSAS	50 33 —	83
OKLAHOMA	50 29 —	79

Officials: John Clougherty, Tim Higgins, Ed Hightower.
Attendance: 16,392

KANSAS – 83

	MIN	FG	FT	REB	PF	TP
Milt Newton	32	6-6	1-2	4	1	15
Chris Piper	37	4-6	0-0	7	3	8
Danny Manning	36	13-24	5-7	18	3	31
Kevin Pritchard	31	6-7	0-0	1	1	13
Jeff Gueldner	15	1-2	0-0	2	0	2
Scooter Barry	9	0-2	1-2	0	1	1
Clint Normore	16	3-3	0-1	1	3	7
Keith Harris	13	1-1	0-0	1	2	2
Lincoln Minor	11	1-4	2-2	1	1	4
Mike Maddox	1	0-0	0-0	0	1	0
TOTALS		35-55	9-14	35	16	83

Three-point goals: 4-6 (Newton 2-2, Pritchard 1-1, Normore 1-1, Manning 0-1, Gueldner 0-1). Assists: 17 (Pritchard 4, Normore 4, Piper 2, Manning 2, Barry 2, Newton, Gueldner, Minor). Turnovers: 23 (Piper 5, Pritchard 5, Manning 4, Harris 4, Barry 2, Normore 2, Minor). Blocked shots: 4 (Newton 2, Manning 2). Steals: 11 (Manning 5, Piper 3, Pritchard, Gueldner, Minor).

OKLAHOMA – 79

	MIN	FG	FT	REB	PF	TP
Harvey Grant	40	6-14	2-3	5	4	14
Dave Sieger	40	7-15	1-2	5	2	22
Stacey King	39	7-14	3-3	7	3	17
Mookie Blaylock	40	6-13	0-1	5	4	14
Ricky Grace	34	4-14	3-4	7	4	12
Terrence Mullins	7	0-0	0-0	1	1	0
TOTALS		30-70	9-13	30	18	79

Three-point goals: 10-24 (Sieger 7-13, Blaylock 2-4, Grace 1-7). Assists: 19 (Sieger 7, Grace 7, Blaylock 4, Grant). Turnovers: 15 (Sieger 6, King 3, Grace 3, Blaylock 2, Mullins). Blocked shots: 3 (King 2, Grant). Steals: 13 (Blaylock 7, Sieger 3, Grant, King, Grace)

Larry Brown and Danny Manning: One keen basketball mind and one extraordinary basketball talent equaled one memorable March for Kansas fans in 1988.

"HE WANTED TO BE A COACH"

For five years, well-known wanderer savored Jayhawks, college atmosphere

The gypsy built a house.

It was 1983, and a new home near Lawrence's Alvamar Country Club gave Kansas men's basketball fans some measure of security when athletics director Monte Johnson hired a man with two reputations: one as a nomad, the other as an outstanding coach.

Wherever his destination, people have always wanted to know when Larry Brown would leave before he even arrived. At Kansas, building a house seemed to answer that question of a man seeking to shed his wandering ways.

For five years, two Final Fours and one NCAA championship, the house – and Lawrence – sufficed. They calmed Brown's urges to roam, silencing the voices that tell him no matter where he is, something better lies elsewhere.

But by June 1988, those urges, and a lavish NBA salary offer, got the best of him again.

"I wasn't surprised that he left," says Chris Piper, whose years as a Kansas forward coincided with Brown's. "He had accomplished a lot. And Danny (Manning) was gone.

"I think the people of Lawrence were wrong to criticize him. He gave them a lot. They should have been happy with it."

Most were, but Brown almost never got the chance to leave his mark on the city and the university it holds dear. Among others, Johnson considered hiring current Oklahoma State coach Eddie Sutton, who then was at Arkansas, and Ralph Miller, a Kansas star in the early 1940s and a coaching legend at Oregon State.

He also contacted longtime North Carolina coach Dean Smith, another Kansas graduate. Smith, one year removed from coaching his first NCAA championship team, said thanks but no thanks.

"We interviewed 10 coaches in Albuquerque, (N.M.), at the (1983) Final Four site," Johnson says. "I came to interview Larry on a Monday in Kansas City. He eventually became the best candidate."

So Thursday, April 7, 1983, Johnson named Larry Brown as the sixth head basketball coach at the University of Kansas.

***

It's not that Brown ever had any trouble deciding what he wanted to do with his life. His only trouble was determining where he wanted to do it.

"Larry Brown as a player for me – he knew he wanted to be a coach," Smith says. "That's all he could talk about."

Smith gave Brown, an honorable mention All-American as a senior point guard in 1962-63, his first opportunity. He hired him as North Carolina's freshman coach, but Brown left that position in 1967 to play for the New Orleans Buccaneers of the American Basketball Association. He was the Most Valuable Player in the ABA's first All-Star game.

LARRY BROWN
Head basketball coach,
1983-88

In 1969, Brown took a job as head coach at Davidson College in North Carolina, but he left after six weeks during a dispute regarding the school's academic admissions policy.

So he returned to the ABA and played three more seasons. In 1972, the Carolina Cougars hired him as head coach. He stayed for two years before Denver hired him in 1974.

Brown moved to the NBA with the Nuggets in 1976. But he left in 1979 when UCLA, only four years removed from John Wooden's coaching dynasty, hired him.

Brown took his first team at UCLA to the 1980 NCAA Tournament final, where the Bruins lost to Louisville. He spent one more year at UCLA, then almost two years with the New Jersey Nets.

Kansas, Brown says, was too alluring to turn down. It was a place Smith had raved about, a place he thought he could spend the rest of his career.

"He made me aware of everything about that school," Brown says of Smith. "There were a lot of similarities between Kansas and Chapel Hill (North Carolina). They're both state schools, good academically and had a wonderful tradition – a campus atmosphere, a college town.

"I was honored I got the job. My main concern: I wanted to get to know the players and the coaching staff. I wanted to build from there. I thought they were the most important things."

Brown didn't take a lot of time to get comfortable in his new surroundings before making waves. First, he did not retain Jo Jo White, a former KU All-American, as an assistant coach. Then, sophomore forward Kerry Boagni, a key recruit of former coach Ted Owens, decided to transfer.

Brown, whose KU teams never could shake a questionable academic reputation, received criticism from the University's faculty in January 1984. It came after he allegedly tried to influence a professor to change a grade for freshman guard Cedric Hunter, who later was declared ineligible.

But the biggest story of Brown's first year, other than taking the Jayhawks to the NCAA Tournament for the first time since 1980-81, occurred before the season started. In September 1983, Brown hired Ed Manning, a truck driver in Greensboro, N.C., with two previous years of experience as an assistant college coach, as White's replacement. Manning, a former professional basketball player, had played for Brown with the Cougars.

Two days later, Manning's son, the best high school player in the nation, announced he would play college basketball at Kansas. Two-and-a-half years later, Danny Manning was named Big Eight Conference player of the year for the first time, KU went 35-4 and made its first Final Four trip in 12 seasons.

Ron Kellogg, an all-conference forward in 1984-85 and 1985-86, recalls Brown's advice after the Jayhawks lost 66-64 to Auburn in the second round of the 1985 NCAA Tournament.

"He told us we had to work a little harder," Kellogg says. " 'Work hard in practice, work hard in the off-season,' and we did. No one went home that summer."

By fall 1985, he says KU players wanted nothing less than the 1986 Final Four. They got it.

Brown, who says, "I don't like to compare teams," nevertheless concedes the 1985-86 squad probably was his best at KU, even better than the national championship squad two years later.

But the Jayhawks lost a 71-67 heartbreaker to Duke in the Final Four in Dallas. The next year, Kansas went 25-11 and advanced to the Sweet Sixteen before losing to Georgetown. Then both Brown and Manning turned down overtures from the NBA for the national title run in 1988.

***

Days after KU defeated Oklahoma in the 1988 NCAA title game, Brown's restlessness returned.

"I was going to UCLA," he says. "I really wanted to go to UCLA. When I went there (to interview), I truly had every intention of going there, but when I came back to KU – we had just had a rally, we had a parade coming up, we had a banquet coming up, we had a meeting with the President. There were a lot of players there that I really cared about, and I thought it was just bad timing."

So Brown said no to the Bruins. Two months later, he became the highest-paid coach in NBA history when he signed with the San Antonio Spurs for $700,000 a year.

Brown and his second wife, Barbara, divorced days after he took the San Antonio job. He also left behind a program that was under NCAA investigation. The NCAA eventually placed KU on probation for three years and refused to allow the school to defend its national title.

Brown says he wouldn't have left KU had he known the probation would be so harsh. He self-reported what he considers the "only real violation," a $364 airplane ticket he bought for Memphis State player Vincent Askew, who was considering transferring to Kansas. Brown paid for the ticket so Askew could fly home to see his sick grandmother, who died shortly afterward.

But the NCAA claimed KU interests paid an additional $880 to lure Askew to Kansas, and an article in *Time* magazine uncovered other improprieties, including small loans former KU player Mike Marshall allegedly made to KU players.

"Of all the things that happened that were good, (probation) is the one thing I'm most disappointed about," Brown says. "Because for one, I don't think the probation was warranted, and two, I never would have left had I known it was going to be that way.

"I left for all the wrong reasons. My personal life was the only reason I left. Unfortunately, I'm disappointed with the way it ended. I should have never left ... The only nice thing, with me leaving, they got an opportunity to get Roy (Williams)."

One person not too sad to see Brown leave was Billy Tubbs, Oklahoma's head coach at the time. The Jayhawks had no bigger rival in the mid-1980s than the

Sooners.

"I've coached against a lot of good coaches," Tubbs says, "but (Brown) brings a high intensity level to the game and he gets his players playing the way he wants them to play. He was always well-prepared. I always thought playing Kansas – it wasn't an easy team to get prepared for."

Former KU guard Mark Turgeon, once an assistant coach for Brown with the Philadelphia 76ers, recalls how Brown never settled for merely being good.

"He was a perfectionist on the floor," Turgeon says. "He would say, 'One more time,' and that meant you had 30 minutes left in practice."

"Offensively, I think he's brilliant. He was phenomenal late in games. We knew we were going to win close games."

Piper also says he can't think of a coach who handles game situations better.

"He was a great fundamental coach, he could see the floor better than anyone," Piper says. "I'd be hard pressed to find a coach who had a better feel for the game while it was going on."

When Brown arrived at KU, men's basketball attendance had fallen to less than 10,000 a game. When he left, a waiting list for season tickets that exists to this day marked the re-emergence of perhaps the nation's most storied program.

Overall, he had a 135-44 record in five seasons at KU. Percentage-wise, he still ranks second only to Williams as KU's winningest coach. Maybe more impressive, though, was KU's 14-4 record in the NCAA Tournament during his tenure.

"He was pretty intense in the regular season," Kellogg says. "But he was more relaxed in postseason play because we knew what we had to do. There was not much he could say to us, except that we had to go out and do the job."

Brown says, "I can be pretty hard on players and pretty demanding, but when I got to the (NCAA) tournament, there was no need getting on guys. I think that's when you have to be the most positive because it's sudden death."

Civically active with the Special Olympics and American Cancer Society during his time in Lawrence, Brown remembers more than just NCAA Tournament glory.

"Every time I walked in Allen Field House, I'd look up at the stands," he says. "I'd see the enthusiasm of the students and then the older people that had been coming during Phog's (Allen) tenure and Ted's (Owens) tenure and mine and appreciated the game and appreciated the people we played against. It's pretty nice to be a part of that.

"I've been involved with three college programs: UCLA, Carolina and Kansas. They stand for all the right things, those schools and those programs. Just being a part of it was my biggest accomplishment.

"Obviously, I'm thrilled that we had some success during that time (at KU). My association with the school ... I had so much respect for Phog Allen and the tradition of the program, it was great from the beginning."

Since leaving KU, Brown has stuck strictly to the NBA. In the spring of 1997, Brown left his job as coach of the Indiana Pacers for Philadelphia. But even in his late 50s, he promises he'll return to college coaching someday.

"Oh yeah, I don't think there's a doubt," he says. "Either that or high school."

There's a new twist – high school coaching. But all should know by now that Larry Brown never rules anything out.

"I've been involved with three college programs: UCLA, Carolina and Kansas. They stand for all the right things, those schools and those programs. Just being a part of it was my biggest accomplishment."

– Larry Brown

The Excellence Continues

Roy Williams greets his mentor, North Carolina's Dean Smith, at the 1991 Final Four. In just his third season as a head coach, Williams guided the Jayhawks to the NCAA title game, a trek that included a 79-73 victory against the Tar Heels in the tournament semifinals.

NO WALK IN THE PARK

Softball coach's attitude paid off in 1992 dream season

KALUM HAACK
Head softball coach,
1988-95

Ask Camille Spitaleri if Kalum Haack was a demanding softball coach at the University of Kansas.

A three-time All-American at third base for the Jayhawks, Spitaleri remembers the beginning of her freshman season, when Haack told her and a freshman teammate to show up at 7 a.m. for "tarp duty" at the KU softball field.

So she did. And Haack suspended her for two games.

"When I got there, they were finished," Spitaleri says, referring to the field duty required of KU softball players. Then she remembers what Haack said.

"He yelled, 'When I say 7, I mean 6:45!' " she says. "After that, I remember having nightmares about being late."

When Haack arrived at Kansas in 1988, the Jayhawks had gone to three NCAA regional softball tournaments in the past six years, winning an average of 38 games in those seasons. In the other three years, they averaged only 24 victories.

In Haack's eight years before leaving for Alabama after the 1995 season, KU finished second or third in the Big Eight Conference six times, went to four NCAA regionals and went to its first NCAA College World Series.

He didn't establish such consistency by coddling his players.

"I have to attribute most of my college success to Coach Haack," Spitaleri says. "I think I would have been a good player had I gone somewhere else, but I don't know that I would have been an All-American.

"He was a really good motivator. He was a tough coach, too. It wasn't just positive motivation all the time. He was really able to find something in me extra."

It might not surprise those who know Haack but don't know his background that he was an all-conference football linebacker at Sam Houston State in Huntsville, Texas, where he graduated in 1980. After graduation, he served as the school's assistant softball coach for four seasons.

He also spent two years as an assistant at Nebraska. He helped guide the Cornhuskers to the World Series both seasons before taking a job as football coach at Taylor High School in Katy, Texas. From there, he took a job as Sam Houston State's head softball coach before going to Kansas.

"When I went to Kansas, I saw the budget compared to what I had at Sam Houston – I was in heaven," he says.

But Haack says he never dreamed the Jayhawks would accomplish what they did in 1992. That year, they made their entrance among the elite programs of college softball by making the World Series, where they arrived with a 45-8 record.

"I didn't ever think we could go through a season losing only eight games, especially with the kind of competition we played," he says. "A lot of things paid off for Kansas that year."

KU lost both games it played in the World Series. Although the Jayhawks returned to the NCAA regionals the next two seasons, they have not returned to the World Series since.

"I'm kind of disappointed we didn't go more often," Haack says. "But that year – it didn't make a difference what signal I flashed at third (base), it was going to work. Everything went our way. I don't even think I hollered at an umpire that year."

Knowing Haack, that's doubtful. Whatever his recipe, he did enough to earn honors as 1992's conference coach of the year, as well as 1992 NCAA Midwest Region coach of the year.

"His coaching philosophy really doesn't work for everybody," Spitaleri says. "But on the team that made it to the World Series, I think we did (make it) because 15-18 people benefited from his style of coaching."

Haack took that style to Alabama in February 1996 after compiling a 283-158 record at Kansas in eight seasons. It was an offer, he says, he couldn't refuse: The starting salary was about 30 percent more than he made at KU. Alabama was just starting its program, too, giving Haack a chance to develop it precisely his way.

It's not a decision he made easily, though. And somewhat abruptly, he resigned from Alabama after the 1998 season.

SWING AND MISS - PLEASE

KALUM HAACK & CAMILLE SPITALERI

The utmost confidence Kalum Haack had in his All-American at third base, Camille Spitaleri, showed in the 1992 NCAA Midwest Regional Final against Oklahoma State.

With a Kansas runner, Kelly Bongatti, on second base, the Cowgirls planned to intentionally walk Spitaleri. With the count three balls and no strikes, Spitaleri thought

Haack had to be kidding when he flashed the next round of signals from the third base coaching box.

"I told her to swing at the next two pitches and miss intentionally," Haack says.

Which Spitaleri did. Utterly confused, Oklahoma State decided to scrap its plans to walk Spitaleri with a full count.

"They did exactly what I wanted them to

do – they pitched to her," Haack says. "She wound up getting a base hit."

Bongatti scored the game-winning run in KU's 4-0 victory, which put the Jayhawks in the 1992 NCAA College World Series.

"I thought he was absolutely crazy," Spitaleri says. "That's something I'll never forget."

LEAVING HER MARK
Skill, intensity set new standard for KU softball players

When Camille Spitaleri decided to attend the University of Kansas on a softball scholarship, she promised herself she would transfer to a more traditional college softball power, Fresno State, if she achieved stardom.

It's one promise she failed to keep, mostly because she didn't think it would happen so soon.

When the eventual three-time All-American at third base first earned that honor at the end of her sophomore season in 1990, transferring was the furthest thing from her mind. By then, she had a different plan: to help take the Jayhawks to their first NCAA World Series.

That didn't happen for two more years. By the time she left in 1992, though, Spitaleri had established a new standard by which KU softball players are judged and played in the World Series – all for a school she had never considered attending while growing up in the San Francisco Bay Area.

"I don't think I thought about Kansas – ever," says Spitaleri, who has given up softball in favor of playing women's professional baseball. "But I had a really good recruiting trip, and I liked Coach (Kalum) Haack's style."

Reviewing Spitaleri's list of personal achievements at Kansas is no small task. As of 1998, she still ranked among the top six in every career offensive category at KU. She had more runs batted in, 114, than any player in school history and maintained a four-year batting average of .337.

But statistics alone cannot measure how she affected Kansas softball, says Haack. As much as anything, he thinks her sheer will to win drove the 1992 squad to a top-15 ranking and a 45-10 record.

"Camille is by far the most intense player I have ever coached," he says. "She's the only player I could ever say played the game with a true passion. She would rather play softball than eat.

"She had desire as well as confidence. She wanted, every game, to be better than who she was playing against."

Equally adept with her glove or her bat, Spitaleri formed the heart of the 1992 Jayhawks along with shortstop Christy Arterburn and pitcher Stephani Williams. Kansas defeated perennial conference favorite Oklahoma State in the NCAA Midwest Regional final, advancing to its first World Series since KU's 1979 team advanced to the World Series of the Association of Intercollegiate Athletics for Women.

Ironically, the Jayhawks faced Fresno State in their first game, which they lost 4-1. Arizona then eliminated the Jayhawks 1-0 in a 17-inning game.

Nonetheless, Spitaleri has no regrets about staying at Kansas, where the Jayhawks won 127 and lost just 41 in her three All-America seasons.

"I always wanted to be remembered as a good softball player," she says. "There are plenty of people who play Division I college athletics and just kind of go through the motions. I wanted to leave a mark."

Despite her personal accolades, she regards playing in the World Series as her crowning achievement at Kansas. It fulfilled a goal she and her teammates set two

"Camille is by far the most intense player I have ever coached. She's the only player I could ever say played the game with a true passion."

– Kalum Haack

CAMILLE SPITALERI

years before it happened.

"It was kind of a sense of relief," she says, referring to the team's reaction after reaching that goal. "I can't imagine what it would have been like not going that last year."

Spitaleri returned to Kansas in 1995 as an assistant coach while finishing a degree in communication. She failed to make the 1996 Olympic team, but that disappointment has faded. Since then, she has concentrated on baseball, playing shortstop for the Silver Bullets, a semipro women's team.

"I don't think I'll ever play softball again," she says. "I'll give the younger people a chance."

When she's not traveling, Spitaleri returns to California. There, she's around a lot of college campuses and a lot of college softball. None compare, she says, with her experience at Kansas.

"I really enjoyed KU," she says. "I see all the schools out here. But they don't compare to the atmosphere at KU."

"I really enjoyed KU. I see all the schools out here. But they don't compare to the atmosphere at KU."

– Camille Spitaleri

RESPECTABILITY RESTORED

But football program's savior failed to establish consistency

When former University of Kansas athletics director Bob Marcum took the same job with South Carolina in January 1982, Joe McGuff, sports editor of the *Kansas City Star*, assessed some of the reasons why Marcum chose to leave.

He included the inability of KU football to regularly compete with Big Eight Conference foes.

"Kansas is not in a position to challenge Oklahoma or Nebraska," McGuff wrote, "and it is at a serious disadvantage in competing with Missouri."

When head football coach Glen Mason left Kansas to take the same job at Minnesota in December 1996, the Jayhawks had won as many bowl games (two) during his nine-year tenure as Oklahoma and Missouri combined.

KU had a 5-4 record against Missouri during the Mason years and beat the Sooners three times in nine tries, including back-to-back victories in Norman in 1995 and 1996. Before Mason, Kansas had beaten Oklahoma three times in the previous 26 seasons.

Granted, severe NCAA penalties and coaching problems toppled Oklahoma from the national prominence it enjoyed in the 1970s and 1980s. In addition, the Tigers had 13 straight losing seasons from 1984 through 1996.

As for Nebraska, no team in the conference outside of Colorado offered it much of a challenge in Mason's tenure, although the Jayhawks came within a two-point conversion of upsetting the Cornhuskers in Lawrence in 1993.

But Kansas, one of nation's worst football programs when Mason arrived in 1988, found a segue that allowed it to compete for bowls and upper-division conference finishes before he left.

"I know there was criticism of Glen and all, but if you step away ... he had just about as much success as any coach that we've had," says Bob Frederick, Kansas athletics director.

Mason, two-time conference coach of the year and two-time finalist for national coach of the year, won't argue.

"You wouldn't have found anybody in 1988 who thought I would be there nine years," Mason says.

Even Mason, though, will admit it could have been better. For all his success against Oklahoma, a 1994 defeat to the Sooners in Lawrence offers a microcosm of why KU football fans grew testy with him after tasting success.

The Jayhawks were 4-2 and competing for a bowl berth entering that game. They led 17-7 in the fourth quarter. They lost 20-17.

Earlier in 1994, Kansas blew a 21-17 fourth-quarter lead at TCU, losing 31-21.

KU finished 6-5 that year and missed a bowl. In 1995, though, the Jayhawks concluded a remarkable 10-2 season with a 51-30 thrashing of UCLA in the Aloha Bowl. Kansas finished No. 9 in the final Associated Press poll, its highest ranking since going to the Orange Bowl and finishing No. 7 in 1968.

But everything unraveled in 1996. After a 3-1 start, Kansas won only one more game. Losses included a humiliating 38-12 loss against Kansas State in Lawrence. It was the first time since the mid-1920s that Kansas, which owned a 61-29-5 lead in the series as the 1998 season began, had lost four straight to K-State.

Before the Wildcats made it five, Mason left for Minnesota.

"The thing that didn't happen," Frederick says, "was that we didn't have that consistency, and he just upset some people with some of the things he said."

***

Frederick's dissertation for a doctorate degree in education studied how institutional private support related to football success at 81 public universities. It included a case study of Kansas football from 1957 to 1981.

So probably no one is more qualified to decide who should run Kansas' football program. In Mason, Frederick found a personality he thought could handle the arduous climb from laughingstock to respectability.

"The guy was energetic," Frederick says. "He was enthusiastic. I thought he was the kind of guy who had enthusiasm and energy to fight through it, because we didn't have many players, and it was going to be a long haul. I took some heat on that because he was from Kent State, but I didn't care."

At the time, Mason says KU football might as well have been dead.

"Apathy had set in that program," he says. "The alumni didn't care, the students didn't care, the faculty didn't care."

While tackling the rebuilding task, Mason promised he wasn't out to make friends.

"You hear a lot of guys say about coaches, 'He's a nice guy,' " he told the *Star* just before his first season. "They can label me what they want, but I'm not a nice guy. You say that about people when you have nothing else to say."

When he arrived at KU, Mason found few players. Fewer still were serious about football. Grueling conditioning and spring practices in early 1988, when he was accused of physically abusing at least one player, weeded out those who weren't totally committed to building the program.

"His objective was to clean house of anybody who had a bad attitude or a poor work ethic – and he did," says Kelly Donohoe, now a high school football coach who was competing for a job as starting quarterback in spring 1988. "The things we did conditioning ... nobody even believes me."

For instance, players had to run "Mount Mason" – the 14th Street incline on the east edge of campus – again and again.

If nothing else, Mason brought a different style to Kansas football. That first year, some thought he was the reincarnation of Woody Hayes, Mason's famous and fiery college coach at Ohio State.

During one spring practice scrimmage, Donohoe remembers calling an ill-advised time out during the middle of a drive. Mason went berserk.

"He just ran onto the field and socked me in the gut," he says. "Actually, it was more of a stiffarm underneath the shoulder pads. But it didn't bother me. I liked his intensity. A lot of guys fed off that."

He says Mason lightened up after that first year, when KU went 1-10. The next season,

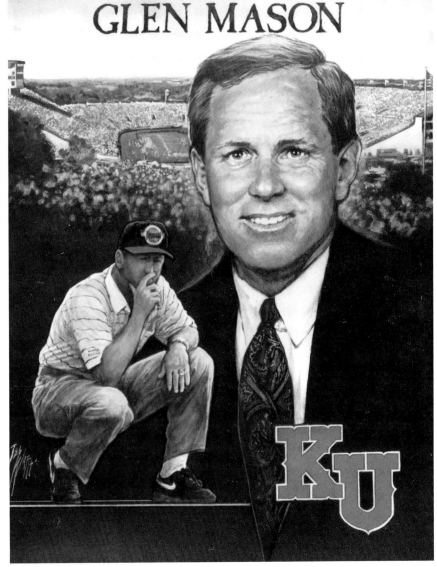

GLEN MASON
Head football coach,
1988-96

GLEN MASON

Donohoe's senior year, the Jayhawks improved to 4-7.

"It was quite an experience," he says of playing for Mason. "I'm glad I did it. I'd never do it again, though."

Chip Hilleary, who took over as quarterback when Donohoe graduated and turned into a first-team all-conference selection, says Mason hated constant campus jokes about the football program in the late 1980s.

"He always took it personally, and he made us take it personally, too," Hilleary says.

Mason's greatest attribute, Hilleary contends, may have been his ability to teach mental toughness.

"One thing that he taught us was to represent yourself and represent your team well," he says. "A lot of things I respected about Coach Mason were things he represented off the field, and he taught us those before we started winning."

***

It wasn't until the last game of 1991, when Tony Sands rushed for an NCAA-record 396 yards in a 53-29 victory against Missouri, that Mason says he saw Kansas turning the corner.

"I lived and died a lot of growing pains with that team," he says. "When we went 6-5 (in 1991), I thought that was huge."

The next season, KU moved into the Associated Press Top 25 for the first time in 16 years. On the way to a victory against Brigham Young in the Aloha Bowl, Kansas pounded K-State 31-7 and beat Oklahoma 27-10. But KU also lost a disappointing Thursday night home game 27-23 against California. It was Kansas football's first game on national television in six years.

"I knew that in '92, we had the makings of a good football team," says Mason, adding he thinks he made a poor decision to agree to the Cal game. Kansas had beaten Tulsa just five days earlier.

"But we had to do anything we could to get on TV," he says. "Before then, nobody wanted KU on TV. A potentially great season ended up being a very good season by KU standards."

Against BYU, the Jayhawks won their first bowl game since 1961. The successful season earned KU a spot in the 1993 Kickoff Classic against powerful Florida State. The Seminoles destroyed Kansas 42-0, and the Jayhawks finished 5-7 in an injury-plagued season. But Mason still defends his decision to play the game.

"If that initial game hurt us, how could we have rallied back and played so well later in the season?" he says, citing the near-upset of Nebraska. In addition, KU ended the season by shutting out Missouri 28-0.

Mason's next three years included some of KU's greatest victories, along with several stinging defeats.

"The 1994 season and 1996 had a lot of parallels," he says. "But in 1994, we lost games in the fourth quarter because of coaching. In 1996, I really think the loss out at Utah was very, very costly. But we were the only top 10 team in the world who played more road games than home games. That was very poor planning.

"In 1995, we won some close games early that built momentum. We very well could have lost to Cincinnati at home. We should have lost the Houston game by all rights."

But after a 20-13 victory against the Cougars, Kansas stunned No. 4 Colorado 40-24 in Boulder, probably the biggest victory Mason enjoyed at Kansas. But a year later, a 20-7 loss to the Golden Buffaloes in Lawrence was just another disappointment as his final year progressed.

Mason almost left a year earlier than he did. He accepted the job as Georgia's head coach just a week before KU's 1995 Aloha

---

"KU was a joke. KU's not a joke anymore."

– Glen Mason

Glen Mason hoisted the Aloha Bowl trophy twice during his nine seasons at Kansas.

Bowl appearance. But he reneged, and Kansas Chancellor Robert Hemenway welcomed him back. Mason formally told his team the news hours before its Christmas Day game, but some players already had learned of the about-face from Pat Ruel, Mason's offensive coordinator.

Many still think the Georgia escapade undermined Mason's team leadership in 1996, contributing to the losing record. But his indecision wasn't entirely uncharacteristic. He often regaled a story of how three days after he started recruiting for Kansas in 1988, he almost called Kent State and asked to return to the school's Ohio campus.

Mason, whose $101,000 salary was the lowest base pay for any head football coach in the conference when he accepted the Georgia job, had flirted with other positions before. During his time at Kansas, he was linked to openings at Miami, UCLA, Louisville, Rutgers, South Carolina and Oklahoma, not to mention about every opening in the Big Ten Conference.

He even encountered rumors in 1992 that he would return to Ohio State. At the time, rumors had Ohio State firing John Cooper, but it didn't happen.

However, Mason says Minnesota, who had courted him once before, proved too alluring. Meanwhile, some Kansas fans wanted him fired anyway.

"Minnesota was very persistent," he says, "and they convinced me the upsides were too good to turn down."

Reflecting on his time at Kansas, Mason has few apologies.

"That program is one heckuva lot better than when I arrived," he said in April 1997 after one of his first spring practices at Minnesota. "That program has improved in every area."

He says he built KU from the ground up without breaking rules at a time when several conference schools were punished by the NCAA.

"I came to the Big Eight when a lot of cheating was going on," he says. "There are some guys who think I'm a good coach, and some guys who think I'm not too good. But there's no one who can call me dishonest.

"I'm proud. We took a program in shambles and built it with a lot of integrity and hard work. KU was a joke. KU's not a joke anymore."

Nevertheless, some Kansas fans and alumni routinely criticized Mason regarding everything from Kansas' poor pass defense in 1994 to his perceived arrogance to the fact he often didn't wear a headset on the sidelines. Conversely, some factions steadfastly praised his efforts.

"My feelings toward KU and the people of Kansas are very positive," he says. "If I didn't think I received enough support, I wouldn't have stayed as long as I did."

However, when the *St. Paul Pioneer-Press* asked him several weeks after Minnesota hired him if Kansas made a significant commitment to football during his tenure, he simply replied, "No." (KU announced a $30.2 million plan to renovate Memorial Stadium shortly after he left.)

MASON'S RECORD AT KANSAS

YEAR	RECORD	NOTES
1988	1-10 (1-6 in Big Eight, 7th)	Mason gets first victory, 30-12 against K-State, Nov. 5 in Lawrence
1989	4-7 (2-5, 6th)	KU beats Missouri 46-44, first victory in series since 1985
1990	3-7-1 (2-4-1, 4th-tie)	KU beats Oklahoma State 31-30 in Stillwater, first victory against Cowboys in 18 years
1991	6-5 (3-4, 5th)	In Manhattan, KU loses 12-3 lead in last four minutes as Wildcats win 16-12, Mason's first defeat versus K-State
1992	8-4 (4-3, 3rd, ranked No. 22)	Jayhawks beat BYU in Aloha Bowl – KU's first bowl victory since 1961
1993	5-7 (3-4, 5th)	Mason eschews tie, but two-point conversion fails in 21-20 loss against Nebraska
1994	6-5 (3-4, 5th)	Blown leads against TCU, Oklahoma doom Kansas bowl hopes
1995	10-2 (5-2, 2nd-tie, ranked No. 9)	Victory at No. 4 Colorado first in series since 1984; KU pounds UCLA 51-30 in Aloha Bowl
1996	4-7 (2-6, 5th in Big 12 North)	KU loses six of last seven, loses to K-State and MU by a combined 43 points
Nine seasons	47-54-1 (25-38-1)	Mason accepts job at Minnesota on Dec. 14, 1996

Many Kansas fans had grown weary of such apparent contradictions. Frederick, though, looks back and considers the Mason years an overall success.

Indeed, no one can argue Mason, whose first Minnesota squad finished 3-9, left KU in better shape than he found it.

"When we hired him, we were really down," Frederick says. "He restored us to respectability, competitiveness. He worked hard at it. He got to two bowl games, which we hadn't been to in a long time, and we had a 10-2 season and were ranked in the top 10 in the country.

"I guess the only frustration was that we were unable to achieve some consistency."

DAVE BINGHAM

DRIVEN TO SUCCEED
Determined coach revived
moribund baseball program

"There's nothing like taking a team and developing it. There's no greater satisfaction than that in athletics."

– Dave Bingham

"Make people pay money to attend Kansas home baseball games? Is this new guy nuts?"

So went the general reaction to one of Dave Bingham's first ideas as head coach of the University of Kansas baseball program.

Let's see, when Bingham took over in May 1987, the Jayhawks were coming off a 15-39-1 season, including a pathetic 3-21 record in Big Eight Conference games. In the six seasons since long-time coach Floyd Temple had retired and left the job to former Kansas City Royals pitcher Marty Pattin, the Jayhawks had finished last or next-to-last in the conference three times, compiled an unsightly overall conference record of 37-88 and made college baseball in Lawrence about as popular as a trip to the dentist.

Charge an admission fee? Why, some fans thought *they* should get paid to watch the Jayhawks play at E.C. Quigley Field, named after the man who presided over Kansas athletics when KU won its last conference championship in 1949. In any case, the mere idea of paying to watch Kansas baseball was foreign to baseball fans throughout northeast Kansas.

But so were NCAA regional and College World Series appearances, and in his eight seasons at Kansas, Bingham introduced those and other new wrinkles to the program.

"I really wanted to charge ... I felt it was important that as we were trying to grow, we needed to develop a product people wanted to come to see," says Bingham, who now operates Sport 2 Sport, a youth sports facility in southwest Lawrence, with former Kansas basketball player Roger Morningstar. "I always felt that if you couldn't charge for it, it really wasn't something that was worthwhile to people."

Charging admission was just another indication that Bingham's arrival coincided with a renewed focus on Kansas baseball. In fact, his arrival hinged on a higher level of commitment by the University.

Renovations costing $300,000 turned Quigley Field, little more than a diamond adjacent to a few bleachers, into Hoglund-Maupin Stadium, which featured lights, a new scoreboard, closed deck seating and concession stands.

"I had a lot of different ideas," Bingham says. "The mentality of baseball at Kansas had been entrenched for a long time. It was a minor sport, something you did when you weren't playing football or basketball. Marty tried to do it, and it began to shift a little. But I pretty much wanted us to be considered a major sport, and I wanted baseball to be in a position with the kind of credibility that other sports had."

Kansas baseball didn't achieve credibility overnight. In Bingham's first season, 1988, the Jayhawks finished last in the conference again. But while making do with junior-college transfers, Bingham and his top assistant, pitching coach Wilson Kilmer, began recruiting the heart of the class that would take Kansas baseball to new heights.

Two years later, the incoming freshman class of 1990 featured pitcher Jimmy Walker, catcher Jeff Niemeier and second baseman Jeff Berblinger. Another new-comer, freshman first baseman John Wuycheck, transferred from Texas A&M. A year later, outfielder Darryl Monroe and pitcher Chris Corn arrived. All eventually played key roles in KU's most glorious spring of baseball.

Niemeier remembers choosing Kansas instead of Missouri because Bingham, who twice served as an assistant coach on the U.S. Olympic Team, set a lofty goal: winning the College World Series.

"Neither (KU nor Missouri) had reason to talk about going to the World Series at that time," Niemeier says. "But he talked about winning a national championship, and he never reduced that goal."

But Bingham almost didn't stay long enough to guide KU to its first World Series trip in 1993. After his third year in 1990, when Kansas again finished next-to-last in the conference, the patience of a man who had turned Emporia State into a small-college baseball power was running thin. However, Bingham's desire to develop his own recruits outweighed any reasons for leaving.

"There's nothing like taking a team and developing it," he says. "There's no greater satisfaction than that in athletics."

Heading into 1993, Kansas had yet to have a breakthrough season, though. But the progress that year of heralded freshman pitcher Jamie Splittorff put the final piece in place, Bingham says.

"The measuring stick for us was always Oklahoma State," he says of the conference's top program at the time. "When we were able to beat them four out of five ... you kind of knew then that this was more than just the average team. It wasn't the best Oklahoma State team. I knew that, but our guys didn't know that."

Two months later, KU lost the conference tournament to the Cowboys. But the Jayhawks rebounded, defeating three high-profile programs – Tennessee, Clemson and Fresno State – in the NCAA Mideast Regional in Knoxville, Tenn. KU also beat Rutgers and avenged its opening-game loss in the regional by beating Fresno State 3-2 in a thrilling, 10-inning game that decided the regional's World Series representative.

Kansas lost both games it played in Omaha, Neb., annual site of the World Series, but finished the season 45-18, the first time a KU team won more than 34 games.

The season also capped a nine-month stretch in which Kansas became the only university to win a football bowl game, go to the NCAA Final Four in men's basketball and make a trip to the World Series in the same academic year.

"The maturity of the players made a big difference in '93," Bingham says. "When we came in, I'd get upset with practices, because they weren't the way I wanted them. By the time we got to 1993, I could walk off the field and they took care of things within the team."

DAVE BINGHAM
Head baseball coach,
1988-95

The Jayhawks returned to an NCAA regional in 1994, when *USA Today* ran a feature detailing the program's rise. But 1995 proved a disappointment as Kansas fell to 24-33, and Bingham abruptly resigned three months after the season.

He says several factors prompted his decision, including the fact he never had more than a one-year contract. But he also wanted to realign his priorities.

"It was a time in my life to go on and do other things," he says, adding he wanted to devote more time to his family. "Probably my intensity level, which at times was my greatest ally, was also my greatest enemy."

Niemeier agrees: "He never wanted to be the way he was when he had to overcoach those first three years," he says. "Being as driven as he is, maybe there were times he needed to get away from it. Some of those losing years, they really tore him up."

Nevertheless, Bingham still watches Kansas knowing he played perhaps the most instrumental part in revitalizing the program. But he also credits KU athletics director Bob Frederick and former chancellor Gene Budig, who left Kansas to become president of Major League Baseball's American League, as well as his former players.

"Maybe we turned the corner," he says, reflecting on his eight years at Kansas. "Because of the things we did, now there is an interest level and it continues to go on. I hope the donors will continue to grow and the quality of the program will continue to grow."

JEFF BERBLINGER

'ROCK-SOLID DEPENDABLE'

Second baseman established tone for KU in early 1990s

Strong up the middle.

Baseball coaches love that phrase. Even more, they love what it represents – good pitching and solid defense at four important positions: catcher, second base, shortstop and centerfield. If flawless fielders at those spots provide clutch hitting as a bonus, their coaches start dreaming about championships.

The 1993 Kansas Jayhawks gave head coach Dave Bingham reason to dream. Consistent pitching finally had arrived, and catcher Jeff Niemeier, shortstop Dan Rude and centerfielder Darryl Monroe all helped fuel KU's offensive engine.

But the Jayhawks' leadoff hitter, senior second baseman Jeff Berblinger, owned the keys to that motor. Fortunately for KU, he rarely misplaced them.

"He was truly a settling force in every way," Bingham say. "On the bus, in practice, on the field: He was rock-solid dependable."

Never more apparent was Berblinger's importance to Kansas than during postseason play. In 1993, for the first time in 10 years, the Jayhawks advanced to the Big Eight Conference Tournament. They made a run at perennial tournament champion Oklahoma State but fell short in the final round. From there, KU traveled to the NCAA Mideast Regional in Knoxville, Tenn., where the Jayhawks went 4-1 and advanced to the College World Series.

In 10 games in the tournament and the regional, Berblinger had 21 hits in 46 at-bats, a .457 average. He scored 11 runs, hit eight doubles, smashed two triples and a home run, had six runs batted in and stole six bases. Kansas won seven of those 10 games.

In KU's two games in the World Series, Berblinger went 0-for-8. The Jayhawks lost both, scoring just one run in each game.

Those two games didn't mirror his stellar college career, but at least Berblinger was playing.

The year before, he missed 25 of KU's 53 games with a broken thumb. An expected breakthrough season for the Jayhawks was delayed a year as they finished 25-28. With Berblinger, the Jayhawks went 16-12. Without him, they were 9-16.

"I had always tried to prepare teams to cover an injury," Bingham says, "but that cut the heart and soul out of us in '92."

In 1993, Berblinger stayed healthy throughout the season, and the Jayhawks went 45-18. He was named All-America after hitting .339 with 20 doubles, nine home runs, 52 RBI, 33 stolen bases and 66 runs scored.

Berblinger finished his four years at KU with a .316 average, and the St. Louis Cardinals selected him in the seventh round of the 1993 major league draft. But Bingham had initial reservations when recruiting him out of high school in Goddard, Kan.

"I loved his athleticism," he says. "He had outstanding speed, quickness and power. But he really started to develop late."

By the end of Berblinger's senior year at Goddard, though, Bingham was convinced he would make a fine college infielder. Grueling hours of practice, Bingham says, turned him into one of the nation's best.

Berblinger started 55 of KU's 58 games during his first season in 1990, but he only hit .244 with 19 RBI and 31 runs scored. Those numbers improved dramatically the next season, when he hit .354 with 36 RBI and 49 runs.

"He was never a kid who was a 'rah-rah' guy," Bingham says. "He just went on the field and did the job. And he'd work until he couldn't work anymore."

During the mid-1990s, Berblinger worked his way through the minor leagues. In 1997, with the Class AAA Louisville Cardinals, he hit .263 with 11 homers and 58 RBI. His first taste of major league action occurred that year when he played in seven games with St. Louis. In January 1998, he signed with the Seattle Mariners and spent the season with the Mariners' triple-A affiliate in Tacoma, Wash.

JEFF BERBLINGER
Baseball,
1990-93

TWO THOUSAND GAMES

Radio analyst's career
spans more than 50 years

Max Falkenstien has almost seen 'em all.

Actually, after 52 years broadcasting Jayhawks' games, Falkenstien has called more than 550 football and about 1,500 basketball games heading into the 1998-99 academic year. Those figures account for more than half of KU football games and more than 60 percent of KU men's basketball games in school history.

KU sports history and the Falkenstien name are almost synonomous. Max Falkenstien was born in 1924 in Lawrence. His father, Earl, was a longtime business manager for the KU athletics department. Max Falkenstien began his radio career in high school at Topeka station WREN, earning $90 a month. He was drafted while attending KU and entered the U.S. Army Air Corps.

After the Army discharged him in 1946, Falkenstien returned to Lawrence and resumed his broadcasting career at WREN. His first assignment was broadcasting the KU-Oklahoma A&M basketball game at the NCAA Tournament in Kansas City, Mo. The Jayhawks lost the game, but the broadcast – and Falkenstien's work – were a success. A career was launched.

Teams change, coaches change, rules change and sites change. But through it all in post-World War II athletics competition at KU, Falkenstien has remained the constant. From 1946 through the 1983-84 season he did the play-by-play on his own broadcast network. When the KU athletics department went to a single sports network, Bob Davis was hired as its play-by-play voice. For awhile it appeared that Falkenstien's broadcasting days were finished. But later he was given the chance to be Davis' color analyst, which he accepted. The two have been inseparable on the Jayhawk Network ever since.

In his 1996 memoir, "Max and the Jayhawks," Falkenstien offers readers an indispensable collection of warm and funny moments throughout his career: a tornado at Texas Tech, bugs at a UCLA football game, two Orange Bowls, two NCAA championships in basketball and a look at the coaches, players and characters that have been a part of Jayhawks' sports – and the 2,000-plus games he has broadcast – since 1946.

***

During Falkenstien's career, he has watched athletes get bigger, stronger, faster. Final scores in basketball games have increased from the 40s, 50s and 60s to the 80s, 90s and 100s. There are no more scoreless ties (or any ties) in football, as was the case in the first Jayhawks' football game he broadcast. He will tell you the attitudes of players and coaches haven't changed, that players want to play ("I think kids were just as competitive in 1940 as they are now") and coaches want to coach. What differences exist, he says, are in people, not eras.

"Doc (F.C. "Phog" Allen) was a great motivator," Falkenstien says while comparing KU basketball coaches. "But he also had the unbelievable ability that when the game was over to put it completely out of his mind. We could lose at Missouri and get on the team bus to ride home, and Doc would take off his shoes, loosen up his necktie, put his feet up on the rail, and five miles out of Columbia he'd be sound asleep. The game was history and gone.

"Larry (Brown) and Roy (Williams) are very, very different than that. Roy probably didn't sleep one minute after the loss to Arizona (in the 1997 NCAA Tournament). He carries the hurt inside him for a long, long time. Larry did, too.

"Ted (Owens) was competitive, but I don't think it gnawed on him forever and

ever, except that time (1978) when we led Kentucky at Lexington by six points with thirty seconds to play and lost the game in overtime."

Concerning players, Falkenstien marvels at how they've grown over the years.

"The players are so much bigger in football and basketball than in the 1940s and 1950s," he says. "We had tackles then that were playing at 230, 240 pounds. Now a guy like that will get absolutely killed out there. He's a hundred pounds short.

"And the height in basketball. Doc (Allen) wasn't so far wrong when he said maybe we should have twelve-foot baskets."

***

Listen to Falkenstien on the radio and you hear a broadcaster who knows history but doesn't dwell in the past. He's quick with a comparison but revels in the now. He appreciates KU's rich sports heritage and tradition but gives today's competitors their due.

Still, as any long-time sports fan will tell you, football and basketball have changed over the years, and not always for the better. Or as Max sees it ...

"Basketball is not near as pretty a game as it used to be. It's just pushing and shoving and rooting with your butt. They say they're palming the ball all the time in college, but they don't call it anymore. It's become so physical, and the referees have been put in an impossible situation: Is it a charge or a block? It's really tough."

Regarding football, Falkenstien says that liberal substitutions are the biggest change he's observed.

"When I started doing the games, guys played both ways. You had 25 or 30 guys who played in the game. I still, in many, many ways, I like that approach to the game. (Former KU stars) Charlie Hoag and John Hadl, were guys who could play on both sides of the football. It's become so specialized now that it takes some of the fun out of it for me, where you have a coach who coaches the offensive tackles, the wide receivers have their own coach, and so on.

"And now it's wide open, substitute any way you want to at any time. They talk so much about how football is bankrupting all the colleges and universities. Of course, that would be one way they could save a lot of money if they wanted: Bite the bullet and do it; they don't need 85 guys on scholarship if you have fellows playing both ways. Why wouldn't it be just as good?"

KU'S ODD COUPLE
Tennis champs displayed potent mix of poise, passion

A stereotypical difference between European and U.S. tennis players manifested itself in a 1994 women's doubles team at the University of Kansas.

Nora Koves, a junior from Budapest, Hungary, typified the reserved on-court demeanor of most Europeans. But her doubles partner, a swaggering junior from Ludington, Mich., named Rebecca Jensen, epitomized rock-and-roll American tennis.

When they were apart, their divergent on-court personalities and enviable talent produced strong results in singles play for the Jayhawks.

But together, Jensen's raging fire and Koves' steady ice yielded the first NCAA women's tennis championship of any kind in the Big Eight Conference.

"Rebecca was the motivator, and she was boisterous," says former Kansas women's tennis coach Chuck Merzbacher. "Nora would really focus on doing her job."

The combination proved overwhelming for opponents in 1994, when Jensen predicted she and Koves would win a national collegiate tennis event.

The prognostication wasn't all that bold. The pair reached the NCAA quarterfinals in 1993, losing to the eventual national champions, Susan Gilchrist and Vickie Paynter of Texas.

The next fall, Koves-Jensen reached the semifinals of the National Clay Court Championships. Months later, in February 1994, they placed second in the Rolex National Indoor Championships. In that tournament, they defeated the No. 1 doubles team in the country, California's Pam Nelson and Keirsten Alley.

By then, Jensen had convinced the sometimes-skeptical Koves they could beat anyone in the country.

"I'm really outgoing on the court," Jensen says. "Nora kept me realistic."

But Koves says, "She was the believer all the time."

At the University of Georgia in Athens, annual site of the NCAA Championships, Koves-Jensen plowed through the doubles field on their way to the final. There they met Mississippi's Marie-Laure Bougnol and Pascale Piquemal.

Merzbacher, now the women's tennis coach at Ohio State, recalls Bougnol-Piquemal playing mainly defensive tennis. That tactic mirrored Koves-Jensen.

"They never really hurt themselves," he says of Koves-Jensen. "They didn't take a lot of chances. They made people beat them. Most good doubles teams are not great shotmakers, but they play smart."

In the final, Koves-Jensen won the first set 6-4 but barely led 6-5 in the second set when the tables turned in their on-court relationship. This time, Koves sparked the fire.

"On the first set point, Rebecca jumped into the point when she shouldn't have and missed a volley," Koves told the *Kansas City Star* just before the pair played in the 1994 U.S Open, a reward for their NCAA title. "I yelled at her, 'Stay where you are.' I kind of surprised myself."

Minutes later, Koves-Jensen won the set and the match, capping their career together at KU. The championship qualified the pair for the U.S. Open, where they won their first match before losing in the second round.

"That was our goal, to win one round, and we did it," Koves says.

Jensen stayed in the professional circuit, joining her famous brothers, Luke and Murphy Jensen, who won the French Open doubles title in 1993. Her twin sister,

NORA KOVES · REBECCA JENSEN

Rachel, also played professionally.

Koves returned for her final college season in 1995, winning the conference's No. 1 singles title and leading KU to its fourth straight conference team championship. She turned professional after leaving Kansas.

Looking back, Merzbacher says KU's solid depth allowed Koves and Jensen to play together regularly for two straight years beginning in 1993. To their credit, they took advantage.

Koves says, "The more we played together on the court, we became better and better friends."

Jensen agrees, adding the pair's confidence in one another grew the longer they played.

"We never gave up on each other," Jensen says. "(That) was one of our biggest strengths."

As professionals, both Koves and Jensen travel across the world playing the game. But again, they agree playing tennis is different now.

"Being on the road, being away from your family ... like any job, it has its highs and lows," Jensen says. "But I enjoy it."

Finally, they also agree on what they yearn for at KU – and it's not classes.

"Basketball games," Koves says, speaking for both, "are the main thing (we) miss."

IN SPITE OF PAIN
Track star overcame muscle disorder, won NCAA title

When Kristi (Kloster) Burritt won the 800-meter run for the University of Kansas at the NCAA Women's Indoor Track and Field Championships in 1996, she couldn't feel her legs and feet down the home stretch.

That's the funny thing about compartment syndrome. In between bursts of pain, sometimes there's no feeling at all. Nothing. During exercise, the fibers that surround most people's muscles expand along with the muscles. But in people suffering compartment syndrome, the fibers don't give, remaining rigid until they eventually cut off circulation.

Burritt didn't know she suffered from the rare disorder until she was a sophomore at Bishop Miege High School in Mission, a suburb of Kansas City. But by the time she was in college, the pain and discomfort in her lower legs got so bad so often, they would fall asleep as she walked atop Mount Oread.

"It just felt like my muscles would pop out of my skin," she says. "It was painful."

Such as the race that put her portrait on a wall inside Allen Field House.

"My feet had been asleep since after the first 200 meters," she says of her NCAA championship laps. "I just felt like I had dead legs to drag around. I took the lead with about 250 meters left. About 70 meters from the finish line, I took a step and there was no strength left at all.

"The very next step, it felt like somebody knocked me behind the knees. I really couldn't feel my legs the last 65 meters or so. I was focusing on lifting my quadriceps and my hamstrings. I knew if I lifted those, the rest would have to come up."

That's how Burritt won a national championship, overcoming years of frustration and bewilderment caused by a condition doctors don't fully understand.

Operations didn't resolve it. Other forms of traditional medicine didn't relieve it. It caused her to sit out the 1993 indoor and outdoor track seasons as a redshirt, and she also missed the 1995 outdoor season. After winning the NCAA championship, she competed in only two meets in the 1996 outdoor season, her last at KU.

Still, she became the first woman in KU track history to win an NCAA title. She's the only KU woman other than Sheila Calmese to win a national title (Calmese won the 300-yard dash in 1978, when women competed in the Association of Intercollegiate Athletics for Women) and was the first Kansas track athlete since 1980 to win an indoor or outdoor NCAA title.

Ironically, Burritt had pictured herself anywhere but KU while growing up in an area thick with Kansas alumni.

"I hate to say this, but I hated KU," she says. "I only went to visit because my high school coach was big on KU. My parents didn't push it. But I knew they would love for me to go to KU. They're big KU fans."

Burritt didn't receive much recruiting attention until the day after she competed in the Kansas state track meet her junior year at Bishop Miege.

"Before I could even think about what I was going to do for college, I had all these options that I never even thought would happen," she says. "The University of Texas actually was the first to call."

Later, she visited Southern Methodist, Drake, Michigan and Kentucky. But her last visit – Kansas – was different.

"The team seemed happy, and I didn't feel any tension between the team members and the coaches," says Burritt, who credits one-time KU assistant coach Steve Guymon for much of her collegiate success. "He was in charge of recruiting. He was incredible. He left his lights on in a blizzard on my visit, and his car was dead. He was like, 'What can I say, I'm an idiot.' It was just really funny to have someone who was down to earth."

By the time she graduated from Miege, Burritt had won five individual state track titles in three different events (200, 400, 800) and participated on four state-champion 1,600-relay teams. She was the Kansas runner of the year in 1989 and never lost a high school 800 while posting the fourth-best prep time in the nation.

At Kansas, it didn't take long for the college track world to notice Burritt. As a freshman, she won the 800 at the Big Eight Conference outdoor meet in 2 minutes, 6.78 seconds.

That time was just short of the school-record 2:04.91 she set winning the NCAA title four years later. She won the NCAA race in a photo-finish so close that the track announcer initially declared a different winner.

"Nationals was probably one of the best races in my life, but it also was probably one of the worst because of the way it ended," she says, recalling how people in attendance questioned whether she actually had won. "That was a point where Coach Guymon had worked so hard for so long to get me there ... that was a time it just all came together, finally."

Besides the NCAA title, Burritt was named second-team academic All-America in 1996 and was one of 10 finalists for NCAA Woman of the Year. A human development and psychology major, she also was KU's Scholar Athlete of the Year.

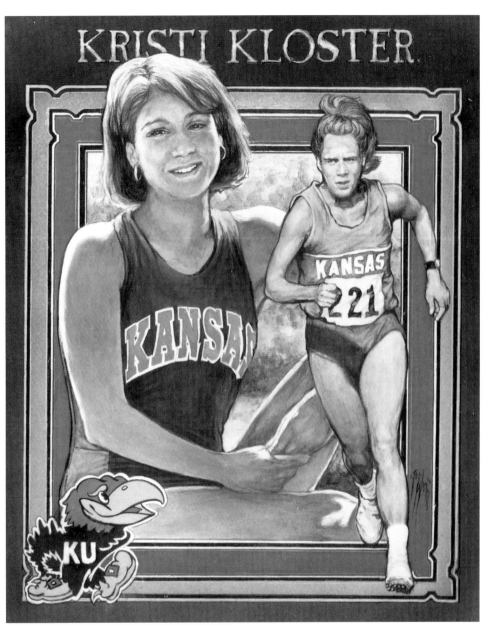

KRISTI KLOSTER
Track and field
and cross country,
1991-96

As she makes a run at the 2000 U.S. Olympic track team, though, Burritt remains perplexed by her biggest nemesis, the one that leaves her shins resembling a mountain range while she trains.

"When I run, I get all kinds of funky bumps," she says, referring to the result of one operation that was supposed to release the compartment pressure. "I think I have more trouble now than I did before the surgery."

However, Burritt thinks a technique called deep muscle integration, a type of physical therapy, may be the key to coping with the disorder. The technique has allowed her to run nine miles without stopping because of pain, twice as far as she could before starting therapy in early 1997.

"The doctors after awhile were clueless," she says. "We finally resorted to a more alternative therapy."

One she hopes will work in time for the Olympic trials in the summer of 2000.

VICTORY THROUGH REDEMPTION

Former gymnast claimed KU's first NCAA diving title

"How do I get on the wall?"

That's the question Michelle Rojohn once asked University of Kansas diving coach Don Fearon while gazing at portraits of Kansas Hall of Fame athletes that line the halls of Allen Field House just outside the KU swimming and diving office.

When Fearon told her she had to win a national championship, the former gymnast who once dreamed of attending UCLA decided she better get serious about diving.

MICHELLE ROJOHN
Diving,
1992-96

"I took up diving on whim," Rojohn says, describing how a high school knee injury ended her hope of landing a college gymnastics scholarship and led her to the diving board. "It came quickly to me because of gymnastics."

So quickly that she finished second in the Kansas High School Championships during her senior season at Olathe South. Despite her injury and a huge knee brace that accompanied it, she still won the all-around competition at the state high school gymnastics competition, as well.

But once she arrived at Kansas in 1992, Rojohn's gymnastics career was over. And Fearon wondered whether her diving career would ever begin.

"I knew she definitely was talented, and she's a quick learner," he says now.

But then, Fearon thought Rojohn might struggle to straighten the learning curve between her and other college divers who had begun competing in grade school. He admits he didn't envision Rojohn winning an NCAA championship.

However, after she placed 13th at the NCAA meet as a junior, both Rojohn and Fearon began to consider the possibility.

What she needed, though, was an attitude adjustment. Rojohn freely acknowledges she often wilted under pressure before her senior year.

"I would get to a big competition and fall apart," she says. "I don't know that I ever really believed I could win (an NCAA title)."

But that changed by the time the 1996 NCAA Swimming and Diving Championships in Ann Arbor, Mich., arrived.

"I went into it knowing I'm going to the final," Rojohn says of the opening one-meter competition.

It didn't happen. She says she "blew a dive" in the preliminary round and missed the cut for the finals.

"I was so ashamed I didn't even want to get in a (swim)suit again," she says. "But something that night told me I had to redeem myself."

That night, she returned to the pool to practice for the three-meter springboard competition the next day. Rojohn practically was the only diver practicing as opposing coaches and the crowd watched.

"She had a great workout," Fearon says, "but she didn't have a very good practice in the morning the following day. I got about as mad as I ever got at her."

Fearon's outburst must have worked. Rojohn put together what she calls "almost my perfect meet." She won the preliminaries and was the last diver among a rotation of eight finalists. In the finals, she trailed by a mere three points when she attempted her last dive as a collegian.

"I didn't know I had won until I climbed out of the pool," she says.

That dive capped a college career in which Rojohn broke all but one Kansas diving record. She barely missed making the 1996 Olympic Trials but is training for the 2000 Olympics.

"The consensus from most every coach around is she should stay in it," Fearon says. "I think she has a great shot."

JOSH KLINER

OUT OF NOWHERE
A delightfully dominating season

JOSH KLINER
Baseball,
1995-96

Joe DeMarco remembers the moment.

An unheralded University of Kansas baseball team, in the infancy of its 1996 season, had just won two of three games in a weekend road series against perennial national power Texas. Contemplating the long season that lay ahead, DeMarco, a junior short-stop, had only one distinct vision: His double-play partner, Josh Kliner, was about to shock the amateur baseball world with one of the best offensive seasons by a second baseman in college baseball history.

"In the Texas series, Josh hit about three doubles off the wall," DeMarco says. "That was the series when I said, 'This guy is for real.' "

It's not as if he really doubted Kliner before that – even when Kliner doubted himself. After all, the transfer from Cypress (Calif.) Community College finished the previous season "on fire," as DeMarco puts it.

Kliner ended 1995 with a .298 batting average. A fine mark, the best of his brief college career. Months later, DeMarco watched him punish pitches during fall practice.

Heading into 1996, though, neither DeMarco nor anyone else could have foreseen Kliner's meteoric rise.

The Texas series sold DeMarco. For Kliner, it took a few more weeks.

"A month into the season," Kliner says, "it got to the point where every time up, I thought I was going to get a hit. In my mind, there was no way the pitcher could get me out. Once you're thinking like that, everything just falls into place."

Kliner had grasped for confidence shortly after

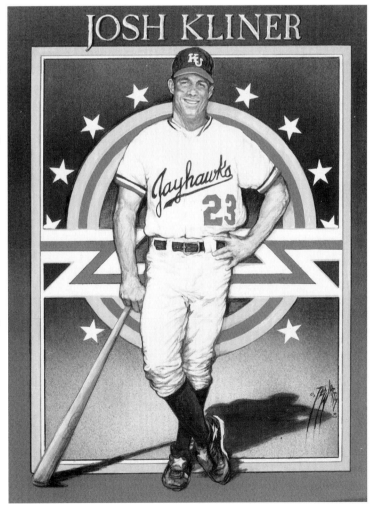

arriving at KU. But after following the advice of then-coach Dave Bingham to relax, and after tearing up a 1995 summer league in Alaska, he simply abused Big Eight Conference pitchers in 1996.

His averaged soared to .438, eighth-highest in NCAA Division I. He set KU single-season records for runs batted in with 85, doubles with 28 – pounding one every two games and ranking fourth in the nation – and total bases with 161. His slugging percentage of .774 ranked 10th in the nation.

Kliner credits fellow KU hitters, who erased the previous school record with a .324 team average, for helping mold his spectacular season. He hit behind DeMarco and future NFL wide receiver Isaac Byrd, an all-conference centerfielder.

"Ike (Byrd) was on base all the time," Kliner says. "I was always hitting with runners in scoring position."

But the switch-hitting Kliner delivered all season for a pitching-thin team that finished 26-30 and needed every run it could muster. He had seven RBI in one game against Iowa State and tied the conference tournament record with five doubles.

Besides runs, Kliner's bat produced numerous All-America honors. But major league teams, citing his average speed and limited fielding range, bypassed him in the annual June draft. He signed with the Arizona Diamondbacks and played one season in that team's minor league system before getting released – even after hitting .308. He most recently played for a Reno, Nev., independent minor league team.

Whether he ever makes the major leagues, Kliner always can reflect on perhaps the most glorious, and certainly the most unsuspecting, season a KU hitter has ever experienced.

"I loved my stay there," the former broadcast major says. "I wouldn't change anything – except for maybe a few more wins."

GARY SCHWARTZ

JAYHAWK LOVE AFFAIR

Coach cites mascot as one reason he chose KU

When he first visited the University of Kansas on a recruiting trip in the early 1960s, two things struck current KU track and field coach Gary Schwartz:

"When I came on campus, probably the two things that really got me interested in this place was how pretty campus was. That really blew me away," Schwartz says. "I came here thinking like most people, that you're going to get here and everything's going to be flat, and there's going to be no trees. Just the whole visual perception of the campus was really appealing."

And the second thing?

"I fell in love with the Jayhawk, too," he says. "For some reason that had a big effect on me."

Big enough for the Wessington Springs, S.D., native to sign with track coach Bill Easton's Jayhawks. Initially, Easton wrote Schwartz about considering KU as Schwartz was dominating South Dakota high school weight competition, winning the state discus title three times and the shot put crown twice. He also was named the 1962 South Dakota high school athlete of the year.

The long line of successful throwers that Easton had produced attracted Schwartz.

"What impressed me and got me real interested in coming here was the rich tradition of the University of Kansas," Schwartz says.

After he enrolled at the University, Schwartz immediately found himself under Easton's spell.

"Coach Easton worked directly with everybody," he says. "Like most athletes, there are certain coaches in their lives that have had a big effect on you and probably shape some of the things you do now.

"Coach Easton was definitely a 'my way or the highway' type of guy. He was in charge, in control. He had strict rules on conduct and behavior (and) a dress code. The dress code thing, and the importance of having rules, were probably two things that I came away with."

During Schwartz's junior year in 1965, Easton was fired after a disagreement with KU athletics director Wade Stinson. Easton saw the outdoor season to its conclusion, and the Jayhawks sent their beloved coach out as a winner with the 12th conference outdoor championship of his 18-year tenure. Schwartz contributed to the victory by winning the conference discus title.

"Things that I have carried over from coach Easton are the importance of tradition and the importance of doing things for the team," he says. "It was a big deal to score points for the team, and it was a big deal to win the conference individual titles. And the whole thing was, we were trying to win the team title. It was a highlight of my career."

***

Schwartz didn't come to Kansas to become a coach, but electrical engineering will do that to a person. Easton suggested Schwartz try physical education for a semester while he tried to figure out what he wanted to do.

"I fell in love with what physical education was all about," he says. "I finally realized that coaching was something I probably would be pretty good at, and it would be a rewarding career."

After graduating in 1966 with a degree in physical education, Schwartz left Lawrence to become an assistant coach at Ohio University while earning a master's degree. He then worked as an assistant at Massachusetts and the U.S. Military Academy.

In 1971, he became men's assistant track and cross country coach at Penn State University. And in 1979, he became a head coach, directing the Nittany Lions' women's cross country and track teams. The promotion prompted some adjustments on Schwartz's part.

"I had no idea what it was going to be like to coach women," he says. "Fortunately, I found out I enjoyed it (and) I was good at it. It offered me the experience of working

GARY SCHWARTZ
Track and field,
1964-66
Head track and field
and cross country coach,
1988 -

with both the men and women and learning the sometimes subtle and sometimes not-so-subtle differences of working with women and men."

Schwartz stayed at Penn State until taking the job as women's track coach at Tennessee. He directed the Lady Vols to second place finishes at the NCAA Indoor Championships in 1986 and 1987. The team took fourth at the NCAA Outdoor Championships those same years.

In 1988, Schwartz returned to Kansas to lead both the men's and women's track and field and cross country teams.

"Coach Easton had been here so long, and Coach (Bob) Timmons had been here even longer, and I just never thought about coming back here," Schwartz says. "Coaches are always talking among themselves about, 'If you had your choice, what two or three schools would you go to?' I'll bet every coach has had that conversation.

"And I had my list, and strangely enough, Kansas was never actually written in – it was an understood thing. The quality of my experience was so good, that it was really one of those 'no brainer' kind of things. When Coach Timmons told me he was going to be retiring, it didn't take me long at all."

Schwartz has proved you can go home again. His first men's track team finished fourth at the 1989 NCAA Indoor Championships. The men's cross country team placed in the top 16 nationally in 1989-91. Both the men's and women's cross country teams appeared together at the 1994 NCAA Championships for the first time in school history. The two squads enjoyed top 20 finishes, too. And the women's indoor track team finished 15th in the 1996 NCAA Championships.

"I like living in Lawrence, and I like the whole quality of life here in Lawrence and at the University," he says. "I know that sounds like a recruiting speech, but what people don't understand is that this place is special. The whole feeling that people come away with from having been here and going to this University is a real special deal."

ANGELA AYCOCK

MAKING A DIFFERENCE
Scorer revitalized Kansas women's basketball

"Not since Lynette Woodard has a player come in and made such a difference."

– Marian Washington
on Angela Aycock

Marian Washington recalls the past and looks forward to the future when discussing Angela Aycock.

"She is 'great people,' " Washington says. "She will always be in my life. My great moment with her, aside from her Kodak All-American team, will be when she gets that degree."

Aycock played for the University of Kansas women's basketball team in 1991-95. She played professionally in Italy before moving to the Seattle Reign of the American Basketball League, a U.S. women's professional league that debuted in 1996. She averaged 7.4 points in her first season with the Reign and averaged 6.3 points in the 1997-98 season. Between seasons, Aycock attends summer school to work toward finishing a bachelor's degree.

When Aycock's playing career ended in 1995, she left Kansas as its third-leading scorer with 1,978 points. She averaged 23.1 points as a senior, scoring 716 points that year. Only Lynette Woodard has exceeded that total in one season for KU.

"Not since Lynette Woodard has a player come in and made such a difference," Washington once said of Aycock.

The 6-foot-2-inch Aycock was named 1991 Texas player of the year at Lincoln High School in Dallas. She progressed steadily during her KU career. As a freshman, she was the team's second-leading scorer, averaging 10.3 points per game. The performance helped earn her a spot on the U.S. Junior National team in the summer of 1992. She was named captain of that team and displayed her leadership abilities by hitting three three-point shots in the final 4 minutes in a semifinal victory against Cuba in Mexico City.

Her teammates thought enough of Aycock to select her as a co-captain her sophomore year. She raised her scoring average to a team-high 16.3 points per game and led Kansas to its sixth Big Eight Conference Tournament championship. Aycock scored 25 points and snared 10 rebounds in the championship game against Nebraska. She earned tournament most valuable player honors.

ANGELA AYCOCK
Basketball,
1991-95

By her junior year, Aycock earned conference co-player of the year honors. She led the team in scoring (16.9 points per game), rebounding (8.7 per game) and minutes played. In the second round of the NCAA Tournament, Aycock played all 40 minutes in an 85-68 loss against Penn State. She scored 27 points and made 11 of 12 free throw attempts.

Aycock picked up as a senior where she left off as a junior. In the 1994-95 season opener, she scored 30 points as the Jayhawks upset No. 8 Virginia 86-84 in Honolulu. Later that season, Kansas faced No. 1 Connecticut on national television. Aycock played tremendously in the 97-87 loss, scoring 29 points and collecting 14 rebounds.

If that performance did not cement a Kodak All-America honor for her, then perhaps her final regular-season game did. Against Missouri, Aycock scored a triple-double with 25 points, 10 steals and 10 assists.

The Jayhawks won 88 games and lost 32 in Aycock's four seasons. She led the Jayhawks in scoring 21 times in 31 games as a senior. She scored 30 or more points seven times, with a season-high 36 points against Southern Mississippi and Houston.

After her senior year, Aycock was named to the U.S. Basketball Writers Association All-America team and the Associated Press All-America second team. When she garnered the Kodak honors, Aycock said, "This award puts all my hard work over the last four years into perspective. I couldn't think of a more incredible way to end my career at Kansas."

TRUE PIONEER

Coach blazes lengthy trail in women's sports

Marian E. Washington has lived – and made – history in her quarter-century as women's basketball coach at the University of Kansas.

Her career, which included six years as women's athletics director at KU, mirrors the great strides that women's athletics programs have made since 1973, the year Washington became the Jayhawks' coach.

Consider:

- The women's sports program belonged to the Health and Physical Education department when KU named Washington as coach. Thanks to federal Title IX legislation and NCAA gender-equity rules, the University now offers 11 women's varsity sports: basketball, soccer, softball, volleyball, swimming, tennis, golf, indoor and outdoor track, cross country and rowing;

- Washington started most of those programs when she became women's athletics director in 1974. Two other sports, field hockey and gymnastics, eventually were disbanded. In time, Kansas added soccer and rowing;

- To supplement early budgets, Washington and female athletes staged car washes and bake sales. Really. Money from coaches' camps was plowed back into the respective sports except for a few dollars. Washington considers today's budget for women's sports at KU as "very competitive" within the Big 12 Conference;

- Most of the women's varsity coaches were professors on campus. Other coaches, such as the local attorney who served as the first volleyball coach, came from outside the University. In time, Washington found some people with "very strong skills" who were willing to take part-time positions as coaches. These part-time positions paid very little, as low as $500 for a season. "It was a tremendous sacrifice," she says.

- Most of KU's competition was statewide, "within reasonable driving distance." This schedule included games or meets with junior colleges and small colleges. Today, KU's women's teams play a competitive national schedule. Some women's basketball games are televised;

- During the "reasonable driving distance" days, women's teams usually traveled in state-owned cars.
  "It was nothing to have a four or five-car caravan," Washington says. "The stress of being responsible as coach and athletics director for that type of travel was enormous."
  Today, KU women's teams travel by chartered bus or fly as they compete on a national basis; and

- No scholarships existed for women's sports in the early 1970s. Today, every women's sport is equipped with a full scholarship allotment as permitted by NCAA rules.

Despite the hardships, obstacles and handicaps that come with being a pioneer, Washington has persevered and succeeded. In 25 seasons at Kansas, she has guided the Jayhawks to a 480-267 record. That mark features one season with 30 victories and 14 seasons with 20 or more victories, including every season since 1990-91.

The Jayhawks captured the first Big 12 Conference regular-season championship

> *"She's such a nice person and such a solid person. She is a real pioneer in women's basketball. She's been fortunate in recent years that people have finally recognized her abilities."*
>
> – Bob Frederick,
> KU Athletics Director

MARIAN E. WASHINGTON

MARIAN E. WASHINGTON
Women's athletics director, 1973-79 • Head women's basketball coach, 1973 -

with a 14-2 mark. Washington and the Jayhawks also won two Big Eight Conference regular season titles and tied for a third. In addition, Kansas won three Big Eight Tournament championships. In 1996, KU advanced to the Sweet Sixteen round of the NCAA Tournament for the first time in school history and repeated the feat in 1998.

Washington came to Kansas in 1972 as a graduate assistant in the health, physical education and recreation department. She taught several classes and earned a master's degree in biodynamics and administration in 1975.

Washington attended West Chester State in her hometown of West Chester, Pa. In 1969, she helped lead West Chester State's basketball team to an undefeated season and a championship in the National Women's Invitational Tournament. Washington graduated in 1970 with a bachelor's degree in physical education and health, and West Chester bestowed an honorary doctorate degree to her in early 1998.

Washington appreciates her success, but she savors the people that helped her succeed.

"I've had some wonderful individuals, stemming from the time I got started, 1973, who are very, very dear to me," she says. "When we talk about teams, it would have to include the (1996-97) team. It's greatly due to the senior class. But I really have fond memories of a lot of people."

The 1997-98 team also was special. For most of the season, the Jayhawks started two freshmen, a sophomore and two juniors. The team went 23-9 and won two games in the NCAA Tournament.

"I thought getting to the NCAA tournament was a great accomplishment," Washington said afterward. "Getting to the Sweet Sixteen was unbelievable."

***

As Washington boils down 25 years of achievement into moments, her thoughts again focus on people instead of games.

"When I find young people who others would write off, when I find them accomplishing things that maybe only a few people can, then I am happy for them," she says.

For example, Lynette Woodard was named to the GTE Academic All-American Hall of Fame in 1992. But as a high school student, a counselor told Woodard that she could not make it academically in college.

"A lot of my athletes have come from some very challenging backgrounds," Washington says. "There are many unbelievable stories. The fact is, that many of them came to Kansas and were able to see some success here. There's no question for me that God has been a part of all of this."

KU athletics director Bob Frederick appreciates what Washington has done for her players and the University.

"She's such a nice person and such a solid person," Frederick says. "She is a real pioneer in women's basketball. She's been fortunate in recent years that people have finally recognized her abilities."

Frederick is referring to two crowning events in Washington's professional life: serving on the women's U.S. Olympic basketball team as an assistant coach in 1996 and leading the Black Coaches Association as president for two terms in 1993 and 1994.

MARIAN WASHINGTON'S BEST SEASONS AT KANSAS

SEASON	W-L	PCT.	NOTES
1978-79	30-8	.789	Lynette Woodard leads team to most victories in school history
1979-80	29-8	.784	Second-straight AIAW tournament appearance
1980-81	27-5	.843	Best winning percentage in school history; Woodard graduates
1991-92	25-6	.806	Big Eight Conference regular season champs at 12-2
1992-93	21-9	.700	Conference post-season tournament champions
1993-94	22-6	.786	Beats No. 4-ranked Colorado before record home crowd of 13,352
1995-96	22-10	.688	Jayhawks reach NCAA Sweet Sixteen for first time
1996-97	25-6	.806	Captures inaugural Big 12 regular season championship at 14-2
1997-98	23-9	.719	Advances to NCAA Sweet Sixteen without any senior starters
Overall	480-267	.643	Ranks in top 30 in victories for an active Division I coach

Tara VanDerveer, head coach at Stanford, directed the 1996 U.S. Olympic team. She tabbed Washington, Ceal Barry of Colorado and Nancy Darsch of Ohio State as assistants. Washington was the first person of color to serve as a coach for the women's basketball team.

"It was very special, as a former athlete and as a coach, to be a part of an experience where you have so many great athletes, that were so motivated, so focused," Washington says. "To be a part of their daily lives, to work with them and see them achieve their goal, it is something I'll always remember."

Washington said the experience was important for her, but to do it for her family and friends was even more important.

"They wanted to see it happen, and they were rejoicing even more so than me," she says.

The women's team enjoyed Washington's presence on the coaching staff, according to comments in the 1996-97 Kansas women's basketball media guide.

"Coach Washington extends beyond the court to the people side of you, and that is very important in life," Teresa Edwards said. "She views you as a person as well as a player."

Edwards' teammate, Rebecca Lobo, agreed.

"Coach Washington commands respect just by the person that she is," Lobo said. "She has a presence about her, and she treats everybody well."

Lenny Wilkens, head coach of the men's Olympic team, called Washington one of the most outstanding coaches in women's basketball.

"She is intelligent, perceptive, disciplined and can communicate well with her players and coaches," he said.

Another significant period in Washington's career occurred when she led the 3,000-member Black Coaches Association. She became the first women to lead the 98-percent male organization, and she was the first person elected to two consecutive terms as president.

Leading the BCA showed Washington how far she has advanced in her career.

"You have to understand, when I got started, there were very few people of color (in coaching)," she says. "As a director of athletics, I had no mentor, really. There was one African-American associate director at Illinois that I didn't call all of the time, but she was at least in the field and encouraged me instead of discouraged me.

"As a person of color in this business, and in most walks of life, there are some very, very definite challenges that we incur. It has nothing to do with our capabilities, and so when I was able to get involved with the BCA, it was really the first time that I was part of a group that has so many people of color.

"We were coming in to hear from other individual's lips the things they had gone through, which made me say to myself, 'My God, I have, too.' When you're going through some challenging periods, it's awfully nice to know that may be others out there that are trying to work on the same challenges, that you're not alone and you get some support from time to time.

"So, the BCA really gave me an opportunity to help some of the younger coaches. But it helped me a great deal, too, in simply reinforcing to me that my persistence really meant something, particularly to the young ones, that I did what I did and I hung in there and that they appreciated it."

***

From Mount Oread to the Olympic pinnacle, Washington has enjoyed success at many levels. As she looks ahead, Washington intends to keep coaching the game she loves at the place she loves while furthering the advancement of women's athletics at KU and across the nation.

"My drive has always been to do my part in helping women's athletics develop where it should, go where it deserves to go and be willing to fight to bring about changes, not just for my sport but for all women's sports," she says. "That's been an ongoing mission of mine."

"My drive has always been to do my part in helping women's athletics develop where it should, go where it deserves to go and be willing to fight to bring about changes, not just for my sport but for all women's sports. That's been an ongoing mission of mine."

– Marian E. Washington

PERFECT TIMING

Big 12 Conference player of the year steps into pro ball

As with one of her 337 assists or one of her 209 steals, Tamecka Dixon ended her University of Kansas basketball career in 1997 as a Kodak All-America selection with perfect timing.

That's because Dixon, Big 12 Conference player of the year in 1996-97, finished college just as two women's professional leagues debuted: the American Basketball League and the Women's National Basketball Association. The Los Angeles Sparks of the WNBA drafted Dixon, the 14th player selected overall, in the second round of its inaugural draft. She signed with the club and contributed 11.9 points, seven assists and three rebounds per game.

As a professional, Dixon also selected an agent and a shoe endorsement contract, two aspects of basketball that were completely foreign to women – until 1997.

TAMECKA DIXON
Basketball,
1993-97

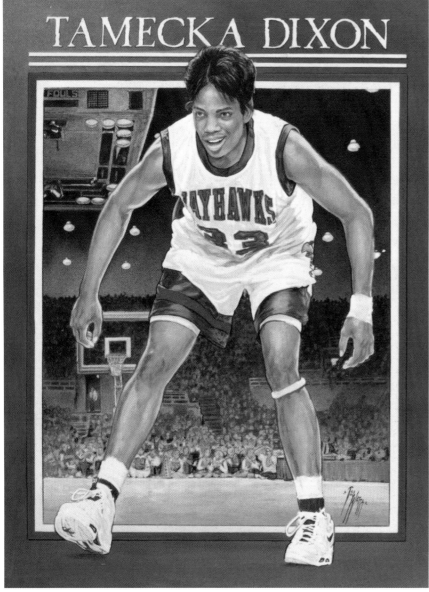

"It means a whole lot," Dixon says of the women's pro league, which plays a 28-game summer season and is supported by the NBA. "I get to represent myself, KU and Coach (Marian) Washington in the pros. It's been really great and very competitive. Every night, I'm matched against another All-American."

Dixon played her way into the pros as a point guard for the Jayhawks. She scored 1,689 points for KU from 1993-94 to 1996-97, fifth in school history, with an average of 14.2 points per game. In her senior season, Dixon led the Jayhawks in scoring in 19 of 31 games. She scored 30 or more points in three games, including a season-high 36 against St. Joseph's. Dixon averaged 20.8 points for the 25-6 Jayhawks, which won the first Big 12 Conference regular season championship.

Besides her Kodak honor, the Associated Press named her second-team All-America. When Kodak chose Dixon for its first team, Washington told the *Lawrence Journal-World*, "Back when Tamecka was being recruited, I knew from her talent that she had the potential to become an All-American. She was very consistent this season and has impacted our program from Day One."

Washington says Dixon learned lessons well on the basketball court.

"She learned how important it was to take directions, to be a positive leader, to discipline herself and deal with challenges, especially when things weren't going well," Washington says. "I saw her improve every single year."

As a junior, Dixon was named Big Eight Conference player of the year, averaging 17 points. The Jayhawks also won the regular season league championship in 1996 and advanced to the Sweet Sixteen of the NCAA Tournament for the first time in school history. Kansas ended that season with a 22-10 record. During Dixon's four years in Lawrence, the Jayhawks won 89 games and lost 33.

Qualifying for the Sweet Sixteen serves as one of her favorite KU memories. Other highlights include Senior Day, the Power Bar Shootout, when both the KU men's and women's teams played highly ranked Connecticut in a nationally televised doubleheader at Kemper Arena; and "Fill the Field House Day" her freshman year on Jan. 9, 1994, when 13,000 fans saw the Jayhawks nip top-10 Colorado by two points.

**

Dixon was born Dec. 14, 1975, to Portia Dixon and Russell "Boo" Bowers. Her father starred in basketball at American University in Washington, D.C., as one of the nation's top scorers. He later played two seasons in the NBA and Europe before injuries cut short his career.

Dixon began learning basketball at her father's knee. She retrieved balls for him as he sank jumper after jumper. She told the *Kansas City Star* in 1997 that she often played basketball with boys while growing up. The early competition often passed her by, but in time she developed her signature crossover dribble, hang time on her jump shot, physical defense and the kind of trash talking that occurs in schoolyard games.

As she grew older and began playing in organized games with girls, Dixon grew bored. She could score and steal at will, often accounting for 30 of her team's 40 or so points.

"Playing with women is fine and all that," she told the *Star*. "But I like going back home in the summer and playing with the guys. It's more challenging. They swat your shots from behind. They can drive by you. I want to play that game."

By her senior year at Linden (N.J.) High School, Dixon was recognized as an All-American and as New Jersey player of the year. She averaged 28.1 points and 13.6 rebounds as a shooting guard.

Dixon credits Washington as the one person for convincing her to move halfway across the country in 1993 to play basketball for Kansas.

"She was like a mother figure to me – someone I could talk to about everything, not just basketball," Dixon says of her college coach. "I fell in love with KU when I met her."

Once in college, Dixon made a huge adjustment in her game, switching from shooting guard to the point. Her lifelong exposure to basketball helped Dixon gain court presence, as did Washington's coaching.

"(Coach Washington) told me that I had all the qualities to be a great point guard," the 5-foot-9-inch guard recalls. "As a point guard, you've got to know everything."

Today, adjusting to life in pro basketball means another challenge. Dixon lives in Los Angeles and travels a lot, playing about three games a week during the WNBA's summer season.

"Back in college, you played a game and then had a week to think about the next game," she says. "Here, there's no time to dwell on anything."

Dixon says she's earning enough money for the year from her "summer job," but she returned to Kansas in fall 1997 and finished her last semester for a psychology degree.

"This is my job now," Dixon says of pro ball.

THE TOTAL PACKAGE

Hard work, dedication strengthen KU's basketball legacy

"He really is special. Kansas fans should be happy: They got a jewel."

– Dean Smith on Roy Williams

Bill Kukuk, a former president of the Jayhawk Roundball Club, couldn't have been less thrilled when Roy Williams succeeded Larry Brown as men's basketball coach at the University of Kansas.

"Needless to say, we would rather have gotten a Gary Williams or a John Chaney or some of the other names we have heard about," Kukuk told the *Dallas Morning News* months after KU athletics director Bob Frederick hired Williams in the summer of 1988. "All of us would like to have seen one with more of a proven track record. We didn't get one, and we will have to wait and see how it all turns out. I think it is causing anxious moments among some people."

Even former KU athletics director Monte Johnson, like many Kansas faithful, questioned Frederick's hiring.

"I am more concerned we have put a man in a position where I am not sure he can win in the eyes of the fans if he doesn't come close to accomplishing what Larry did," Johnson told the *Morning News* in the same article. "I don't think they will be as patient with a guy who hasn't been a successful head coach on the college level, who would get his system in, and in three to four years then win."

Patience on the part of KU fans wasn't necessary. Early in his second season, despite NCAA penalties from violations that occurred during Brown's tenure, Williams had KU ranked No. 1 in the nation. By his third year, KU advanced to the NCAA Tournament title game.

So much for not coming close to what Brown accomplished. A decade later, Johnson's view of Williams has turned 180 degrees.

"I'm not sure I've seen a better total package than Roy," Johnson says. "Roy would be as comfortable as a business executive as he is as a coach. He relates extremely well to all alumni.

"Larry wanted to coach. Period. And he was most comfortable when he was coaching. Roy seems as comfortable in a booster setting or a business. I've heard him speak to a group of utility company training specialists, and it was the best talk I'd ever heard anybody – not just a coach but a businessman – give. He recruits better, he works harder than anybody.

"What he's done in the time he's been here is awesome."

***

Kukuk, Johnson and myriad other skeptics didn't have the luxury of knowing in 1988 what Dean Smith had told Frederick. They didn't know what Dick Harp had seen with his own eyes. And they had no idea what Williams regarded as the best basketball advice anyone ever gave him.

"If you choose to not work hard, someone else will," Williams wrote on a KU Sports Information Office questionnaire in 1990, "and he might be the person you have to compete with."

Dick Harp, KU's former head coach of the late 1950s and early 1960s, worked as an assistant coach alongside Williams for Smith at North Carolina in the mid-1980s.

"Dean picked up Roy when he was coaching high school," Harp says. "He told me Roy was going to make it and make it big."

After watching Roy work with North Carolina's players, Harp understood why Smith was so certain about Williams.

"I knew Roy was going to be a great coach," he says. "There was no question in my mind."

Smith says Williams proved himself worthy of future accolades from the time he worked at North Carolina's basketball camp when he still was a high school coach in Swannanoa, N.C., just east of Asheville, where he grew up.

"I never worried about him running the camp properly," Smith says. "He was always organized. He knew everybody's name. As a coach, he was extremely competent from Day One."

Smith told these things to Frederick. Conventional wisdom is that Williams was the leftover choice after some higher-profile names turned down the KU job. Indeed, Ohio State's Gary Williams withdrew his candidacy after early consideration, but many other coaches – Purdue's Gene Keady, Wichita State's Eddie Fogler, Georgia Tech's Bobby Cremins and Kentucky's Eddie Sutton, to name a few – expressed little interest in the job.

Smith was the first person Frederick called when Brown left for the NBA's San Antonio Spurs. However, North Carolina had just named its new arena after Smith. Needless to say, he quickly turned down a chance to return to Kansas.

"But he said, 'I'm interested in helping you if I can.' " Frederick says. "And he said, 'Who are some of the people you're interested in?' And I mentioned Gary Williams and I mentioned Charlie Spoonhour. He said good things about Gary Williams. And he said, 'You know, I'd like you to think about Roy Williams.' "

The rest, as they say, is history.

"I flew to Atlanta to talk to Roy, and I got real interested in him after I talked to him," Frederick says. "So we brought him in for an interview, and I offered him the job just as soon as the interview was over."

Williams accepted right away.

"He didn't even ask what the salary was," Frederick says. "And he said, 'I want to call Jerry Green (Williams' top assistant during his first few years at Kansas).' So he called Jerry Green before he called his wife."

***

During his interview with KU, Williams broke down when professing his love for North Carolina. At that point, Frederick says he thought Williams would turn Kansas down.

But the episode probably proved something more – something Smith, discussing whom he thought Kansas should hire, told the *Lawrence Journal-World* when Brown left for San Antonio.

"He has so many of the characteristics of Larry, and he (Williams) would be there *forever*," Smith said. "He's the permanent type."

Before accepting the KU job, Williams had interviewed at Mississippi State, James Madison, Furman, Tennessee-Chattanooga and George Mason. Instead, he waited for a bigger chance, and since arriving at Kansas, he's turned down numerous NBA and college coaching overtures.

He stayed with Smith for 10 seasons before taking a head coaching position. Once he did, he quickly lived up to his reputation for organization and outworking fellow coaches, especially after the NCAA stunned KU with a harsh, three-year probation on Halloween 1988. Williams, his wife, Wanda, and their children, Scott and Kimberly, had lived in Lawrence for only three months.

Frederick says he told every coaching candidate about possible NCAA penalties, but not even he thought they would be so severe: no postseason play in 1988-89, meaning KU could not defend its NCAA championship, and no on-campus

"When you consider everything – the way he recruits, the way he coaches, the way he treats people in this department – I just can't imagine anybody who is better."

– Bob Frederick
on Roy Williams

ROY WILLIAMS
Head basketball coach, 1988 -

recruiting visits in 1989.

The harshness of the penalties stemmed partly from the fact KU's football program had received probation amid serious recruiting violations in the early 1980s. But the reasons offered no sympathy for Williams and KU's players.

So Williams worked. And worked. And worked some more. With no on-campus visits allowed, he had to recruit twice as hard.

"When he first came to KU, he never went to lunch," says Mark Turgeon, an assistant coach on Williams' first Kansas staff. "You were afraid to go to lunch. You'd bring stuff and stick it in your desk drawers just to get through the day."

Kansas, despite an eight-game losing streak, went 19-12 in Williams' first season. The Jayhawks lost to Kansas State in the first round of the Big Eight Tournament, ending their season.

That year represents, by far, the fewest victories and most losses of any season during Williams' tenure heading into 1998-99. But Smith still regards it as his best coaching job at KU.

"That was a sensational job that won't go down in history, but it does with me," Smith says.

The next season, KU reeled off 19 straight victories to start the season, including upsets of Louisiana State and Nevada-Las Vegas in winning the Preseason NIT tournament. In addition, the Jayhawks pounded Kentucky, also suffering from NCAA probation, 150-95 in Allen Field House. No Kentucky team before or since surrendered as many points in one game.

ROY WILLIAMS' RECORD

SEASON	W/L	CONFERENCE	FINAL AP RANKING	NCAA TOURNAMENT
1988-89	19-12	6-8, Sixth	—	None (NCAA probation)
1989-90	30-5	11-3, Second-tie	No. 5	1-1, advanced to second round
1990-91	27-8	10-4, First-tie	No. 12	5-1, advanced to NCAA title game
1991-92	27-5	11-3, First	No. 2	1-1, advanced to second round
1992-93	29-7	11-3, First	No. 9	4-1, advanced to Final Four
1993-94	27-8	9-5, Third	No. 13	2-1, advanced to Sweet Sixteen
1994-95	25-6	11-3, First	No. 5	2-1, advanced to Sweet Sixteen
1995-96	29-5	12-2, First	No. 4	3-1, advanced to Elite Eight
1996-97	34-2	15-1, First	No. 1	2-1, advanced to Sweet Sixteen
1997-98	35-4	15-1, First	No. 2	1-1, advanced to second round
Overall	282-62 (.820)	111-33, 7 titles (.771)	7 Top 10 finishes	21-9, 2 Final Fours, 3 Elite (.700) Eights, 6 Sweet Sixteens

- 1989-90 National Coach of the Year (U.S. Basketball Writers Association)
- 1991-92 National Coach of the Year (Associated Press)
- 1996-97 National Coach of the Year (*The Sporting News*)
- 1989-90 Big Eight Conference Coach of the Year (United Press International, AP)
- 1991-92 Big Eight Conference Coach of the Year (AP)
- 1994-95 Big Eight Conference co-Coach of the Year (Voted by league coaches)
- 1995-96 Big Eight Conference Coach of the Year (League coaches)
- 1996-97 Big 12 Conference Coach of the Year (AP)

KU stayed No. 1 or No. 2 in most national polls for 13 consecutive weeks and finished 30-5. The next year, Kansas advanced to the NCAA title game before losing to Duke 72-65.

In 1988, Frederick had warned Kansas fans it might take two or three years for KU basketball to recover from the NCAA penalties. But he recalls how soon Williams showed his recruiting prowess, even as penalties loomed.

"Still one of the most amazing accomplishments that he had," Frederick says, "one thing that gets lost about all this stuff about Roy: He got oral commitments from Adonis Jordan, Thomas Hill (who later helped Duke win consecutive NCAA titles) and Harold Miner (a first-team All-American at USC in 1991-92). And if that probation had come a week later, we would have signed all three of those to national letters of intent. That is amazing, considering where he started."

But only Jordan kept his commitment. A year later, Williams corralled forward Richard Scott without the benefit of a campus visit. Scott, who chose Kansas instead of his home-state school, Arkansas, and Jordan formed two-fifths of KU's starting lineup when the Jayhawks again went to the Final Four in 1993.

Even Smith learned how difficult it was to recruit against his former aide.

"When we recruited Rasheed Wallace (North Carolina's former center who left college early for the NBA in 1995)," Smith says, "his mother told me during the recruiting process, 'I like you, but that Roy Williams is still my favorite.' I said, 'Well, he's my favorite, too.' "

Frederick, one of Williams' closest friends, says, "You know, after he had some of those early recruiting successes, I thought he'd let up. I thought he'd give more responsibility to his assistants, and they have a lot of responsibility.

"But he's always involved in it. When Raef LaFrentz came along, the guy was just unbelievable. The more success he had, the more committed he was.

"I just didn't realize how driven he is to be successful."

***

Williams' drive and commitment remain the biggest factors behind KU's reputation as one of the elite men's basketball programs in the nation. But those who know him have learned much more.

"The No. 1 thing Roy Williams taught me is to treat people the way you want to be treated," Turgeon says. "Coach Williams taught me how to be a competitor as a coach. He challenges his players and gets more out of them than maybe any other coach.

"I truly believe he was born to be a basketball coach. He truly loves his players. It's not a fake thing, which happens a lot in our business."

Williams defends his players to the limit. Witness the game at Oklahoma in February 1995, when an Oklahoma student harassed KU's Jerod Haase, who had slid on the floor out of bounds into an area occupied with Oklahoma student-fans.

Williams leapt from the KU bench and ran to Haase's aid, pointing a finger and yelling at the student. He received a technical foul but no further disciplinary penalties.

On at least three occasions, Williams has voiced displeasure with Allen Field House fans: when he thought they were too quiet during an 84-72 victory against Oklahoma State in February 1993, when a less-than-capacity crowd filled the arena for a Saturday game against last-place Colorado in February 1994 (KU won that game 106-62, breaking a three-game losing streak), and when he didn't think KU fans gave Jayhawks' point guard Jacque Vaughn a proper reception before a home game against Texas A&M in January 1997. Vaughn had broken the Big Eight Conference assist record three days earlier in a victory against Connecticut.

On each occasion, Williams mentioned his players when deriding fans for an apparent lack of support. And on the far more numerous occasions he has called Allen Field House the best place to play college basketball, support for his players tops the list of reasons why.

KU players have said time and again Williams is more than just their basketball coach.

"The great thing about Coach Williams and his staff is that they teach you how to conduct yourself in certain situations," LaFrentz says. "They teach about life. That's as important as teaching you how to properly execute a pick and roll. That's what Coach Williams gives you that not a lot of other coaches do."

Sutton, now one of Williams' Big 12 Conference coaching nemesis at Oklahoma State, says few coaches do the things Williams does.

"When you play Kansas, you know they'll be well prepared and you know the players will give 100 percent," Sutton says. "I know that Roy wouldn't like to be compared with Dean (Smith). But I don't think there is anybody in the college game who coaches better than he does."

Frederick, whom Smith recruited out of high school, agrees.

"When you consider everything – the way he respects the University, the way he recruits, the way he coaches, the way he treats people in this department – I just can't imagine anybody who is better," Frederick says. "He's so caring about other people. He's just been amazing."

Amazing enough to average 28 victories and just six losses in his first 10 years at Kansas. Amazing enough to lead KU to seven conference championships in those 10 years. Amazing enough to lead the Jayhawks to a total of two Final Fours, three Elite Eight and six Sweet Sixteen appearances in nine NCAA Tournaments since he arrived. No other college basketball coach won more games in his first 10 seasons. As of 1998, only one coaching feat had hauntingly eluded him: the coveted NCAA Tournament championship.

The son of a wayward, alcoholic father and a poor, hard-working mother, Williams mostly credits other people for his success – Wanda; his mother, who died in 1992; his high school coach and Smith, the head varsity coach when Williams played on the freshman team at North Carolina in 1968-69. (A generation later, Williams' son, Scott, played for Smith as a Tar Heels' walk-on.)

Smith says he and Harp do deserve credit for helping Williams get the KU job. Otherwise, they claim Williams, named Distinguished Kansan of the Year for 1997, is the one responsible for his outstanding career.

"It makes me feel good that he respects me, but I want him to take credit for the job he's done," says Smith. "He really is special.

"Kansas fans should be happy: They got a jewel."

MUSICAL CHAIRS

Larry Brown and Roy Williams on the same coaching staff.

That combination never has happened, but it almost did at the University of Kansas in the mid-1980s.

Ironically, had Williams taken a position as an assistant on Brown's staff, KU probably wouldn't have won the NCAA championship in 1988.

When Brown took the job as KU's men's basketball coach in 1983, he tried to hire Williams, then an assistant to Brown's college coach, Dean Smith, at North Carolina. But after contemplating the offer, Williams decided to remain at Chapel Hill.

Brown hired Ed Manning a couple weeks after Williams turned him down. The Manning family, including a high-school aged boy named Danny, moved to Lawrence.

Had Williams accepted the position on Brown's staff, Danny Manning probably would have attended college in ... North Carolina. The Manning family lived in Greensboro, N.C., before they moved to Lawrence.

Instead, Manning became the leading scorer in KU men's basketball history, a two-time consensus first-team All-American and national player of the year in 1987-88, when he led KU to its second NCAA title.

Five years after telling Brown no, Williams replaced him at Kansas. Smith says its obvious that Williams, a North Carolina graduate, now loves KU.

"I knew he would," says Smith, a Kansas alumnus. "He's a real Jayhawker now. But he's still a Tar Heel, too.

"You can be both. Look at me."

PRIME EXAMPLE
Pasadena point guard personified the good in college sports

"Jacque's greatest asset to our team was not what he could do on the floor. It was his leadership."

– Raef LaFrentz

Years from now, University of Kansas basketball fans must choose what they remember most about him.

It's easier now. Although his KU days are over, the memories are fresh. But after he's dealt his last no-look pass, after he's made the last of his patented start-at-the-waist-scoop-finger roll layups, after the sun has set on his NBA career, they'll have to decide what they recall most distinctly about Jacque Vaughn.

It could be a pass he made, but selecting which one is difficult. Because Vaughn shattered the Big Eight Conference record for career assists with 804, recalling any Vaughn dish that stands above another is like choosing ice cream: no matter the flavor, it's usually good.

The top memory could encompass mere seconds, such as the three-pointer he made against Indiana at Allen Field House in his 12th game as a freshman in 1993-94. With just two seconds left in overtime, the shot beat the Hoosiers 86-83 in one of the most dramatic games ever played on KU's hallowed home court.

Or the memory could comprise an entire game. While KU's other players struggled, Vaughn single-handedly kept the Jayhawks in the contest against Syracuse during the second half of the 1996 NCAA Western Regional final.

Kansas lost 60-57 that Sunday afternoon. But not before Vaughn, who averaged 9.6 points per game in 126 games at KU, made eight of 12 field goal attempts, hit three three-pointers, contributed four assists and scored a game-high 21 points.

Only relishing on-court achievements by Vaughn does him injustice, though. His impact on Kansas and all of college basketball transcended the way he tucked his head and shoulders while dribbling through a blur of flat-footed defenders. More than anything, the manner in which he carried himself when he was nowhere near a basketball court defined Jacque Vaughn.

These are the days of pouting NBA rookies, Dennis Rodmans and overhyped college recruits. And these are the days parents from Sarasota to Seattle tell their kids they should emulate players – make that people – such as Vaughn.

He provided the ultimate example.

"Jacque and Jerod (Haase) as a combination backcourt, both being academic All-Americans, having (college basketball commentator) Dick Vitale pumping them all the time on national television – I really believe that there are people all over the country who weren't Kansas fans or had no Kansas connection that took a real interest in our team because of how they conducted themselves, in particular those two guys," says Bob Frederick, KU's athletics director.

"They had the right priorities. People just clutched onto them. I think that men's basketball team and the way they conducted themselves brought as much credit to the University as any aspect ever of our athletics programs.

"In a time when there's a lot of question about the way professional athletes conduct themselves, to see a group like that was so outstanding in every respect."

***

At Kansas, which went 34-2 in Vaughn's senior year and 115-21 in his four years in a KU uniform, no one questioned who was the team's leader behind head coach

Roy Williams.

"Jacque's greatest asset to our team was not what he could do on the floor," says Raef LaFrentz, the former All-American power forward who received many of Vaughn's lightning-quick feeds. "It was his leadership."

Off the court, Vaughn graduated with a 3.7 grade-point average on a 4.0 scale and a degree in business administration. His classroom success should not have surprised KU fans who knew Vaughn as more than one of the nation's top high school point guards when he arrived at Kansas in fall 1993.

He had won the Dial Award as the nation's top high school athlete of 1992-93, the first men's basketball player to do so. But he also graduated second in his class of 350 at John Muir High in Pasadena, Calif.

A poetry lover who quoted Robert Frost when announcing his decision not to enter the NBA draft after his tremendous junior season, Vaughn was an atypical college basketball player from the moment he stepped on the Kansas campus.

He started every game, 100 straight, in his first three years. When he ran onto the court against Western Michigan as a starter on Nov. 17, 1993, he was the first KU freshman to start his first game since Danny Manning nine years earlier.

JACQUE VAUGHN
Basketball,
1993-97

In 1993-94, the only year Vaughn played that KU did not win a conference championship, he guided Kansas to the first of his four career NCAA Tournament Sweet Sixteen appearances. He was voted conference newcomer of the year and made honorable mention all-conference.

During the next two seasons, he made first-team all-conference. He was conference player of the year as a junior in 1995-96 and made second-team Associated Press All-America, as well as first-team Wooden All-America. He was a finalist for the Naismith Award as college basketball's best player. By the end of his junior year, he had done about everything a college basketball player can do.

Except go to a Final Four.

But Vaughn barely mentioned basketball when announcing his decision against turning pro before graduating. Instead, he cited a desire to "take a stand." Rather than shun being a role model, he welcomed it.

"I'd rather a father and mother be a role model," he said at that May 7, 1996, news conference. "But I've been put in a situation where kids look up to me. I'm going to carry a little more weight on my back."

Oklahoma coach Kelvin Sampson praised Vaughn's decision.

"I enjoy competing against the best, and he's the best," Sampson told the *Lawrence Journal-World*. "He is worth his weight in gold for your program without even dribbling a basketball. He's good for college basketball. He represents the great qualities other kids would like to have."

Four months later, in an off-season pickup game, Vaughn suffered torn ligaments in his shooting wrist. The injury caused him to miss the first 10 games of his senior season. The naysayers who said he should have entered the NBA draft crowed louder.

At Kansas, Jacque Vaughn was a leader off the court, as well. He joined Darnell Valentine and Ken Koenigs as the only KU men's players named first-team academic All-America more than once. He earned the honor in 1995-96 and 1996-97.

By the end of the season, which ended with a heart-breaking 85-82 defeat to eventual NCAA-champion Arizona in the Sweet Sixteen, some still said Vaughn shouldn't have returned.

KU finished the regular season No. 1 in the AP poll, the first Kansas team to accomplish the feat. But the season ended in another NCAA Tournament disappointment for Vaughn and the Jayhawks. Despite their regular season dominance, he and KU's other senior regulars – Haase, Scot Pollard and B.J. Williams – never made a Final Four.

Despite falling short of that goal again, Vaughn said he had no regrets about staying at Kansas for four years. He and LaFrentz, as finalists, went to Los Angeles for the presentation of the Wooden Award honoring college basketball's player of the year.

"The experience I gained, friendships I made and sense of accomplishment from finishing my senior season and getting my business degree are all things you can't trade," he told the *Jayhawk Insider*. "I've always dreamed of playing in the NBA, but my degree is something basketball can't take away from me."

Playing at Allen Field House also is something the NBA never can take away from Vaughn. When the 1997-98 season opened – KU's first without Vaughn since the 1992-93 Final Four team led by Rex Walters and Adonis Jordan – the Jayhawks had a 44-game home winning streak, the second-longest in school history. (By the end of the season, that streak stood at a school-record 60.)

"If there's one thing I appreciate most, it's the support I got here," he told the *Topeka Capital-Journal* before his last home game. "I'll always remember that."

Above all, Williams will remember Vaughn's dedication.

"I've always said the three best competitors I've been around are Michael Jordan, Rex Walters and a girl where I coached in high school," Williams told the *Journal-World* shortly before the Utah Jazz reunited Vaughn with former college teammate Greg Ostertag by making him their first-round choice in the June 1997 NBA draft. "I'm adding a fourth – Jacque Vaughn. He's the most disciplined person I've been around in my life."

But discipline didn't translate into preparation when Vaughn, voted the Big 12 Conference men's athlete of the year for 1996-97, spoke at his final team banquet April 10, 1997.

"The reason I didn't prepare anything," Vaughn told his teammates and the crowd, "is this is the last time I'll address you guys in Allen Field House, and I wanted what I had to say to typify how I played on the court: with instinctiveness, with intuition, with passion.

"And with my heart."

MONONA'S PRIDE

Two-time All-American proved small-town players can make it big

In late May 1997, three weeks after announcing his decision to stay at the University of Kansas for his senior season instead of entering the NBA draft, Raef LaFrentz had retreated to his hometown.

Monona, Iowa (pop. 1, 520), sits comfortably in northeast Iowa, about 15 miles east of the Mississippi River. Similar villages dot the territory surrounding Monona, but the closest city with more than 10,000 people is Dubuque, 70 miles to the southeast.

LaFrentz was born in Hampton, Iowa, but spent his formative years in Monona. It's where, in the space of a couple years in high school, he went from the best player in Clayton County to the most-coveted high school center in the nation. His feathery, left-handed touch, the fluid nature with which he ran the floor and his 6-foot-11-inch frame had college coaches scrambling for Iowa road maps.

Eventually, LaFrentz narrowed his choices to Iowa – "I sure wasn't an Iowa State fan, and I'm not now," he says – and Kansas. But the remoteness of Monona may not hit home until one realizes that when he announced his decision to attend KU on an Iowa radio station, LaFrentz traveled an hour southwest to Oelwein to do it.

So it's understandable that in late May 1997 in Monona, days after sports pages and television stations in northeast Kansas blared the news that KU would get a rematch with Arizona in ESPN's Great Eight spectacle the following December, LaFrentz had not yet heard the news.

"Who? What? We are? We're playing them in the Great Eight?" he said. "Yes! I told Coach (Roy) Williams that's what I wanted to do."

LaFrentz knew Arizona well. He fired the last shot, a desperation three-pointer that couldn't find its way into the basket, when the Wildcats stunned the Jayhawks with an 85-82 upset in the 1997 NCAA Southeast Regional semifinals.

A year earlier, when KU beat Arizona 83-80 in the semifinals of the NCAA Western Regional in Denver, LaFrentz played his only game at KU in which he didn't score a field goal. He finished the game with one point and four rebounds.

So before the 1997-98 season, LaFrentz admitted he was hungry for some revenge against Arizona, which eventually won the 1997 NCAA championship – a title practically everyone had thought KU would win. The '96-97 Jayhawks finished 34-2, ranked No. 1 in the final Associated Press poll, and won their third straight Big Eight/Big 12 Conference title in the process.

Even though it couldn't erase the hurt of an early exit from the 1997 NCAA Tournament, LaFrentz and the Jayhawks got their revenge nine months later. He scored 32 points on 12-of-17 shooting and grabbed eight rebounds as Kansas defeated the defending national champions 90-87.

Unfortunately, in his final game at Kansas, LaFrentz would endure another unexpected, heartbreaking March defeat.

***

LaFrentz pulls no punches about one of the goals he had when choosing Kansas instead of Iowa.

"The bottom line is one reason players come to KU is to go to a Final Four, the possibility that you can get that far in the tournament," he said before the 1997-98 season.

"He is like a third-grade kid at times when he hits you with that smile. When he smiles out there on the court, that's worth more than any kind of money you could give me."

– Roy Williams

RAEF LaFRENTZ
Basketball,
1994-98

As KU fans everywhere know, that dream never became reality for LaFrentz. Despite never losing a game in Allen Field House and winning four consecutive consecutive conference championships, the Jayhawks always fell short in March during the LaFrentz Era. His final act as a KU player was dunking a rebound with one second left, the last points in KU's stunning 80-75 loss against Rhode Island in the second round of the 1998 NCAA Tournament.

But the chance to play in a Final Four is far from the only reason the most-widely known prep star in Iowa history left his home state. On the day he announced his decision, more than 2,000 people called a *Des Moines Register* hotline to find out LaFrentz would play at Kansas.

"Ideally, I would have liked to stay in my home state," he says. "It was very hard leaving. But I couldn't turn down the people and the things I saw at Kansas."

He says the overriding factor behind his choice was Williams, who targeted LaFrentz harder than any player he previously recruited at Kansas.

"Coach Williams was *the* factor," LaFrentz says. "Coach Williams was the coach I really couldn't turn down."

His choice sent shock waves through Iowa. Even Iowa football coach Hayden Fry chastised the decision.

Whenever LaFrentz played conference foe Iowa State in Ames, he was showered with catcalls and boos – even though he never considered attending Iowa State. In his first game there as a freshman in 1994-95, LaFrentz scored only five points but grabbed nine rebounds in a 69-65 loss. After the game, in a measure of class, Cyclones' star Fred Hoiberg criticized Iowa State fans for booing LaFrentz.

But LaFrentz and KU dominated the senior-laden Cyclones in 1996-97. The Jayhawks defeated them three times, including a 72-48 thrashing in the conference tournament semifinals in what Williams called the best defensive performance of any KU team he has coached. In those three games, LaFrentz averaged 17.7 points, nine rebounds and two blocked shots. And in his senior year, his final basket against the Cyclones in an 83-62 victory in Ames was a rare three-pointer.

***

The progress LaFrentz made against the Cyclones offers a microcosm of his steady evolution as a college player.

At MFL Mar-Mac High School, he used his sheer height and superior athleticism to batter smaller, less-gifted opponents.

But LaFrentz quickly noticed a change at Kansas, even though he had learned "a small-town kid can play with big-city boys" when he attended numerous summer basketball camps during high school.

"The intensity level and the constant grind of the season was the toughest adjustment," he says.

As a freshman, LaFrentz started every game, averaging 11.4 points and 7.5 rebounds. He vividly remembers what he calls his "wake-up call" to college basketball.

"I think I'll always remember the UMass game when they were ranked No. 1," he says, referring to his second game with the Jayhawks. "At the time, I was kind of starstruck. But I put together a good game."

Against celebrated sophomore center Marcus Camby and senior forward Lou Roe, LaFrentz held his own with 18 points and nine rebounds. The Jayhawks beat Massachusetts 81-75 in a nationally televised game in Anaheim, Calif.

But the length of the season and physical nature of college basketball took a toll on LaFrentz by the end of his freshman year, when he weighed only 220 pounds. In the season's last six games, he scored in double digits just three times after scoring more than 10 points in 19 of KU's first 25 games. He made only 19 of 50 field goal attempts in those six games; he shot 53.4 percent from the floor for the entire season.

Nonetheless, he was named as the conference's freshman player of the year and was named honorable mention all-conference. As a sophomore in 1995-96, he led KU with 13.4 points and 8.2 rebounds per game and was named first-team all-conference.

"I just wanted to enjoy the college experience, to be a Jayhawk one more year. There are not too many better feelings than playing in Allen Field House."

– Raef LaFrentz

LaFrentz boosted his weight to 235 pounds before his junior season. He says the extra weight and the experience of two years as a starter made the biggest difference as he established himself as college basketball's elite power forward in 1996-97.

Early in the season, he began piling up big numbers. In an 82-53 victory against Louisiana State, he had 23 points and 13 rebounds. When KU pounded UCLA 96-83 in Los Angeles, he had 31 points and 11 rebounds.

But it wasn't until senior starting center Scot Pollard sat out with a broken bone in his foot that LaFrentz began dominating every game. As KU's lone scoring option inside, he averaged 23.1 points and 10.3 rebounds in the eight games Pollard missed, turning into KU's most automatic inside scoring threat since Danny Manning.

"He was as important to us in that stretch as any player we've ever had," Williams told the Associated Press.

That stretch sealed LaFrentz's choice as a first-team All-American. It included an 82-77 victory against Nebraska in Allen Field House, when he scored 11 of KU's 22 overtime points.

It included a 96-94 double-overtime loss at Missouri – KU's only regular season defeat – when he played 47 minutes, scored 26 points, grabbed 16 rebounds and sent the game into overtime with a rebound and basket off a missed free throw with only seconds remaining.

It included the rematch with Missouri at Allen Field House, when he hit 11 of 15 shots, made nine of 11 free throws, scored 31 points, grabbed 10 rebounds, blocked four shots and survived a skirmish with Missouri forward Derek Grimm. KU won 79-67. (Grimm later issued a written apology for what most thought was a cheap shot on LaFrentz late in the game.)

LaFrentz, who averaged 18.5 points and 9.3 rebounds for the season, was named conference player of the year and was a finalist for the Wooden Award as college basketball's player of the year.

"I think the thing that's so much better about him this year is that little things don't bother him, and he doesn't make them into bigger things," Williams told the *Topeka Capital-Journal* in March 1997. "He's a much more mature youngster and a much more confident youngster."

LaFrentz agrees he matured during 1996-97, especially during the conference portion of the schedule.

"When Scot went down, I knew I was going to have to be a bigger presence inside," he said after the season. "Every player likes that feeling of four other players depending on your efforts. I've always been confident of my ability and most of the time, I answered the call."

Perhaps more than anything about Raef LaFrentz, Kansas fans will remember his nearly unstoppable turnaround jumpers.

He definitely answered the call of KU fans who wanted him to stay for his senior season. He and forward Paul Pierce did so through hand-written notes, which longtime KU radio announcer Max Falkenstien read to about 5,000 KU fans attending a charity exhibition game at Allen Field House.

"Rather than looking for reasons to leave, I was looking for reasons to stay," says LaFrentz, who talked repeatedly about his decision with Jacque Vaughn, the former KU point guard who made the same decision in May 1996.

One last opportunity to make the Final Four certainly enticed LaFrentz to return to Kansas. But he says he still would have returned had KU won the NCAA title during his junior year.

"I just wanted to enjoy the college experience, to be a Jayhawk one more year," he says. "There are not too many better feelings than playing in Allen Field House."

Returning also gave Williams one more year to enjoy LaFrentz's smile.

"He is like a third-grade kid at times when he hits you with that smile," Williams once told the *Lawrence Journal-World*. "When he smiles out there on the court, that's worth more than any kind of money you could give me."

With LaFrentz and Pierce returning, KU again bulldozed most opponents in 1997-98. Going into the season, NBA draft analyst Don Leventhal rated KU's two biggest stars as the top two NBA prospects, and LaFrentz was favored to win numerous honors as college basketball's top player.

But LaFrentz saw his season derailed the day after Christmas. In a practice at the Rainbow Classic in Honolulu, he broke a bone in his right hand. He missed nine games; two of KU's three regular season losses occurred during his absence. In addition, the injury probably cost him any chance at a college player-of-the-year award.

LaFrentz returned to the KU lineup with flare a month later, though, scoring 31 points and garnering 15 rebounds as the Jayhawks throttled Texas Tech 88-49 before a raucous home crowd.

KU cruised through the rest of the regular season and won its second straight conference tournament, the first school to accomplish that feat. The return of LaFrentz ignited a 14-game winning streak. In 10 of those games, he posted a double-double in points and rebounds.

However, during the ninth game of that streak versus Oklahoma, his last home game at KU, LaFrentz injured his left shoulder. He played with pain the rest of the season, especially when shooting his patented turnaround baseline jumper.

After winning the conference tournament, KU pounded Prairie View in its opening NCAA Tournament game. But the Jayhawks couldn't overcome poor outside shooting against Rhode Island. Even more, they couldn't stop the Rams' hot shooting guards.

LaFrentz, however, ended his career in typical fashion – with a double-double. His 22 points and 14 rebounds were the highlight of an otherwise dismal day for the Jayhawks, which ended the season 35-4, tying the school record for most victories in a season.

After the game, a disappointed LaFrentz answered the same question he answered when he broke his hand and hurt his shoulder: Do you regret coming back for your senior season?

He replied, simply and sincerely, "No," just as he had each time before.

A Final Four berth was about the only thing LaFrentz left Kansas without. He was KU's first two-time All-American since Manning and became only the second KU player besides Manning to score 2,000 points. He also finished second to Manning on KU's all-time rebound list.

As a senior, LaFrentz averaged 19.8 points and 11.4 rebounds a game, the first KU player to average a double-double since Roger Brown and Dave Robisch both did it in 1970-71. At KU, he had 56 double-doubles in his 131 games, a school record. For his career, he averaged 15.8 points per game. And most importantly, in games that he played, the Jayhawks went 116-15.

For KU, the LaFrentz chapter ended March 15, 1998. But for LaFrentz, who was chosen by the Denver Nuggets with the third pick in the 1998 NBA Draft, another chapter awaited: a professional basketball career. Thankfully for Kansas fans, he extended the first and delayed the second.

WHY "RAEF?"

Maybe a million.

Maybe that's how many times people have asked Raef LaFrentz how he received his unusual name.

So here's the answer, one which LaFrentz no doubt will have to repeat a million more times:

Raef's parents, Ron and Ellen LaFrentz, named their son after Raef Honeycutt, a character played by George Peppard in the movie, "Home From the Hill."

That's it. It's that simple.

By the way, the LaFrentz surname in not French, as many people think. It's German.

HAIL TO THE STUDENT-ATHLETE

Athletics director balances numerous issues, but one always takes priority

Since May 1987, when Robert E. Frederick took over as athletics director at the University of Kansas, the school's athletics program has enjoyed it finest era of overall success while growing larger than ever, encompassing about 500 athletes and 20 sports.

Since May 1987, among other achievements, KU teams have: won an NCAA championship in men's basketball, gone to two other Final Fours, won two football bowl games, advanced to the College World Series in baseball and softball, advanced to NCAA final rounds in men's tennis, women's tennis and men's golf and produced individual NCAA champions in women's track, women's diving and women's tennis.

Since May 1987, KU's athletics programs have helped make the University the 31st-best college sports school in the United States, according to *Sports Illustrated*. Despite an athletics budget that ranks in the bottom half of the Big 12 Conference, *SI* says only two conference schools – Texas and Nebraska – rank ahead of KU.

Since May 1987, KU's athletics programs have developed more opportunities for varsity women athletes than any other in the conference. In the 1996-97 school year, 246 athletes participated in women's sports at Kansas. No other conference school had more than 200 women competing in varsity athletics.

Since May 1987, Frederick has attained recognition as one of the nation's most prominent athletics directors. In April 1996, *College Sports Magazine* named him one of the 50 most influential people in college athletics. The magazine placed only two athletics directors higher than Frederick, who was ranked No. 37.

Since May 1987, KU's athletics department has been on NCAA probation once, when the men's basketball team received penalties in 1988. Violations that caused that probation occurred before Frederick arrived. Since then, no KU program has incurred NCAA penalties.

Who then, should Kansas alumni and fans thank for KU's success during Frederick's tenure? Maybe his wife, Margey.

Frederick was the athletics director at Illinois State when Monte Johnson resigned as KU's athletics director in March 1987. At the same time, Wisconsin, a Big 10 Conference school with 10,000 more students than Kansas and an impeccable academic reputation, also was searching for an AD.

"It just happened that the Wisconsin job and the Kansas job came about at the same time," he says. "I was sort of intrigued by the Big Ten and the great academic reputation of Wisconsin.

"But my wife said, 'You have to go back to try at Kansas because you'll never forgive yourself if you don't.' I just got intrigued by the Wisconsin job; she kind of got me back on track. I'm really grateful I made that decision."

So is KU.

BOB FREDERICK

BOB FREDERICK
Basketball, 1959-62 • Assistant basketball coach, 1962-64 and 1971-72
Assistant athletics director, 1981-85 • Athletics director, 1987 -

***

Academicians and professionals, citing the need for variety, often advise against obtaining bachelor's and master's degrees from the same institution, let alone getting those two and a doctoral degree from the same university.

Perhaps those who don't know Dr. Bob Frederick, those who chastise him for having turned down opportunities to lead other athletics programs – such as Michigan, Arizona State, and, in June 1997, North Carolina – ought to look at his résumé. It lists a bachelor of science in education, a master's in education and a doctorate in education.

He acquired all three degrees from KU.

"I have a great affection for the University," Frederick says. "I have a lot invested here. I really struggled when the Big 12 thing came up, whether we (his family) really wanted to give up being on a university campus."

"The Big 12 thing" to which Frederick refers is the job as commissioner of the conference formed when four schools of the Southwest Conference joined the Big Eight in 1996. Frederick and Steve Hatchell, commissioner of the old SWC, were finalists for the position. Conference presidents chose Hatchell in a split vote.

Frederick admits some disappointment at not getting the job. But it gave him a chance to reflect on what he believes is his true mission as an athletics director: providing the optimum college experience for student-athletes.

"I've seen my role evolve as one in which I could bring the focus back to the student-athlete and the student-athlete's welfare, in trying to make this a quality environment for kids to compete in and to get a degree in," he says. "When I didn't get (the Big 12 job) I tried to really, really reflect on my own job and what I wanted to do differently.

"The one thing that I had consistently been saying to myself but not doing was spending more time with student-athletes. So since then, I've really made an effort to spend more time with student-athletes ... still not as much as I'd like."

Critics of college athletics no doubt cringe at the number of times Frederick uses the term "student-athlete." But he gives it more than lip service. He participates as a mentor in the KU athletics department's student support services program, which has grown exponentially in the past decade. He visits various campus student groups, and KU fans can spot him as often at a women's soccer game as they can among the throng in Allen Field House.

Renewing the focus on student-athletes was one of Frederick's two main concerns in 1989, when he publicly warned that college athletics were on the verge of "self-destructing" if "drastic changes" didn't occur in the next five years.

Changes have happened, not only at KU but throughout college athletics.

"I think our student-athletes have better opportunities now to compete to earn a degree," he says, shifting from college athletics as a whole to KU in particular. "We're in a stronger conference, we have stronger competition, we have better facilities, we have better athletic support programs. We have more opportunities for women. We have more programs that put the focus on the students themselves. I think being a student-athlete now is a better situation that it was 10 years ago."

Although he's satisfied with progress on the student-athlete front, the other worry he addressed in 1989 – finances – remains a problem.

***

The No. 1 dilemma facing most college athletics departments is money.

Adding women's sports costs money. Refurbishing facilities, such as KU's $30.2 million plan to update and redesign Memorial Stadium, costs money. Scholarships cost more money each year as tuition soars.

How to meet those costs is Frederick's top concern.

"The expenditures just scare me to death," he says. "We went through and made a bunch of cuts and saved about $1.98. It just keeps going up, and travel costs are skyrocketing."

In KU's first year in the Big 12, Frederick notes that the KU Athletics Corp., which pays for KU sports and receives their revenue, used three-fourths of its additional projected revenues from the new conference to pay for increased travel costs.

"You don't go to Lubbock in a van," he says, referring to the home of Texas Tech, one of KU's new conference foes.

In 1997-98, KU's athletics budget of $20 million was $12 million more than when Frederick arrived. But it still ranked seventh among the 12 conference schools.

"Nebraska, Texas, Oklahoma ... they're in the mid-$20s (million)," he says. "I just don't know how we can keep going like this."

In that environment, stipends for student-athletes are unrealistic, Frederick says.

"We're still getting a lot of criticism for not giving stipends to student-athletes," he says, somewhat discouragingly. "The critics sometimes must think that the administrators are spending it. Actually, all the income the Jacques, the Scots and the Jerods (former KU basketball players Vaughn, Pollard and Haase) of the world generate are paying for tennis programs, pay for our soccer programs, etcetera."

In 1959-60, KU's athletics department revenues totaled $514,021. Then, football and basketball supported the entire athletics program. While the budget has increased, what supports it remains essentially the same.

"If you could get a (football) season-ticket base that assures financial success every year – your problems aren't over, but they're a long way toward getting there," Frederick says.

He hopes the stadium renovation that began in late 1997 helps sell more season football tickets and elevates that program. Of course, the two go hand-in-hand: win more games, sell more tickets.

But Frederick also points out that great facilities don't guarantee success. Likewise, what some consider outdated facilities don't necessarily cause losing. Take Allen Field House, for example, or Notre Dame's football stadium, which finally is undergoing a facelift in the late 1990s.

"You don't have to have a Cadillac budget and Cadillac facilities to have a Cadillac program," he says. "We're going to continue to work as hard as we can and do as much as we can with our resources. There's a lot in our conference in our same situation."

Despite his desire to cover expenses, Frederick is not consumed with finding revenue sources, especially at the expense of integrity. When Notre Dame secured its own television contract with the National Broadcasting Company in early 1990, Frederick ended KU's basketball series with the Fighting Irish and wrote a scathing editorial criticizing Notre Dame's decision in the *New York Times*.

"I was really down about that, really upset," says Frederick, recalling how Notre Dame abandoned the College Football Association, a group of schools that collectively bargained for television rights. "I took a lot of flak about that. That was the only time in 10 years I was sorry I had a listed phone number. I had people calling from New Mexico and Florida – they were all Notre Dame, I assumed, 'subway' alumni. They called and just raised Cain with me about it.

"But you know what, a bunch of people from Notre Dame told me in subsequent years that they thought I was right."

***

Frederick has made other unpopular decisions as the Kansas AD, ones that struck closer to home. Tony Redwood, a business professor and chairman of the KU Athletics Corp. board that hired Frederick, resigned when Frederick fired football coach Bob Valesente. The KU football team's woeful academic reputation improved while Valesente was coach, but the team's performance on the field was dreadful.

The man Frederick hired to replace Valesente, Glen Mason, guided KU to two bowl victories, the first KU coach to accomplish that feat.

Before gaining national notoriety as an athletics director, Bob Frederick (right) coached basketball for almost 20 years. He was an assistant with Sam Miranda (center) on KU head coach Ted Owens' (left) staff in 1971-72.

Frederick also received a mountain of criticism in the summer of 1988 when he hired an unproven men's head basketball coach to replace Larry Brown. But his choice, Roy Williams, had the highest winning percentage of any active college basketball coach heading into the 1998-99 season.

"I've always felt like I've had a good sense of people and how they are going to work in different situations here," Frederick says. He regards hiring good coaches as one of his greatest accomplishments at Kansas because "they have helped me and our staff provide a greater quality of experience for our student-athletes."

A pretty fair coach, Dean Smith, began Frederick's route to Kansas 40 years ago. After Frederick graduated from Kirkwood (Mo.) High School in 1958, he wanted to attend the Air Force Academy to play basketball. Smith, a Kansas alumnus and an assistant coach at Air Force, recruited Frederick, then steered him to KU after he failed an eye exam for entrance into the academy.

At Kansas, Frederick played on the freshman team – and not much else. But Dick Harp, the head coach at KU, noticed something about him.

"Bob endears himself to everybody," he says. "He was not a very good basketball player. But he's a great person."

Early in his career, Frederick, who always had wanted to be a teacher and coach basketball, jumped from job to job. He coached high school basketball in suburban Chicago and Russell, Kan. He was the coach at Coffeyville (Kan.) Junior College for a year. Then, in the early 1970s, he got what he thought was his big break as an assistant coach to Ted Owens at Kansas.

He only stayed with Owens for a year, though, before moving to Provo, Utah, where he was an assistant at Brigham Young for three years. Then he worked as an assistant at Stanford, where the seedier side of college athletics almost got to him.

"I was somewhat discouraged in the late '70s, as I was out recruiting, about some of the cheating and so forth that was going on," he says. "I wasn't positive at that point that I wanted to stay in athletics."

But then the coaching position at Lawrence High opened in 1977, and Frederick grabbed it. In April 1981, KU athletics director Bob Marcum hired Frederick as assistant athletics director for fund raising and executive director of the Williams Educational Fund, KU's athletics scholarship program.

In the meantime, Frederick worked toward a doctorate. He took the Illinois State job in June 1985 and returned to KU two years later when Chancellor Gene Budig hired him.

Marcum now is athletics director at Massachusetts. He proudly says – with a laugh – that he's the man who brought Frederick back to Kansas. But he turns serious when he assesses Frederick's impact at KU.

"You look at the total sports program under Bob's administration," he says. "No one's done a better job."

Frederick, who survived a serious bicycling accident in the mid-1990s and has given up his beloved midday jogs because of arthritic knees, was the the first Kansas AD to sign a multiyear contract. The former chairman of the NCAA Men's Basketball Committee contemplates his future role while sitting in the KUAC boardroom in Parrott Athletics Complex, another project he supervised.

Looking down on Frederick is a portrait of F.C. "Phog" Allen, KU's legendary basketball coach and also the school's athletics director from 1919 to 1936.

"I want to be able to make a difference in student-athletes' lives," Frederick says. "As long as I can keep doing stuff that's going to help them have a positive situation, then I want to be here.

"If our two oldest sons (Frederick has four, two in their early 20s and two teenagers) were our only two sons, I might even start to think about retiring. But that's not the case. I think I'm here for the long haul."

With that statement, if only for a brief moment, the smile on Allen's face grows wider.

"You look at the total (KU) sports program under Bob's administration. No one's done a better job."

– Bob Marcum

'ALMOST UNSTOPPABLE'

Smooth forward made basketball look easy

People recognize Inglewood, Calif., mostly for one thing. It's the home of the Great Western Forum, which in turn is the home of the NBA's Los Angeles Lakers, a franchise that has captured more league championships than any besides the Boston Celtics.

The 17,505-seat Forum is Inglewood's most famous and cherished building. But a different structure, Inglewood High School, offers more significance in University of Kansas lore.

PAUL PIERCE
Basketball,
1995-98

Not far from where Earvin "Magic" Johnson, Kareem Abdul-Jabbar and James Worthy once dazzled Lakers' fans, another gifted basketball player honed his skills in the high school's gymnasium. More than a simple court and a few seats, it is the alpha and omega of that player's time with the Kansas Jayhawks.

That player was Paul Pierce.

It was there Jan. 27, 1995, that Pierce told about 40 reporters he had chosen KU instead of UCLA as the school at which he would play college basketball. One thousand one hundred sixty-one days later, he told many of the same reporters gathered in the same gymnasium that he was leaving the Jayhawks after his junior season to pursue an NBA career.

For three years in between, he redefined the standard by which KU small forwards are measured.

"One of the things he does better than anything else," said KU guard Ryan Robertson after Pierce announced he would turn professional, "is that when you get him in an isolation situation, where he is one-on-one, he's almost unstoppable."

No one had to tell that to Oklahoma coach Kelvin Sampson after the Sooners played the Jayhawks in Allen Field House on Feb. 23, 1998. It was Senior Night, the annual love-fest marking the last home game for KU's four-year players.

This night, however, a junior took center stage.

Many KU fans suspected the game might also be Pierce's last home court appearance with the Jayhawks. He had turned down overtures from the NBA after his sophomore season, when he averaged 16.3 points and 6.8 rebounds per game. The Jayhawks went 34-2 that season, but on a team with All-Americans Raef LaFrentz and Jacque Vaughn, Pierce garnered no better than third-team all-Big 12 Conference honors.

A year later, Pierce left little doubt he was among the best college basketball players in the nation. But if any existed, he erased it in a 3-minute span during the second half on Senior Night.

The Sooners were giving Kansas, playing for its fourth consecutive outright conference title, a stern test with about 9-and-a-half minutes left in the game. Then Pierce erupted.

He hit 10-foot jump shot from the baseline. Less than 30 seconds later, he hit a three-pointer. About a minute later, he hit a jumper from the free throw line. Another three-pointer followed. Then another.

Sampson called timeout, but the damage was done. In perhaps the most unforgettable individual offensive explosion by any KU player in the Roy Williams era, Pierce had scored 13 straight points.

As he turned to head toward the Kansas bench, Pierce raised his arms to the deafening crowd, belying his almost sullen on-court demeanor. Sampson met him halfway, and in a rare gesture by an opposing coach in the heat of battle, honored the effort with a quick slap to Pierce's backside.

Kansas fans then commenced a sing-song chant: "One more year, one more year." After the timeout, Pierce ended his run at 15 by scoring in the lane off a rebound. KU cruised the rest of the way, winning 83-70.

During the game, Pierce made 14 of 17 shots. About the only offensive skill he didn't showcase during his one-man, second-half show was an in-your-face dunk. But then again, he had done that in the first half, after which Sampson called another time out.

That's how it was with Pierce. For three years, he forced KU's opponents to pick their poison. Get a hand in his face on the wing, and his deceivingly quick first step could free him for a 15-foot jumper in one direction or catapult him to a baseline jam in the other. But lay off him on the perimeter, and he could swiftly yet effortlessly bury a three-pointer.

When LaFrentz broke his hand midway through the 1997-98 season, Pierce often played power forward. The stint proved he also could post up and score inside, and the 6.3 rebounds he averaged in his 108 games at KU testified to his prowess in that department.

But Kansas basketball fans always will remember Pierce as the most versatile scorer in the history of the rich program. He was the antithesis of scrappy, the essence of smooth. He barely broke stride when canning pull-up jumpers on a secondary fast break. Even to the trained eye, the grace with which he glided across the court or unleashed a silky jumper from the top of the key made basketball look easy.

Growing up in Oakland, Calif., Pierce found basketball was far from easy. In fact, he never played the game much before he and his family moved to Inglewood while he was in junior high. There, he avoided the gang and drug-related pitfalls kids easily can encounter on that city's streets. But he didn't start making a name for himself in basketball until jumping from the junior varsity team to the varsity squad midway through his sophomore season in high school.

By the end of his senior season, college basketball recruiting analysts widely considered Pierce the best player in California and one top 10 players in the country. He averaged 27 points and 11 rebounds a game that year. At the 1995 McDonald's High School All-American all-star game, he scored 28 points, the highest individual total since Michael Jordan scored 30 in the 1981 game.

Pierce didn't immediately dominate games in college. In his first two college contests, he made just five of 20 shots. But by the time the conference portion of the schedule began, he had scored 24 points against San Diego, 21 points against Indiana and 30 points against East Tennessee State. By the end of the season, in an NCAA Tournament Sweet Sixteen game against Arizona, he scored 20 points and hit four three-pointers.

He finished the 1995-96 season with per-game averages of 11.7 points and 5.3 rebounds. He made just 41.9 percent of his field goal attempts and only 60.6 percent of his free throw opportunities. For every assist he made, he made 1.31 turnovers. Still, he exhibited numerous flashes of brilliance and shared conference freshman-of-the-year honors with Colorado's Chauncey Billups.

Pierce progressed steadily but quickly. During his junior year, when he finally made first-team all-conference and became only the fifth KU player to make first-team Associated Press All-America, he led KU in scoring with 20.4 points per game. It represented only the 15th time in KU history that a player averaged 20 points a game and the first time since Danny Manning did a decade earlier.

He also averaged 6.7 rebounds a game during his junior season, hit 51.3 percent of his shots from the floor and made 73.8 percent of his free throws. His turnover-to-assist ratio fell to 1.12-to-1, and he and LaFrentz both were finalists for virtually every college player-of-the-year award.

In only three seasons, Pierce scored 1,768 points, fifth-highest on KU's all-time scoring chart. He finished his career by scoring in double figures in 51 straight games.

But he did not finish his career with an appearance in the Final Four. KU lost as a No. 1 seed in the NCAA Tournament each of his last two years, first against eventual national champion Arizona in the 1997 tournament. Pierce single-handedly kept the Jayhawks breathing during the second half of that game and finished with a game-high 27 points and 11 rebounds.

The Arizona loss stunned the KU faithful. It also was a prelude to a month of decision making for both Pierce and LaFrentz, who heard the NBA beckoning.

But as with LaFrentz, Pierce announced in early May 1997 at an exhibition game in Allen Field House that he would return to Kansas for the 1997-98 season.

"Raef and I talked throughout the time we were deciding," Pierce told the *Topeka Capital-Journal* a month afterward. "I think we both wanted to to fulfill a dream we both had – to go to the Final Four."

Everyday life, though, is a reminder that dreams don't always come true. The All-American pair led KU to a 35-4 record and a No. 2 ranking heading into the 1998 NCAA Tournament. Again, the Jayhawks fell short of the Final Four, losing to Rhode Island in the second round.

Pierce hardly was responsible for KU's postseason struggles during his career. In nine NCAA Tournament games during his three seasons, he averaged 18.3 points and 7.8 rebounds. He led the Jayhawks in scoring in six of those games, contradicting the notion that seniors dominate the tourney. He scored 23 points in his last game at Kansas.

This time, 18 days after the season-ending loss – one of just 11 he experienced at KU – Pierce announced at a news conference that he would take his talent to the NBA. Most pundits predicted he would be one of the first five players chosen in the league's June draft; Boston Celtics' coach Rick Pitino considered it a steal when he grabbed Pierce with the 10th overall pick.

Williams accompanied Pierce at the news conference, during which Pierce

"In introducing Paul Pierce to you, I'm introducing one of the outstanding players that I've ever dealt with. But above all that, I'm introducing you to a youngster who is a far better person than he is a basketball player. My life has been enriched as a coach for having the privilege of being able to say that I have coached Paul Pierce."

– Roy Williams at the news conference when Pierce announced his decision to leave Kansas for the NBA.

In the 1997-98 season, Paul Pierce averaged 20.4 points per game, just the ninth player in Kansas history and the first since Danny Manning in 1987-88 to average 20 points a game in a single season.

announced his decision to turn pro:

"In introducing Paul Pierce to you, I'm introducing one of the outstanding players that I've ever dealt with," Williams said. "But above all that, I'm introducing you to a youngster who is a far better person than he is a basketball player. My life has been enriched as a coach for having the privilege of being able to say that I have coached Paul Pierce."

The gym at Pierce's high school alma mater served as the launching pad for both his college basketball playing days and an NBA career. He'll likely get his first chance to play in Inglewood's larger arena in the 1998-99 season.

THANKS FOR THE MEMORIES

Swim coach remembers people more than performances

Names from the past stream out of Gary Kempf's mind, rolling off his tongue like copies from an overambitious Xerox machine.

Jenny Wagstaff, Celine Cerny, Tammy Thomas.

Swimmers. At the University of Kansas. Kempf has made them his career for almost 25 years. But asking him to pick a most memorable moment or declare a personal favorite from his years as KU's men's and women's swim coach is a request that will go unheeded.

"Each year carries its special moments," he says. "I've just been blessed with wonderful kids and a great opportunity from the University of Kansas."

The special moment in 1983 was watching Cerny and Wagstaff, fine swimmers both, complement Thomas, a U.S. recordholder, at the NCAA Championships. Thomas' two record-setting performances led the way to a seventh-place finish for KU's women's team.

"Tammy had a great meet, but that whole group that went along really swam well," Kempf says.

Tom Kempf.

Gary Kempf distinctly remembers why swimming turned into a lifelong love. He grew up in Bartlesville, Okla. His father worked for Phillips 66, which sponsored a swim club that competed in Amateur Athletic Union meets. Also an accomplished runner, he watched his older brother, Tom, earn All-America honors in 1971 as a KU swimmer. That led Gary to Mt. Oread.

"I have often wondered if I would have ever swum in college or ever been a coach had I not gone to KU," Kempf says.

Debbie Bunker.

Kempf graduated from KU in 1976 with a bachelor's degree in biology. Originally a pre-med student named the Big Eight Conference's Swimmer of the Year in 1973, Kempf says he was "tired of going to school" by the time he graduated. So instead of

GARY KEMPF
Swimming
1972-76
Head women's swimming coach, 1976 -
Head men's swimming coach, 1981 -

medical school, he took over as head coach of the fledgling KU women's program.

He recalls Bunker, later a captain, as an inspirational leader of his first team at Kansas, which won a conference championship. The women's team won conference titles every year from then through 1984 and again in 1988, 1989, 1992 and 1993.

Dick Reamon.

Kempf's first year was Reamon's second-to-last as KU's men's coach. In 15 years at Kansas, Reamon's teams won eight conference championships. Those titles occurred consecutively from 1968 to 1975. Bill Spahn followed Reamon, then Kempf took over as both men's and women's coach in 1981.

Ron Neugent.

Neugent, an All-American and an Olympic qualifier in 1980, was the glue that held together Kempf's first few men's teams at KU.

"One of the greatest memories is the opportunity to coach athletes like Thomas and Neugent," Kempf says.

Chris McCool, Glenn Trammel, Dan Mendenhall, Marc Bontrager.

With Kempf in command, conference titles have eluded KU's men's teams. However, as team captains in the late 1980s, McCool, Trammel and Mendenhall revitalized the men's program. Trammel, from Topeka, was an All-American three straight years, and he and Mendenhall led KU to a 13th-place finish at the 1990 NCAA Championships. Bontrager, KU's captain in 1995, earned All-America honors four straight years.

Despite their achievements, Kempf says it's more gratifying to observe those and other swimmers after they leave KU.

"I love the kids I work with," he says. "I don't just coach swimmers. I coach people. Watching kids grow up, to watch how their lives change ... you know somewhere along the line, KU served a purpose in their lives."

Tammy Pease, Seth Dunscomb.

Twice as KU's coach, Kempf has mourned the death of swim team captain. Pease, a 1986 captain, died in a car accident. Dunscomb, a 1997 captain, collapsed and died after a workout.

"That doesn't only change your program, it changes your life," he says. "Hopefully, you can grow from it and move on."

Kristen Nilsen.

Nilsen, an All-American, an honorable mention academic all-conference selection and a 1998 captain, embodies what Kempf cherishes perhaps more than anything as a coach.

"She's had as big an impact on our program as any swimmer I've ever had," he says. "Not in victories, maybe, but as a person."

Quincy Adams, Jeanine Wilk, Brad Artis, Chad Sunderland ...

Sixty-two names appeared on the 1997-98 women's and men's swimming rosters at Kansas. Sixty-two names Kempf will catalog in his mind, filed for future remembrance.

He's had chances to move to other coaching positions, but he thinks none offered more than the one he's had for his entire adult life.

"This is my home," he says of KU. "I plan on finishing my career here. I've told (KU athletics director) Bob Frederick that."

Kansas, then, is where Kempf will continue compiling memorable swimmers. And to him they're all memorable.

"I don't have two or three favorites," he says. "I have hundreds of favorites."

About The Authors

LYLE NIEDENS

Lyle Niedens has compiled 11 years of experience as a journalist. After covering high school sports as a correspondent with the *Great Bend (Kan.) Tribune*, he covered University of Kansas sports as a staff writer with the *University Daily Kansan* and as a correspondent with *The Kansas City Star*.

A 1993 KU graduate with a B.S. in journalism, Niedens currently covers business and financial news as a senior reporter with Bridge News Service in Overland Park. He lives in Westwood with his wife, Caryl.

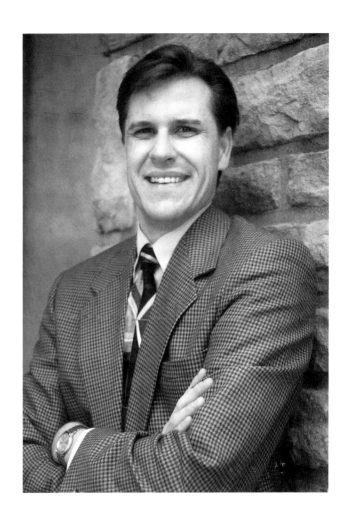

STEVE BUCKNER

Steve Buckner has accumulated 15 years of experience as a journalist. He covered high school and junior college sports for his hometown *Independence (Kan.) Daily Reporter* and was a student assistant with the University of Oklahoma sports information staff. He also has covered Douglas County government for the *Lawrence Journal-World*.

A 1980 graduate of OU with a B.B.A. in business and a 1990 KU graduate with a M.S. in journalism, Buckner currently is editor of *The Grower* magazine with Vance Publishing Corp. in Lenexa. He lives in Lawrence with his wife, Tammy, and their two children.

TED WATTS
Sports Artist

Ted Watts of Oswego, Kan., has literally painted his way into the forefront of American illustrators with a no-nonsense approach to his favorite subject... sports.

At age 27, Watts was unpublished as an artist. Two years later, he opened his own free-lance art studio specializing in sports illustrations and drawings prepared specifically for college and university sports information and athletic departments. Today, the 55-year-old former football and track athlete from Miami, Okla. is considered a pioneer for transforming college sports art publicity from a cartoon dominated market during the mid-century to an illustration art preference on campuses during the '80s and '90s.

His clients include the United States Olympic Committee, the National Collegiate Athletic Association and more than 150 college and university clients from coast-to-coast. His works hang in the Baseball Hall of Fame – Cooperstown, N.Y.; Basketball Hall of Fame – Springfield, Mass.; Pro Football Hall of Fame – Canton, Ohio; USA Wrestling Hall of Fame – Stillwater, Okla.; and the College Football Hall of Fame – South Bend, Ind.

In 26 years, Watts' sports art "stats" are prodigious. He's completed more than 5,000 pieces of finished art; more than 1,250 cover illustrations (including 65 national award winners); 1,350 display paintings, portraits and murals; 600 posters and calenders and 81 limited edition art prints.

Watts was born Dec. 12, 1942, in Anthony, Kan. He is a 1960 graduate of Miami High School. He received his AA degree from Northeastern Oklahoma A&M College in Miami in 1962, where he studied with famed Oklahoma muralist and lithographer, Charles Banks Wilson. He completed his college education at Pittsburg State University (BFA 1966).

The artist celebrated his 26th year in business May 2, 1998. Watts and his wife, Faye live in Oswego. They have two sons, Thom, 27, and Brad, 23.

INDEX